"This superb collection leverages Africa – the most dynamic and understudied region for world constitutionalism – for a sophisticated examination of the promises and perils of public participation. With its rigorous framing and rich case studies, the book provides a major advance in our understanding of constitution-making in the 21st century." – *Tom Ginsburg, Leo Spitz Professor of International Law and Professor of Political Science at the University of Chicago, and a member of the American Academy of Arts and Sciences, USA*

"Demands that constitutional reform must be people driven are now ubiquitous in Africa but does participatory constitution-making strengthen constitutionalism in Africa? What makes it meaningful? What is its impact on minorities? Can it effectively challenge elite interests? What are its risks? This wide-ranging volume explores these and related questions with case studies that challenge the usual platitudes and enrich our understanding of constitution-making in Africa. It is a wonderful contribution!" – *Christina Murray, Professor of Constitutional and Human Rights Law, University of Cape Town and Senior Advisor on constitutions and power sharing, Mediation Support Unit, Department of Political Affairs, UN*

"An African proverb says that you cannot shave someone's head in his absence. Africa's post-independence constitutions were hurriedly crafted and imposed by the departing colonial powers with very limited involvement of the people. From the 1990s a new era of 'made in Africa' constitutions based on popular participation began. Tania Abbiate *et al*'s book provides the first fresh and much-needed insightful and thoughtful analysis that goes beneath the rhetoric to reveal the realities of popular participation in the making of the new generation of African constitutions. Written by a group of eminent scholars and accomplished practitioners, the book is a timely and highly valuable contribution that could not have come at a better time. As the UN Office of the High Commission for Human Rights has embarked on drafting guidelines to promote more effective public participation in public affairs, this book is bound to put the African experience at the centre of the global debate. Because it takes account of and reflects the experiences of Africa's diverse constitutional traditions, the book makes compelling reading to all legal and political theorists, practitioners and all those who are interested in the increasingly important discourse on public participation in constitutional processes and public affairs in general." – *Charles Manga Fombad, Professor of Comparative African Constitutional Law at the Institute for International and Comparative Law in Africa, Faculty of Law, University of Pretoria, South Africa*

T0320228

Public Participation in African Constitutionalism

During the last decade of the 20th century, Africa has been marked by a "constitutional wind" which has blown across the continent giving impetus to constitutional reforms designed to introduce constitutionalism and good governance. One of the main features of these processes has been the promotion of public participation, encouraged by both civil society and the international community.

This book aims to provide a systematic overview of participation forms and mechanisms across Africa, and a critical understanding of the impact of public participation in constitution-making processes, digging beneath the rhetoric of public participation as being at the heart of any successful transition towards democracy and constitutionalism. Using case studies from Central African Republic, Egypt, Kenya, Libya, Malawi, Morocco, Senegal, Somalia, South Africa, South Sudan, Tanzania, Tunisia, Zambia and Zimbabwe, the book investigates various aspects of participatory constitution making: from conception, to processes, and specific contents that trigger ambivalent dynamics in such processes. The abstract glorification of public participation is questioned as theoretical and empirical perspectives are used to explain what public participation does in concrete terms and to identify what lessons might be drawn from those experiences.

This is a valuable resource for academics, researchers and students with an interest in politics and constitution building in Africa, as well as experts working in national offices, international organizations or in national and international NGOs.

Tania Abbiate is a Senior Researcher at the Max Planck Institute for Social Law and Social Policy, Germany.

Markus Böckenförde is Executive Director and Senior Researcher at the Centre for Global Cooperation Research, Duisburg, Germany, and a Visiting Professor at the Central European University (CEU), Budapest, Hungary.

Veronica Federico is Researcher of Comparative Public Law in the Department of Legal Studies at the University of Florence, Italy.

Routledge Global Cooperation Series

This series develops innovative approaches to understanding, explaining and answering one of the most pressing questions of our time – how can cooperation in a culturally diverse world of nine billion people succeed?

We are rapidly approaching our planet's limits, with trends such as advancing climate change and the destruction of biological diversity jeopardising our natural life support systems. Accelerated globalisation processes lead to an ever-growing interconnectedness of markets, states, societies and individuals. Many of today's problems cannot be solved by nation states alone. Intensified cooperation at the local, national, international and global level is needed to tackle current and looming global crises.

Series Editors:

Tobias Debiel, Claus Leggewie and Dirk Messner are Co-Directors of the Käte Hamburger Kolleg/Centre for Global Cooperation Research, University of Duisburg-Essen, Germany. Their research areas are, among others, Global Governance, Climate Change, Peacebuilding and Cultural Diversity of Global Citizenship. The three Co-Directors are, at the same time, based in their home institutions, which participate in the Centre, namely the German Development Institute/Deutsches Institut für Entwicklungspolitik (DIE, Messner) in Bonn, the Institute for Development and Peace (INEF, Debiel) in Duisburg and The Institute for Advanced Study in the Humanities (KWI, Leggewie, former Director, now retired) in Essen.

https://www.routledge.com/Routledge-Global-Cooperation-Series/book-series/RGC

Titles:

American Hegemony and the Rise of Emerging Powers
Cooperation or Conflict
Edited by Salvador Santino F. Regilme Jr. and James Parisot

Moral Agency and the Politics of Responsibility
Challenging Complexity
Edited by Cornelia Ulbert, Peter Finkenbusch, Elena Sondermann and Tobias Debiel

Public Participation in African Constitutionalism
Edited by Tania Abbiate, Markus Böckenförde and Veronica Federico

Public Participation in African Constitutionalism

Edited by Tania Abbiate, Markus Böckenförde and Veronica Federico

LONDON AND NEW YORK

Centre for
Global
Cooperation
Research

SPONSORED BY THE

Federal Ministry
of Education
and Research

First published 2018 by Routledge

2 Park Square, Milton Park, Abingdon, Oxfordshire OX14 4RN

52 Vanderbilt Avenue, New York, NY 10017

Routledge is an imprint of the Taylor & Francis Group, an informa business

First issued in paperback 2019

British Library Cataloguing-in-Publication Data
A catalogue record for this book is available from the British Library

Library of Congress Cataloging-in-Publication Data
Names: Abbiate, Tania, editor. | Böckenförde, Markus, editor. | Federico, Veronica, editor.
Title: Public participation in African constitutionalism / edited by Tania Abbiate, Markus Böckenförde and Veronica Federico.
Description: New York : Routledge, 2017. | Series: Routledge global cooperation series
Identifiers: LCCN 2017027851 | ISBN 9781138745872 (hb) | ISBN 9781315180540 (ebook)
Subjects: LCSH: Constitutional history—Africa , | Democracy—Africa. | Political participation—Africa.
Classification: LCC KQC527 .P83 2017 | DDC 320.9609051—dc23
LC record available at https://lccn.loc.gov/2017027851

ISBN: 978-1-138-74587-2 (hbk)
ISBN: 978-0-367-33293-8 (pbk)
ISBN: 978-1-315-18054-0 (ebk)

DOI: 10.4324/9781315180540

Typeset in Goudy
by Deanta Global Publishing Services, Chennai, India

This work and its open access publication has been supported by the Federal Ministry of Education and Research (BMBF) in the context of its funding of the Käte Hamburger Kolleg/Centre for Global Cooperation Research at the University of Duisburg-Essen (grant number 01UK1810).

Contents

Tables

Contributors

Tania Abbiate holds a PhD in comparative public law from the University of Siena, Italy, and she is currently Senior Researcher at the Max Planck Institute for Social Law and Policy in Munich, Germany. She is the author of a book on Tunisian participatory constitution-making processes (La partecipazione popolare ai processi costituenti. L'esperienza tunisina, *Editoriale Scientifica*, 2016), as well other articles and book chapters on the topic. Her research interests include constitutional and democratic transitions, African comparative constitutional law, and fundamental and human rights.

Mohamed Abdelaal is Assistant Professor of law at Alexandria University Faculty of Law in Alexandria, Egypt, and Adjunct Professor of law at the University of Indiana Robert H. McKinney School of Law in Indianapolis, Indiana, USA. He focuses his teaching and scholarship on the areas of constitutional law, administrative law, comparative law and Islamic law. Abdelaal has published widely on constitutional law and comparative law and he served as a presenter and panelist in several law conferences and workshops in USA. Meanwhile, he is licensed to practice law in Egypt, and he is admitted as a certified arbitrator under the Egyptian law. He is also a permanent member of the Egyptian American Rule of Law Association (EARLA), Washington, DC, and has been invited for three consecutive years (2012, 2013, 2014) to serve as an Egyptian expert to draft the Rule of Law Index Report sponsored by the World Justice Project (WJP).

Francesco Biagi is a postdoctoral research fellow in comparative public law at the University of Bologna's School of Law, and a researcher at the Center for Constitutional Studies and Democratic Development. From October 2015 to January 2017 he was a senior research fellow at the Max Planck Foundation for International Peace and the Rule of Law (Heidelberg). In 2017 and 2015 he was visiting professor at the College of Law of the University of Illinois. He is the author of a book on the role of constitutional courts in the processes of transition to democracy (*Corti costituzionali e transizioni democratiche. Tre generazioni a confronto*, il Mulino, 2016), as well as several articles and book chapters in the field of comparative constitutional law.

Markus Böckenförde is currently working as Executive Director and Senior Researcher of the Centre for Global Cooperation Research, Duisburg

(Germany) and as Visiting Professor at the Central European University (CEU), Budapest, where he is also the course director of the annual summer course on "Constitution Building in Africa". He holds a law degree and a PhD from the University of Heidelberg and a Master of Laws degree from the University of Minnesota (Fulbright scholarship) as well as the equivalent of a Bachelor's degree in political science (University of Freiburg). He has been involved in various constitution-building processes, including in Afghanistan, Nepal, Sudan, Somalia, Tunisia and Libya, working in part together with the pertinent constitutional assemblies. He has published widely in the area of constitutional law and constitution building.

Boniface Cheembe holds a Bachelor of Arts from the University of Zambia with a major in political science and a minor in development studies. He also holds a Master of Arts degree, attained as a Fulbright Scholar from Eastern Mennonite University in Harrisonburg, Virginia, in the United States of America with a focus in conflict transformation. He is a civil activist currently working as the executive director for a Zambian-based nongovernmental organization called Southern African Centre for the Constructive Resolution of Disputes – dealing with issues pertaining to peace and democracy in Zambia and the sub-region. He is also a part-time lecturer of political science at the UNZA in the Department of Political and Administrative Studies in the school of Humanities and Social Sciences. Boniface Cheembe is also a researcher.

Nedra Cherif is a graduate of Sciences Po Paris from which she holds a Master's degree in International Relations/Security Studies. N. Cherif is currently a PhD researcher in political science at the European University Institute in Florence, Italy. She focuses her research on the Tunisian and Egyptian constitution-making and democratization processes following the Arab uprisings of 2011. She previously worked as political analyst for The Carter Center's Constitution Monitoring Team in Tunisia.

Jill Cottrell is currently one of the directors of the Katiba Institute in Nairobi, a body committed to the implementation of the 2010 constitution through litigation, research, lobbying and education. Educated at the University of London and Yale Law School she taught law for 40 years at universities in Nigeria, the United Kingdom and Hong Kong before she retired in 2006. She has been a consultant on constitution-making for Timor-Leste, Maldives, Iraq, Libya, Fiji, South Sudan and Somalia. From 2006 to 2008, Jill was a consultant with the Constitution Advisory Support Unit, UNDP, Kathmandu, Nepal. She has also been involved with International IDEA on a project for women members of the constituent assembly. She is author of several publications on constitution-making, public participation in constitution-building and womens' engagement.

Leopoldine Croce holds an LLB (honors) from the University of London, and an MA and PhD from the University of Salzburg. Leopoldine grew up in Europe, emigrated to the United States, and now lives in Senegal. She has served numerous nongovernmental and governmental organizations in supporting citizen participation in public affairs in 35 countries so far.

Veronica Federico is Researcher of comparative public law with the Department of Legal Studies of the University of Florence. She holds a PhD from the Ecole des Hautes Etudes en Sciences Sociales in Paris. Research associate with the School of Social Sciences, University of the Witwatersrand (Johannesburg) from 2000 to 2004, she has been awarded a NATO scholarship, a United States Institute of Peace scholarship and several prestigious research grants. Author of three monographies, four edited books and special issues, and a number of chapters and articles, her research interests include African studies, African comparative constitutional law, fundamental and human rights, constitutional and democratic transitions, French constitutional law and politics, and citizenship studies.

Yash Ghai is a Kenyan constitutional lawyer. For most of his professional life he has been a law teacher at universities in Africa, US, Europe, Asia and South Pacific and has advised a number of governments and political parties on dispute settlement and constitution making. His research interests include constitutionalism and human rights, ethnic conflicts, sociology of law, and autonomy. He has published extensively on these and other areas. Yash was the Special representative of the UN Secretary General on human rights in Cambodia and has been a consultant to the UNDP, UNRISD, International Institute for Democracy and Electoral Assistance, the Ford Foundation and various other foundations on human rights and constitutionalism. He is a co-founder and co-director of an NGO, Katiba Institute, which is dedicated to the protection and promotion of Kenya's 2010 Constitution.

Omar Hammady was country director of Democracy Reporting International for Libya between 2014 and 2015. In this capacity, he was responsible for providing legal advice to the Libyan Constitution-drafting Assembly as well as to Libyan CSOs involved in the constitutional process. As a fellow researcher at the Max Planck Institute for Comparative Public Law and International Law between 2011 and 2013, he was coordinator of the Institute's North Africa projects under which he advised the Libyan and Tunisian Assemblies on constitutional issues. He is currently the constitutional advisor of the United Nations' Special Envoy for Yemen and is a visiting professor at the European University Institute in Florence and visiting scholar at the Max Planck Institute for Comparative Public Law and International Law.

Heinz Klug is Evjue-Bascom Professor of Law at the University of Wisconsin Law School, and an honorary senior research associate in the School of Law at the University of the Witwatersrand, Johannesburg, South Africa. Growing up in Durban, South Africa, he participated in the anti-apartheid struggle, spent 11 years in exile and returned to South Africa in 1990 as a member of the ANC Land Commission and researcher for Zola Skweyiya, chairperson of the ANC Constitutional Committee. He has published two books on the South African Constitution, *Constituting Democracy* (Cambridge University Press, 2000) and

The Constitution of South Africa (Hart Publishing, 2010). He has taught at Wisconsin since September 1996.

Rose W. Macharia is an advocate of the High Court of Kenya and a former law clerk of the Supreme Court of Kenya. She holds an MA in International Relations from the United States International University and a Master of Public Policy from the Blavatnik School of Government, University of Oxford. Rose has engaged in extensive constitutional research both in legal practice and during her term at the Supreme Court of Kenya.

Philipp Michaelis is a research assistant at the Käte Hamburger Kolleg/Centre for Global Cooperation Research in Duisburg where he is currently working on constitution-building processes in sub-Saharan Africa as well as on migration dynamics within and from West Africa. Philipp holds a Master's degree in political science, African Studies and English from the University of Cologne. His research interests include constitution-building, statehood and state fragility, causes of armed conflict and forced migration.

Douglas Togaraseyi Mwonzora is a practicing lawyer and currently the secretary general of the Opposition Movement for Democratic Change. He is also a former co-chairperson of the Parliamentary Select Committee that spearheaded the drafting of the Constitution of Zimbabwe between 2009 and 2013, former member of Parliament in Zimbabwe, and former law lecturer at the University of Zimbabwe and the Great Zimbabwe University.

Matteo Nicolini is Assistant Professor of comparative public law at the University of Verona (Italy) and researcher at the Institute for Comparative Federalism of the European Academy of Bolzano/Bozen (EURAC). His main fields of research include regionalism and federalism, constitutional litigation, Southern African common law, legal geography, law and literature. He is author of three monographs and articles and contribution in Italian, Spanish and English.

H. Kwasi Prempeh is a Ghanaian legal scholar whose scholarship focuses on the prospects and challenges of building democracy and constitutionalism in Africa's post-authoritarian states. A 2011 Reagan-Fascell Democracy Fellow at the National Endowment for Democracy, Washington, DC, Prempeh was professor of law at Seton Hall University School of Law, Newark, New Jersey (USA), from 2003 to 2015 and a visiting professor at Ghana's GIMPA Law School in 2010. He has co-taught the "Constitution-Building in Africa" course at the Central European University in Budapest, Hungary, since 2014. From 2013 to 2014, he served as a constitutional adviser to the UN Special Envoy to Yemen, assisting the Yemeni National Dialogue Conference and the Constitution Drafting Commission to design and draft a new federal constitution for the country. Prempeh has published and consulted on a wide range of democratization, rule of law and governance issues. A former corporate attorney, Prempeh is a graduate of Yale Law School, where he was note editor of the

Yale Law Journal and an assistant-in-instruction/Coker Fellow. He is currently an international legal and governance consultant based in Accra, Ghana.

Abrak Saati is a senior researcher at the Department of Political Science, Umeå University, and a visiting research fellow at the British Institute of International and Comparative Law and the Bingham Centre for the Rule of Law. She specializes in constitution building in post-conflict states and in states in transition from authoritarian rule, and has a particular interest in participatory constitution making in such contexts. She is the author of *The Participation Myth: Outcomes of Participatory Constitution Building Processes on Democracy* (2015). Saati has also worked with constitution building outside of the academia, in policy-making in international contexts.

Jan Amilcar Schmidt is a German and UK trained lawyer and research fellow at the Max Planck Foundation for International Peace and the Rule of Law in Heidelberg, Germany. Based in Nairobi, Kenya, Jan Amilcar Schmidt currently serves as the project manager for the Somalia projects of the Foundation supporting the Somali constitutional review and implementation process. Before joining the Max Planck Foundation for International Peace and the Rule of Law, he worked at the Institute for Federal Studies at the University of Hannover, the Max Planck Institute for Comparative Public Law and International Law as well as for the United Nations Development Program and the United Nations Political Office for Somalia. He has more than nine years of working experience in supporting rule of law programs, including constitutional processes in Somalia, South Sudan and Sudan.

Katrin Seidel is a post-doctoral research fellow at the Department of Law and Anthropology, Max Planck Institute for Social Anthropology, and was a fellow at Käte Hamburger Kolleg/Centre for Global Cooperation Research (2015–16). Based on her interdisciplinary background (law and African/Asian studies), her research is situated at the intersection of legal pluralism, heterogeneous statehood and governance. Her studies are concerned with interdependent relationships between plural normative and judicial orders at different levels of regulations and with intertwinements of respective social actors involved. Seidel's current research focus is on "South Sudan's and Somaliland's constitutional geneses: A comparative analysis of post-conflict constitution making processes".

Martina Trettel is a researcher at the Institute for Studies on Federalism and Regionalism at European Academy of Bolzano/Bozen (EURAC) and has a PhD in European and international legal studies. Her main research interests are institutional innovation and participatory democracy, autonomy and Italian regional law, comparative fiscal federalism and comparative constitutional justice.

Acknowledgments

This publishing project has been in production for almost eighteen months. It originated in a panel on public participation and constitution-making at the European Conference on African Studies 2015 in Paris, and it developed along the months in a snowball effect to finally take the form of this volume. As it is almost inevitable given the substantial number of authors whose contributions appear here, and the various conflicting demands on editors, the process has taken longer than anticipated, and the list of obligations we incurred has become long.

We are indebted to all the authors for the enthusiasm with which they have accepted to be part of the project, and for their patience in complying with editors' requests and waiting for latecomers, and to Margaret Farrelly and her colleagues at Routledge, for waiting while some deadlines passed.

We are greately indebted to Philipp Michaelis, Research Assistant at the Centre for Global Cooperation Research in Duisburg, for all his assistance in the process of reviewing a number of chapters. Without his learned support, the overall quality of the volume would have suffered and the bulk of work on the editors' shoulders would have been much heavier. If Routledge's publication policy had permitted, we would have included him as an Assistant Editor of this volume.

We are also grateful to Patricia Rinck, Susanne Brunnbauer, and Saina Klein from the publication team at Centre for Global Cooperation Research in Duisburg, who have supported the project since the very beginning. Without their help, especially in the final process of editing, the production process would have been further delayed.

We dedicate the volume to all those women and men who struggle with the peaceful weapons of knowledge, education and wisdom, to make Africa a better place to live.

Tania Abbiate, Munich
Markus Böckenförde, Duisburg
Veronica Federico, Firenze
29 May 2017

Introduction

Tania Abbiate, Markus Böckenförde
and Veronica Federico

During the last decade of the 20th century, Africa has been marked by a 'constitutional wind' which has blown across the continent giving impetus to constitutional reforms – designed to introduce constitutionalism and good governance. One of the main features of these processes has been the promotion of public participation, encouraged by both civil society and the international community. While the former has sought to ensure that the views of the populace come to be reflected in the constitutional text in particular cases, with demands also being filed through the courts, the international community has primarily been involved in designing and supporting the implementation of these constitutional processes.

Public participation has become a 'must have' in recent constitutional reforms and the vast majority of processes have at least pretended to respect this norm as part of their roadmap – primarily so as to subsequently be viewed legitimate. Yet, despite growing international support, what is still lacking in comparative research is solid empirical evidence regarding the merits of public participation as well as a critical theoretical discussion of how it may work to ensure better democratic performance and the emergence of constitutionalism subsequent to the process.

The volume investigates various aspects of public participation in African constitutionalism and aims to offer a systematic overview of participation forms and mechanisms across the continent. It seeks to provide a more nuanced understanding of the impact of public participation in constitution-making and constitutional-reform processes on the African continent, digging beneath the rhetoric of public participation as a simple panacea for any successful process. Moreover, by regarding Africa as a multifaceted continent, the volume wants to give voice to the different Africas and to revisit the all-too-often emphasised cleavages between Northern Africa and sub-Saharan countries, Eastern and Western countries, Anglophone and Francophone regions. Noticeably, to various degrees, the processes in all countries addressed in this volume have been influenced by international interventions and by the participation of international or foreign players. Insofar, the volume also reflects on the ambivalence of external participation in participatory constitution-making processes in the context of global cooperation.

DOI: 10.4324/9781315180540-1

Motivations and needs to draft a new constitution differ: for countries coming out of civil war, authoritarian rule or dictatorship, constitutions are vehicles for change and testimonials of a new beginning; for new states, they may serve as founding documents or as signals of hope in fundamental reform processes. Though embedded in particular historical contexts, they are commonly perceived as initiating a fresh start into the future. In most cases, the impetus to draft a new constitution have not emerged out of amendment processes to existing constitutions, but rather as the result of independent processes, marked by their own rules and dynamics.[1] In terms of constitutional theory, it is the people acting as constituent power (*pouvoir constituant/constitution-making power*) in the creation of the foundational document as opposed to their occasional participation as a constituted power (*pouvoir constitué*) in an amendment process of the constitution.[2] Because the inclusion of the public in exercising the role of the constitution-making power is centre-staged, but remains critical in its concrete application, it is taken the central point of departure for the studies in this volume. Ten of the twelve recent, or even still ongoing, processes are constitution-making processes. Though in the end Zambia's process has been finalised through the existing amendment rules, the long-lasting process has been continuously promoted by the government as an exercise to create a new people-driven constitution and has therefore been included in the volume. Senegal was added in the chapter on the constitution-making process in the Central African Republic so as to contrast approaches from two Francophone countries and in order to shed light on the specific role of France in these processes.

In general, arguments made in favour of ensuring public participation in constitution-making processes are manifold: constitutions, in order to create ownership and to be regarded as legitimate, need to include in the process of writing those who will subsequently be bound by it; participatory processes are an educational exercise in democracy and a means to promote the growth of a democratic political culture in a society; they can also provide political antagonists with an arena in which to collectively address past grievances and structural inequities that stand at the heart of a given conflict. But to what extent have processes indeed been designed to ensure that these positive dimensions are realised? And in cases in which the processes have effectively been designed to ensure just this, has the result nevertheless been one of ambitious but unfulfilled promises?

1 This is often reflected in the date of birth of a given constitution. See, for example, 'La Constitution du Royaume du Morroc de 2011'; La Constitution de la République centrafricaine de 2015; the Constitution of Egypt 2014; the Constitution of Kenya 2010.
2 Some constitutions generally require the direct involvement of the people in a constitutional amendment procedure through referendum (Algeria, Egypt). In other countries, direct public participation is reserved for cases in which specifically entrenched provisions are affected (Botswana, Kenya, Ghana), in which it is deliberately established by presidential decree (Cameroon, Tunisia), or in which a super-majority in Parliament cannot be achieved (Benin, Niger). Again, other constitutions do not foresee a direct public involvement at all (Burundi, South Africa, Central African Republic).

Moreover, should all constitutional contents be open for participation or should specific fields – such as the rights of minorities or the death penalty, for example – be excluded from public participation? What has to be regarded as 'participation'? Are there minimum standards in terms of timing, openness of the political system, accessibility of participatory mechanisms, inclusiveness, etc. in order for participation to be an effective tool in the hands of the people and so that constitutions are drafted in a manner that may make a difference?

Habermas noted that 'the entitlement to political participation is bound up with the expectation of a public use of reason: as democratic co-legislators, citizens may not ignore the informal demand to orient themselves towards the common good' (Habermas, 2001:779). Have the citizens of the African countries included in the volume behaved as democratic co-legislators? Are there requirements that need to be met in order to allow for participating in the interest of the common good and so as to ensure that these are not compromised by parochial interests and expectations?

The book systematically analyses the mechanisms and processes of public participation, as well as the effects, merits, and challenges of participatory constitution-making. It thereby makes empirical and theoretical contributions in several areas that do not only boost further academic debate in a still under-explored area of comparative constitutional law, but also provides findings to initiate a more effective international and national support in those processes that are currently still unfolding or that will occur in the future.

The objective of providing a better understanding of public participation is pursued in a threefold manner. First, the term public participation is conceptualised: namely, what does it actually imply and how might one classify different degrees of participation? What are the merits and challenges of providing the 'public' with the final say in a constitution-making process through a referendum? To what extent may the recent experiences serve as viable antidote against the longstanding African experience of having 'constitutions without constitutionalism'?

Second, by analysing twelve recent or even ongoing processes in several African countries (Central African Republic, Egypt, Kenya, Libya, Morocco, Senegal, Somalia, South Sudan, Tanzania, Tunisia, Zambia and Zimbabwe), the book highlights the plurality of settings under which public participation has been able to unfold. Though the contributions accentuate the individual character of each of the processes and their specific dynamics, they are guided by four common questions: (1) 'how was participation envisaged in the drafting process?', (2) 'how did it translate into practice?' – highlighting whether the model was followed, and what the most relevant discrepancies were, (3) 'what role did the international community and foreign countries play in terms of shaping participation in the constitution-making processes?', and (4) 'what influence did previous or contemporary experiences of other countries have?' – with a special focus being paid to the influence of other African countries.

Third, by looking at how participation has impacted controversial themes (e.g., death penalty, religion, LGTB rights), by exploring the role of specific stakeholders in the process (e.g., women), by turning the focus to participation as a means of civil resistance or by inquiring into specific terrains and into the participation strategies of particular actor groupings (e.g., women, LGBT organizations), the book enables an analysis and critical reflection on the limits, merits and impact of participation. The different contributions confirm the value of participatory mechanisms in terms of promoting new notions of African constitutionalism. At the same time, to paraphrase the words of Justice A. Chaskalson in the memorable case *S v Makwanyane and Another* (CCT 3/94), there might, however, be issues – as, for example, pertaining to social outcasts and marginalised people – with respect to which participation *per se* does not guarantee 'the rights of minorities and others who cannot protect their rights adequately through the democratic process' [para. 88]. Equally, a closer look at successful stories of participation may reveal the limits of fostering social change through the law, which means, in other words, that the struggle for rights and liberties through inclusive participation should neither be confined to constitution-making or law-making processes.

What have been the motivations behind shifting the focus to Africa? From Bolivia to Iceland, an increased demand for citizen and civil society participation has emerged in the course of the first decades of the 21st century. We have witnessed calls for the direct involvement of citizens and social organisations in the decision-making processes at all levels, from constitution-making to local-level regulations around the globe. Traditional forms of political representation through mass political parties – which are facing a severe legitimacy crisis – have been strongly challenged almost worldwide. Moreover, the notion of 'public space' (Habermas, 1962) has constantly expanded, and in the early 21st century it has come to largely exceed the mere circle of public institutions and their acts. Civil society has become a very relevant element of the 'public space', with its diversity of organizations as well as its repertoire of actions and actors. In turn, traditional forms of participation, through electoral processes and the typical activities of political parties, have come to constitute a too narrow terrain to voice civil society's multiple claims. When the fundamental law of a country is at stake, the so-called backbone of the political community, or, more emphatically, 'the soul of the nation' (Ebrahim, 1998), then the quest for new forms of civil society involvement in decision-making processes becomes more imperative. As Hart has fittingly observed: 'in a changing world, constitutional practice is also changing. Twenty-first century constitutionalism is redefining the long tradition of expert constitution-making and bringing it into the sphere of democratic participation' (2003:1). What is the contribution of the African continent to this process of redefining constitutionalism, both in its contents and in its forms?

Africa as a continent has borne testimony to the highest diversity of constitutional reforms in the last decades. Diversity pertains to the factors that drove constitution-making processes (new country, end of civil war, violent election, coup d'etat, end of authoritarian rule, reform agenda), the actors involved (national actors, international community, but also individual foreign states), and the political context in which the processes then unfolded (dictatorship, absolute monarchy, failed state, military rule, democratization process). By itself, this suffices to uphold the choice of concentrating on the African continent, as it provides – to put it in a nutshell – a specific diversity with a number of very different cases and experiences. But there are two further considerations supporting the focus on Africa. First, 'Africa as a whole, more than other world regions, lends itself to a broadly comparative approach' (Young, 2012:5), due to a remarkable mix of similarities and differences among the countries. Much has been written on differences and also on the notion of *Afrique au pluriel* (Bayart, 2003), which highlights a number of realities each with its own history, traditions, social order, political and legal institutions, and developmental process. On the other hand, similarities lie in the 'cultural patterns [. . .] that underpin the regular invocation of an African society'; in the 'defining impact of the colonial occupation'; in the contemporaneity of decolonization, whereby 'once the dam broke, decolonization was quite rapid; thirty-five of the fifty-three states achieved independence during the decade between 1956 and 1966'; as well as in the 'similarity of regime structures', whereby the 'decolonization process grafted onto the robust trunk of colonial autocracy weakly implanted constitutional frames modeled on the imperial centers'. Finally, we may note that similarities lie in the 'high degree of political diffusion in the African arena' (Young, 2012:5–7).

Second, drawing on Comaroff and Comaroff's reflection on theories from the Global South, and their emphasis on a dialectic centre-periphery relationship between the Global North and Africa, we argue that the continent has often been the first to 'feel the effects of world-historical forces', so that 'old margins are becoming new frontiers, and [. . . Africa in many respects is] running slightly ahead of the Euromodern world, harbingers of its history-in-the-making' (Comaroff and Comaroff, 2012:13). In other words, exactly due to its peripheral position – in terms of economic development, geopolitical strategies, technological advancement, etc. – contemporary Africa is a true laboratory for the elaboration of new forms and new content of the so-called globalised constitutionalism. As the Comaroffs suggest, 'Africa has come, in significant respect, to anticipate the unfolding history of the global north' (Comaroff and Comaroff, 2012:15). Against this backdrop, a sound investigation of participation in constitution-making processes in contemporary African experiences may unveil relevant lessons for the rest of the world. The chapter authors are both African scholars and foreign scholars who have extensive experience in constitution-building processes on the continent. Among the former are some of the most internationally renowned scholars on constitutionalism and constitution-building in Africa as well as scholars who have played a very prominent role in negotiating the respective processes and practitioners who have actively been involved in constitutional experiences. With regard to the latter, they have pursued long-standing academic research on matters of constitution-building in Africa. The contributions by African and European scholars entail overlaps, which in turn have contributed also to a cross-pollination of both analytical and explanatory tools, strongly boosting the added value of the volume. Fourteen contributors in this volume participated in various forms and functions in the annual summer course called 'Constitution Building

6   *Tania Abbiate* et al.

in Africa' at the Central European University in Budapest. Many of the thoughts shared in this book were enriched by discussions in these courses.

The book starts by exploring the gap existing between the rapid rise in the popularity of public participation and the current efforts to increase levels of public participation, and its low theoretical conceptualization. Despite the expectations that have come to be attached to 'participatory constitution-making', the concept of public participation still remains fairly vague and actual practices vary considerably as one explores different empirical cases. Abrak Saati analyses what 'public participation' actually entails in the context of constitution-making, by considering a number of crucial questions, such as: What does it mean to participate? How can we approach this notion analytically? Are we better advised to refer to *different types* of participation instead of referring to public participation as a uniform concept? Through this conceptual investigation, she notes that participation assumes different forms and she proposes a typology of different types of participation in constitution-making. This effort of reconceptualization is complemented by Markus Böckenförde's reflection on the referendum and whether this in fact comes to mark the constituent power's decisive involvement in the process. Mirroring the African experiences against the (assumed) merits and challenges of this form of participation offers fresh and at times surprising insights to the experiences and dynamics of African constitutionalism.

The chapters in the second section of the book are dedicated to country studies, organised along two categories of accomplished and ongoing processes. The discussion starts with an in-depth analysis of the processes unfolding in Egypt, Morocco and Tunisia, which had all begun to find expression during the Arab Spring but which show in an exemplary way the diversity of outcomes. Mohamed Abdelaal's contribution highlights the difficulties and ambiguities of the Egyptian process, wherein the military-backed government sought to control and direct public attitude and input. Moreover, when participation in constitution-making processes is not recognised and guaranteed as a fundamental right, but rather taken as a 'grant to be awarded pursuant to the pleasure of the authorities', public participation can only be flawed and defective. Morocco is a paradigmatic case where public participation was promoted 'from above', and Francesco Biagi argues that this played an instrumental role in terms of strengthening the *status quo*. Herein, those who participated could not really influence the content of the constitutional reform, as even the approval referendum was unable to turn the process into a fully democratic one. By contrast, Nedra Cherif's enquiry into the Tunisian process sheds light on some of the concrete contributions made by the public in terms of constitutional content, and points to the manner in which the participatory initiatives promoted by public authorities and those promoted by the active civil society fruitfully intertwined. The Tunisian process was a paramount moment of higher law-making, in which even constitution-makers demonstrated a high sense of responsibility.

Moving south on the continent, Yash Ghai and Rose Macharia compare the 2005 and 2010 constitution-making processes in Kenya by analysing the difference in forms and structures, scope and extent of public participation. Interestingly, among other very relevant issues – such as civil society's reaction against the political hijacking of the process – this contribution discusses two elements that are closely intertwined: the time and education dimension of constitution-making processes. As the authors highlight, while they may appear long and very complex, 'processes educate people in democracy'.

Comparing the most and the least stable African Francophone democracies (Senegal and Central African Republic), Leopoldine Croce reaches extremely interesting conclusions: even though very different actors initiated and drove public participation processes, both experiences involved similar institutional devices – including blanket adoption by referendum – and even though in both countries public participation set new benchmarks, neither Senegal nor CAR adopted constitutions that entrench citizen participation for future constitution-making processes. Whether this might be a legacy of French colonial rule remains to be further investigated.

The chapters on Zimbabwe and Zambia add new, crucial elements to the volume with respect to its critical approach. On the one hand, they discuss the challenges that constitution-making processes may face when operating in authoritarian structures (Zimbabwe). On the other hand, they illustrate how it may happen that processes which are undertaken with the objective to allow the people to equally participate in constitution-making and which are characterised by a rather impressive and commendable record of citizens' participation, may end up failing (Zambia). As argued by Boniface Cheembe, in fact, since the start of the reform processes, the people of Zambia have not felt like they have obtained a people-driven constitution as promised beforehand. Similarly, Mwonzora's chapter analysing Zimbabwe's constitutional review process shows some of the most controversial aspects of participation: in this particular case, people's enthusiasm about the constitutional reform provoked a sudden change of mind in the dominant political party – testifying to the success of broad public engagement into policy-making at the constitutional level – and yet this enthusiasm has not contributed towards enhancing people's knowledge of the content of the constitution that they so massively supported.

Ongoing processes highlight the most severe challenges for meaningful public participation processes. Indeed, all countries included in this section, except for Tanzania, have recently been (or still are) ravaged by violent conflicts. In all countries, public participation has been perceived as a *conditio sine qua non* for a constitution-making process that could also entail conflict resolution and democratization. And this is already a very important contribution to the broader debate on participation, which confirms the hypothesis concerning participation's multidimensional added value. Nonetheless, the most interesting aspects of the Libyan, Somali and South Sudanese constitution-making processes are the questions they raise regarding content, forms, mechanisms, purposes and the timing of the participation programme in very delicate and unstable environments. To different degrees, all three cases show the ambiguities that characterise the intervention of international actors.

In addition to providing a critical insight into legal systems that are often neglected by mainstream comparative law research, the three studies broaden the scope of inquiry on public participation in constitution-making. Omar Hammady investigates whether the 'needs of constitution-making linked to a peace-making process could justify a limited involvement of civil society at certain stages in order to protect the peace deal to be reached, first, amongst the major warring parties' (Hamady).

Against the backdrop of Somalia's protracted crisis of complete state collapse – characterised by an extreme political fragmentation with a high number of small but powerful political elites – Schmidt's contribution argues that internationally empowered political elites finalised the constitutional process through political negotiations, without taking the results of the public consultation process into account. The analysis of the Somali experience raises one of the most critical and radical questions: might the failure of participation processes not only frustrate people's expectations, but also have a significant negative effect on peace and state-building as such?

An analysis of the process of drafting a citizen-driven constitution in South Sudan leads Katrin Seidel to discuss the dilemma of providing a quick, permanent constitution which respects international standards, while simultaneously being driven by the desire to draft a constitution which derives its legitimacy from public participation. According to the author, the recourse to public participation in South Sudan's constitution-making process has mainly served the interests of a few dominant local actors, whereby local ownership became a tool that legitimised and fuelled the political struggle as well as the violent (re)negotiation.

Tanzania differs from the other experiences in the sense that the unaccomplishment of the constitution-making process was not due to violent conflict, but rather due to opposition from the ruling elite. Noticeably, according to Philipp Michaelis, 'the entire constitutional reform process was conceptualised in a fashion that left ample room for participatory elements and the Tanzanian people in fact vividly took these up'. However, people's contributions touched issues so crucial – such as the structure of the union, presidential powers, separation of powers and checks and balances – that the ruling elite unilaterally decided to alter or drop several public proposals and postponed *sine die* the final referendum that was scheduled for 2013. Tanzania's experience is one of the best examples, *a contrario*, of how participation may be extremely destabilising and come to pose serious challenges for dominant political actors.

Finally, the third section explores some controversial issues that have emerged out of participatory constitutional experiences as well as the role that was played by specific stakeholders in the processes. The objective is to shed light on the effective impact of participation on specific constitutional provisions, and the importance of participatory constitution-making processes for democratic stability and resilience. Cottrell's discussion of women's engagement in the 2010 Kenyan constitution-making process shows that women's groups can be effective even in rather hostile environments, but that the success of an active mobilisation and participation depends also on the specificity of the issue at stake.

Participation tools do not have the same effective impact on every terrain – for example, successes pertaining to land rights were not coupled with an equal success in abortion matters, which are still deemed too sensitive.

The case of Malawi adds a new perspective: the impact of public participation on democratic endurance. Despite the frequent problems that affect the transition to democracy and the establishment of constitutional democracy in Malawi, Matteo Nicolini and Martina Trettel demonstrate that engagement in the public sphere is the primary and most effective instrument of civil resistance. Building on this, the two chapters on South Africa engage in a discussion on the limits and merits of successful public participation. South Africa's constitutional transition and its multifaceted participation program have become the paradigm of the new African constitutionalism, and much has been written on the lessons learned from its experience. Heinz Klug and Veronica Federico's chapters go beyond the celebration of the South African outstanding experience to discuss, on the one hand, whether there might be issues that shall be better ruled without echoing public opinion (and this is the case for the death sentence). On the other hand, they investigate the consequences of a very critical mismatch between the slowness of social change and the relative speed of legal change, that might even be a radical change, as it happened for LGBT rights, strongly influenced by specific stakeholders through skilled participation in constitution-making and in law-making processes.

The circle of our analysis closes by going back to North Africa and discussing the centrality of religion in the Tunisian constitution-making process. The "secularist" policies imposed by the state since independence, especially in terms of civil liberties, were strongly challenged during the constitution-making process that ended with the adoption of the 2014 Constitution. Much debate in both the academic literature and in public debate was focused on the role of religion in the new legal system, and the participatory mechanisms could in fact be seen to have represented a sort of Trojan horse for the Islamization of society and of the public sphere. Tania Abbiate's analysis shows, on the contrary, that an enlarged public space, where secularists and stakeholder's organizations – such as women's groups – mobilised and voiced their claims, counterbalanced the most conservative pleas.

Does participation matter in African contemporary constitutionalism? Yes, it does, but with very diverse effects and implications. Diversity is defined first and foremost by the respective sociopolitical, economic, cultural and historical contexts. It is self-evident that participation in Somalia and Libya finds more obstacles than in Tunisia, Senegal or South Africa. However, our research shows that, for example, the failure of participatory mechanisms in Somalia is by and large due to a tension between internal and international stakeholders, the fragmentation of the territory, and, last but not least, the intrinsic characters of Somali political culture that struggles with the very concept of representative democracy. Second, diversity depends on the very nature of participatory mechanisms, which are at times more or less inclusive, and which are in some cases defined by specific targets – as was the case in Tunisia, where students were directly consulted on the constitution's second draft by the National Constituent Assembly – based on oral or written submissions, etc. In relation thereto, the accessibility of those mechanisms and processes plays a role – taking into consideration the urban-rural divide, the illiteracy question, the media reach issue and the lack of reliable web connections. Third, diversity depends on the timing. Informing people of the contents of the constitution, distributing constitutional drafts, collecting submissions and organising hearings requires an adequate time span that, however, should also not be too long. When the timing is too tight, the risk of mere facade participation is very high; but if the deadlines are too far away – as it happened in Tanzania – participation loses its momentum. Fourth, diversity depends on people's willingness to engage in the constitution-making processes and on their commitment to participate. It is the question whether people's participation is fueled by interests of democratization, and effort to advance and enforce constitutionalism or whether it rather comes to be defined by very specific stakeholders, to the detriment of social cohesion.

The impact of public participation on African constitutionalism remains critical. Borrowing Kwasi Prempeh's words, 'Meaningful public participation, if it is to have an enduring impact on constitutionalism, must not end with the conclusion of the constitution-making process and the coming into effect of a new constitution'. As a matter of fact, the adoption of a new constitutional text does not solve once and for all the political struggles that characterise constitution-making process and these may become object of everyday politics. Moreover, constitutions, also those that are the product of participatory constitution-making processes, are a tool in the hands of the people. Participation in constitution-making is not a guarantee that these constitutions are implemented and interpreted as to ensure democracy, social justice, the quality and the effective enhancement of fundamental rights and freedom. Rather, 'public participation remains necessary even after a constitution has been adopted, so as to monitor, defend, and enforce the bargains made and rights secured in the constitution-making process' (Kwasi Prempeh, chapter 19).

References

Bayart, J.F. (2003). *L'Afrique: Continent Pluriel*. Paris: Sedes.
Comaroff, J., and Comaroff, J. (2012). *Theory From the South*. London: Boulder.
Ebrahim, H. (1998). *The Soul of a Nation. Constitution-making in South Africa*. Cape Town: Oxford University Press.
Habermas, J. (1962). *Struktuwrwandel der Oeffentlichkeit*. Neuwied: Luchterhand.
Habermas, J. (2001). 'Constitutional Democracy. A Paradoxical Union of Contradictory Principles?' *Political Theory*, 29(6) 766–81.
Hart, V. (2003). *Democratic Constitution-making*. Washington: United States Institute of Peace.
Young, C. (2012). *The Postcolonial State in Africa*. Madison: The University of Wisconsin Press.

Part I

Conceptualizing public participation in constitution-making processes

1 Participation – to unveil a myth

Abrak Saati

Introduction

About twenty years ago James Tully stated that constitution making is the single activity in "modern politics that has not been democratized" over the last three centuries (Tully 1995, 28). The ink on the paper on which those words were written had hardly dried when a sea change on this very matter occurred. Indeed, much has happened during the past twenty years, and today constitution making is no longer limited to the smoke-filled chambers of political elites and lawyers; an utterly secretive matter to be deliberated and decided far from the public eye – rather the opposite has evolved into a new norm. Nowadays, an increasing number of constitution-making processes are conducted by the assistance of ordinary men and women. This holds particularly true for many countries on the African continent, in which we have witnessed, and continue to do so, participatory constitution making. Cases of public involvement in constitution-making processes include Rwanda, Eritrea, Ethiopia, Kenya, Uganda, Zimbabwe, Nigeria, South Africa, Tunisia, CAR, Egypt, Morocco and Tanzania. Some of these cases are elaborated in the following chapters of this volume. Though the idea to include the general public in the making of their founding laws is now considered best practice, particularly when constitution making takes place in times of transition from war to peace or from authoritarian to democratic rule, the concept of "public participation" remains fairly vague and actual practices of participation vary extensively between empirical cases. This chapter aims to bring conceptual clarity to this terrain and to discuss and analyse what public participation in the context of constitution making entails. A number of questions will be addressed, such as: Why is public participation even sought after? What does it mean to participate? How can the notion of participation be approached analytically? Are we perhaps better advised to refer to *different types* of participation rather than referring to public participation as a uniform concept? Having discussed these issues, the chapter ends with a classification table that illustrates characteristic features of different types of participation in constitution-making processes. In the table, a number of African cases are also classified as demonstrative examples of these different types of participation.

DOI: 10.4324/9781315180540-3

The rationale for participation

The idea to allow the general public to participate directly in political decision making has a long tradition in the field of political science and derives from the ideas of classical liberal theorists such as John Stuart Mill and Jean Jacque Rousseau (Mill 1862; Rousseau 1971). In the writings of these philosophers, direct citizen involvement in matters of public relevance is emphasized and encouraged, primarily because of its educational merits. To be directly involved in public affairs is hypothesized to teach people how to work together and how to reflect on their wishes and concerns with respect to the needs and interests of other members of society. Participation is believed to develop responsible and politically aware citizens who recognize that participation with other members of society will in the long and in the short run be beneficial for one's own interest. As such, participation is even envisioned to remedy the individual's narrow and selfish interests to only look after his/her own concerns and it has therefore been argued that it is the responsibility of government to install institutions that facilitate direct participation because it is *this* that fosters responsible and moral citizens (Mill 1862). Many of the ideas that were originally developed by Mill and Rousseau have been echoed by contemporary participation theorists such as Pateman (1970), Arnstein (1969), Mutz (2002) and Finkel (2003), to name a few. However, while Mill and Rousseau as well as those writing in the 1960s and 1970s focused their attention to participatory practices in the United States and the rest of the industrialized world, the focus today is broader and includes the exercise of participation in the so-called developing world. In addition, the normative underpinnings of participation theorists, past and present, have made their way into policy documents of international organizations in which it is often emphasized that public participation is more than the involvement of recipients of aid in the implementation of projects, but as a development strategy in its own right.[1] Indeed, public participation, not only in the arena of constitution making but in general, is part of a broader development and peacebuilding agenda that emphasizes "the local" (Mac Ginty and Richmond 2013), "peacebuilding from below" (Ramsbotham et al. 2016), and "grassroots peacebuilding" (Heathershaw 2008). This in response to failed, or at least broadly perceived as such, top-down approaches to development and peacebuilding (see for example Khwaja 2004).

The rationale for participation in constitution making

When it comes to the arena of constitution making specifically, the reasons that are advanced by advocates of public participation in such processes can be

---

1 The 1993 Human Development Report, for example, states: "Participation, from the human development perspective, is both a means and an end. Human development stresses the need to invest in human capabilities and then ensure that those capabilities are used for the benefit of all. Greater participation has an important part to play here: it helps maximize the use of human capabilities and is thus a *means* of increasing levels of social and economic development. But human development is also concerned with personal fulfilment. So, active participation, which allows people to realize their full potential and make their best contribution to society, is also an *end* in itself".

summarized into five main points. To begin with, public participation for the sake of increasing the *legitimacy* of the constitution is a frequently emphasized argument. The claim is quite straightforward: people need to be included when formulating the rules that will govern them, otherwise they will not consider the document as a legitimate one (Hart 2003; Samuels 2009; Widner 2008). Secondly, public participation in constitution making as an *educational exercise* in democracy is also a commonly cited argument in the literature (Ghai and Galli 2006; Widner 2005). Thirdly, supporters of public participation argue that when individuals in a society repeatedly engage in discussions and deliberations about the content of the constitution, *social capital* is simultaneously being built – this since ownership induces a sense of influence and trust (Widner 2005, 506). Fourthly, just as repeated series of deliberations is assumed to build social capital, it is also anticipated to *reconcile* former adversaries of violent conflict. By being exposed to each other's ideas, it is expected that former enemies will be able to put their differences aside and focus on a common vision for the future of their country (Ghai and Galli 2006, 13; Hart 2003, 3). Lastly, practitioners and scholars alike support public participation in constitution-making processes because it is presumed to lead to *higher levels of democracy* after the finalization of the process (Wing 2008, 2; Banks 2008, 1055; Samuels 2009).[2] Having briefly reviewed the arguments for public participation in political decision making in general and in constitution-making processes in particular, the next section discusses what is actually meant by "participation."

What does it mean to participate?

Though public participation in constitution-making processes, in times of transition from war to peace or from authoritarian to democratic rule, is widely endorsed, *what* participation actually means is an issue that still remains vague. What does it mean to participate, and how can it be determined that a constitution-making process has been more or less participatory? Other than making the process accessible for ordinary women and men regardless of their social class, their economic status, their ethnicity and their religious beliefs, not much is specified in the literature as to how participation is to take form or how we can determine that a specific constitution-making process was particularly successful in terms of including members of society. The lack of conceptual clarity has, in turn, made it convenient to construe participation as an issue primarily concerned with quantity, implying that the more people who have been involved in the making of the constitution, the more participatory it has been. For example: a process in which one million constitutional submissions have been gathered from the public might be considered more participatory compared to a process in which 400,000 constitutional submissions were solicited. Though this might possibly say something about the extent of public excitement to engage in the process, it leaves many questions unanswered, the most important one being: how much *influence*

---

2 In Saati (2015), this argument is investigated by the empirical analysis of forty-eight cases.

does the participation of the people allow? I have argued elsewhere (Saati 2015; Saati 2016) that the possibility for the public to influence the process of making the constitution as well as the content of the actual document should be at the front and centre of our focus when we set out to determine how participatory a constitution-making process is. Measuring influence is, however, not easily made by the use of quantitative measures; rather, a qualitative approach is needed. In an effort to systematically approach the notion of participation, I have at an earlier time (Saati 2015) compared twenty cases of constitution-making processes in post-conflict states and in states in transition from authoritarian rule in order to understand which generic factors to look for in order to be able to categorize cases as having been more or less participatory depending on the extent of influence granted to participants. I will in the following sections summarize my main points as far as these generic factors are concerned.

The initiators of the process

All constitution-making processes are initiated by someone; be it an individual (the executive, for example), a political party, a civil society organization or an international actor. Regardless of who the initiators are, they arguably have manoeuvre space to form the constitution-making process in a manner that decides the extent of public influence on the process itself as well as on the final draft. In the flurry of different types of initiators, an initial distinction can be made between initiators who are outsiders (international actors, regional actors and/or individual states) and those who are insiders (national actors). These can be further distinguished into different types of actors. As far as the outsiders are concerned, there is, on the one hand, outside actors who are quite dominant to the extent that they even formulate constitutional content for the country in which they are operating in, and on the other hand there are outside actors that limit their involvement to guiding the set-up of the constitution-making process by determining, for example, the constitution-making bodies that are to be used, the sequencing of events and the timeframe of the process. Between these two, the former is needless to say more influential and, more importantly, more influential at the expense of national actors as well as ordinary citizens in the country in which the process is taking place. When it comes to insiders as initiators, these too vary from one case to the other and at times constitute a mix of different actors – but on a general level, either one of three different types of inside actors appear as initiators. Either national elites (military or political elites), civil society organizations, or a broad array of national actors that unite and together initiate constitutional reform (Saati 2015). To sum up, the initiators of the constitution-making process have the possibility to design the process such that public influence is reduced or increased. Their aspiration (or lack thereof) to involve the general public so that genuine participation becomes a viable option depends on how the initiators communicate and inform the people about the constitution-making process. It is to this issue I direct my focus next.

The forms of communication

As simple as it is true, people cannot participate if there are no avenues for participation. Therefore, the channels through which a constitution-making process reaches out to the population is crucial, and even more so if participation is envisioned to actually solicit input to the constitutional draft. However, such aspirations are not always the case. To be sure, a number of countries, both on the African continent and elsewhere, have designed their constitution-making processes such that the "participation" of the public has merely been a matter of keeping members of society informed about events rather than seeking input that is to influence the content of the constitution.[3]

When referring to various ways that a constitution-making process can be communicated to the public, one of four general modes of operation are frequently used. As just hinted, some constitution-making processes employ a *one-way model of communication*, which only serves to keep the public informed about the process without allowing feedback. In such instances, it is pretty safe to say that those who are in charge of the process are speaking *to* the people rather than *with* them; consequently, people are not allowed to provide input that can affect the content of the constitution even in the least. Other constitution-making processes have employed a *two-way model of communication*. This procedure at least signals that communication channels run both ways – from those in charge of drafting the constitution to the general public and from the general public back to the drafters. Yet other processes employ what I refer to as a *two-way model of communication with proactive measures*. In such instances, constitutional education programs have been included in the process. As far as public influence on the content of the constitution is concerned, such educational programs are far from insignificant, rather the contrary. For people to be able to participate in a constitution-making process, not only must there be a two-way model of communication that allows them to provide constitutional submissions to the drafters, but people must also be equipped with the necessary skills to be able to do so. Here, it must be remembered that quite a few countries that are in transition either from protracted conflict or from authoritarian rule, have populations that are perhaps only vaguely familiar with the concept of constitutionalism; an issue that must somehow be remedied if genuine participation is to be possible (Brandt et al. 2011). Hence, instances in which the design of the process has been constructed such to provide members of society the necessary knowledge *before* soliciting their opinions as to constitutional content signals that there is a genuine interest in allowing people to participate with influence. Finally, there are constitution-making processes in which the forms of communication subscribe to the description of what I refer to as *consultation*. This is a strategy that resembles the one just described but in which the comprehensiveness

---

3 Such was the case in for example the 1999 Nigerian constitution-making process and the Iraqi process of 2005 (Saati 2015).

of the communication plan distinguishes it a bit. In such instances, the communication strategy also involves mechanisms for reviewing the feedback of the public in order to make it possible to gather additional information from individuals and organizations as regards specific suggestions on constitutional provisions. Constitutional education programs have furthermore been carried out throughout the country and been designed such that individuals with varying degrees of previous knowledge about the concept of constitutionalism can benefit from them – this involves making education programs available in all spoken languages as well as developing alternative ways of communication than solely through written channels. To sum up, different forms of communication affect the degree to which the public are able to participate in a constitution-making process, and the form of communication also indicates if those in charge of drafting aim to solicit input to the draft or if they merely wish to give an impression of including the people. In the next section I turn my attention to the third factor that impacts the extent of public participation in constitution-making processes.

The degree of inclusion

In order to be able to make an assessment of how participatory a constitution-making process is, the extent of inclusion is also a factor that must be considered. When referring to inclusion in this context, the aspect under consideration is whether or not all groups in society have actually been allowed (and accepted) to participate. Though it is true that inclusion, in and by itself, does not equal influence, it is nevertheless an aspect worth considering, because if some groups are banned from participating and/or some groups boycott the process then this impacts on the public's overall degree of influence on the content of the constitution. In relation to the matter of inclusion specifically, there is also a normative understanding among many proponents of participatory constitution making that all segments of society should be invited to participate regardless of their social status (see for example Brandt et al. 2011, 84–85; Hart 2010, 20). To conclude, if one sets out to distinguish between different types of participation one must also consider the matter of inclusion. In the next section, the last factor that must be taken into consideration in order to assess the extent of public participation in constitution making is elaborated.

The question of final authority

Having taken into consideration who the initiators of the constitution-making process are, how the forms of communication with the public have been constructed, if all segments of the population have been invited (and accepted) to participate in the process, one critical issue remains; namely, in who's hands does the ultimate fate of whether or not the constitutional draft enters into force lie? Indeed, to be able to determine how participatory a constitution-making process is, the question of final authority is an essential aspect to consider. The public may be allowed to accept or reject the constitutional draft directly through a referendum, or indirectly by voting for members of a constitution-making body who then make decisions on their behalf, or perhaps not at all in cases where an executive body resides over final authority. The matter of "to do, or not to do" when it comes to referendums deserves some further attention as it is a contentious issue. On the one hand, there is probably always going to be those who insist that a referendum is a poor instrument for securing public participation in a constitution-making process. Is it really "participation" to vote yes or no on a political package of constitutional provisions that one has not been part of influencing even in the slightest? Even though this is a valid argument it must be remembered that elections still lie at the heart of the conception of democracy (Hart 2010, 32–33). Moreover, if approval through a referendum is decisive for the adoption of a draft constitution, then it is a manifest of public influence that is relevant to consider. Nevertheless, I do not argue that the question of whether the public are allowed to vote on the draft is the *only* factor that must be considered when we set out to assess the extent of participation in a given constitution-making process, but that it is one of four factors that must be given attention next to who the initiators are, how the forms of communication are constructed and how inclusive the process has been.

Differentiating participation

The four generic factors elaborated above are qualitative indicators that serve to assist in understanding how participation in a given constitution-making process has taken form and it is important to stress that when one analyses a constitution-making process all of these four factors must be given due consideration before a case can be referred to as having been more of less participatory in comparison to another case. Table 1.1 is a framework that can be used for analysing participation in such processes. In the left side column, we find the four factors elaborated earlier; in the column to the right, the different forms that these factors can play out are listed.

In Table 1.2, we see that depending on who the initiators of the process have been, how the forms of communication have been constructed, the degree to which the process has been inclusive and where the ultimate faith of the constitution has been vested, five different *types* of participation appear. I name these general types of participation in constitution-making processes *false, symbolic, limited, consultative* and *substantial* participation. Each participation type, as we move from false to substantial, implies an increasing level of influence for participants. In the final row of the table, some empirical cases from the African continent are categorized in the participation type that best fits their individual circumstances. These categorizations are also briefly elaborated below.[4]

As seen in Table 1.2, two main features set false participation apart from symbolic participation. The first concerns the identity of the initiators of the process.

---

4 For further reading on the categorization of these cases, please be referred to Saati 2015, 307–18.

Table 1.1 Framework for analysing public participation in constitution-making processes

Factors that affect public participation in constitution-making processes	Forms that the factors can take
• Initiators of the process	• Outside actors who influence constitutional content • Outside actors who determine how the constitution-making process will be carried out • National elites (political or military elites) • Civil society organizations • Political elites from the ruling party, military elites, political parties in the opposition and civil society organizations
• Forms of communication	• One-way model of communication • Two-way model of communication • Two-way model of communication with integrated proactive measures • Consultation
• Degree of inclusion	• Constitution-making process bans certain groups/political parties from participation • The constitution-making process open to all groups/political parties, some of whom voluntarily decided to boycott the process • Constitution-making process open to all groups/political parties and all groups/political parties interested in participating do so
• Question of final authority	• Final authority vested in the hands of an appointed or executive body • Final authority indirectly vested in the hands of the people (e.g., through a popularly elected constitutional assembly) • Final authority directly vested in the hands of the people (through a referendum)

Source: Saati, A. (2015) "The Participation Myth: Outcomes of Participatory Constitution Building Processes on Democracy". (Dissertation) Umeå. Print & Media. Page 36.

While outside actors are, generally, the primary initiators in cases of false partici-pation, this is not as common in cases of symbolic participation, where different types of inside actors typically perform the role of initiator. The second main difference between false and symbolic participation concerns the degree of inclu-sion. Whereas some groups are banned from partaking in the constitution-making process in cases of false participation, all segments of the population are allowed to participate in cases of symbolic participation (though some voluntarily choose not to). In false and in symbolic types of participation the forms of communica-tion are similar: generally, a one-way model of communication is employed with no possibilities for the public to provide feedback to drafters. These two types of participation are also similar to each other as regards final authority over the

Table 1.2 Typology of different forms of participation in constitution making

	False participation	Symbolic participation	Limited participation	Consultative participation	Substantial participation
Initiators of the process	Outside actor (determines the content of the constitution or the process)	Outside actor (determines the constitution-making process)/different types of inside actors	National elites (political or military)	National elites (political or military)	Civil society organizations/a broad array of national actors
The forms of communication	One-way model of communication	One-way model of communication	Two-way model of communication, or two-way model of communication with integrated proactive measures	Two-way model of communication, or two-way model of communication with integrated proactive measures/Consultation	Two-way model of communication with integrated proactive measures/Consultation
The degree of inclusion	Certain groups banned from participation	All segments of the population/political parties allowed to participate, but some chose to boycott the process	All segments of the population/political parties allowed to participate, but some chose to boycott the process	All segments of the population/political parties allowed to participate, and all interested in doing so participate	All segments of the population/political parties allowed to participate, but some chose to boycott the process/All segments of the population/political parties allowed to participate, and all interested in doing so participate
The question of final authority	Final authority rests with the executive/indirectly in the hands of the public	Final authority rests with the executive/indirectly in the hands of the public	Final authority indirectly vested in the hands of the people	Final authority indirectly vested in the hands of the people	Final authority directly vested in the hands of the people through a popular referendum
	Empirical case(s): Nigeria	*Empirical case(s)*[1]:	*Empirical case(s):* Rwanda, Uganda, Ethiopia	*Empirical case(s):* South Africa, Eritrea	*Empirical case(s):* Kenya, Zimbabwe

Saati, A. (2015) "The Participation Myth: Outcomes of Participatory Constitution Building Processes on Democracy". (Dissertation) Umeå. Print & Media. Page 37.

1 Some empirical cases outside Africa fit this general description (e.g., East Timor, Fiji, Colombia)

constitutional document. Decision-making power either rests with the executive or is indirectly in the hands of the public. As far as empirical cases on the African continent are concerned, the 1999 Nigerian constitution-making process quite well captures the general description of false participation, though the initiators of the process were military elites rather than outside actors. A timespan of merely two months to produce a constitution made it difficult to include Nigeria's large population, and the forms of communication were not constructed such to enable genuine participation either. The CDCC (Constitution Debate Coordinating Committee) which was in charge of drafting did not engage the opposition or civil society organization and, moreover, it chose a posh hotel in the capital of Abuja as the venue for people to come and propose submissions which made it impossible for most Nigerians to participate. In addition, final say over the constitution was vested in the hands of the executive (Ihonvbere 2000; Jega 2000). Hence, the circumstances that characterized the process implied that the public were not allowed to exert influence on the constitutional document. Therefore, one may refer to the 1999 process as an instance of false participation.

Directing our attention back to Table 1.2, we see that limited participation differs from false and symbolic participation mainly as regards the initiators of the process and the forms of communication. Initiators in cases of limited participation are generally national elites and they usually establish a two-way model of communication, or even a two-way model of communication with integrated proactive measures, thus making it possible for people to get engaged in the process and provide feedback. When it comes to the degree of inclusion, cases of limited participation are generally similar to symbolic participation; all segments of the population are allowed to participate, but some groups (for various reasons) choose not to get involved. Final authority is typically indirectly vested in the hands of the public. Applying this participation type to an empirical context, Uganda, Rwanda and Ethiopia albeit with some deviations, fit the general description of limited participation. The constitution-making process in all of these three cases was initiated by national elites. In Uganda and Ethiopia, a two-way model of communication with integrated proactive measures was employed. Though the extent of constitutional education programs was more comprehensive in Uganda, this was also a distinct feature of the Ethiopian process (see, for example, Moehler 2006; Tripp 2010; Abebe 2013). In Rwanda, on the other hand, a two-way model of communication was employed, but constitutional education programs were left out and hence it is difficult to know how well prepared the Rwandese were to genuinely participate. The Ethiopian constitution-making process was open for all groups. In mid-1992, however, the Oromo Liberation Front (OLF) withdrew its participation. In Uganda and Rwanda, the process was never open for everyone; in the former, politicians were allowed to engage in their capacity as Ugandan citizens, but they were not allowed to engage as representatives of a political party because political parties as such were banned from the process. In Rwanda, none of the political forces who had actively engaged in the genocide were allowed to take part in the commission that was in charge of drafting. However, whereas final authority over the adoption of the constitution was indirectly vested in the hands of the people in Ethiopia and Uganda, it was directly vested in the hands of the Rwandese people through a referendum. To conclude, even though these three cases are not identical to each other and do not exactly conform to the general description of limited participation, when taking all factors into account and analysing the manoeuvre space for influence granted to participants, it may be argued that this participation type still fits these cases.

Returning yet again to the general descriptions found in Table 1.2, we see that consultative participation differs from the three earlier participation types mainly as regards the forms of communication and the degree of inclusion. In instances of consultative participation, a more developed form of communication is employed, providing not only well designed constitutional education programs, avenues for feedback, but also mechanisms that enable constitution-making bodies to contact individuals who have provided opinions in order to ask additional questions about their ideas on particular issues. When it comes to the degree of inclusion, this participation type not only welcomes all groups in society to participate but also manages to get those who wish to contribute on board (hence, voluntary boycotting of any sort is generally not found in instances of consultative participation). Eritrea and South Africa are cases that capture the general description of this particular participation type. In both cases, national elites were the initiators of the process; the scope, design and the innovative ways of conducting constitutional education programs also characterizes these two cases; the process was open to everyone; and final authority was indirectly vested in the hands of the public (see for example Selassie 2010, Ebrahim 2001, Haysom 2001).

Lastly, as depicted in Table 1.2, the main, and most important, difference that sets substantial participation apart from consultative participation is that final authority over the constitution rests directly in the hands of the public. Looking at empirical cases in Africa, Kenya (the 2001–2005 process) and Zimbabwe (the 1999–2000 process) capture this participation type quite well. Both of these processes were initiated by civil society organizations in their respective countries; both processes included forms of communication with integrated proactive measures including well-designed constitutional education programs; both processes welcomed everyone to participate, but in both cases some segments voluntarily decided to refrain[5]; both processes ended with a public referendum on the constitutional draft (see for example, Bannon 2007, Ndulo 2010).

Concluding remarks

My main argument here has been that when referring to "participation" in constitution-making processes, we ought to approach this notion in an analytical,

---

5 In Kenya, a number of government ministers boycotted the proceedings of the National Constitutional Conference; in Zimbabwe the National Constitutional Assembly refused to participate in the government-led constitutional reform process.

sharp and distinct way that allows us to acknowledge and distinguish different practices of participation in empirical cases – such as has been illustrated with anecdotal examples above. Clearly, participation is not always exercised with the same amount of influence for participants, rather significant differences appear between cases. Hence, it is hoped that the typology of different types of participation in constitution making presented here can be useful in terms of unpacking this notion and be helpful for other researchers interested in analysing participatory constitution-making processes.

References

Abebe, A. K. (2013) "From the 'TPLF Constitution' to the 'Constitution of the People of Ethiopia': Constitutionalism and Proposals for Constitutional Reform", in Mbondenyi, M. K., & Ojienda, T., eds., *Constitutionalism and Democratic Governance in Africa: Contemporary Perspectives from sub-Saharan Africa*. Pretoria: Pretoria University Law Press, 51–88.

Arnstein, S. R. (1969) "A Ladder of Citizen Participation", *Journal of the American Institute of Planners*, Vol. 35 (4), 216–24.

Banks, A. M. (2008) "Expanding Participation in Constitution Making: Challenges and Opportunities", *William and Mary Law Review*, Vol. 49 (4), 1043–69.

Bannon, A. L. (2007) "Designing a Constitution-Drafting Process: Lessons from Kenya", *The Yale Law Journal*, Vol. 116 (8), 1824–72.

Brandt, M., Cottrell, J., Ghai, Y. & Regan, A. (2011) *Constitution Making and Reform: Options for the Process*. Switzerland. Interpeace.

Ebrahim, H. (2001) "The Public Participation Process in South Africa", in Hyden, G., & Venter, D., eds., *Constitution-Making and Democratisation in Africa*. Pretoria: Africa Institute of South Africa, 153–61.

Finkel, S. E. (2003) "Can Democracy Be Taught?", *Journal of Democracy*, Vol. 14 (4), 137–51.

Ghai, Y., & Galli, G. (2006) "Constitution Building Processes and Democratization", International Institute for Democracy and Electoral Assistance: Stockholm.

Hart, V. (2003) "Democratic Constitution Making" United States Institute of Peace.

Hart, V. (2010) "Constitution Making and the Right to Take Part in a Public Affair", in Miller, L. E., & Aucoin, L., eds., *Framing the State in Times of Transition: Case Studies in Constitution Making*. Washington, DC: United States Institute of Peace, 20–56.

Haysom, F. (2001) "Special Features and Mechanisms in Negotiating the South African Constitution", in Hyden, G., & Venter, D., eds., *Constitution-Making and Democratisation in Africa*. Pretoria: Africa Institute of South Africa, 93–113.

Heathershaw, J. (2008) "Unpacking the Liberal Peace: The Dividing and Merging of Peacebuilding Discourses", *Journal of International Studies*, Vol. 36 (3), 597–621.

Ihonvbere, J. O. (2000) "How to Make an Undemocratic Constitution: The Nigerian Example", *Third World Quarterly*, Vol. 21 (2), 343–66.

Jega, A. M. (2000) "Popular Participation in Constitution Making: The Nigerian Experience", in Alemika, E. E. O., & Okoye, F., eds., *Constitutional Federalism and Democracy in Nigeria*. Human Rights Monitor: Kaduna, 1–19.

Khwaja, A. I. (2004) "Is Increasing Community Participation Always a Good Thing?" *Journal of the European Economic Association*, Vol. 2 (2–3), 427–36.

Mac Ginty, R., & Richmond, O. P. (2013) "The Local Turn in Peace Building: A Critical Agenda for Peace", *Third World Quarterly*, Vol. 34 (5), 763–83.

Mill, J. S. (1862) *Considerations on Representative Government*. Norrköping: Föreningens boktryckeri.

Moehler, D. (2006) "Participation and Support for the Constitution in Uganda", *Journal of Modern African Studies*, Vol. 44 (2), 275–308.

Mutz, D. C. (2002) "Cross-Cutting Social Networks: Testing Democratic Theory in Practice", *American Political Science Review*, Vol. 96 (1), 111–26.

Ndulo, M. (2010) "Zimbabwe's Unfulfilled Struggle for a Legitimate Constitutional Order", in Miller, L. E., & Aucoin, L., eds., *Framing the State in Times of Transition: Case Studies in Constitution Making*. Washington, DC: United States Institute of Peace, 176–206.

Pateman, C. (1970) *Participation and Democratic Theory*. Cambridge: Cambridge University Press.

Ramsbotham, O., Woodhouse, T. & Miall, H. (2016) *Contemporary Conflict Resolution* (4th ed). Cambridge: Polity.

Rousseau, J. J. (1971) The Social Contract and Discourse on the Origin and Foundation of Inequality among Mankind. New York: Washington Square Press.

Saati, A. (2015) "The Participation Myth: Outcomes of Participatory Constitution Building Processes on Democracy". (Dissertation) Umeå. Print & Media.

Saati, A. (2016) "Different Types of Participation in Constitution Making Processes: Towards a Conceptualization", *Southern African Journal of Policy and Development*, Vol. 2 (2), 18–28.

Samuels, K. (2009) "Postwar Constitution Building: Opportunities and Challenges", in Paris, R., & Sisk, T., eds., *The Dilemmas of Statebuilding: Confronting the Contradictions of Postwar Peace Operations*. New York: Routledge, 173–95.

Selassie, B. H. (2010) "Constitution Making in Eritrea: A Process-Driven Approach", in Miller, L. E., & Aucoin, L., eds., *Framing the State in Times of Transition: Case Studies in Constitution Making*. Washington, DC: United States Institute of Peace, 57–80.

Tripp, A. M. (2010) "The Politics of Constitution Making in Uganda", in Miller, L. E., & Aucoin, L., eds., *Framing the State in Times of Transition: Case Studies in Constitution Making*. Washington, DC: United States Institute of Peace, 158–75.

Tully, J. (1995) Strange Multiplicity: Constitutionalism in an Age of Diversity. Cambridge: Cambridge University Press.

UNDP (1993) *United Nations Human Development Report 1993*. New York, Oxford: Oxford University Press.

Widner, J. (2005) "Constitution Writing and Conflict Resolution", *The Round Table*, 94, (381), 503–18.

Widner, J. (2008) "Constitution Writing in Post-Conflict Settings: An Overview", *William & Mary Law Review*, Vol. 49 (4), 1513–37.

Wing, S. (2008) Constructing Democracy in Transitioning Societies in Africa: Constitutionalism and Deliberation in Mali. New York: Palgrave Macmillan.

2 Letting the constituent power decide?

Merits and challenges of referenda in constitution-making processes in Africa

Markus Böckenförde

Introduction

Forms of public involvement in constitution-building processes are manifold and serve different purposes. Some of them focus on the deliberative character of the process, by providing citizens with a *voice* through different means of communication and consultation. Others emphasize the element of *voting*, be it through the direct election of a constituent assembly or through referendum at the end of the process (LeDuc 2015, 129). Here, in the latter, citizens are ascribed a decisive role in the process, either by determining the composition of the body relevant for drafting the constitution through election, or by approving the work of the drafters at the final stage. Though voting on a political package of constitutional provisions has its limitations, (Lenowitz 2013) for many, meaningful public participation in a constitution-making process still cannot be thought of without the direct involvement of the people in this final act. A referendum is often regarded as "best practice" in constitution-making today (Tushnet 2013, 1999) and considered the only acceptable conclusion to such a process (Kirkby and Murray 2016, 108). Some scholars even argue that popular ratification is an emerging soft norm of international law (Tushnet 2013, 1999).

To some degree, the typology of different forms of participation in constitution-building processes that was introduced in the previous chapter by Saati is based on this intuitive understanding: "substantial participation"[1] in a process can only be achieved "if the final authority [is] directly vested in the hands of the people through a referendum".[2] Based on the African experiences, this chapter aims to explore the different roles of referenda as a final up or down vote on the

---

1 It is important to highlight that this doesn't apply in reverse. The mere fact that a referendum was held at the end of the process doesn't yet guarantee a substantial participation. In the view of this author, the term "substantial participation" may be misleading due to the limited direct influence of most referenda on the substance. "Decisive participation" might be an alternative.
2 See Chapter 1, Table 1.2. Saati does not explicitly make the claim that the extent of participation can be measured simply through the availability of a referendum at the end of the process. But she argues that substantial participation, as the strongest form of participation, cannot be achieved without a referendum.

DOI: 10.4324/9781315180540-4

constitutional document. It does so in two parts. Part one reflects on the theoretical underpinnings of the people acting as the constitution-making power in a democratic setting. To what extent does the people's sovereignty in a constitution-building process translate into mandatory activities in the process, wherein the referendum plays an essential one? In the African context, this debate is not a mere academic exercise, but, for instance, defined a Kenyan High Court judgement. In *Njoya and others vs. Attorney-General and others*, the court had to decide *i.a.* whether the Constitution of Kenya Review Act was unconstitutional by not providing the people of Kenya with an institutional mechanism to exercise their constituent power. The second part of this chapter examines to what extent the positive and negative aspects generally ascribed to referenda at the end of a constitution-building process are mirrored in the experiences of those African countries that have recently undertaken the process of writing or adopting a new constitution. Some of them have designed their referenda in a manner that minimizes some of the negative aspects.

Referenda in constitution-making processes: A mandatory expression of the constituent power?

There has been an increasing trend of popular ratification of constitutions over the last decades, to which Africa is no exception (Suksi 2010, 3). Out of the 54 national constitutions currently in place, 26 were directly approved by the people (CIA 2016), and a vast majority of new African constitutions in the 21st century were ratified by referendum.[3] Beside the political decision of whether citizens should be granted popular imprimatur on the country's founding document, or the general normative claim that some form of participation in constitution-building processes is required by international law (Dann et al. 2011, 3), a fundamental question of *democratic* constitutional theory is whether a final vote by the people at the end of the process is a mandatory legal requirement. This claim is based on the idea of the people as the primordial "constitution-making power" (constituent power).[4]

The constitution is the fundamental law of the state, containing the principles upon which the polity is founded and spelling out the basic rules under which it operates. Considered as the supreme law of the land at the apex of a legal hierarchy that authorizes lower norms,[5] a constitution's own normative

---

3 In the new millenium, out of 19 new permanent African constitutions, 15 were adopted/ratified (not amended!!) by referendum (CIA 2016).

4 The German term *Verfassungsgebende Gewalt* (constitution-making power) captures more accurately the malleability that underlies the role of the people as "constituent power". In the following text, "constituent power" and "constitution-making power" are used interchangeably.

5 Notable exception can, *i.a.*, be found in the Constitution of Somalia stipulating in Art. 3 para. 1, which reads: "The Constitution of the Federal Republic of Somalia is based on the foundations of the Holy Quran and the Sunna of our prophet Mohamed (PBUH) and protects the higher objectives of Shari'ah and social justice".

authority and regulating force cannot derive from a legal norm that stands above it. A core question of constitutional theory remains: From where does the constitution gain its special status and on which normative basis is the constitution's claim to validity premised? In a secular and democratic setting, it can neither directly derive from a monarch, nor from a divine source. In turn, the concept of the people as the constituent power was developed by Abbé Sieyès to counter the French king's sovereign powers in 1788–89[6]: humans, out of their will and sovereign decision, take their fate and the order of their polity into their own hands (Böckenförde 1991a, 94). This inherently democratic concept expresses the most fundamental act of self-determination of a people (Dann et al. 2006, 426). But as the constituent power of the people precedes the constitution, it cannot be legally established by the constitution itself (Schmitt 2008, 76). Not existing within or on the basis of the constitution, it is to be distinguished from the institutions established by it as constituted powers. The powers that are regulated in the constitution, including the statute-making and constitution-altering powers, differ from those of the constitution-making power. The former are limited by and subject to the constitutional order. This may lead to a double identity of "the people", who may act as institutionalized power within the constitution and are thereby bound by it,[7] or as an extra constitutional entity with constitution-making power. From this distinction between constituent power and constituted powers, it follows that the power to eliminate a constitution and to replace it with a new one can reside only in the people, who come to arrive at a "political consciousness" in the latter form (Stacey 2011, 602). The expression of this consciousness, in turn, mandates the development of democratic settings in which the bearer of the constituent power can express itself adequately. For some scholars, envisaging a "constituent power" as an extra constitutional entity belongs to the world of myths. In their view, law acquires its authority from intrinsic qualities, making the concept of constituent power in the form of "the people" as an authorizing agent redundant (Dyzenhaus 2012, 233). They argue that "in constitutional democracy, the constituent power must be construed as emanating

---

6 As highlighted by several authors with reference to Bodin, Locke (Loughlin 2014, 220), and Lawson (Kay 2011, 3), there had been earlier versions of the idea of constituent power. Though Sieyès hadn't been the first one, he provides a refined distinction between constituent power and constituted power.
7 In this context, judgement DCC 14/199 of the Constitutional Court in Benin is noteworthy. It emphasized that neither the immutable clauses (those explicitly written into the constitution as well as those identified by the court) nor the entire constitution can be removed by the people through a referendum in the amendment process – as in this case the people would act as constituted power (*que la révision de la Constitution résultant de la mise en œuvre du pouvoir constituant dérivé ne peut détruire l'ordre constitutionnel existant et lui substituer un nouvel ordre constitutionnel*). This decision stands in marked contrast to French constitutional jurisprudence, which does not differentiate between originary constituent power and amending power (Baranger 2011, 402; CC decision No. 92-313DC, § 19). The Benin Court even argued that due to the initial weight of the National Conference's consensus in 1990, any amendment made by a state organ borne of that consensus would be unable to create a new constitution (Stroh 2015, 43).

from the organs of the constitution and not in conflict with them" (Juma and Okpalu 2012, 314). And indeed, why should an exercise of the constituent power at an early stage prevail over an exercise of the same people, constituted differently at a later stage (Tushnet 2013, 2005)? From a civil law perspective, the answer is immanent in the concept of immutable clauses (sometimes referred to as eternity clauses).[8] Existing amendment procedures cannot lawfully change or repeal these clauses. They are truly eternal from the perspective of constituted powers within a constitutional framework, but they are admissible for the constituent power while replacing the old constitution by a new one. Common law countries instead have to rely on the judge-made "basic structure doctrine", which distinguishes between "amendments" and "replacement" (see below).

This academic debate was mirrored in the Kenyan High Court judgement in *Njoya and others vs. Attorney-General and others* that was handed down in the context of the constitutional reform process in Kenya between 2001 and 2004. In a nutshell, the reform was based on the Constitutional Review Act 2001 (CRA),[9] which supplemented the constitutional provisions on constitutional amendment by outlining a process of constitutional review and potential amendment in which several institutions were to be involved. The Constitution of Kenya Review Commission (CKRC)[10] was empowered to "compile its [review] report together with a summary of its recommendations and on the basis thereof, draft a Bill to alter the Constitution".[11] The report and the bill were to be referred to the National Constitutional Conferences (NCC)[12] "for discussion, debate, amendment and adoption"[13] before they were then to be submitted to the "National Assembly for enactment".[14]

Njoya in his successful application to the High Court of Kenya argued that the outcome of the CKRC's work and the conference was a draft constitution rather than a bill amending the existing constitution.[15] Making reference to the "basic structure" doctrine developed by the Indian Supreme Court in *Kesavananda vs.*

8 In Africa, all civil law countries do have immutable clauses in their constitutions while – with the exception of Namibia – none of the common law countries have unamendable provisions (Gambia's eternity clause safeguards the savings of the commission of inquiry as long as based on a military decree and is not considered an substantive immutable clause in this context).
9 In the preparation of the process and due to political and civil society driven interventions, the Act was amended three times between 1997 and 2001.
10 The CKRC was composed of 27 commissioners nominated by the National Assembly and appointed by the president (Sec. 6 (4b) CRA).
11 Sec. 26 (7) CRA.
12 The NCC was composed of 629 delegates, including all CKRC commissioners and members of the NA, 126 civil society delegates, 41 political party representatives, and 210 district delegates (Sec. 27 (2) CRA).
13 Sec. 27 (1b) CRA.
14 Sec. 28 (4) CRA.
15 The draft altered, *i.a.*, the system of government from a presidential to a parliamentary system, substantially reducing the powers of the executive (Stacey 2011, 597).

State of Kerala,[16] he claimed that the Kenyan Constitution authorized the National Assembly as a constituted power only to "alter" the constitution, but not to replace it. The majority opinion (Ringera J and Kasango Ag. J) of the judgement shared this interpretation and by and large also followed the subsequent line of Njoya's argument, which highlighted "that the alteration of the constitution does not involve the substitution thereof with a new one or the destruction of the identity or existence of the constitution altered" (Ringera 2004, para. 60). Consequently, the draft had to be considered illegitimate without the participation of the Kenyan people acting as the constituent power. An institutional mechanism and framework for the people of Kenya, which would allow them to exercise their constituent power and to make and adopt a new constitution, was neither reflected in the constitution nor in the Constitutional Review Act. The two ways in which the constituent power could have been exercised were through a constituent assembly directly elected by the people for the purpose of making the constitution or through a mandatory referendum before it was ratified. The National Constitutional Conference failed "the test of being a body with the peoples' mandate to make a Constitution" (Ringera 2004, para. 30), since it neither had a direct mandate from the people nor the ultimate say in the process, due to the need for final approval by the National Assembly. As the constituent power was not able to manifest itself through a constituent assembly, the adoption through a referendum was indispensable.[17] The hypothetical question of whether a referendum would have been required – even if such a body had been elected – was not at stake in this case and thus not explicitly answered by the High Court. Considering that the majority ruling followed quite closely the line of argument of the Supreme Court of India, which expressly relied on a constituent assembly to overcome a constitution's basic structure, one might assume that either of the decisive involvements of the people would have been considered satisfactory (Brandt et al. 2011, 297).

Conceding that mainstream democratic constitutional theory[18] attributes the constituent power a decisive involvement in the constitution-making process at the beginning (election of the constituent assembly) and/or end (referendum), the question remains to what extent mandatory referenda are the preferable option in such a process? The next section will reflect on the African experiences and the potential advantages and challenges of a constitutional referendum.

16 *Kesavananda Bharati vs. The State of Kerala and Others*, AIR 1973 SC 1461.
17 The dissenting opinion (Kubo J) dismissed the idea of the constituent power as a juridical constitutional concept outside the written law. There are several alternative ways of legitimizing a constitution. Relying on a constituent assembly or a mandatory referendum can be one way, having trust in the National Assembly another. This issue is predominately a political one that requires a political solution (Kubo 2004, 16). If Kenyans prefer one specific mode to another, they should explicitly provide for it in the constitution or the law. Thus, the questions before the Court required resolution through a legislative as opposed to a judicial process (Kubo 2004, 15). In order for the Court to determine that a referendum was mandatory, it had to be expressly provided for in the legislation (Kubo 2004, 17).
18 This theory is based on the – contested (see note 8) – finding that there is a distinction between the people acting as constituted power or as constituent power.

Merits and challenges of referenda in constitution-making processes: African experiences

Referenda: People as gatekeepers against elite capture

Referenda provide citizens with the opportunity to act as gatekeepers in approving or rejecting the final constitutional document (Elkins et al. 2008, 367).[19] Their decision in favour of or against the constitution may be motivated on various grounds. For some there is a considerable distrust of the direct involvement of the people at the end of the process, due to their potential irrationality or even inability to understand inherently complex issues. But actually, there are sufficient examples from the African continent of people using their "veto power" against the constitution for reasons that are, to a great extent, ascertainable, and which were, at least, not unpredictable. The four cases listed below, to various degrees and without ignoring other relevant and context related factors, had one common denominator: first, in the view of the people, promises pertaining to the participatory nature of the process were not kept; and second, the process was perceived as being hijacked by the governing elites. As a consequence, and not irrationally, they refused approval. Describing these ratification defeats as failures may be inapt (Tushnet 2013, 2000). In the Seychelles (1992), the new constitution was drafted in closed sessions during which the opposition remained predominantly marginalized. Critics charged the democratic features of the text as sham and opposition parties campaigned successfully against it (Elkin et al. 2008, 380). The required majority for approval in the final referendum was not obtained.[20] In Zimbabwe (2000), the initially people-driven process for constitutional reform in the late 1990s was subsequently captured by President Mugabe. In order to gain control over the process and its outcome, he used his powers under the Commissions of Inquiry Act to establish a government-led constitutional commission that was tasked with writing recommendations (Saati 2015, 141). Despite its biased composition, the commission produced a draft that was generally considered as "in many respects a progressive and impressive document and might have formed the basis of a new constitutional order" (Hatchard 2001, 213). Making use of the powers granted to him under the Act, Mugabe, however, then altered the content of the text considerably, leaving it to be rejected by 54 percent of those who voted. In Kenya (2004), the draft adopted by the National Conference in the course of an inclusive and people-driven process was amended substantially by the government and passed by Parliament. The government draft was finally put to the people – and rejected – in the referendum (Kirkby and Murray 2016, 109). In Zambia (2016), the promise by the newly elected president

---

19 Not all referenda held in African constitution-making processes have been legally binding or were so at the very end of the process (see Zimbabwe in 2000 and in 2013). But to the knowledge of the author, no African constitution was ratified despite a "no vote" in the referendum.

20 The process required 60 percent of total votes for approval, but only some 54 percent voted in favour of the constitution.

in 2011 to deliver "a new people-driven constitution" remained unredeemed. In the course of the process, the governmental commitment shifted towards preferring a mere constitutional amendment with limited public influence. The initial idea of holding a stand-alone referendum on the entire document was dropped accordingly and the ordinary constitutional amendment clause applied (see chapter on Zambia in this volume). Most parts of the constitutional reform package were amended through a parliamentary process by a two-thirds majority. The manner in which the government's party used its numbers to push amendments through fuelled discontent within the opposition party and parts of civil society (Lumina 2016, 3). For amendments on the specially entrenched Part III (Bill of Rights) of the constitution, a popular referendum had to be held with a minimum turnout of 50 percent of eligible voters.[21] This threshold wasn't met and the referendum failed, also due to the fact that the opposition campaigned for a boycotting of the referendum.[22] Quite a few see this result not as a missed chance, but rather as an opportunity to revisit the constitution-making process in a more inclusive fashion and to reconsider issues that the ruling party unilaterally rejected (Lumina 2016, 3).

As the cases above illustrate, it is not only politically unwise but – due to the instrument of a referendum – also fundamentally counterproductive for a government to draft its own constitution. In the Seychelles, the ruling elite seems to have learned its lesson: following the rejection of the draft constitution, the Constitutional Commission resumed its work, with the opposition now participating fully in its sessions (Hatchard 1993, 606). Proceedings were more open, live coverage through the media was permitted and interest groups were able to put forward proposals (Elkins et al. 2008, 380). The members of the commission unanimously adopted a new and thoroughly revised constitution and in a referendum held in June 1993, it received the approval of around 73 percent of the votes cast (Hatchard 1993, 606). In Kenya, after several years and through "major changes both in the legal framework for and attitudes towards popular ratification in the follow up process" (Kirkby and Murray 2016, 110), the people approved their constitution in 2010 by 68 percent.[23]

It remains to be seen whether the political elite in Tanzania anticipates similar dynamics in that country under the new president and whether it will work to

---

21 Art 79 (3) of the Constitution of Zambia reads:

(3) A bill for the alteration of Part III of this Constitution or of this Article shall not be passed unless before the first reading of the bill in the National Assembly it has been put to a National referendum with or without amendment by not less than fifty percent of persons entitled to be registered as voters for the purposes of presidential and parliamentary elections.

22 Only 44,4 percent of eligible voters participated in the referendum (out of which some 71 percent of valid votes were in favour of the amendment). See EISA 2016.

23 Though Brandt et al. argue that "it does not seem that Kenyan politicians, acting through the parliamentary select committee, were particular concerned about the reaction of the people (even shortly before the 2010 referendum was due), but the committee of experts, realizing that the last word lay with the people, felt emboldened to restore some people-oriented provisions that had been removed by the committee." (Brandt et al. 2011, 300).

redirect a currently gridlocked and elite-captured process, before the people decline the draft constitution in the referendum. As outlined in the chapter on Tanzania in this volume, the Constituent Assembly (assembled in a manner that guaranteed a super majority to the then existing ruling elite) redrafted much of the constitutional text submitted to it after a rather extensive and participatory review process.

Referenda: Downstream constraint

Referenda are generally held at the end of a constitution-making process.[24] However, this does not mean that their relevance is limited to yes/no voting in the final stage. One crucial effect that a referendum may have on the dynamics of a constitution-making process is what Elster has described as a "downstream constraint". If constitutional drafters "know that the document they produce will have to be ratified by another body, knowledge of the preferences of that body will act as a constraint on what they can propose" (Elster 1995, 374). The cases discussed above do not affirm an anticipatory sensitivity or pressure of the political elites towards the will of the people, when they put to referendum their own version of the constitution (occasionally having altered participatory drafted previous versions). But there are other, more concrete and content-specific examples that can be seen to confirm this effect: during the post-conflict constitution-making process in the Central African Republic (CAR), some NGOs urged for the abolition of the death penalty in the constitution. The drafters, who declined this suggestion, argued that due to the genocidal incidents in the CAR, the majority of people would reject the constitution if capital punishment were to be abolished as a legally permissible sanction.[25] In Zimbabwe, the opposition party (MDC) was careful not to be regarded as opposed to the expropriation of land for redistribution to the landless black majority. It premised its stance on the need to provide adequate compensation and to advance de-racializing of the land issue (see chapter on Zimbabwe). In Senegal, the idea of including the principle of *laïcité* in the catalogue of immutable clauses was dropped after heavy protests from the National Federation of Associations of Senegal Koranic Schools who threatened to boycott the referendum (Ndao 2016). It is obvious from these examples that the downstream constraint on constitutional content is in a sense ambivalent as it may also respond to illiberal sentiments. This ambivalence holds true not only with regards to single issues, but can more generally also apply to the drafting of an overall coherent and comprehensive document: the pressure to accept the various views of the people on too many different issues in

---

24 Occasionally, referenda in constitution-building processes can also be initiated to settle a contentious issue emerging in the drafting body. The process in Uganda (1995) and Kenya (2005) provided for the opportunity to adjourn the proceedings and refer the contentious issue for resolution by the people (see Art. 27 (5) of the Kenyan Constitutional Review Act as of 2002). In both cases, it wasn't taken up (Brandt et al. 2011, 297).

25 Interview with an international advisor being involved in the transitionary process between 2013 and 2015.

order to guarantee its success in the referendum may become counterproductive due to the simultaneous creation of internal inconsistencies and institutional mismatches (Elster 1995, 388; Elkins et al. 2008, 371).

A rather productive "downstream constraint" of referenda seems to be their conditioned activation. Here, the constraint felt by the drafters does not unfold on the basis of anticipating certain preferences of the populace, but precisely through the fact that, under particular circumstances, a referendum could be staged at the end of the process. In South Africa, Uganda, and Tunisia, directly elected constituent assemblies were tasked with adopting the final constitutional text. A referendum was included only as an option of last resort in case the respective assembly failed to adopt the text by the required majority. In both South Africa and Tunisia, this mechanism had a reinforcing effect on the desire of the members of the assemblies to forge a common understanding on the relevant issues, in order to receive the required majority vote and avoid the referendum. There was consensus in both countries among the drafters that a referendum should be avoided by all means in order to prevent a potential collapse of the constitution, particularly through the influence that extremists may end up having on the referendum (Brandt et al. 2011, 300; chapter on Tunisia in this volume).

One might also deliberately trigger some sort of downstream constraint by instituting specific requirements on approval thresholds of referenda. In countries with a dominant religious or ethnic group and strong group identification, constitutions may be drafted to privilege this group at the expense of minorities. Though, by definition, referenda do have a majority bias; in such contexts, tailoring the approval requirements to prevent a single group from dominating the outcome may contribute to more consensus-driven negotiations. Instead of relying on a simple majority of those voting, one may increase the threshold either on the side of turnout (50 percent of registered voters or even 50 percent of eligible voters (Zambia) have to participate) or on the kind of majority to be gained (absolute majority (Congo) or 60 percent (Seychelles) of votes). Another approach was taken in Kenya where apart from an overall majority of votes nationwide, the draft needed to get a support of at least 25 percent in a minimum of five of the eight provinces (Brandt et al. 2011, 299).[26] In an ethnically divided country like Kenya, constitutional drafters have to consider the views of regionally located minorities if they do not want the draft to fail in the referendum.

Referenda: Whose voice?

Referenda are seen as the modal form of participation in constitution-making processes (Elkins et al. 2008, 364). Yet, there is scepticism about this instrument.

26 In Switzerland, rules are even stricter. According to Art. 195 of the Swiss constitution, the passing of a new constitution requires that, in addition to the majority of the people at the national level, a majority in more than half of the 26 cantons (regions) must vote in favour. This idea of double majority voting can also be delinked from the territorial concept. One might, for example, require that next to an overall majority, the majority from one specific ethnic minority or religion – regardless of where they are situated in the country – must consent.

Some concerns are of a general nature, while others are limited to the specificities of voters facing a binary decision as to what is to constitute the foundations for their society – by nature always complex and multidimensional.

Constituent power's voice or autocratic plebiscite?

One concern is with its frequent employment by autocrats and thereby the use using referenda to legitimize their authoritarian control, rather than to allow citizens to render a verdict on their constitution (Blount 2011, 50). In authoritarian contexts, referenda campaigns and elections are to a considerable degree facing the same challenges: the use of official resources for campaigns, monopolization of airtime, executive control over media, intimidation and the use of militia, bribery and other forms of corruption, etc. On top, the draft text is often deliberately handed out only shortly before the referendum in order to avoid independent assessment and public debate. Often, governmental pressure and its control of the ballot boxes leaves no space for people to articulate discontent by voting "no", or by boycotting the referendum completely. Examples are abundant: in the Sudanese process of 1998, the draft text of the commission was considerably altered by the president and when submitted to a highly manipulated and controlled referendum, where the outcome was an approval rate of 96.7 percent of voters with 91.9 percent of eligible voters participating.[27] Rwanda (2003), and the recent processes in Congo Brazzaville (2015), in Morocco (2011), and in Egypt (2014) have a similar track record in capturing people's votes, ranking in Saati's typology between "symbolic" and "false" forms of participation (Saati chapter 1). As difficult as it is to prevent the misuse of a democratic device for undemocratic means in autocratic contexts, this risk shouldn't be taken as an argument against referenda or elections more generally. The sporadic success, sometimes rather unexpected and surprising, in blocking the executive's attempt in this direction should be reassuring.

Right tool for the wrong purpose?

Apart from the outright misuse of the referendum, there remains the more general question as to the adequacy of a referendum to ensure participation, if participation is understood to mean something deeper than just expressing a yes/no vote on a given political package or on provisions negotiated by others (Saati 2015, 34). It has been stated earlier that referenda offer citizens a vote at the end of the process but not a voice within the process. They are ill adapted to adjust or fine-tune a complex and multidimensional document and the risk remains that an entire document may get rejected due to a rather minor constitutional issue that has been blown out of proportion in the campaign.

In only a few cases have African countries tried to overcome the binary option on an entire document by offering different choices. One example is the

---

27 See the country report Sudan of the Widner's Constitution Writing and Conflict Resolution Project. Available at: https://www.princeton.edu/~pcwcr/reports/sudan1998.html.

referendum for approval of the draft constitution in Benin in 1990. Voters had three choices: declining the constitution altogether or choosing between two versions of the constitution, which differed on one single issue that the National Conference hadn't been able to agree on: namely, the incorporation of a clause stipulating upper and lower age-limits for presidential candidates[28] (Gisselquist 2008, 797).[29] Since the number of invalid votes was quite low (3 percent), one might assume that the multiple choices hadn't been too confusing for voters. But it is also obvious that this bricolage of multiple questions in a final referendum had inherent limitations.

Generally, and as addressed above, a strong participatory effect of a referendum comes to be dependent on the logic and expectation that an effective downstream constraint will exist. It is based on the assumption that in order to be successful, a referendum requires a process design with a high degree of buy-in and ownership of the gatekeepers. Or, the power of the vote creates room for the voice. In turn, the argument concerning the limits of citizens' competence to decide on complex issues runs in a similar vein. If constitutional literacy is low, respective education programs are needed[30] in order to allow for a better understanding on the part of citizens, rather than washing out the basic idea of the people as the constituent power. Case studies have illustrated the increase of constitutional knowledge through respective programs and participatory involvement (Moehler 2008, 233).[31]

But there is an additional, partly overlapping aspect relevant for assessing the appropriateness of referenda and adequate alternatives. While in theory, a clear distinction exists between people voting (electing representatives who will make decisions on behalf of the people as the constituent power) and issue voting (though referenda), this distinction is rendered more ambiguous and complex in practice (Morel 2012, 501). Referenda are seen as a form of direct democracy that is commonly believed to be the true and real form of democracy, expressing the immediate and genuine will of "the people", and as uncovering the legitimate national interest. In comparison, where the will is expressed through representatives, it is perceived to be mediated, often deficient, and to be justifiable only by technical necessities (Boeckenfoerde 1991b, 381). This categorization of different degrees of "full" democracy may be based on a romanticized understanding of

---

28 Though this clause initially reads as being of minor relevance, it had a strong impact since it aimed to keep the leaders who had dominated since the 1960s out of electoral politics (Gisselquist 2008, 797).

29 93.2 percent of votes were in favor of the new constitution and 6.8 percent against it. Out of the 93.2 percent yes votes, 73.3 percent opted for age limitation and 19.9 percent against age limitation. See African Elections Database, available at: http://africanelections.tripod.com/bj.html

30 In a country with a high illiteracy rate, visual depictions in graphic form (cartoons), radio, television, and occasionally different forms of theatre plays are used.

31 As learned in the case of Zimbabwe (see country report in this volume), those in control of the radio and television stations may use these means of communication to manipulate and redefine constitutional content.

the concept of the "people" as the incarnation of a popular will standing above partisan politics. The existence of a body of representatives is seen to dilute the "self" in self-governance – and the autonomy and political affirmation ascribed thereto – when it is assumed that these representatives may also act against the will of the people. But the people as a monolithic entity is fiction. As Ghai and Galli have pointed out, "There is no such thing as the people". Instead, it is a collection of groups and identities with complementary and contradictory interests. There are religious and ethnic groups, women, youth, farmers, pastoralists, workers, business persons, "indigenous people", lawyers, failed or aspiring politicians, family members, etc. all pursuing their agenda (Ghai and Galli 2006, 15). Individual voters, rather, align to one of the parties, groups, or identities they feel best represented by, or are most dependent on. These entities may organize in support of or against ratification, often by significantly simplifying the constitution's diverse and complex content and by occasionally focusing on only single issues. *De facto*, referendum campaigns to approve a new constitution often end up supporting a specific group or political party. Considering that in practice a certain form of representation is always inherent, the distinction between "direct" and "represented" becomes gradually blurred and hardly justifies the former's status as superior.

Conclusion

Constitutional theory, as interpreted by some courts on the African continent, requires a decisive role of the constituent power in the process. A referendum is one admissible instrument next to a directly elected constituent assembly. The paper highlights that the existence of referenda in a process has had its merits in several African countries for it has allowed the people to halt elite captured processes. It also illustrates that in some countries, process design limited some of the potential pitfalls of referenda (divisive nature of yes-or-no votes). Balancing positive dynamics – that were in part triggered by downstream effects – with its inherent shortcomings, it may be fruitful to explore further whether a directly elected constituent assembly, composed through a system of proportional representation, would serve the purpose of having a substantial impact on the process. This might especially be the case, if a referendum isn't categorically avoided, but would rather be used for a specific question at an intermediate stage of the process and would come to serve as a fallback option when broad consensus can't be achieved in the assembly.

References

Baranger, D. (2011). "The Language of Eternity: Judicial Review of the Amending Power in France (or the Absence Thereof)", 44 *Israel Law Review*, 389–428.

Blount, J. (2011). "Participation in Constitutional Design". Ginsburg and Dixon, *Comparative Constitutional Law*, Cheltenham, 38–56.

Boeckenfoerde, E.W. (1991a). *Die verfassungsgebende Gewalt des Volkes – Ein Grenzbegriff des Verfassungsrechts*. Staat, Verfassung, Demokratie, Frankfurt, 90–114.

Boeckenfoerde, E.W. (1991b). *Demokratie und Representation: Zur Kritik der heutigen Demokratiediskussion*. Staat, Verfassung, Demokratie, Frankfurt, 379–405.

Brandt, M., Cotrell, J., Ghai, Y., and Regan, A. (2011). *Constitution-Making and Reform – Options for the Process*. Interpeace.

CIA (2016). "Constitutions". In: "The World Factbook". Available at: https://www.cia.gov/library/publications/the-world-factbook/fields/2063.html.

Dann, P., Riegner, M., Wortmann, M., and Vogel, J. (2011). "Lessons Learned from Constitution-Making: Processes with Broad-Based Public Participation". Democracy Reporting International, Briefing Paper No. 20.

Dann, P., and Al-Ali, Z. (2006). "The Internationalized Pouvoir Constituant: Constitution-Making Under External Influence in Iraq, Sudan and East Timor". In: Bogdandy and Wolfrum (eds), 10 *Max Planck Yearbook of United Nations Law*, 423–63

Dyzenhaus, D. (2012). "Constitutionalism In an Old Key: Legality and Constituent Power". 1 *Global Constitutionalism*, 229–60.

Electoral Institute for Sustainable Democracy in Africa, Eisa (2016). Zambia: 2016 Referendum Results. Available at: https://www.eisa.org.za/wep/zam2016referendum.htm.

Elkins, Z., Ginsburg, T., and Blount, J. (2008). "The Citizen as Founder: Public Participation in Constitutional Approval". 81 *Temp. L. Rev.*, 361–82.

Elster, J. (1995). "Forces and Mechanisms in the Constitution-Making Process". 45(2) *Duke Law Journal*, 364–96.

Ghai, Y., and Galli, G. (2006). "Constitution Building Processes and Democratization". International IDEA. Available at: http://www.idea.int/sites/default/files/publications/constitution-building-processes-and-democratization.pdf.

Gisselquist, R.M. (2008). "Democratic Transition and Democratic Survival in Benin". 15(4) *Democratization*, 789–814.

Hatchard, J. (2001). "Some Lessons on Constitution-Making from Zimbabwe". 45(2) *Journal of African Law*, 210–16.

Hatchard, J. (1993). "Re-Establishing a Multi-Party State: Some Constitutional Lessons from the Seychelles". 31(4) *The Journal of Modern African Studies*, 601–12.

Juma, L., and Okpalu, C. (2012). "Judicial Intervention in Kenya's Constitutional Process". 11 *Washington University Global Studies Law Review*, 287–364.

Kay, R.S. (2011). "Constituent Authority". 59 *Americal Journal of Comparative Law*, 735–55.

Kirkby, C., and Murray, C. (2016). "Constitution-Making in Anglophone Africa: We the People?" In: Ndulo and Gazibo, *Growing Democracy in Africa: Elections, Accountable Governance, and Political Economy*, Cambridge Scholars Publishing, Newcastle upon Tyne, 86–113.

Kubo, J. (2004). "Dissenting Opinion". In: *Reverend Dr. Timothy M. Njoya and 6 others vs. Honourable Attorney-General and another* .

LeDuc, L. (2015). "Referendums and Deliberative Democracy". 38 *Electoral Studies*, 139–48.

Lenowitz, J.A. (2013). *Why Ratification? Questioning the Unexamined Constitution-making procedure*. Columbia University.

Loughlin, M. (2014). "The Concept of Constituent Power". 13 *European Journal of Political Theory*, 218–37.

Lumina, C. (2016). "Zambia's Failed Constitutional Referendum: What Next?". Available at: www.constitutionnet.org/news/zambias-failed-constitutional-referendum-what-next.

Moehler, D. (2008). *Distrusting Democrats: Outcomes of Participatory Constitution Making.* Ann Arbor.

Morel, L. (2012). Referendum. Rosenfeld and Sajó (eds), *The Oxford Handbook of Comparative Constitutional Law.* Oxford University Press, 501–28.

Ndao, S.D. (2016). "Revision Constitutionelle: Les maitres coraniques exigent le retrait du concept de Laïcité". *Jotay*, 5 February 2016. Available at: http://jotay.net/revision-constitutionnelle-les-maitres-coraniques-exigent-le-retrait-du-concept-de-laicite/.

Ringera, J., and Kasango Ag. J. (2004). "Majority Opinion". In: *Reverend Dr. Timothy M. Njoya and 6 others vs. Honourable Attorney-General and another.*

Roznai, Y. (2017). *Unconstitutional Constitutional Amendments: The Limits of Amendment Powers.* OUP.

Saati, A. (2015). *The Participation Myth: Outcomes of Participatory Constitution Building Processes on Democracy.* Umeå University.

Schmitt, C. (2008). *Constitutional Theory* (translated by J. Seitzer). Duke University Press.

Stacey, R. (2011). "Constituent Power and Carl Schmitt's Theory of Constitution in Kenya's Constitution Making Process". 9 *International Journal of Constitutional Law,* 587–614.

Stroh, A. (2015). "Benin". In: S. Elischer, R. Hofmeier, A. Mehler, and H. Melber. *Africa Yearbook 11: Politics, Economy and Society South of the Sahara in 2014.* Brill, 41–47, 43.

Suksi, M. (2010). "Referendums in Constitution-making Processes". Constitution-making in Focus: Issue Paper. Interpeace.

Tushnet, M. (2013). "Constitution-Making: An Introduction". 91 *Texas Law Review,* 1983–2013.

Part II

Participation in constitution-making processes

3 The flawed public participation in the Egyptian constitutional process

Mohamed Abdelaal[*]

Introduction

It is critical to distinguish our understanding of public participation in constitution-making process from any other competing conception. One should regard public participation in particular as different from the concept of having a quite participatory constituent assembly in general that is usually charged with the task of writing the constitution. The concept of having a participatory constituent assembly is, in fact, a scheme of participation that determines the degree of involvement by different actors in the constitution-making process, typically in the drafting stage. Public participation, however, implies a wider understanding regarding the guarantee of more accessibility in different stages of the constitution-making process that goes beyond the initial drafting step. Specifically, in a brilliant leap, Jennifer Widner (2008) identifies five stages of the process of constitution making, which she names the drafting, the consultation, the deliberation, the adoption, and the ratification.[1] Among these five stages, the significance of creating a participatory constituent assembly could be witnessed in the drafting and the deliberation stages. However, public participation, with more or less degree, plays a pivotal role in the five different stages. This is a distinction that I will discuss further in the pages to follow.

In setting the boundaries between public participation and a participatory constituent assembly, it is worthwhile to mention that the former is concerned only with the participation of the general public. The latter, however, calls for the involvement of different actors, such as the government, political parties, interest groups and lobbyists, societal elites, professional syndicates, and constitutional experts, in addition to the public itself. Although, representatives of these different actors will contribute to the process of public participation through popular referendum; however, at this time they will lose their institutional affiliation and vote as ordinary citizens.

---

[*] Assistant Professor, Alexandria University Faculty of Law, Alexandria, Egypt. Adjunct Professor of Law, Indiana University Robert H. McKinney School of Law, Indianapolis, Indiana, USA.

1 Some scholars summarized the process of constitution making in only three stages, the drafting, the deliberation, and the ratification (Eisenstadt and LeVan 2012). Other scholars prefer to add pre-negotiations and bargains to different stages of constitution-building process (See, e.g. Banting and Simeon 1985).

DOI: 10.4324/9781315180540-6

Techniques vary on how a constitution-making process is to be structured and conducted. They range from having an assembly that is composed of mostly experts or elite groups, or a representative assembly whom its members may be selected through either elected legislatures or direct elections. These techniques are not fundamentally heterogeneous; however, a modern constitution-making process could blend them altogether in an attempt to confer more legitimacy and to avoid foreseeable shortcoming results (Democracy Reporting International 2011).

In 1787, an elite-dominated group gathered in Philadelphia to craft the Federal Constitution of the United States. Members of this group, who were later known as Founding Fathers of the United States and the Framers of the Constitution, were all white males and most held slaves. After they completed their drafting work, they sent the written document to the states for an approval process to be conducted by popularly elected legislatures (Dahl 2001, 102–8). In a modern constitution-making process, this approval step is known as the ratification process (Ginsburg et al. 2008, 362).

Contrary to the paradigm introduced by the drafting process of the American Constitution, however, still motivated by the American Revolution and fascinated by the Enlightenment ideas introduced by the American Constitution, the task of drafting the French Constitution of 1791 was vested in the elected legislative assembly to confer more legitimacy (see Elster 1995). In 1789, the newly formed French National Assembly gathered to draft the short-lived French Constitution of 1791. The Assembly would later appoint a twelve-member committee and charged it with the task of writing the new constitution.[2]

Although the purpose of the ratification process introduced in the making process of the American Constitution was to lessen the severity of not having the public represented in the drafting process (Rakove 1996, 96), it has been periodically the target for many critics who see popular participation as the most effective tool in regard to the right of citizenry (Ghai 2004, 7).

Guided by the revolutionary spirit, likewise, the drafting of the French Constitution of 1791 seemed to avoid the negative outcomes that were likely to be generated from designating the king as the institution to ratify the constitution (Elster 1995). Specifically, the power of writing the constitution was granted to the elected legislative national assembly as a feature of the now-widely accepted concept that public input could be achieved indirectly through a representative body that acts on behalf of the people (see e.g. Samuels 2006, 668).

The previous two examples, the US Constitution of 1787 and the French Constitution of 1791, are not necessarily inclusive in seeing the involvement of popularly elected assemblies, either in the ratification process or the drafting process per se, in the constitution-making process as a tool to witness the public input, but many constitutions adopted the same approach. Although constitutional ratification through public referendums has gained more popularity in the

2 The delegates of the 1791 French Constitution adopted a proposal that renders them ineligible to run for the first ordinary legislature to shield themselves against self and partisan interests (Elster 1995, 385).

making process of modern constitutions (see Ginsburg et al. 2009), the fact that the constitution-making process is not only limited to the approval process, but rather extends to accommodate the drafting and consultation processes, makes public participation, with different degrees, a must in these latter stages as well.

Why public participation?

Public participation in the process of constitution making is generally theorized to strengthen democratic practices and skills by educating citizens about their political participation, building bridges of trust between individuals and governmental institutions (Finkel 1987, 441, 461), enhancing the concepts of self-realization and self-government (see Kariel 1969),[3] making individuals aware of the content of the constitution and different ways to oppose the government (see Barber 1984), and creating positive political culture. However, in the case of Egypt, the importance of public participation goes beyond that.

Given the circumstances that surrounded the process of making the current Egyptian Constitution, ensuring the legitimacy of the document was a matter of great concern. Precisely, the constitution was drafted in a time of crisis where an elected president has been ousted after nationwide protests and a military-backed interim government was ruling the country. Additionally, at this time, the Egyptian society was best described as a post-conflict dismembered society where Islamists faced sectarian recriminations from liberals whilst the latter as well as the military has been accused of bringing the democratic process to a fail by ousting the elected president and seizing power.

Further, supporters of the Muslim Brotherhood as well as the West have regarded the process of forcing President Morsi of the Muslim Brotherhood out of power as well as the suspension of the 2012 Constitution as a full military coup which turned Egypt backwards and which should be categorically rejected by all free men. Consequently, both the interim government and the military were placed in the position of the defendant who always needs to negate the coup accusation and ensure the legitimacy of the political transition and the regime change.

Given these riotous circumstances, public participation was an urgent demand in the making of Egypt's current Constitution of 2014. Specifically, in a time of crisis that Egypt experienced when it entered a political transition period following the toppling of the Muslim Brotherhood's regime, a constitution-making process that is not observed by the public and a constitution that is not deliberated on by the people would simply contribute to worsening the crisis.

Likewise, public participation was of huge importance in the making of the Egyptian Constitution, that is to send a message to the West that the removal of the former regime was not the outcome of a military coup but a popular uprising. Thus, public participation would simply be handing a powerful cover of

---

3 Describing the process of self-realization as "the testing of the boundaries of one's identity."

legitimacy. Similarly, public participation was crucial for Egypt to confirm the national unity and to obliterate the negative idea that the society is divided into a pro-Islamist camp verses an anti-Islamist camp.

Finally, and most prominently, after two popular uprisings that toppled two defiant regimes in 2011 and 2013 respectively, where people were frustrated by the actions of government and the deteriorated political and economic situations, it was necessary to involve them in the making process of the constitution. Having said that, an intuitive claim for mass participation in the recent constitution-building process in Egypt was essential for future renegotiation (see Voigt 2004) and for allowing people to monitor actions of the government to curb any attempt to violate limits on governmental power (see Carey 2000). Moreover, mass participation was necessary to convince the public that they are among the stakeholders in political life as well as to promote the principle of self-government since it enhances the idea that people are the real owner of the constitution (Hart 2003).[4]

Participation in the Egyptian constitution-making process

The constituent assembly: Was it participatory?

Pursuant to a constitutional declaration issued by the military on July 8, 2013 after the president's ouster, two committees were to be involved in the drafting of the new constitution. A ten-member committee of legal experts was formed by a presidential decree to amend the Constitution of 2012[5] before having these amendments discussed by a fifty-member committee representing major stakeholders in Egyptian society (Abdelaal 2015).

According to Article 29 of the constitutional declaration, the Committee of Fifty should represent political parties, workers, peasants, members of labor unions and federations, national councils, churches, Al-Azhar institute, armed forces, police, and public figures. The committee should also include at least ten youth from both sexes. Thus, the formation of the Committee of Fifty reveals the commitment of the interim government to install a diverse constituent assembly.

However, unlike the former Constitution of 2012, which was drafted by a Constituent Assembly in which the first democratic Islamist-dominated House of Representatives elected most of its members, the Constituent Assembly of the current Constitution of 2014, including both the Committee of Ten as well as the Committee of Fifty, was formed by a presidential decree.[6] Having this in

---

4 Arguing that "a claim of necessity for participation is based on the belief that without the general sense of 'ownership' that comes from sharing authorship, today's public will not understand, respect, support, and live within the constraints of constitution government" (Hart 2003, 4).

5 According to Article 28 of the declaration, the Committee of Ten is to be formed of two members of the Supreme Constitutional Court and its College of Commissioners, and two of the judges of the State Council, and four constitutional law professors.

6 The first 2012 Constituent Assembly was composed of 100 members: 39 seats for parliamentary members and 61 seats for independent members (6 seats for judges, 13 seats for labor unions, 21 seats

mind, public participation was more evident in the 2012 Constituent Assembly since its members were to be elected by the legislature that acted on behalf of the people. However, since members of the 2013 Constituent Assembly were to be appointed pursuant to a presidential decree, a mechanism that may negatively affect the degree of public participation, the assembly had to incorporate different societal stakeholders in which the public input was to be seen in the participation of the political parties, national councils, and the youth.

The deliberation process

After the appointment of the Committee of Fifty, this latter was divided into five committees: The Fundamental Principles and the State Committee, The Regime and Public Authorities Committee, The Drafting Committee, The Rights and Freedoms Committee, and The Communication and Community Dialogue Committee. The Communication and Community Dialogue Committee was charged with the task of communicating with the general public and receiving their comments, suggestions, and criticisms about the content of the constitutional draft.[7] The committee tried to conduct an effective consultation process by holding various public hearing sessions with different sects of the Egyptian society, such as the Nubians and Bedouin people, surveying their opinion about the content of the constitution.

In addition, as a part of the consultation process, the State Information Service Institute, an institute that is affiliated with the Office of Presidency, launched several campaigns and held numerous panels and colloquiums that toured Egypt's different cities and provinces with the purpose of familiarizing the people with the constitution and making them aware of its content. Further, the official website of the Committee of Fifty provided an option for the public to submit their suggestions and criticisms of every single article of the constitutional draft.[8]

Beside the official consultation process, supporters and opponents of the constitutional draft were able to launch unofficial campaigns to mobilize in favor or against the draft. For instance, entities that support the constitutional draft, such as Al-Nour Party of the Salafists, the Dignity Party, the Trade Union, and the National Salvation Front launched campaigns and held several meetings to

for public figures, 9 seats for law experts, 5 seats for the Al-Azhar institute, 4 seats for the Coptic Orthodox Church, a seat for the armed forces, a seat for the police, and a seat for the Ministry of Justice). However, this Assembly was dissolved by the Supreme Council of Armed Forces (SCAF) after a ruling from the Supreme Constitutional Court dissolved the elected Parliament. In the formation of the second Constituent Assembly, only 39 out of the 100 members were elected by the Parliament (Abdelaal 2013, 203).

7 Similarly, the 2012 Constituent Assembly responsible for the drafting of the 2012 Constitution was made up of five committees in which one of them, the Drafting and Research Committee, was responsible for communicating with the people and receiving their opinions and suggestions regarding the constitutional draft.

8 The Committee of Fifty's Official Website, available at (http://dostour.eg/).

persuade the people to vote up the draft. Likewise, those who oppose the draft, specifically members of the Muslim Brotherhood, Egypt's Revolutionary Socialists, and the Revolution Front publicly denounced the constitutional draft asking the people to vote it down (Ahram Online 2014; Ahram Online 2013). Further, some of the constitutional draft's opponents, such as the Anti-Coup Alliance, the Strong Egypt Party, and the April 6 Youth Movement inaugurated a campaign to boycott the referendum process (Egypt Independent 2014; Mada Masr 2014).

International community and the constitution-making process

A number of dependent variables collectively control the exercise of the constitution-making process. One of these variables is whether an external actor could influence the making process of the constitution. Such external actor is always associated with the possibility of reserving a role for the international community to be played in the constitution-making process. The influence of the international community could be directly witnessed if foreign actors were allowed to take part in the drafting process of the constitution, or indirectly by allowing international organization to direct the constitutional drafters to the importance of including some international fundamental standards in the constitutional draft. For instance, in the process of building the current Afghan Constitution of 2004, the international community was directly involved through the participation of the United Nations, the Center on International Cooperation at New York University, and foreign diplomats in writing the constitution (Al-Ali 2011, 81). However, in the making of the Rwandan Constitution of 2003, international participation was indirectly acknowledged when the Legal and Constitutional Commission (LCC) invited the UN Development Fund for Women (UNIFEM) to help educate the constitutional designers as well as the public about Rwanda's international obligations under the UN Convention on the Elimination of All Forms of Discrimination Against Women (CEDAW).[9]

In Egypt, given the many domestic and international calls that described Morsi's ouster and the overthrow of the Muslim Brotherhood's regime as a military coup, and thus denying the legitimacy of the constitution-writing process, ensuring a broad base of international participation was to be expected in an attempt to legitimize the entire process. However, the constitution-making process was after all a strict closed affair where the international community's participation was kept at the minimum (Moustafa 2012, 11). In fact, with a long constitutional history dating to 1882 when it was an Ottoman province,[10] a large population, and several legal practitioners and experts, Egypt should not be

---

9 The UN Development Fund for Women (UNIFEM) held several workshops and meetings throughout the country to help raise women's rights public awareness (see Banks 2008).
10 Egypt's first encounter with modern constitutions can be traced to the era of Ottoman Egypt, when Khedive Tewfiq, ruler of Egypt and Sudan, issued the Constitution of 1882, before being repealed by the British occupation. The Constitution of 1882 was a modest attempt to implement a democratic system under an Ottoman rule, as embodied in the family of Muhammad Ali.

blamed for limiting participation in the constitution-writing process on the nationals. Moreover, throughout the different stages of the constitution-making process, the position of Islamic Sharia and the issue of political accountability were the most often confronted, which are all matters related to the internal affairs of the state that should not be decided by foreign actors.

If that is the case, the role of the international community was witnessed only in the referendum process. The US government, the European Union, NGOs, and many international observers were allowed to monitor the referendum as well as to examine the public attitude during the drafting process. These international actors, with the cooperation of Egypt's official and judiciary that supervise the voting process, were granted access to places where pooling and voting took place in order to document any violation (Dunne 2014).

For instance, Democracy International, one of the international institutes that was allowed to monitor the voting process, had serious concerns about the political atmosphere in which the referendum took place. Specifically, the institute expressed its fears towards the draconian Public Protest Law of 2013, which was issued by the interim government and resulted in a wide police crackdown on the opposition figures, activists, and protestors (Abdelaal 2014). Additionally, the institute criticized the Egyptian media for being biased in ignoring criticisms directed towards the constitutional draft, spending much time praising it, and directing the voters to vote it up (Democracy International 2013).

Similarly, before being approved, the constitutional draft has been heavily criticized by Human Rights Watch, an international nongovernmental organization, as it failed to provide more guarantees for equality between men and women and to address the state's commitment towards the rising phenomenon of sexual harassment (Human Rights Watch 2014). Further, international and domestic women's rights organizations condemned the composition of the fifty-member constitutional committee that only 10 percent of its seats is reserved for women and the youth (Equality Now 2014). It is worth noting that many concerns have been raised by the international observers regarding the state's conduct in imposing further restrictions on the work of civil society organizations, which have resulted in banning many of them from participating in the constitution-making process through monitoring and observing the drafting as well as the voting stage.

In sum, it is safe to say that the role played by the international community in the process of making the Egyptian Constitution was, after all, neutral. As mentioned earlier, the international community and foreign actors did not have access to the drafting process for issues related to preserving the state's sovereignty and reducing external influences. However, the role of the international community was only observed in the participation of the state-approved international actors and organization observed in the referendum stage, a participation that has nothing to do with the content of the constitution. The neutrality of the international community was more evident in that the legitimacy of the constitution has never been disputed by any of the international organizations and actors, notwithstanding the many concerns raised by some of them.

Evaluation

Judging from the relevant circumstances and methodologies adopted in the making process of the Egyptian Constitution, it was envisaged from the outset that the public was consulted throughout most of the stages of the process. Nevertheless, the ridiculously low turnout rate of only 32.9 percent among residents and expatriates suggests that something definitely went wrong.[11]

In fact, a careful examination of the mechanism adopted in forming the Egyptian Constituent Assembly reveals that it does not expressly advance for including the public in the making process of the constitution. Public input in constitutional design could take different forms; among them is the direct participation, which represents a feature of direct democracy in which the public can be directly involved in the making process of the constitution by being members of the constituent assembly. However, direct mass participation remains an unrealistic option in the making process of modern constitutions, including that of Egypt, given its logistic and financial difficulties as well as the high population and its continuing growth.

Public participation in the constitution-making process could also be guaranteed though the mechanism of representation, as a form of representative democracy, by electing representatives to the body responsible for drafting the constitution. This mode of public participation could be achieved either by allowing the public to directly elect those who would represent them in the constituent assembly or indirectly by designating an already established elected legislature as the constitutional drafting committee. The latter model was adopted in the making of Egypt's former Constitution of 2012, when the Parliament was vested the power to elect members of the constituent assembly. However, the mechanism adopted in the formation of the constituent assembly responsible for the drafting of the current Constitution of 2014, by installing its members pursuant to a presidential decree issued by the interim president, does not support the purpose of public participation through representation.

Another mode of public participation is consultation. Despite the fact that ample evidence supports the position of Egypt's authorities in consulting the public throughout the constitutional drafting process, serious concerns could be raised regarding the effectiveness of this consultation process. Across a broad range of consultation mechanisms – including public hearing sessions, official and unofficial campaigns, and an informative official website for commenting on the work of the drafting committee, the consultation process failed to confer a convinced legitimacy on the constitutional text and thus, to ensure a strong sense of public ownership.

11 The official results of the 2014 Egyptian Constitutional Referendum is available at (http://www.atlanticcouncil.org/blogs/egyptsource/official-results-98-1-percent-vote-in-favor-of-egypt-s-new-constitution-with-38-6-percent-voter-turnout).

Right from the beginning, it seems that the authorities failed in considering one of Egypt's deeply rooted problems; that is the high rate of illiteracy.[12] After the creation of its website, the constituent assembly invited the public to submit their comments on the content of the constitutional draft using the online system provided by the website. According to the database of the assembly's website, the 90,286 who actively engaged in commenting on the constitutional articles equaled only less than one percent of the 55 million civilian noninstitutional population who have the right to vote in Egypt. In fact, such low participation raises great concerns regarding the mechanism adopted in consulting the public since it ignored the high illiteracy rate among the Egyptian population, which consequently entails digital illiteracy. Thus, by expecting the public to participate in the constitution-making process through submitting their comments and criticisms online, the state assumed the availability and accessibility of digital knowledge and skills in the Egyptians, which was a huge mistake after all.

Moreover, as mentioned earlier, most of the several campaigns launched to educate the public about their constitutional rights and make them aware of the content of the constitution were state-sponsored and urged the people to vote up the constitutional draft, a matter that significantly contributed in hurting the neutrality of the consultation process, rendering it a biased one. Additionally, when the constituent assembly sought to allow some relevant stakeholders in the Egyptian society to participate in the making process of the constitution through consultation, such participation was limited on inviting actors/actresses and lawyers to share their thoughts regarding the constitution (Abdelaal 2013). Further, the invitation of the constituent assembly to these stakeholders to take part in the deliberations of the constitutional draft should not be counted towards an effective consultation process simply because Egypt's actors/actresses and lawyers were already represented in the assembly through the head of their syndicate (Abdelaal 2013).

In fact, a fair and impartial examination of the constitution-making process in Egypt reveals that public participation is not an inherent right that the public must enjoy; however, it is no more than a grant that is awarded subject to the discretion of the authorities. Further, if being granted, public participation in Egypt would likely still be subject to the discretion of the authorities regarding how it should be controlled and directed. Ample evidence supports this view; that is, the military backed interim government in Egypt tried desperately to control the attitude of the public throughout the constitutional drafting process and to direct the public input towards a favored outcome through the designation of a so-called fearful atmosphere where police are in violent crackdown against opposition and the media is so biased trying to push the public to approve the constitutional draft.

12 According to the International Literacy Data 2014 provided by the UNESCO Institute for Statistics (2014), Egypt's illiteracy rate ranges from 70 percent to 79 percent, available at (http://glossary.uis.unesco.org/literacy/Pages/literacy-data-release-2014.aspx).

The idea of interpreting public participation in the constitution-making process as not being a fundamental right but rather a grant to be awarded pursuant to the pleasure of the authorities places Egypt in direct violation with its international obligations. Strictly speaking, Article 25 of the International Covenant on Civil and Political Rights (1966), which was ratified by Egypt in 1982, provides mandate for mandatory public participation in public affairs and public service, which accommodates participation in legislation-making process including the constitution.[13] Unlike the situation in Egypt, the South African Constitutional Court settled the issue of public participation in its infamous decision in *Doctors for Life International v Speaker of the National Assembly & Others*,[14] when it held that the right of public participation in the law-making process is a fundamental right guaranteed by the South African Constitution of 1996 as well as the international legal standards (Czapanskiy and Manjoo 2008).

On the international level, as mentioned earlier, I am not trying to argue against the constitution-making process being a highly concaved affair; however, with the many challenges facing the military-backed interim government after the deposition of the former regime, and given the fact that Egypt is still groping its way towards democracy as well as the escalating tension between Egypt's Islamists and liberals, the participation of the international community would have helped in alleviating some of these problems. Precisely, the participation of international organizations, such as the United Nations or the National Endowment for Democracy (NED) could have been wisely formulated to tackle and publicly denounce any attempt to militarize the governance through a constitutional provision (Moustafa 2012, 11). Likewise, given the huge wave of human rights violations and forced disappearance that Egypt witnesses to date, teaming up with the United Nations would have been of a great benefit to address Egypt's international obligations as well as to hold nationwide workshops to raise public awareness regarding the International Convention for the Protection of All Persons from Enforced Disappearance (ICCPED).[15]

References

Abdelaal, M. (2015). "Reforming the Constitution of Egypt: An Ugly Institutional Competition", *Cambridge International Law Journal*.

Abdelaal, M. (2014). "Egypt's Public Protest Law 2013: A Boost to Freedom or a Further Restriction?", *US-China Law Review*, 11(9).

13 International Covenant on Civil and Political Rights, Art. 25, Dec. 16, 1966, 999 U.N.T.S. 171 ("Every citizen shall have the right and the opportunity, without any of the distinctions mentioned in article 2 and without unreasonable restrictions: (1) To take part in the conduct of public affairs, directly or through freely chosen representatives; (b) To vote and to be elected at genuine periodic elections which shall be by universal and equal suffrage and shall be held by secret ballot, guaranteeing the free expression of the will of the electors; (c) To have access, on general terms of equality, to public service in his country.").

14 *Doctors for Life Int'l v Speaker of the Nat'l Assembly & Others* 2006 (12) BCLR 1399 (CC) (S. Afr.).

15 Egypt neither signed nor ratified that International Convention for the Protection of All Persons from Enforced Disappearance (ICCPED).

Abdelaal, M. (2013). "Egypt's Constitution: What Went Wrong?", *Vienna Journal on International Constitutional Law*, 7(2), 200–13.

Ahram Online (2014). Way of the Revolution Front to Vote No to Constitution, January 8, 2014.

Ahram Online (2013). Egypt's Pro-Morsi Coalition to Boycott Constitutional Referendum, December 22, 2013.

Al-Ali, Z. (2011). "Constitutional Drafting and External Influence", in T. Ginsburg, R. Dixon (eds.) *Comparative Constitutional Law*, 77–95.

Atlantic Council (2014). *Official Results: 98.1 Percent Vote in Favor of Egypt's New Constitution with 38.6 Percent Voter Turnout*, January 18, 2014, (http://www.atlanticcouncil.org/blogs/menasource/official-results-98-1-percent-vote-in-favor-of-egypt-s-new-constitution-with-38-6-percent-voter-turnout).

Banks, A. M. (2008). "Expanding Participation in Constitution Making: Challenges and Opportunities", *William & Mary Law Review*, 49(2), 1043–69.

Banting, K. G., and Simeon, R. (1985). Redesigning the State: The Politics of Constitutional Change in Industrial Nations.

Barber, B. (1984). *Strong Democracy: Participatory Politics for a New Age*, University of California Press, Berkeley.

Carey, J. M. (2000). "Parchment, Equilibria, and Institutions", *Comparative Political Studies*, 33, 735–61.

Czapanskiy, K. S., and Manjoo, R. (2008). "The Right of Public Participation in the Law-Making Process and the Role of Legislature in the Promotion of the Right", *Duke Journal of International and Comparative Law*, 19(1), 1–40.

Dahl, R. A. (2001). *How Democratic Is the American Constitution*, Yale University Press, New Haven.

Democracy International (2013). *Preliminary Statement: Democracy International Observation Mission to Egypt Constitutional Referendum*, December 31, 2013, (http://democracyinternational.com/resources/preliminary-statement-democracy-international-observation-mission-to-egypt-constitutional-referendum/).

Democracy Reporting International (2011). Lesson Learned from Constitution-Making Processes with Broad Based Public Participation, Briefing Paper No. 20.

Dunne, M. (2014). *Legitimizing an Undemocratic Process in Egypt, Carnegie Endowment for International Peace*, January 9, 2014, (http://carnegieendowment.org/2014/01/09/legitimizing-undemocratic-process-in-egypt).

Egypt Independent (2014). *Strong Egypt, April 6 boycott referendum*, January 13, 2014.

Eisenstadt, T. A., and LeVan, C. (2012). "Democracy's Missing Link: Interest Representation and State-Society Relations in Latin America and Africa", Apsa Annual Meeting Paper.

Elster, J. (1995). "Forces and Mechanisms in the Constitution-Making Process", *Duke Law Journal*, 45, 364–96.

Equality Now (2014). *Egypt: Ensure Women's Full Participation in the Constitutional Process and Promote Their Rights*, February 7, 2014, (http://www.equalitynow.org/take_action/discrimination_in_law_action384).

Finkel, S. E. (1987). "The Effects of Participation on Political Efficacy and Political Support: Evidence from a West German Panel", *The Journal of Politics*, 49(2), 441–64.

Ghai, Y. (2004). *Toward Inclusive and Participatory Constitution Making*, Presentation at the Constitution Reform Process: Comparative Perspectives, Kathmandu (Nagarkot).

Ginsburg, T., Elkins, Z., and Blount, J. (2009). "Does the Process of Constitution-Making Matter?", *Annual Review of Law and Social Science*, 5, 201–23.

Ginsburg, T., Elkins, Z., and Blount, J. (2008). "The Citizen as Founder: Public Participation in Constitutional Approval", *Temple Law Review*, 81, 361–82.

Hart, V. (2003). *Democratic Constitution Making*, United States Institute of Peace, Special Report, (http://www.peacemaker.un.org/sites/peacemaker.un.org/files/Democratic ConstitutionMaking_USIP2003.pdf.).

Human Rights Watch (2014). *Human Rights Watch World Report 2014: Egypt – Events of 2013*, (https://www.hrw.org/world-report/2014/country-chapters/egypt).

Kariel, H. S. (1969). *Open Systems: Arenas for Political Actions*, Peacock Publishers, Itasca, Illinois.

Mada Masr (2014). "Strong Egypt Party members arrested after posting 'no' campaign material," January 8, 2014.

Moustafa, T. (2012). *Drafting Egypt's Constitution: Can a New Legal Framework Revive a Flawed Transition?*, Brookings Doha Center-Stanford Project of Arab Transitions.

Rakove, J. N. (1996). *Original Meanings: Politics and Ideas in the Making of the Constitution*, Knopf, New York.

Samuels, K. (2006). "Post-Conflict Peace-Building and Constitution-Making", *Chicago Journal of International Law*, 6(2), 663–82.

UNESCO Institute for Statistics (2014). *International Literacy Data*, (http://glossary.uis. unesco.org/literacy/Pages/literacy-data-release-2014.aspx).

Voigt, S. (2004). "The Consequences of Popular Participation in Constitutional Choice – Towards a Comparative Analysis", in A. van Aaken, C. List, and C. Luetge (eds.), *Deliberation and Decision: Economics, Constitutional Theory and Deliberative Democracy*, Ashgate, Aldershot, 199–229.

Widner, J. (2008). "Constitution Writing in Post-Conflict Settings: An Overview", *William & Mary Law Review*, 49, 1513–37.

4 The 2011 constitution-making process in Morocco

A limited and controlled public participation

Francesco Biagi

Introduction

In his speech given on June 17, 2011, while presenting the project of the new constitution, King Mohammed VI declared that "for the first time in the history of our country, the constitution [was] made *by the Moroccans for all the Moroccans*."[1] This statement, however, corresponded only to a limited extent to what really happened during the 2011 Moroccan constitution-making process. Indeed, as this chapter will attempt to prove, even if the rhetoric of the regime deeply relied on the principle of public participation, in actual fact political parties, trade unions, social organisations and civil society had the possibility to influence the content of the new constitution only marginally. Public participation was certainly higher compared to previous constituent processes, but was strictly controlled by the regime so as not to hinder by any means the supremacy of the monarchy in the constitution-making process.

The first section of this chapter will show that the decision of the King to adopt a new constitution was clearly aimed at calming the growing dissent among the population and containing the protests which started to break out after February 20, 2011. The second part will analyse the major features of the constituent process, highlighting how and to what extent the public was involved in this process. In particular, the following aspects will be discussed: the lack of a democratically elected constituent assembly, the lack of transparency and the rapidity of the process, the higher level of participation by political parties and social organisations compared to the past, and the fact that the consultation through which the constitution was ratified was more similar to an authoritarian plebiscite than to a democratic referendum. A few final remarks will conclude the chapter.

The "20 February Movement" and the regime's reaction

Before the 2011 Constitution, Morocco had adopted five constitutions (in 1962, 1970, 1972, 1992 and 1996), which all entered into force under the

---

1 Emphasis added. The speech of June 17 is available, along with all other official speeches of the sovereign, online at http://www.maroc.ma/fr/discours-du-roi.

DOI: 10.4324/9781315180540-7

reign of Hassan II, the father of Mohammed VI. All these five constitutions granted to the King almost unlimited powers. In particular, the constitutional provision – defined within the literature as the "Supra-Constitution" (Boukhars 2011, 42) or "a Constitution within the Constitution" (Tourabi 2011, 6) – on which the "hard core" (Cubertafond 2011, 7) of the Sovereign's power was based was given by Article 19. This provision granted to the monarch both temporal and spiritual powers, as he was defined both as the Head of State and supreme representative of the nation, and "*Amir Al Mouminine,*" that is the "Commander of the Faithful."[2]

The need to adopt a new constitution had become apparent since Mohammed VI came to the throne in 1999. It was in particular the *Mouvement de Revendication d'une Constitution démocratique*, made up mainly of members of left-wing parties, which pushed for the adoption of a new constitution providing for greater protection for fundamental rights and freedoms, a more robust recognition of the pluralist nature of Moroccan identity and a far-reaching reform of the system for distributing political power.

There appear to be two main reasons why, despite a rather intense debate on this issue, a new constitution was adopted only following the King's March 2011 speech. The first reason results from the fact that the adoption of a new constitution did not represent a priority for the major parties represented in Parliament; in fact, these parties considered the 1996 Constitution to be satisfactory, "and that what needed to be changed was not the constitution, but practices; compliance with the [then] constitution was all that was needed" (Storm 2007, 157).

The second – and more important – reason resulted from the fact that the King did not have any interest in making any amendments to the 1996 Constitution, and even less in adopting a new one when he was not under any political pressure to do so (Storm 2007, 157). It was not, therefore, particularly surprising that Mohammed VI had no intention of debating constitutional reforms. Besides, history has demonstrated that democratic reforms are only implemented in Morocco when the monarchy is put under significant pressure (from the army, the political parties, the population or the international community), and it is for this reason that the literature uses the expression "top-down democratization" (Storm 2007, 157).

Unexpectedly, Mohammed VI announced on March 9, 2011, a "global constitutional reform" (to use the King's expression), which represented a strategic decision so as to ensure the regime's stability and continuity. In other words, the Moroccan monarch gave rise to what can be defined as "*surviving constitutionalism,*" i.e., a constitutionalism whose main purpose was not to democratise

---

2 Art. 19 stated: "The King, Amir al-Mouminine [that is, the Commander of the Faithful], Supreme Representative of the Nation, the Symbol of the unity thereof, Guarantor of the perpetuation and continuity of the State, shall ensure the respect for Islam and the constitution. He shall be the Protector of the rights and freedoms of the citizens, social groups and organizations. He shall guarantee the independence of the Nation and the territorial integrity of the Kingdom, within its authentic borders."

the country, but to guarantee the regime's own survival (Biagi 2014b, 1240ff.). Indeed, through the adoption of a new constitution the sovereign aimed at calming the growing dissent among the people and containing the protests which started to break out after February 20, 2011 – the date from which the eponymous movement "*Mouvement du 20 Février*" took its name.

This movement, largely comprised of young people, was supported by numerous nongovernmental organisations, human rights associations, political parties from the left and the extreme left, the Islamic movement *Al Adl Wa Al Ihssane*, trade unions, associations of emigrant communities resident abroad, intellectuals and businessmen. These actors, who had participated in the past in other protest movements against the regime, subsequently founded the "National Council of Support for the 20 February Movement."

The protestors denounced in particular the systematic and endemic corruption, the high cost of basic products, low wages and increasing poverty; they also called for greater social justice, free access to healthcare, greater employment opportunities and the right to housing. Young Moroccans also hoped for the achievement of profound and radical constitutional and political reforms, the construction of a state based on the rule of law and a free and independent legal system in order to enable the country to turn into a parliamentary monarchy (Fernández Molina 2011, 436–37). Therefore, the 20 February Movement did not call into question the sovereign, but called for change in the form of government: what was requested was indeed the move to a parliamentary monarchy based on the Spanish or British model, where the King "*règne, mais ne gouverne pas.*"

With the goal of calming the protests and the growing dissent within the country, the regime – which was concerned by the revolts and revolutions breaking out in neighbouring countries – decided to step up contacts with the major political and social players: the Prime Minister and the Interior Minister met with representatives of the main political parties, various trade unions, several associations of unemployed graduates, the Moroccan Human Rights Association and the Forum for Truth and Justice. Certain "preventive measures" (Fernández Molina 2011, 437) were adopted, such as a wage increase for public sector employees, the creation of new jobs, the guarantee of unemployment benefit, provision for mandatory medical insurance and free access to the health service for a greater number of citizens. The Economic and Social Council was also established, a body provided for under the 1992 Constitution but which had remained "on paper" until that moment.

Moreover, the Advisory Council on Human Rights (created in 1990 by Hassan II) was transformed into the National Council on Human Rights. Chaired by the renowned human rights activist Driss el-Yazami, this body had the purpose of addressing all questions relating to the protection of human rights, the guarantee of their full exercise and promotion, and the preservation of the individual and collective dignity, rights and freedoms of citizens. Alongside the power to pursue investigations and inquiries, and to submit the relative reports to the competent authorities, the council was requested to verify how Moroccan legislation could be brought into line with the international human rights treaties and conventions which had been ratified by Morocco.

Furthermore, it must be noted that the King's announcement of a far-reaching constitutional reform on March 9, 2011, occurred less than three weeks after the first protest demonstrations, which broke out on February 20 of the same year. Thus, Mohammed VI managed to turn the time factor to his advantage, catching the demonstrators off balance.[3]

However, alongside the carrot, the regime did not hesitate to use its stick. Members of the 20 February Movement, who were depicted as enemies of the state and accused of jeopardising its territorial integrity, were subjected to various forms of intimidation and harassment. In addition, the terrorist attack in Marrakesh on April 28, 2011, was used in some cases as a pretext for prohibiting anti-regime demonstrations.

It is important to underline that, compared with other neighbouring Arab countries, the protests which took place in Morocco involved decidedly fewer demonstrators[4] and made more moderate requests: in particular, it is sufficient to consider the fact that the position of Mohammed VI was not called into question.[5] One should not be taken by surprise, since the King was still "genuinely popular" (Mezran and Alunni 2012, 29).[6] According to a survey carried out in 2009 by the Moroccan newspapers *TelQuel* and *Nichane* and by the French newspaper *Le Monde*, 91 percent of Moroccans considered "positive" or "very positive" the first ten years of Mohammed VI's reign (Benchemsi 2013, 25–26). His popularity appears to be due essentially to three reasons. The first lies in the fact that the Moroccan sovereign, as a member of the Alaoui dynasty, claims direct descent from the Prophet Mohammed, and this gives him a very strong legitimacy. Second, in contrast to other countries such as Tunisia, Egypt or Libya, Morocco had initiated an important process of democratic reform in 1999 when Mohammed VI came to the throne[7] (and in some senses even in 1989, when Hassan II initiated a

3 On the various measures adopted by the King to calm the protest demonstrations, see also Biagi 2015, 54ff.
4 For example, the demonstrations of February 20 that took place in fifty-three cities and towns were attended by 240,000–300,000 people according to the organisers, or 37,000 people according to the Interior Ministry. In any case, these figures are decidedly lower than those registered in Tunisia or Egypt.
5 In Egypt, Libya and Tunisia on the other hand, there were immediate calls for their respective presidents to be replaced.
6 It should be stressed that a high degree of legitimacy is enjoyed not only by the Moroccan King, but also more generally by all monarchs and ruling families in the Arab world (see Ottaway and Muasher 2011).
7 The fundamental pillars of the reform process included a deep reform of the Code of Personal Status (the *Moudawana*), as well as the creation of a Truth Commission (the "Equity and Reconciliation Commission") in charge of investigating cases of "disappearances" and arbitrary imprisonment between 1956 (the year in which the country gained independence) and 1999 (the year in which Hassan II died). For a discussion of the reform process pursued by Mohammed VI, see Centre d'Études Internationales (ed.) 2010; Boukhars 2011.

cautious process of reform).[8] Third, the idea according to which without the King and his "unifying role" the country would be ungovernable, is very strong among the population (Benchemsi 2013, 24).

The 2011 constitution-making process

On March 9, 2011, Mohammed VI gave a genuine "constituent speech," in which he asserted the "seven key elements" on which the constitutional reform was to be based: (1) a guarantee of the pluralist nature of Moroccan identity, including the *Amazigh* component; (2) consolidation of the rule of law, the promotion and expansion of the scope of fundamental rights and guarantee of their exercise; (3) guarantee of the independence of the judiciary and reinforcement of the powers of the Constitutional Council; (4) consolidation of the principle of the separation of powers through the transfer of new powers to the Parliament and the appointment as prime minister of a member of the party obtaining the largest number of votes in elections, and the reinforcement of the prime minister's status as the head of the executive branch; (5) consolidation of the role of political parties within a pluralist system, reinforcement of the role of the parliamentary opposition and civil society; (6) bolstering of mechanisms intended to guarantee moral integrity within public life and to favour responsible conduct within public office; and (7) guarantee of the institutions addressing the issues of good government, human rights and protection of freedoms.[9]

On March 10, the day after the speech was delivered, the King appointed an *ad hoc* body, the Consultative Commission on Constitutional Reform, which was charged with the task of preparing a new draft constitution. The commission was chaired by Abdellatif Mennouni, a renowned constitutionalist and former member of the Constitutional Council, and was comprised of eighteen members, all appointed by the King. Most of these members were university professors and activists from human rights associations. It should be stressed that, with the exception of Rajae Mekkaoui,[10] the commission lacked any religious members or *oulema*, thereby stressing the path towards secularisation which the new constitution was intended to pursue.

In parallel with the appointment of the commission, Mohammed VI ordered the establishment of a "Political Mechanism Accompanying the Constitutional Reform," a body directed by his advisor Mohammed Moatassim, a university professor and expert in constitutional law, which was comprised of representatives of

---

8 Indeed, two new constitutions were adopted (in 1992 and in 1996); the Advisory Council on Human Rights – a body intended to provide protection to individual rights – was established; several – albeit extremely limited – changes were introduced in 1993 to the Code of Personal Status (the *Moudawana*) in order to improve conditions for women; in 1998 the policy of "*alternance*" was implemented for the first time, according to which members of the opposition parties could be appointed to government office. See Storm 2007, 54ff.

9 For an analysis of the 2011 constitution-making process, see also Biagi 2015, 56ff.

10 A Member of the High Council of the *Oulema*.

political parties and the trade unions. This *"mécanisme de suivi"* was expected to facilitate dialogue and concerted action between the various political actors, and was intended to operate as a channel for communication between the commission and the political forces and trade unions.

All of the political and social organisations within the country – including the 20 February Movement (that the King had not mentioned in his speech of March 9) – were invited to submit proposed constitutional amendments to the commission, which also organised around one hundred meetings in order to enable the representatives of the organisations to present their requests orally (Fernández Molina 2011, 439). Only a small number of minor parties failed to reply to the commission's invitation (such as the United Socialist Party (PSU), and the Democratic Way Party (*Annahj*)) (Tourabi 2011, 5), along with some associations and the 20 February Movement, complaining that the commission lacked democratic legitimacy and that the constitution was being granted as an act of "largesse."

The work of the commission, the meetings of which were not open to the public, was completed with particular speed, given that in his speech the King had stated that he expected an initial report to be presented to him before the end of June. The commission met with the political parties and trade unions on June 7, 2011: on that occasion, Commission President Mennouni only made an oral presentation of the key features of the reform, without distributing a written version of the new text of the constitution. This resulted in the decision by some political parties and trade unions to walk out of the meeting in a sign of protest (Tourabi 2011, 9).

Subsequently, on June 10, Mennouni presented the plan for constitutional reform to Mohammed VI, whilst Moatassim informed the sovereign of the decisions adopted by the Political Mechanism Accompanying the Constitutional Reform. Most political parties and trade unions were strongly critical of the fact that they had only received a written draft of the constitution on the day before the King's speech to the Nation (June 17), when the sovereign set out the key elements of the reform, inviting the population to participate in a constitutional referendum to be held on July 1, and to approve the new text.[11]

The referendum result was a success for Mohammed VI, given the approval of the new constitution by 98 percent of the population. With some rare exceptions (consider the 20 February Movement), political parties, trade unions and social organisations invited the population to vote "yes" in that consultation. The turnout of 73.5 percent may be read in diametrically opposed terms depending upon one's point of view: whilst on the one hand it is double the rate registered at the 2007 parliamentary elections (which was a meagre 37 percent), it did, however, represent the lowest rate in the history of the constitutional referendums held in the country, being more than 11 percentage points lower than the 1996 consultation.[12]

---

11 It also appears that Moatassim had made certain changes to the draft constitution a few hours before the King's speech on June 17 (Fernández Molina 2011, 439).

12 See the data reported by Montabes Pereira and Parejo Fernández 1999, 632–33.

The lack of a democratically elected constituent assembly

The constituent process was strongly criticised both by certain political parties and social organisations as well as within the literature. The main objection, as had already been asserted, regarded the lack of democratic legitimacy of the Commission on Constitutional Reform, since it had been appointed entirely by the sovereign. Once again, in fact, the requests to elect a constituent assembly were disregarded.

It should be pointed out that some political parties, trade unions and associations had been calling for the election of a constituent assembly since the 1962 Constitution. Indeed, the *Union Nationale des Forces Populaires*, the *Parti Communiste Marocain*, the *Parti Démocratique Constitutionnel* and the trade union *Union Marocaine du Travail* rejected that constitution since it was not the outcome of a constituent assembly but it came directly from the palace (and indeed it was often defined as *"Constitution mon bon plaisir"* (Rousset 2012a, 31)). In a speech given on November 18, 1962, Hassan II defended the principle of an *"octroyée"* constitution by stating that "the Constitution that I built with my own hands, that will be diffused over the entire Realm and that in twenty days will be subject to your approval, this Constitution is first of all the renovation of the sacred covenant that has always united the people and the King."[13] The difficulties – which were practically insurmountable – in electing a constituent assembly may be summarised by a commentator writing in 1963: "The Constituent Assembly is vested with supreme power and, in Morocco, *such supreme power lies with the King alone.* This power of His Majesty was not challenged even prior to the Protectorate."[14] Indeed, it is well known that Hassan II has always considered himself "the holder of the power to propose new rules on the organisation of the society" (Rousset 2012b, 50).

Mohammed VI continued to pursue this tradition of a "constituent King" (Cubertafond 2011, 3); indeed, it was he who decided to engage in far-reaching constitutional reform, to identify the "key elements" on which that reform was to be based, to appoint the Commission on Constitutional Reform and finally to grant his approval to the draft presented to him by Mennouni. Thus, the sovereign had the first and the last word. Therefore, down to the present day, *"octroyées"* constitutions have been a constant feature of Moroccan history.[15]

It should be pointed out that the constitution-making process in Morocco was very similar to the procedures followed to reform – respectively in 2011 and 2016 – the 1952 Jordanian Constitution and the 1996 Algerian Constitution. Indeed, as occurred in Morocco, in both Jordan and Algeria the constitutional reforms seemed to be a "concession" by the Head of State and not so much the

13 Cited by Tozy 1999, 89.
14 Guédira 1963, 67, cited by Tozy 1999, 90–91 (emphasis added).
15 It should be noted that part of the literature has praised the constituent procedure adopted in Morocco, defining the process of drafting the constitution through a constituent assembly as "cumbersome, ineffective and disappointing" (Rouvillois 2012b, 67).

result of the popular will. The members of the commissions on constitutional reform established in both countries were indeed nominated respectively by King Abdullah II and by President Abdelaziz Bouteflika, both of whom had the final say concerning the contents of the reform. Thus, as in Morocco, the approach followed was "top-down" and not "bottom-up."[16]

By contrast, a diametrically opposed constitution-making process was followed to adopt the new Tunisian Constitution in 2014, which has been aptly regarded as an example of a "participatory constitution": voters were indeed able to participate directly in that process through, for example, public demonstrations, meetings between MPs and students and the so-called *"e-participation"* (Groppi 2015, 203ff; Abbiate 2016; Sherif 2017).

The lack of transparency and the rapidity of the process

A further objection addressed the lack of transparency within the work of the commission, since its meetings were not open to the public. It should be specified that secrecy in itself is not an absolute evil, whilst on the contrary, "debates in front of an audience tend to generate rhetorical overbidding and heated passions that are incompatible with the kind of close and calm scrutiny that ought to be the rule when one is adopting provisions for the indefinite future. By denying the public admission to the proceedings and by keeping the debates secret until the final document has been adopted, one creates conditions for rational discussion that are less likely to prevail in the presence of an audience" (Elster 2006, 191).

However, initial secrecy should be offset by subsequent publicity, for example in the form of discussions in a plenary assembly. In fact, with total secrecy, "partisan interests and logrolling come to the forefront" (Elster 1995, 395).[17] In this sense, the Spanish constituent process was considered by Jon Elster as one which came closest to striking an "optimal balance" (Elster 1995, 395) between secrecy and publicity.[18] In Morocco, on the contrary, as noted above, the second – public – stage was entirely lacking.

From this point of view, the difference with the Tunisian constituent process – which was characterised by a very high degree of transparency and openness – could not be more evident. Indeed, in Tunisia, even external actors played a role in this process; for example, on June 3, 2013, the Speaker of the National Constituent Assembly requested the opinion of the Venice Commission on the

---

16 On the case of Jordan see Hammouri 2016, 725; on the case of Algeria see Biagi 2016b.
17 With regard to this aspect two diametrically opposed processes of constitution-making are the 1787 Federal Convention in Philadelphia (which met in complete secrecy) and the 1789 French Constituent Assembly (which was fully public). On this point see Elster 2000, 345ff.
18 Initially, in fact, the Constitutional Affairs and Public Freedoms Committee appointed a *Ponencia* (comprised of seven members from the main political parties) with the task of drawing up a draft constitution, and the decisions of this body were taken in secret. The draft constitution was only subsequently presented to the *Cortes* and discussed publicly in both houses of Parliament (de Esteban 1989, 275ff.).

final draft of the Constitution of Tunisia. The observations of the commission were made public on July 17, 2013 (Venice Commission 2013).

Another criticism that has been made is that the Moroccan constituent process was too short. Indeed, it took just three months to prepare the draft constitution and to consult with the representatives of political parties and trade unions.[19] In particular, the timeline set by the King "made it impossible for various political actors to criticize the draft [of the constitution] effectively or delay its presentation in the referendum" (International Institute for Democracy and Electoral Assistance 2012, 15; on this point see also section "Higher level of participation by political parties and social organisations"). Although this "time indicator" can hardly provide definite answers – either in one way or another – on the democratic character of the process, the case of Morocco seems to confirm that very rapid constitution-making periods are one of the distinguishing features of "non-democracies" (Blount, Elkins and Ginsburg 2012, 41).[20]

Higher level of participation by political parties and social organisations

For a very long period of time, the principal – if not only – instrument available to the parties in order to submit proposed constitutional amendments to the King was to send him "*memoranda*." This practice "affirmed the domination and authority of the King in the process of drafting the constitutional text, but at the same time it allowed other parties to get involved in the process and add their remarks and demands to the reform agenda" (Tourabi 2011, 3). Hassan II underlined several times the *consultative* dimension of this practice, by pointing out that it only consisted of "taking into account the points of view and the suggestions that we spontaneously asked the political parties in order to enrich the project of revision of the Constitution."[21]

The level of public participation in the drafting of the 2011 Constitution was undoubtedly higher compared to the past. Indeed, political parties, trade unions, associations representing civil society, women, youth and other organisations had the opportunity not only to submit *memoranda*, but also to meet with the members of the Commission on Constitutional Reform and to present their requests orally. Moreover, dialogue and concerted action were also promoted by the presence of the Political Mechanism Accompanying the Constitutional Reform.

The reality, however, is that this form of public participation affected the content of the 2011 Constitution only marginally. First of all, the political and the social organisations never really had the chance to make any comment or recommendation on the draft of the constitution, since they only received a copy of it on the day before the King's speech to the nation (June 17), when

---

19 *Contra*: Rouvillois 2012a, 351, who argues that the rapidity of the process "did not affect the democratic legitimacy of the consultation at all."
20 On the timeframe in the Tunisian and Egyptian constitution-making processes see Frosini and Biagi 2015, 137–38.
21 Speech given by Hassan II on July 10, 1982, cited by Tozy 1999, 102.

the latter announced the constitutional referendum of July 1. This is a major difference with respect, for example, to the Tunisian constitution-making process, where four drafts of the constitution were made public, discussed and revised (in August 2012, December 2012, April 2013 and June 2013) before the final version was adopted.

Second, it has been rightly stressed that, in the light of the strong tie between the King and Mohammed Moatassim (the President of the Political Mechanism Accompanying the Constitutional Reform), the role of this body was not only to facilitate dialogue between the Commission on Constitutional Reform and the political forces and trade unions, but also to identify what was "politically acceptable to the palace and what was not" (Rousset 2012b, 60).

In any case, it should be noted that the requests presented by the political and social organisations were largely of the same tone as the "constituent speech" delivered by Mohammed VI on March 9, 2011. Indeed, most of the proposals were already stated in the King's speech, and therefore they did not introduce any significant novelty in the debate.[22] Therefore, the practical consequence was that the commission merely wrote the text of a constitution whose content had been to a large extent "dictated" directly by Mohammed VI.[23] One of the most significant exceptions was given by the opposition of the Islamic moderate party *Parti de la justice et du développement* (PJD)[24] to the constitutional provisions which were considered in contrast with the Islamic identity of the country (Tourabi 2011, 9–10).

It should be noted that this *passive position* of the vast majority of the political parties is an excellent example of their "domestication" (Maghraoui 2013, 182) by the King, thus confirming the "politics of consensus" that has been characterising Morocco for many years. According to this notion, the role and the absolute powers of the sovereign are not the object of discussions and divergence among the parties. The latter, regardless of their ideological orientations, "seem comfortable with not taking the initiative and leaving the palace in full control of the political game and orientations of the country" (Maghraoui 2013, 182).

Democratic referendum or (more likely) authoritarian plebiscite?

An argument which may be proposed in support of the position that the 2011 Constitution did not result from an act of "largesse" flows from the fact that

22 A proposal that was diametrically opposed to the King's speech was the one presented by the leftist Vanguard Party to eliminate the "old" Art. 19 of the Constitution, which granted unlimited powers to the King (Tourabi 2011, 6).
23 For an analysis of the 2011 Moroccan Constitution, see Bouachik, Degoffe, Saint-Prot (eds.) 2012; Centre d'Études Internationales (ed.) 2012; International Institute for Democracy and Electoral Assistance 2012; Azzouzi and Cabanis 2011; Biagi 2014a. More specifically, on the form of government provided for by the new constitution see Ruiz Ruiz 2014, 33ff.; Biagi 2016a, 495ff.
24 The *Parti de la justice et du développement* is the party which won the parliamentary elections in November 2011 and October 2016. On the role played by the PJD and its leader Abdelilah Benkirane, see Biagi 2016a, 505.

it was ratified by popular referendum (as happened with the previous five constitutions adopted in the country). However, this argument is decidedly weak, above all in the light of the fact that during the two weeks running up to the consultation, the monarchy took every effort to promote the reform as much as possible, and strongly restricted the space available to those (such as the representatives of the February 20 Movement) who by contrast promoted a boycott of the vote. Even sermons by imams in mosques across the kingdom invited the population to vote "yes." Moreover, on election day, reports of fraud came from all over the country. Thus, there was never going to be any doubt over the referendum result. It is evident, then, that this consultation was much more similar to an authoritarian plebiscite than to a democratic referendum. Indeed, authoritarian plebiscites are "motivated more by a desire to legitimise the autocrat's control of a polity than to allow the citizens to render a considered verdict on the constitution" (Blount 2011, 50).[25]

It should also be noted that the process that led to the adoption of the constitution was characterised by certain legal irregularities, as witnessed by the fact that the day before the consultation three provisions of the new constitution were "furtively corrected" (Fernández Molina 2011, 439). Indeed, the Official Gazette of June 30, 2011, contained a "correction of *material* errors"[26] concerning Articles 42(4), 55 (last paragraph) and 132(3) of the new constitution. The "corrected" version of Article 42(4), however, introduced the appointment of the president of the Constitutional Court among the royal decrees (*dahirs*) that do not require the countersignature of the head of government. It is evident that this change can hardly be qualified as a "material error."

It must be stressed that in Morocco this popular consultation has also an extremely important religious meaning, as it is considered a "modern redefinition" (Abouchi 2013, 56) of two traditional institutes, the "*bay'a*" (pledge of allegiance to the king) and the "*shura*" (consultation). This instrument is therefore aimed at consolidating the spiritual link, the sacred covenant between the monarch – who is the "*Amir al Mouminine*" (Commander of the Faithful) – and the people. As a consequence, contesting "the project of the King would mean to commit a crime and to leave the community. It would mean to breach a divine duty and to commit a sacrilege" (Madani 2012, 225).

A limited and controlled public participation

By using expressions such as "collective mobilisation," "participatory approach" and "enlarged national debate," Mohammed VI – in his speech given on March 9, 2011 – seemed to launch a constitution-making process in which public participation would have played a significant role. On the one hand, it

---

25 On the differences between plebiscite and referendum, see also de Vergottini 2011, 244–48; Biagi 2017, 713ff.
26 Emphasis added.

is true that the involvement of political parties, trade unions, civil society and social organisations was much higher compared to previous constituent processes; on the other hand, however, this form of public participation controlled "from above" affected the content of the 2011 Constitution only to a very limited extent. The monarchy was the guiding force of the constitution-making process, steering its progress, stipulating time-scales and above all having the final say on its content. Thus, the constitution – far from being developed "in perfect communion with all the living forces of the Nation" (as Mohammed VI proclaimed in his speech given on June 17, 2011, while presenting the project of the constitutional reform) – continued to be a "concession" made by the sovereign.

Having said that, the form and the degree of participation of political parties, trade unions and civil society in the process that led to the adoption of the 2011 Constitution should not be underestimated. Indeed, this type of participation was undoubtedly a considerable advancement, especially if compared to the previous practice of the "*memoranda*." Therefore, should Morocco amend the constitution in the future, this benchmark will hardly be disregarded by the regime.

References

Abbiate, T. (2016), *La partecipazione popolare ai processi costituenti. L'esperienza tunisina* (Napoli: Editoriale Scientifica).

Abouchi, E.H. (2013), "La pratique référendaire dans le régime constitutionnel marocaine, 1962–2011: une analyse du contenu," in *Cinquante ans de vie constitutionnelle au Maroc. Quel bilan?* (Publications de l'Association marocaine de droit constitutionnel).

Azzouzi, A., and Cabanis, A. (2011), *Le néo-constitutionnalisme marocaine à l'épreuve du printemps arabe* (Paris: l'Harmattan).

Benchemsi, A. (2013), "Mohammed VI, despote malgré lui," *Pouvoirs*, no. 145.

Biagi, F. (2014a), "The 2011 Constitutional Reform in Morocco: More Flaws than Merits," *Jean Monnet Occasional Papers* (Malta: Institute for European Studies), no. 7, http://www.um.edu.mt/__data/assets/pdf_file/0020/208307/JM_Occasional_Paper_no._7_final,_5th_March_update.pdf.

Biagi, F. (2014b), "Will Surviving Constitutionalism in Morocco and Jordan Work in the Long Run? A Comparison with Three Past Authoritarian Regimes," *Cambridge Journal of International and Comparative Law*, vol. 3, no. 4.

Biagi, F. (2015), "The Pilot of *Limited* Change. Mohammed VI and the Transition in Morocco," in J.O. Frosini and F. Biagi (eds.), *Political and Constitutional Transitions in North Africa. Actors and Factors* (London: Routledge).

Biagi, F. (2016a), "The Separation and Distribution of Powers Under the New Moroccan Constitution," in R. Grote and T.J. Röder (eds.), *Constitutionalism, Human Rights, and Islam after the Arab Spring* (Oxford: Oxford University Press).

Biagi, F. (2016b), "Tra innovazione e continuità: la riforma costituzionale algerina del 2016," *Osservatorio costituzionale*, no. 3, http://www.osservatorioaic.it/tra-innovazione-e-continuit-la-riforma-costituzionale-algerina-del-2016.html.

Biagi, F. (2017), "Plebiscite: An Old but Still Fashionable Instrument," *University of Illinois Law Review*, vol. 2017, issue 2.

Blount, J. (2011), "Participation in Constitutional Design," in T. Ginsburg and R. Dixon (eds.), *Comparative Constitutional Law* (Cheltenham-Northampton: Edward Elgar).

Blount, J., Elkins, Z., and Ginsburg, T. (2012), "Does the Process of Constitution-making Matter?" in T. Ginsburg (ed.), *Comparative Constitutional Design* (Cambridge: Cambridge University Press).

Bouachik, A., Degoffe, M., and Saint-Prot, C. (eds.) (2012), *La Constitution marocaine de 2011. Lectures croisées*, Publications de la Revue marocaine d'administration locale et de développement, Série "Thèmes actuels", no. 77.

Boukhars, A. (2011), *Politics in Morocco: Executive Monarchy and Enlightened Authoritarianism* (London: Routledge).

Centre d'Études Internationales (ed.) (2010), *Une décennie de réformes au Maroc (1999–2009)* (Paris: Karthala).

Centre d'Études Internationales (ed.) (2012), *La Constitution marocaine de 2011. Analyses et commentaires*, (Paris: L.G.D.J.).

Cherif, N. (2017), "Participation in the Tunesian constitution-making process," in this volume.

Cubertafond, B. (2011), "La transition marocaine après le printemps arabe et la nouvelle Constitution," *Les Etudes et Essais du Centre Jacques Berque*, no. 5, November 2011, http://www.cjb.ma/images/stories/publications/Cubertafond_EE_5.pdf.

de Esteban, J. (1989), "El proceso constituyente español, 1977–1978," in J.F. Tezanos, R. Cortarelo and A. de Blas (eds.), *La transición democrática española* (Madrid: Editorial Sistema).

de Vergottini, G. (2011), *Diritto costituzionale comparato* (Padua: Cedam).

Elster, J. (1995), "Forces and Mechanisms in the Constitution-making Process," *Duke Law Journal*, vol. 45.

Elster, J. (2000), "Arguing and Bargaining in Two Constituent Assemblies," *University of Pennsylvania Journal of Constitutional Law*, vol. 2, no. 2.

Elster, J. (2006), "Legislatures as Constituent Assemblies," in R.W. Bauman and T. Kahana (eds.), *The Least Examined Branch. The Role of Legislatures in the Constitutional State* (Cambridge: Cambridge University Press).

Fernández Molina, I. (2011), "The Monarchy vs. the 20 February Movement: Who Holds the Reins of Political Change in Morocco?" *Mediterranean Politics*, vol. 16, no. 3.

Frosini, J.O., and Biagi, F. (2015), "Transitions from Authoritarian Rule following the Arab Uprisings: A Matter of Variables," in J.O. Frosini and F. Biagi (eds.), *Political and Constitutional Transitions in North Africa. Actors and Factors* (London: Routledge).

Groppi, T. (2015), "La Costituzione tunisina del 2014 nel quadro del 'costituzionalismo globale,'" *Diritto pubblico comparato ed europeo*, no. 1.

Guédira, A.R. (1963), "Une constituante ni nécessaire ni possible," *Confluent*, no. 27, January.

Hammouri, M. (2016), "Constitutional Reform and the Rise of Constitutional Adjudication in Jordan," in R. Grote and T.J. Röder (eds.), *Constitutionalism, Human Rights, and Islam after the Arab Spring* (Oxford: Oxford University Press).

International Institute for Democracy and Electoral Assistance (IDEA) (2012), *The 2011 Moroccan Constitution: A Critical Analysis* (Stockholm).

Madani, M. (2012), "La reforme constitutionnelle sous le règne de Mohammed VI: le processus et l'aboutissement," in A. El Messaoudi and M.J. Terol Becerra (eds.), *El Poder Constituyente en el mundo árabe* (Sevilla: Centro Euro-árabe de Estudios Jurídicos Avanzados de la Universidad Pablo de Olavide).

Maghraoui, D. (2013), "Constitutional Reforms in Morocco: Between Consensus and Subaltern Politics," in G. Joffé (ed.), *North Africa's Arab Spring* (London: Routledge).

Mezran, K., and Alunni, A. (2012), "Power Shifts in the Arab Spring: A Work in Progress," *The Bologna Center Journal of International Affairs*, vol. 15, Spring.

Montabes Pereira, J., and Parejo Fernández, M.A. (1999), "Morocco," in D. Nohlen, M. Krennerich and B. Thibaut (eds.), *Elections in Africa: A Data Handbook* (Oxford: Oxford University Press).

Ottaway, M., and Muasher, M. (2011), "Arab Monarchies: Change for Reform, Yet Unmet," *The Carnegie Papers*, December, http://carnegieendowment.org/files/arab_monarchies1.pdf.

Rousset, M., (2012a), "L'évolution constitutionnelle du Maroc de Mohammed V à Mohammed VI," in A. Bouachik, M. Degoffe and C. Saint-Prot (eds.), *La Constitution marocaine de 2011*. Lectures croisées, Publications de la Revue marocaine d'administration locale et de développement, Série "Thèmes actuels", no. 77.

Rousset, M., (2012b), "L'interprétation des pouvoirs du roi dans la nouvelle Constitution," in Centre d'Études Internationales (ed.), *La Constitution marocaine de 2011. Analyses et commentaires* (Paris: L.G.D.J.).

Rouvillois, F. (2012a), "Les règles relatives à la révision dans la Constitution marocaine de 2011," in Centre d'Études Internationales (ed.), *La Constitution marocaine de 2011. Analyses et commentaires* (Paris: L.G.D.J.).

Rouvillois, F. (2012b), "Réflexions sur la monarchie démocratique à la marocaine," in A. Bouachik, M. Degoffe and C. Saint-Prot (eds.), *La Constitution marocaine de 2011*. Lectures croisées, Publications de la Revue marocaine d'administration locale et de développement, Série "Thèmes actuels," no. 77.

Ruiz Ruiz, J.J. (2014), "La Constitución marroquí de 2011 y el ensayo de parlamentarización de la monarquía," *Revista de estudios políticos*, no. 164.

Storm, L. (2007), *Democratization in Morocco: The Political Elite and Struggles for Power in the Post-independence State* (London: Routledge).

Tourabi, A. (2011), *Constitutional Reform in Morocco: Reform in Times of Revolution*, November, http://www.arab-reform.net/en/node/526.

Tozy, M. (1999), *Monarchie et Islam politique au Maroc* (Paris: Presses de Sciences Po).

Venice Commission (2013), *Opinion on the Final Draft Constitution of the Republic of Tunisia*, October 17, http://www.venice.coe.int/webforms/documents/?pdf=CDL-AD(2013)032-e.

5 Participation in the Tunisian constitution-making process

Nedra Cherif

Introduction

In an article published a few months after the adoption of the Tunisian constitution, T. Abbiate defined this new fundamental law as "The Constitution of the people" (Abbiate, 2014). Tunisia had indeed adopted a constitution widely acknowledged as a breakthrough in the Arab world's constitutional history not only for some of its most progressive provisions – notably those related to rights and freedoms – but also for the unprecedented inclusiveness of its drafting process, thus meeting what has now turned into an "established trend" in the field of constitution-making (DRI, 2011: 1; Interpeace, 2011: 9). In a country – and a region – where citizens' voices have long been silenced by authoritarian rulers and where the prerogative of issuing legal and political norms has remained in the hands of a powerful elite, the participatory dimension of the constitution-making process indeed provided more space than ever for the expression of Tunisia's multifaceted society.

Though assessing the direct and effective impact of public participation on the final constitutional text remains difficult, this chapter will attempt to explore the various participatory mechanisms developed in the Tunisian constitution-making process,[1] as well as the tools used by the drafters to translate citizens' contributions into the constitutional document. It will then provide a tentative assessment of some constitutional provisions that have effectively been influenced by and modified according to citizens' recommendations.

The challenging path towards participation

Participation in the Tunisian constitution-making process has been a varied as well as challenging process. The direct election of a National Constituent

---

1 This chapter will, however, not address an aspect of the drafting process that has been widely regarded as a successful contribution by civil society organizations, namely the Nobel Prize-winner Quartet (UGTT, UTICA, LTDH, Bar Association). The author indeed considers that the role played by the Quartet during the 2013 political and constitutional crisis should be analyzed as an act of crisis management or conflict resolution rather than an attempt to participate in constitution-drafting process and influence its final wording. The chapter will thus focus more specifically on efforts by individual or organized groups of citizens to a have a direct impact on the text itself, leaving other dimensions for further research.

DOI: 10.4324/9781315180540-8

Assembly (NCA) on October 23, 2011, had indeed raised great enthusiasm among Tunisians, not only as their first opportunity to vote in a free and democratic election, but also as it offered them a chance to be involved in the drafting of their country's fundamental law.[2] But the initial enthusiasm quickly faded, as the drafting process – initially set to last only one year, and which effectively began in February 2012 – started to flounder and fall into fruitless debates, making only slow progress after months of work.[3] Lacking political and constitutional skills for most of them, the constitution drafters also proved inefficient in communicating to the public the reasons for this delay. While people had expected a swift constitutional process that would enable the country to quickly turn the page of the transition and recover stability, the lengthy process and the increased disconnection between the society and its elected representatives contributed to a climate of resentment and distrust towards the assembly. Regular reports by the media of delayed plenary sessions and elevated rates of absenteeism among the deputies did little to improve the already grim picture of the constitution-making process.[4]

The NCA's uncertain position on participation

While various organizations of the civil society as well as legal and constitutional experts had, early on in the process, suggested comments and advice to the drafters, and requested access to the constituent commissions' work and plenary sessions of the assembly,[5] they initially faced some reluctance from (part of)

2 Some schools of thought consider the direct election of a Constituent Assembly as an initial form of public participation. Though not denying this point of view, this chapter will be dedicated to the activities that enabled the direct involvement of citizens in the constitution-drafting process and their interaction with the drafters. See DRI, 2011: 2; Miller, 2010: 630.

3 From the outset, the timeframe of the process has been a controversial issue. While the decree No. 2011–1086, taken by transitional President F. Mebazaa at the time and calling for the NCA election, had set the assembly's mandate to one year, the law on "the Provisional Organization of Public Authorities" (OPPP), later adopted by the NCA and which had primacy over all other laws, made no such provision, leaving the length of the drafting process without limit. See TCC, 2015: 26.

4 «Séance plénière de l'ANC retardée d'une heure, le quorum n'étant pas atteint», *Business News*, 16 November 2012: http://www.businessnews.com.tn/Tunisie-%E2%80%93-S%C3%A9ance-pl%C3%A9ni%C3%A8re-de-l%E2%80%99ANC-retard%C3%A9e-d%E2%80%99une-heure,-le-quorum-n%E2%80%99%C3%A9tant-pas-atteint,520,34579,3; «Tunisie: Absences massives à l'ANC, séance plénière levée», *African Manager*, November 29, 2012: http://africanmanager.com/tunisie-absences-massives-a-l%C2%92anc-seance-pleniere-levee/. About a year after the start of the constitutional process, the CSO Al *Bawsala* – the observatory of the NCA – released a report assessing the NCA's effective work and deputies' attendance that reaches the same negative conclusions. For a summary of the main findings of the report, see: «Le rendement de l'ANC à la loupe», *La Presse de Tunisie*, March 6, 2013: http://www.lapresse.tn/20062016/63672/le-rendement-de-lanc-a-la-loupe.html.

5 An estimated 10 constitution projects (in addition to some constitutional articles) were submitted to the NCA by various organizations and independent personalities, such as constitutional law professors, the UGTT or the *Doustourna* network; author's interview with Law Professor Chafik Sarsar, Tunis, November 3, 2016. See, for example, the constitution project of the *Doustourna* network,

the assembly. The close-minded attitude of many deputies was mostly based on a lack of experience, legislators in Tunisia not being used to the principles of openness and transparency. Parliaments under the previous regime had indeed been mostly used as mere rubber stamps dominated by the ruling party, for which there was no access, not even interest or request by the civil society to monitor the work. Other conservative-minded deputies, keen to protect their constituent prerogatives, were as well unwilling to share their task of drafting the constitution with nonelected actors (TCC, 2015: 59). Under the pressure of national as well as international organizations to foster greater transparency and public participation, the NCA was thus faced with the challenge of reforming deeply entrenched mentalities and adapting to the requirements of a democratic process.[6]

Participatory elements in the NCA's organizational framework:
From theory to (non)practice

The constitution-making process had, however, initially been thought (at least theoretically) as one that should be participative. Various provisions of the assembly's Rules of Procedures (RoP) indeed foresaw that commissions' meetings as well as plenary sessions should be "public" (art. 54 and 76, respectively).[7] To maintain the link between the members of the assembly and the citizens, the RoP had provided for the so-called "week in the regions" – one week per month dedicated to deputies' visit to their constituents in the field.[8] The RoP also gave the possibility for commissions to organize field visits related to their areas of competence, and which should involve deputies elected from the region (RoP, art. 63). These initiatives, however, rarely concretized and the "week in the region" was never implemented due to lack of time and resources. The NCA indeed provided no administrative, financial, or logistical support for outreach activities. The occasional meetings that took place between deputies and their

based on a two-day gathering with about 350 lawyers, experts, and ordinary citizens to draft together a "citizen constitution": http://doustourna.org/index.php/fr/projets/notre-constitution.
6 The Carter Center, in its statement of May 10, 2012 entitled "The Carter Center Encourages Increased Transparency in the Constitution Drafting Process" observes that "while the NCA acknowledges the importance of transparency, it does not ensure civil society organizations' full access to debates and relevant information. . . . Queries of civil society organizations to attend NCA plenary and commissions' sessions were met with unresponsiveness." The center reiterated its call for increased participation in a following statement ("The Carter Center Recognizes Tunisia's National Constituent Assembly Progress; Calls for Increased Public Participation, Outreach, and Transparency"), released on September 26, 2012, while DRI had also made similar recommendations in its report of November 2011 (DRI, 2011: 8).
7 Early on in the process, however, article 54 proved controversial, as NCA members had widely different understandings of what "public" meant. CSOs' observatory role in particular was highly debated, and whether they should be allowed to attend commissions' sessions or only submit their comments to them. See the debate during the NCA plenary session, February 28, 2012.
8 "The calendar of meetings of the Assembly and the commissions is established in such a way as to dedicate one week per month to contacts of members with the citizens," RoP, art. 79.

constituents remained the fact of individual members of the assembly or the initiatives of some civil society organizations (CSOs) rather than the result of an institutionalized process (TCC, 2012: 5, 58).

Interestingly, holding a popular referendum on the adoption of the constitution – as an ultimate form to involve the people in the process, a now common practice in constitution-making processes, though not a systematic choice[9] – was not envisioned in Tunisia as complementary to the NCA's vote but rather as an option of last resort in case of failure of the assembly to adopt the text (RoP, art. 107).[10] Having been directly elected by the people and thus mandated by it to write the new constitutional document, drafters obviously considered there was no need for additional popular legitimacy. Acting in a very polarized environment some might also have feared the outcome of an instrumentalized referendum that could have sanctioned political actors rather than the constitutional text itself.[11]

Only progressively and under the effect of increased pressure, the drafters started to overcome their concerns and see external actors as potential partners rather than rivals in the constitution-drafting process. The already regular auditions of national and foreign experts – which had started as early as March 2012 (in accordance with article 59 of the RoP)[12] – were gradually completed with more systematic interaction with the civil society. Visits, interviews, one-on-one meetings with deputies, and lobbying in the corridors of the assembly started to become part of the NCA's routine. Representatives of specialized CSOs as well as delegations from various professional organizations made their way to the assembly to defend their views on specific provisions of the constitution draft. For instance, a delegation of imams came to the assembly to lobby against the enshrinement of the freedom of conscience during the article-by-article vote on the constitution in January 2014.[13] Civil society actors and citizens sometimes made their opinions more vocally heard through demonstrations in front of the assembly building or in the capital's main squares. Therefore, feminist organizations and women demonstrators mobilized in August 2012 on Tunis' main Bourguiba Avenue to denounce the flaws of an article related to women's rights

---

9 For details on the debates related to the advantages and flaws of constitutional referenda, see Interpeace, 2011: 298–99.

10 RoP, art. 107 refers to art. 3 of the OPPP, which states that in case NCA members fail twice to adopt the constitution by a two-thirds majority, the text should be submitted to a popular referendum to be adopted by a majority of voters. This actually follows the South African model.

11 This fear was further deepened by the fact that no legal provision had been envisioned in case of negative referendum, and in spite of this obvious legal loophole acknowledged by all, no initiative was taken to solve it. However, this concern, which was hanging over the drafters' heads like a sword of Damocles all along the process, eventually proved positive in that it clearly pushed them towards reaching a consensus. (This is based on interviews conducted by the author throughout the process with various NCA members, who regularly reiterated the necessity to agree on conflicting issues in order to avoid going to the referendum).

12 About 160 hearings of experts and CSOs' representatives were held throughout the whole constitution-making process; see Abdelkafi, 2016: 2.

13 Author's participant observation, NCA, January 2014. See also TCC, 2015: 73.

in the constitution draft, while supporters of the Salafi party *Hizb Al-Tahrir* demonstrated in front of the assembly in January 2013 to denounce the "concessions and compromises" of the constitution and criticize "the absence of any reference to Sharia law" in the text.[14] In spite of this significant improvement, procedures to regulate the flow of ideas and comments that were entering the assembly through different channels remained weak. The few participatory mechanisms envisioned by the NCA indeed proved not to be adapted to systematically give voice to the citizens and hear their opinions on the constitutional process, hence the need for more relevant tools.

Structuring the NCA-civil society relation

Under the lead of Baddredine Abdelkafi, an NCA member from the Islamist party Ennahdha appointed deputy to the NCA president in charge of the relationship with citizens, civil society, and Tunisians living abroad, new initiatives to foster public participation started to emerge. Abdelkafi set a diverse team composed of members from the different political currents represented in the assembly, which started to reflect on how to strengthen the participatory dimension of the Tunisian constitutional process. As there was no clear provision in the NCA's RoP concerning citizens' direct involvement in the drafting process, the team had to elaborate an outreach project from scratch. In this purpose, it sought opinion from various international organizations on comparative experiences of participatory constitution-making processes, and received direct advisory, logistical, and financial support from the UNDP.[15]

As a first step, the team launched in September 2012 an online consultation platform on the NCA official website to allow citizens to send comments and suggestions on constitution-related issues.[16] Though a positive start, it proved poorly efficient as the platform received only 217 contributions along the following year and a half of drafting process (TCC, 2015: 68–69). This virtual tool was, however, aimed to be combined with other activities on the ground. Two major projects were thus developed and successively implemented by the Abdelkafi team: an initial open-door initiative at the NCA targeting civil society actors, followed by a national dialogue on the constitution held throughout the various regions of the country.

The NCA opens its doors

Under the title "Towards a participatory writing of the constitution," the first participatory project undertaken by the NCA took place on September 14–15, 2012. During two days, the NCA's constituent commissions opened their doors

---

14 Ibid.
15 Author's interview with B. Abdelkafi, Tunis, April 6, 2016.
16 http://www.anc.tn/site/main/AR/contribution/contribution_citoyen_constit.jsp. (Link not functional anymore).

to civil society representatives, who could participate in the debate and directly interact with the drafters on the various constitutional issues discussed within each commission. At the exception of a few international organizations explicitly invited to observe the event and ensure its transparency, national CSOs were not invited individually, but had to go through an online registration process, by filling in a form available on the NCA website. Despite limited communication around the event in the media the event proved successful, with representatives of some 300 CSOs attending the two-day event, including some organizations from outside the capital, as well as organizations representing Tunisians living abroad.[17]

The event, however, did not go without some difficulties. From the outset, the NCA Bureau expressed little support for the initiative, not really convinced of its potentiality for success.[18] The general atmosphere in which the NCA started its work was also shaped by a lack of confidence of some civil society actors towards the assembly who decided to boycott the event. Their opposition was based both on their doubts that the NCA would actually take into consideration the civil society's views, as well as a broader ideological disagreement in particular of some liberal and secular CSOs towards what they saw (especially at the beginning of the process) as an Islamist-dominated assembly that would attempt to enforce conservative views on the drafting process. In spite of this tense climate, further worsened by the general political context,[19] the event went smoothly. Participants took the opportunity to present numerous suggestions and recommendations on the different articles of the first constitution draft that had been released on August 14, 2012.

The success of the event gave new impetus to the organizing team to further develop the participatory dynamic of the constitutional process. The main demand that had emerged from the civil society during this first event was indeed that deputies would show reciprocity and make the effort to come visit citizens on the ground, now that the people had come visit the NCA. More and more, constituents had the feeling to have lost any proximity with their elected representatives, who seemed to have left to the capital to never return. There was, therefore, a manifest need to retake contact with the field, which the CSOs were certainly the best vehicle to convey to the deputies. Hence the idea emerged that deputies should visit their constituents on the ground.[20]

---

17 More organizations had actually expressed their interest, but the number of participant organizations had to be limited to 300, represented by one person each – in addition to the 21 invited international organizations – due to the lack of capacity of the NCA. See TCC, 2015: 69.
18 Author's interview with B. Abdelkafi.
19 The American embassy in Tunis had been attacked on September 14, 2012, by a group of demonstrators associated with Salafi movements denouncing the release of an Islamophobic movie, and the Islamist-led government had been accused of laxity by the secular opposition in dealing with the issue.
20 Author's interview with B. Abdelkafi. See also Abdelkafi, op. cit.: 3.

The NCA reaches out to citizens

Following the release of the second constitution draft on December 14, 2012, two new initiatives to reach out to citizens came into being. The first step consisted of several meetings between drafters and students on university campuses, while the second one entailed a round of national consultations in the different regions of the country and abroad.

Investing in the future: Meeting with students

The project as initially prepared and presented to the NCA Bureau in October 2012 included a first round of meetings between NCA members and high school students, and a second one dedicated to university students. The idea behind this initiative was that youth, as an essential component of the Tunisian society and the driving force of the 2011 uprising, should have a chance to express their views and concerns, as well as feel represented in a constitutional text that was aimed to last for the coming generations. The NCA Bureau, however, proved reluctant to open the dialogue to "normal citizens" in spite of the success it had already encountered with CSOs' representatives. Other deputies also feared that a large-scale consultation process would further slow down the drafting process (TCC, 2015: 69). Due to the delay in the response of the Bureau, who approved the project only two months later, the initial meeting with high school students had to be canceled, but the second part dedicated to university students could still be implemented.[21]

On December 16, 2012, two regional sessions were held in the two main cities of the country, the first one in the capital at the Faculty of Law of the University of Tunis, and the second one in Sfax – the so-called "capital of the South" – at the Faculty of Sciences. To avoid large crowds of students, the organizers decided to target only the elected student representatives in the academic councils from all universities around the country.[22] A group of deputies – including representatives of the various constituent commissions and deputies elected from the constituencies of Tunis and Sfax – went to the campuses to meet the student delegates for a daylong event. Logistical support was provided by the UNDP in cooperation with the Ministry of Higher Education.

Discussing with students proved a more difficult task than debating with civil society representatives. Not only because students had long felt marginalized by the NCA and the political class in general and thus initially displayed little eagerness to cooperate with the NCA members, but also due to the extreme politicization and polarization of the Tunisian university. The majority of the attending delegates were indeed affiliated either with the leftist student

21 Author's interview with B. Abdelkafi.
22 This represents about 500 delegates nationwide, of which some 300 – about 200 in Sfax and some 100 in Tunis, at the peak of the event – attended the consultations.

union UGET (*Union Générale des Etudiants Tunisiens*) or with the Islamist-oriented UGTE (*Union Générale Tunisienne des Etudiants*), known for their conflicting relationship. It thus resulted in heated debates that sometimes went beyond constitution-related issues and almost turned violent at certain moments.[23] The event, however, proved relatively successful, as students were able to raise a number of constitutional issues, including those related to students' conditions, prospects for employment, and academic rights, and had an opportunity to discuss them directly with the deputies, who in turn realized the importance to be confronted back to the reality of the field.[24]

The NCA in the regions and abroad

The students' sessions were followed by a round of 24 sessions covering the 24 governorates of Tunisia, as well as 18 additional sessions held in France and Italy targeting Tunisians living abroad.[25] The consultations unfolded at a rate of six governorates per weekend from December 23, 2012, to January 13, 2013, for the national dialogue and from January 19 to the end of February 2013 for the meetings held abroad.[26] They were opened to any citizen that would have registered on the NCA website (within the limit of 300 participants per session – later extended to 500). As previously, a delegation of NCA members composed of deputies from the region, as well as a member of the organizing team and NCA counselors, would come to the governorate and hold a one-day meeting with the citizens. Deputies were prepared in advance and provided with guidelines on how to handle the meetings, in order to avoid discrepancies from one governorate to another. These included essentially paying careful attention to people's points of view and avoiding expressing personal opinions not mentioned in the constitution draft (Abdelkafi, 2016: 5).

With a few exceptions (Nabeul, Ben Arous, Medenine), citizens' participation was low in the first sessions of the dialogue, increasing only near the end of the process. This was partly due to the lack of communication around the event – only well-informed civil society organizations and interested citizens actually knew of the consultations – as well as the limited initial involvement of some political parties (TCC, 2015: 70). Opposition parties in particular continued

23 Author's participant observation, University of Tunis, December 16, 2012.
24 Author's discussion with various deputies attending the session, University of Tunis, December 16, 2016.
25 Due to financial and logistical reasons, consultations abroad had to be limited to these two countries, which host the largest communities of Tunisian emigrants. A project of videoconference targeting Tunisians living in other countries was submitted to the NCA Bureau but never got a response.
26 The sessions were held as follow: December 23: East and coastal cities (Sousse, Monastir, Mahdia, Kairouan, Sfax, and Gabès); December 30: West and Center-West (Gafsa, Jendouba, Beja, El Kef, Siliana, Zaghouan); January 6: Tunis and suburbs (Ariana, Ben Arous, Manouba), as well as the Northern cities of Nabeul and Bizerte; January 13: Center and South (Kasserine, Sidi Bouzid, Tozeur, Kebili, Medenine, and Tataouine). Eleven sessions were also held in France and seven in Italy.

to doubt that peoples' comments would seriously be taken into consideration and still perceived the whole outreach project as a "form of populism" from Ennahdha's side (Abdelkafi, 2016: 4). One could thus observe a clear ideological unbalance during the first weeks of the event, with religious supporters represented in larger number – having been informed and/or mobilized by the Islamist party or affiliated CSOs.[27] Yet starting from the third week, as opposition parties realized that the output of the dialogue could effectively have an impact on the constitution-drafting process, they started mobilizing and encouraging their supporters to participate in the dialogue sessions.

From the outset, the dialogue indeed appeared to be not ideologically neutral. If the NCA members generally showed neutrality and objectivity in their presentations, defending the constitution draft from a common voice rather than along partisan lines, a large number of attendants displayed a clear ideological or partisan orientation, sometimes leading to a polarization of the debates. Some participants seemed to have even been briefed in advance by their respective parties, as they not only presented the same recommendations and suggestions across the different regions, but also used exactly the same wording from one session to another.[28] Such a politicization of the dialogue is problematic in that it casts doubts on the actual spontaneity of people's interventions, and raises questions on how much the final result of the dialogue reflects citizens' personal views rather than political positions of some parties that would have used them as intermediaries.

In spite of this, the consultations did not turn into an ideological battlefield as was initially feared by some critics. Discussions went smoothly, citizens listening to each other even when they disagreed with opposing views. Participants made relevant comments and constructive recommendations to the NCA members, both on the form and the content. Recurrent issues related to the universality of human rights in the constitution, rights and freedoms, the role of religion and the Arab/Muslim identity of the state, the army and security forces, and provisions for amending the constitution. Participants also raised local issues of concern: for instance, the right to water (art. 34 of the second draft) did not have the same resonance in the arid region of Tozeur as in the green governorates of Beja or Zaghouan. Discussions also went beyond the sole constitutional text, citizens taking the opportunity of the dialogue to complain about their difficult living conditions as well as express their grievances towards the NCA members, whom they accused to have neglected the population and failed to fulfill their electoral promises and the goals of the Tunisian revolution. Some voices were also critical towards the organizational and financial support provided by the UNDP, which they considered as a foreign interference.[29]

27 Author's participant observation in various locations of the national dialogue, December 2012–January 2013.
28 Ibid.
29 Ibid. See also TCC, 2015: 70.

Overall, about 5,000 citizens were able to participate to the various stages of the consultation process. This participatory dynamic thus gave the opportunity both to make citizens' voices heard and to remind deputies of their representative role. But following the event and to ensure its long-term credibility, deputies had to keep the promise reiterated throughout the sessions of the dialogue that views expressed by citizens would actually make their way to the constitutional text.

From the field to the text: Translating citizens' recommendations into constitutional provisions

From the outset, the participatory initiative was thought by Abdelkafi's team as one that should be effective and not merely cosmetic. Early on, the team had, therefore, to think of a mechanism to translate citizens' views into concrete constitutional input. This was first and foremost made possible through the careful attention paid to reporting along all the sessions with civil society actors, students, and citizens. Each of the session was indeed accompanied by a rapporteur in charge of taking note of the citizens' comments and recommendations, which were later organized in a final report prepared with the aid of the UNDP.[30] The report was then published on the NCA website and transmitted to the presidents of the constituent commissions, alongside with a partial report containing the main comments related to the respective chapters of which they were in charge.

The second step was the translation of the compiled recommendations into constitutional provisions. For this purpose, agreement was reached among the drafters to revise the NCA RoP in order to include a mechanism ensuring that citizens' recommendations would be taken into consideration in the revision of the constitution draft. During a round of RoP amendments adopted by the assembly in March 2013, a new provision was thus added to article 104 of the document, stating that "Constituent commissions shall commit to review the comments and propositions that emerged from the general debate and the national dialogue on the constitution, and this within 10 open days of the date of reception of the reports" (art. 104 new, para. 2).

A specific legal mechanism was thus in place. What remains to be seen though is to what extend the popular input was deemed sufficiently relevant by the drafters so as to effectively contribute to modifications in the revised constitution draft. The section on page 79 provides a preliminary assessment of some of the main issues that do actually reflect citizens' views.

---

30 Author's interview with B. Abdelkafi and participant observation in the various phases of the consultation process. The UNDP hired external rapporteurs – usually law professors – who, alongside with NCA-appointed counselors, attended the different sessions of consultations and wrote down participants' suggestions, which were later compiled in the report. See the final report: UNDP, 2013. Available in French and Arabic.

Impact of the participatory process on the constitution draft: An assessment

The third constitution draft that was issued on April 22, 2013, did actually include some new or revised provisions based on citizens and CSOs' recommendations. These related to both the form and the content of the text and covered most chapters of the constitutional document. But to assess with exactitude how much the changes brought to the text reflect exclusively citizens' views remains difficult, as propositions expressed by the participants to the consultations actually coincided in many cases with issues previously raised by political parties or even mentioned in the media. Sorting out which point directly related to citizens' concerns is therefore challenging, and below is only a preliminary attempt to do so.

In this regard, the NCA and the UNDP made a meaningful contribution to assess the impact of the dialogue on the third draft through the production of a joint report entitled "Effect of the National Dialogue on the third constitution draft: An analytical reading."[31] This report attempts to review, chapter by chapter, the main points raised by citizens that were directly translated into the third draft. Most of the following analysis is based on this report.

Interestingly, we note various types of comments from the participants. Some are clearly a reflection of the predominant views expressed by political parties, civil society actors, and even international organizations, and citizens merely joined their voices to the dominant opinion. An obvious example concerns the addition of the term "universal" to the human rights principles mentioned in the preamble of the constitution draft. This had been a highly debated issue both within and outside the NCA, and the drafters had been subject to intense pressure, including from the international community, to make this addition. Some Islamist and other conservative members of the assembly were initially opposed to the idea, fearing that such a wording could contradict some principles of Islam.

Other changes, however, appear more clearly linked to citizens' daily concerns, as well as their previous experience of living under an authoritarian regime, whose return they wished to prevent. This is reflected in a number of provisions related to the neutrality of public administration and educational institutions, of the army and the internal security forces, the independence of the judiciary, or an increased role for citizens in the management of local affairs. Some of these points will be discussed more thoroughly here.

Neutrality of the public administration and educational institutions

While the issue of the neutrality of places of worship had already been highly debated within the assembly and addressed in the second constitution draft (art. 4), citizens put an emphasis on a more concerning issue for them, namely

---

31 NCA/UNDP, 2013. Available only in Arabic.

the neutrality of the public administration, which they wanted to see expressed with more details (the issue was already shortly addressed in article 14 of the second draft). Though they could not obtain more specification on this point, a new provision was added according to their demands, which dealt with the neutrality of educational institutions, providing that the state "shall ensure the neutrality from partisan instrumentalization."[32] Educational institutions had indeed more recently started to reflect partisan or ideological bias, notably in the religious field, and a heated debate had even arisen regarding the emergence of anarchic schools and kindergartens providing religious teaching.[33]

Army and security forces

Article 10 of the second draft dealt with the role of the army and ensured its "political neutrality," but popular pressure pushed for an additional provision that would cover internal security forces as well.[34] This demand should be read in the context of the dark memories of the Ben Ali era, during which the police in particular was used as the armed wing of the regime to tightly control the population and prevent any attempt of contestation. Having been the main victims of the state security apparatus, citizens thus took the opportunity of drafting the new constitution to enshrine the principle of its neutrality and clearly define its responsibilities. A new article was thus added that deals specifically with the national security forces, which it defines as "republican," in charge of "maintaining security, public order, protecting individuals, institutions and properties, law enforcement while ensuring the respect of freedoms, in total neutrality."[35]

Political parties and opposition

At the request of citizens, article 24 of the second draft on the creation of "parties, syndicates and associations" was reinforced by a clause stating that these organizations, in their status and activities, shall not only respect the provisions of the constitution, the law and the principle of financial transparency, but also "reject violence."[36] The period of transition had indeed been shaped by several cases of political parties' and trade unions' offices being attacked by illegal armed

---

32 In the final Constitution, art. 6 deals with the neutrality of the places of worship, art. 15 with the neutrality of the public administration, and art. 16 with the neutrality of educational institutions.
33 On the debate about anarchic religious schools, see for instance Sbouaï, S., «Jardins d'enfants coraniques: zone de non droit?», *Nawaat*, November 23, 2012: https://nawaat.org/portail/2012/11/23/jardins-denfants-coraniques-zone-de-non-droit/.
34 This recommendation was expressed in various locations of the national dialogue, including in the governorates of Manouba, Ariana, Tunis, Kasserine, and Siliana. See UNDP, 2013: 23, and NCA/UNDP, 2013: 5.
35 Art. 17 of the third draft; art. 19 of the final Constitution.
36 Art. 30 of the third draft; art. 35 of the final Constitution.

groups, and this addition was thus an attempt to prevent such incidents from occuring in the future.

This comes in addition to a brand new article constitutionalizing the role of the opposition in the legislative assembly, which emerged in large part from the regional dialogue.[37] With a view to remedy to decades of political desertification and crackdown on the opposition, the third draft thus defines the opposition as an "essential component" of the legislative assembly, in whose structure and work it should be "adequately represented."[38] The fourth draft (June 1, 2013) would later grant to the opposition "the right to create and preside over an inquiry commission every year," while the final constitution eventually provides for a member of the opposition to head the strategic finance committee of the assembly.[39]

Youth's participation

As the 2011 uprising had been mainly carried out by the young generation, citizens expressed the wish to see youth's place and role in society enshrined in the new constitution. Various propositions were made, including dedicating a fixed number of seats to youth in the legislative assembly[40] or establishing a "High Council for Youth" among the "constitutional bodies" provided for by chapter 6 of the draft.[41] From these suggestions, one was eventually retained, consisting in a new article defining youth as an "active force in building the Nation," whom the state shall provide with the conditions to "expand its participation to the social, economical, cultural and political development."[42] The role of youth at the local level was also reinforced by a provision stating that the "electoral law shall ensure youth representation in local councils."[43]

Through the participatory process, citizens thus eventually managed to influence the constitutional text – with more or less success depending on the topic. As appears from this preliminary assessment, both issues of general interest and more specific concerns of particular groups of citizens found an echo in the final document. This achievement was made possible through the serious attention given to them by the drafters and the mechanisms provided to turn people's recommendations into an effective input in the constitution-making process. But, in spite of the actual effect on the text, what also needs to be questioned is whether Tunisians eventually identified with the final document.

37 This demand was raised notably by attendees in the governorates of Monastir, Bizerte, and Sidi Bouzid. See UNDP, 2013: 35; NCA/UNDP, 2013: 6.
38 Art. 57 of the third draft.
39 Art. 59 of the fourth draft; art. 60 of the final Constitution. See also TCC, 2015: 89–90.
40 A proposition made by some participants in Kairouan. See UNDP, 2013: 51.
41 Proposition made in Beja, Zaghouan, and Gafsa. See UNDP, 2013: 168.
42 Art.12 of the third draft; art. 8 of the final Constitution.
43 Art. 125 of the third draft; art. 133 of the final Constitution. See also UNDP, 2013: 177.

A constitution for all Tunisians?

In spite of the initial lack of internal support, time pressure, and limited means, the NCA managed to put in place an innovative participative project, which proved successful to a large extent and should indeed be praised in regard to the country's history of decades of de-politicization and inexistent public participation. This chapter attempted to provide an assessment of this original process by answering a number of questions, including how participation was envisaged in the drafting process, how it was translated into practice, the role of the international community, and the influence of other constitution-making experiences on the way participation unfolded. Below is an attempt to offer some conclusions, while also highlighting the limits of the Tunisian experience.

The discrepancy between the way a participatory approach of constitution-making was initially envisioned in the organizational framework of the NCA and how it eventually was implemented reflects the NCA's initial uncertainty and lack of commitment to public participation. As a result, various actors progressively set up their own ways to influence the process through different informal channels, before a varied and motivated team of deputies eventually put in place a more structured outreach project that gave voice to the people.

Though coming late in the process and initially encountering limited support, the project succeeded in overcoming both NCA members and citizens' skepticism about its usefulness and actual impact on the constitution-making process. Overall, both participants and organizers expressed satisfaction for this opportunity that enabled making the constitutional text known to the people, hearing from them, and thus helping forge a national consensus on the main political principles on which to rebuild the Tunisian State.[44] It also proved a useful occasion for constitution drafters to reconnect with the reality of the field and made them realize the "informative and innovative potential of public participation"[45] – convincing even the most reluctant deputies of its benefits.[46] Drafters' commitment to translate citizens' comments into constitutional provisions – which went through the amendment of the NCA RoP and the actual consideration and inclusion of some recommendations that stemmed out of the dialogue into the text – also contributed to make public participation effective.

But above all, the participatory experience proved a unifying moment for the drafters. As previously noted, the constitution-making process unfolded in an extremely polarized environment, and outreach events saw the participation of a number of ideologically positioned citizens who were keen on expressing and defending their views. Such a tense atmosphere could have easily got out of hand had the NCA members adopted a divisive stance along these ideological lines. On the contrary, they demonstrated an impressive sense of unity – rarely observed during the debates at the NCA – and the pedagogy they used

44 NCA/UNDP, 2013: 2.
45 DRI, 2011: 4.
46 Author's interview with B. Abdelkafi.

during all the events proved extremely valuable in preventing any potential conflict. Being aware of their common responsibility to defend and promote the constitutional project, they put aside their ideological disagreement, even in time of serious political crisis,[47] to carry the project together. It is interesting to note that, at this point of the process, the dividing line had shifted from an initial one between the drafters themselves (mainly Islamist/secular), towards a drafters/citizens divide, where all the NCA members would find themselves on the same side.

Last but not least, the participatory process was entirely indigenous in its content; as defined by its initiator, it was "a Tunisian process for Tunisian people."[48] In spite of the critics raised against the UNDP's financial and logistical support, the international organization never interfered in any substantive issue. Influence of other constitutional experiences was also limited. If various international organizations following the Tunisian process at the time encouraged more participation based on the examples of previous successful cases – among which South Africa was always presented as a model – none was strictly followed to develop the Tunisian approach and no foreign organization was directly involved in its implementation either.[49]

Limits and lessons to be learned

However, this bright picture should not overshadow a number of dark zones, especially when looking at the long-term effects and implementation phase of the constitution. The aftermath of the drafting process and participation project indeed seem to reveal that the Tunisian Constitution was still not fully perceived as the constitution of the whole Tunisian people.

The participatory project, as innovative as it was, indeed remained limited in scope and obviously did not reach all citizens. Although there is no set numerical threshold to determine whether a participatory process is sufficiently inclusive, the dissemination of information in the Tunisian case remained limited due to the absence of a wide information campaign around the various events, and the whole project ended up being unknown to a large fringe of the population (TCC, 2015: 68). Fearing that it could not manage large crowds of people, the NCA eventually communicated timidly, and *de facto* limited the number of participants at outreach events, thus leaving many people with a continued sense of marginalization. While broadening these events might not have been a realistic option, communicating on a more regular basis around the NCA's daily work

---

47 Since the beginning of the constitution drafting process and even more so at the time of implementation of the participatory project, the NCA and the overall Tunisian political scene were extremely polarized between supporters of the Islamist party and of the secular opposition. This tension was further aggravated by the political assassination of leftist leader Chokri Belaïd on Feb. 6, 2013, i.e., during the last weeks of the national dialogue in Italy. In spite of this, the process went forward and was concluded peacefully.

48 Author's interview with B. Abdelkafi.

49 Ibid.

could have helped to keep citizens informed and interested in the constitution-drafting process. Monthly encounters with the citizens in the field – as initially provided for by the RoP – would also have contributed to "bridge the information gap" between the elected officials and their constituents (TCC, 2015: 156). Such a gap actually became clearly visible in the post-adoption phase.

In May 2014, the NCA indeed organized a last outreach event in the regions – the so-called "Month of the Constitution" – aimed at presenting to the people the constitutional text that had been adopted by the NCA a few months earlier. However, the debacle of its launching day in the central city of Sidi Bouzid, the birthplace of the Tunisian uprising – where protesters prevented the delegation headed by the NCA President from holding the event, calling "not for a constitution but for employment and development"[50] – and the low attendance during all the unfolding sessions[51] reveal limited interest as well as deep frustration amidst the population. The fact that those who attended the meetings did comment as much (and sometimes more) on the political and economic situation as on the constitutional text itself clearly indicates that the constitution was eventually not everyone's main issue of concern.[52]

This reflects a broader difficulty common to many constitution-making processes taking place in times of transition, and hardly manageable by the constitution drafters. This has to do with the overall environment in which constitution-drafting processes unfold. Constitution-making indeed occurs more often than not in contexts of profound political change and also economic and social turmoil, and sometimes high levels of insecurity, which render all authorities not trustworthy in the eyes of people. Such periods also redefine people's priorities, which for many is not the constitution but more immediate concerns such as employment and security. It is understandably difficult for people to focus on such a long-term project as a constitution when short-term needs and problems remain unsolved.

Eventually, if participatory constitution-making processes do not necessarily lead to "better" constitutions in a normative sense, they could still have a positive impact in the sense that they re-give a voice and place to the citizens in the public debate and thus create documents that are closer to the people. An identity card of a people, where anyone could find the basic common ground that unites him to his fellow citizens. Or to put it simply, a constitution of the people, for the people. In this regard, the Tunisian experience, in spite of its flaws, has partly succeeded in giving a popular imprint to its new constitution. Overcoming the remaining feeling of marginalization will require time and efforts to further sensitize people to the importance of the constitution – in particular the younger generation – as well

---

50 «Le lancement du mois de la Constitution perturbé par un mouvement de protestation», *Babnet Tunisie*, May 10, 2014: http://www.babnet.net/cadredetail-85029.asp.
51 3,479 citizens in total attended the event throughout the country. See TCC, 2015: 95.
52 Authors' participant observation in various locations of the outreach event. See also TCC, 2015: 95–96.

as to urgently deal with more pressing issues such as the dire economic situation. The Tunisian experience, however, offers rich lessons – both through its successes and failures – to other countries in transition, which could draw on it and seek to improve it, while also developing their own national participatory approach.

References

Abbiate, T. (2014), "La nuova Costituzione tunisina, la Costituzione del popolo", *Diritti Comparati*, March 10, 2014: http://www.diritticomparati.it/2014/03/la-nuova-costituzione-tunisina-la-costituzione-del-popolo-.html.

Abdelkafi, B. (Sept. 2016), "The National Constituent Assembly and the Civil Society: What Is the Relationship?," in the United Nations Development Program (UNDP), *The Constitution of Tunisia: Processes, principles and perspectives*, Tunis: http://www.arabstates.undp.org/content/rbas/en/home/library/Dem_Gov/the-constitution-of-tunisie-.html.

Democracy Reporting International (2011), "Lessons Learned from Constitution-Making: Processes with Broad Based Public Participation," Briefing Paper No. 20, November 2011: http://dann.rewi.hu-berlin.de/doc/Dann_2011.pdf.

Interpeace Handbook (2011), *Constitution-Making and Reform: Options for Process:* http://www.constitutionmakingforpeace.org/sites/default/files/Constitution-Making-Handbook.pdf.

Miller, L.E. (ed.) (2010), *Framing the State in Times of Transition: Case Studies in Constitution Making*, Washington DC: USIP Press.

National Constituent Assembly (NCA) & United Nations Development Program (UNDP) (2013), "*Athr al-hiwar al-watany 'ala miswadat machrou' al-doustour al-thalitha: kiraa tahliliya*, [Effect of the National Dialogue on the third constitution draft: An analytical reading] June 2013. Only in Arabic (Doc. provided by the NCA).

The Carter Center (TCC) (2015), *The Constitution-Making Process in Tunisia*, Final Report, 2011–2014: https://www.cartercenter.org/resources/pdfs/news/peace_publications/democracy/tunisia-constitution-making-process.pdf.

The Carter Center (TCC) (2012), "The Carter Center Encourages Increased Transparency in the Constitution Drafting Process," May 10, 2012: http://www.cartercenter.org/news/pr/tunisia-051112.html.

United Nations Development Program (UNDP) (2013), *Dialogue National sur le Projet de Constitution, Le Rapport Général*, Tunis, March 2013. Available in French and Arabic (Doc. provided by the NCA).

6 The role of participation in the two Kenyan constitution-building processes of 2000–2005 and 2010

Lessons learnt?

Rose W. Macharia and Yash Ghai

Introduction

Participation in the 2000–2005 and 2010 constitution-building processes in Kenya was characterised by different institutionalised[1] and spontaneous[2] models across different social and political spheres. Before the formal constitution-building process formally began in 2000, various individuals, groups and institutions had been agitating for constitutional reform for some years.[3] This chapter analyses those models, their scope and influence upon the resulting draft constitutions. It also discusses participation[4] as initially envisaged in the Constitution of Kenya Review Act 1997: where the Organs of Review comprised the the Constitution of Kenya Review (CKRC) Commission, District Forums and the National Forum (later conference) and how this model changed during the elaborate processes of the CKRC and the Committee of Experts (CoE).

Drawing from the resulting draft constitutions, we make conclusions regarding the role of various actors and the character of participation, noting distinctions between the CKRC (and Bomas) and CoE processes. This chapter concludes with a summary of the different pressures for change as well as resistance to change, and the circumstances in which reform is possible.

Kenya's struggle for a new constitution was undoubtedly intensified by the global political shifts of the 1960s to the 1990s. The Nkrumah African revolution first raised the possibility and then realised the actuality of African independence in the full glare of the colonised world (Ogoth/Ochieng 1995). On 3 February 1960, the British Prime Minister, Maurice Harold MacMillan, delivered the famous "wind of change" speech. He acknowledged that the

---

1 In this chapter, the institutionalised models are those which are formally prescribed, by law, and can be traced in Kenya to the Constitution of Kenya Review Acts of 1998, 2002 and 2009.
2 For the purpose of this chapter the spontaneous models are those drawn from events and opportunities that enabled the public to voice their views and exert influence at the various stages of constitutional reform in Kenya.
3 For an excellent account of the role of civil society prior to the formal process, see Mutunga 1999.
4 Participation in this case refers to the various methods employed to enable collective public engagement in the constitution-making process such as public debate, dialogue and civic education.

DOI: 10.4324/9781315180540-9

processes which gave rise to nation states of Europe were being repeated all over the world. He referred to the National African Consciousness (International Relations and Security Network (ISN) 2016) in his acclaimed proclamation: "The wind of change is blowing through the continent, and whether we like it or not, this growth of national consciousness is a political fact. We must all accept it as a fact and our national policies must take account of it." He posed, "Will the great experiments in self-government that are now being made in Asia and Africa, especially within the Commonwealth, prove so successful, and by their example so compelling, that the balance will come down in favour of freedom and order and justice?" (Ogoth/Ochieng 1995). Soon after, the air of freedom filled the entire African continent.

Kenya gained independence on 12 December 1963 following several years of unrest and resistance. The independence constitution was an elite agreement between Kenya's political class and the British administration in the Lancaster House Constitutional Conference in London, which took place between 1960 and 1963 (Maxon 2011). Although the process for the independence constitution is outside the scope of this chapter, it is worth noting that the British process for that constitution discouraged popular participation. The key decisions were made in London, between the British government and delegates of political parties from the colony. It is as if the British philosophy was that the further the political leaders were removed from their supporters, the more compliant they might be to British proposals (for the fact is that the British were not merely a neutral umpire – they had their own interests, so that negotiations were not only between competing local parties, but also with the British). The British may also have assumed that it would be easier to develop or coerce agreements among parties or groups away from their supporters.

Post-independence, various constitutional amendments were made between 1963 and 1999; notably, the 1982 amendment meant to stifle any opposition by making Kenya a *de jure* one-party state. These amendments were inserted into the constitution to protect existing power structures such as an imperial presidency. The president had power to appoint members of Parliament (MPs) as ministers and assistant ministers. Another tool was the persecution of anyone who criticised the government. It is no wonder that when the formal constitution-making process began, reform of the executive and form of government (devolved or centralised) took centre-stage as did a strong and inclusive Bill of Human Rights.

During this period, there was outcry from twenty-nine trade unionists and parliamentarians who defected from the Kenya African National Union (KANU) (Ghai/McAuslan 1970; Okoth-Ogendo 1972) and formed the Kenya People's Party (KPU) to oppose the actions of the president and the constitutional amendments which had curbed human rights and democracy. As a consequence, the Constitution of Kenya (Amendment) (No. 2) Act No. 17 of 1966 was enacted to remove from Parliament a parliamentarian who resigns from the party on whose platform he or she had been elected, thus effectively causing the removal of the members who crossed over from the ruling party

(Okoth-Ogendo 1972). The "turn coat rule" as it was popularly known as, was introduced to intimidate any MP who joined the opposition. In effect, it worked because 13 of the 29 MPs who had defected, went back to KANU (ibid.).

The pre- and post-2005 models of participation

In this section, we discuss two periods of attempts to adopt a new constitution. The first (from 2000 to 2005) involved the appointment of the Constitution of Kenya Review Commission (CKRC) to consult the people and also, abiding by a set of pre-agreed values, to prepare a draft constitution for further consideration in a constituent assembly and ultimately adoption by the National Assembly. Two distinct drafts were prepared, the first essentially by a constituent assembly based on the CKRC's draft and the second by the National Assembly ("Wako draft" after the Attorney-General), but neither became the constitution – the first scuppered by the judiciary, and the second by the people (rejected by a majority 58.12 percent).

The second period started in 2008 headed by a committee of experts appointed by politicians, in the aftermath of acute violence including the killing of over 1,500 people in essentially ethnic conflicts and the displacement of 500,000 people from their homes, following the 2007 elections. The starting points of the new draft were the 2004 draft of the CKRC and the so-called Wako draft of 2005. It ended with the adoption of a constitution by a 68.55 percent majority in August 2010 – which is now Kenya's constitution.

There were unfulfilled promises of a new constitution by the second and third presidents, Arap Moi and Mwai Kibaki (during his first term). The latter assumed office after a unique multi-party union – the National Rainbow Coalition (NARC) – was formed and negotiated to provide a united front to oust President Moi. Constitutional reform was sustained by strong criticism of the *status quo* by the civil society, academia, religious groups, the opposition and foreign states who threatened to withdraw foreign aid.

In 1994, faith-based groups and civil society organizations under the umbrella Citizen's Coalition for Constitutional Change (4C's), developed a proposed constitution.[5] Instead, President Moi proposed that a team of foreign experts develop a new constitution. This proposal was rejected. Ahead of the 1997 general elections, there were more calls for reform. In 1998, the Constitution of Kenya Review Act, 1998,[6] was enacted to "facilitate the comprehensive review of the Constitution by the people of Kenya and its eventual alteration by Parliament."[7] The Act established the CKRC, whose mandate was to engage in nationwide consultations with the view of preparing a people's constitution. At first, CKRC's composition did not include members of the civil society and faith-based groups, who had been involved in the previous movement for change.

5 See Mutunga 1999.
6 This Act was amended in the year 2000.
7 The long title to the 1998 Act.

Initially, the government wanted a politically driven process managed by politicians and political parties. Civil society, on the other hand, was keen to have a participatory process, with the people at its centre (Cottrell/Ghai 2007). It is no wonder that the Constitution of Kenya Review Act was amended thrice. In 1998, it was amended after civil society protested the exclusion of the people from the review process. However, following this amendment, political parties could not agree on representation in the review commission, stalling and frustrating the process. As a result, religious leaders under the aegis of the Ufungamano initiative comprising members from the civil society and religious organisations formed a parallel process, and embarked on an intensive public-view collection exercise.[8] This prompted the government to commence another process (2000 amendment), adequately engaging public participation. An independent commission, drawn largely from civil society, was to collect views from the public, including political parties, before drafting the constitution; the opposition and religious leaders were not entirely happy with this model.

The notion of two competing and antagonist processes was only likely to cause further conflict and invoke violence, as was beginning to happen when Yash Ghai, who was offered the chair of the statutory commission, refused to accept it unless the two commissions were merged. After protracted negotiations with both factions, he was able to bridge the differences between the two factions, setting the stage for a joint and a highly participatory process, with heavy emphasis on the values of the new constitution, including human rights, gender equality, devolution and an accountable executive (introduced in further amendments in 2001 to the Act).[9]

This inspired adoption of a unified road map that would guide the review process based on the principles of: (a) trust and national consensus; (b) peace and non-violence; (c) respect for human rights and freedoms; (d) police protection; (e) regard to the independence of the commission and its members; and (f) restraint from any political or administrative action that would adversely affect the success of the review process (CKRC 2003). These values would mark the character of the process.

Constitution of Kenya Review Commission and the National Constitutional Conference

The Constitution of Kenya Review Act was to "facilitate the comprehensive review of the Constitution by the people."[10] Five organs were instrumental to this process: the Constitution of Kenya Review Commission (CKRC), the Constituency Constitutional Forum (CCF), the National Constitutional Conference (NCC), Referendum and the National Assembly.[11] CKRC was

8 See Cottrell/Ghai 2014.
9 For a detailed account of the negotiations, see Mati 2012.
10 The Constitution of Kenya Review Act (CAP 3A).
11 The Act provided for twenty-nine members (twenty-seven commissioners appointed by the National Assembly, the attorney general and secretary to the commission). According to

mandated to collect views from the public, conduct civic education, compile research drawn from other jurisdictions and draft a bill amending the constitution to be presented to the National Assembly for debate and enactment.[12] The CKRC review process was the most participatory of the three stages leading to the first constitutional referendum in 2005. The nationwide consultations yielded more than 35,000 memoranda from the public. The terms of reference of the commission necessitated a process that would strengthen the following values: peace, integrity, national unity, clear separation of powers, participation of the people in governance, inclusiveness, equity and equitable access to national resources, national integration and unity, rights and freedoms, management of public affairs and consensus for nation-building.[13]

The features of the CKRC-led process were: first, that participation would be prioritised through the *processes and procedures* guiding the organs of review and their mode of conduct, and second, collection and collation of people's views. Public participation during this phase was structured as follows: the Constituency Constitutional Forum (CCF), whose mandate was to enable "debate, discuss, collect and collate views from the public at the district level"[14] and the National Constitutional Conference on the draft constitution developed by CKRC at the national level.[15] The resulting draft constitution would thereafter be presented to the National Assembly for adoption. The National Assembly would be able either to accept or reject the document as a whole, but not make changes.

The constitution-making process was the embodiment of hope for economic growth, political freedoms, stability and individual and societal fulfilment. In particular, the people expressed fourteen critical issues to be included in the draft constitution: (1) the guarantee of a decent life, with the fundamental needs of food, health-care, water, clothing, shelter, security and basic education; (2) peace and stability; (3) a fair system of access to land and justice remedying past wrongs; (4) inclusion in decision-making; (5) shared power; (6) good leadership and integrity; (7) corruption-free society; (8) police respect and protection; (9) equality of men and women' (10) sustainable future for children and future generations; (11) complete inclusion and treatment of persons with disability; (12) freedom of culture and belief; (13) government accountability; and (14) strong institutions (CKRC 2005, 63).

---

the Constitution of Kenya Review Act, 1998, the commission was designed to include members drawn from the inter-parties Parliamentary Committee (IPPC), the Muslim Consultative Council and the Supreme Council of Kenyan Muslims, the Kenya Episcopal Conference, the protestant church in Kenya, the Kenya Women's Political Caucus, the National Council of Non-Governmental Organisations and at least two representatives from each of the eight provinces in Kenya. The CAP 3A formula, however, provided a leaner and centrally appointed membership. It should be clarified that the referendum referred not to people's verdict on the final draft, but to the power of the constituent assembly to hold a referendum during its tenure, as a way to resolve varying differences among its members. The assembly made no use of it, partly to save time.

12 CAP 3A, Section 17.
13 CAP 3A, Section 3.
14 CAP 3, Section 20.
15 CAP 3A, Section 27(1)(b).

CKRC published its first report and draft constitution on 27 September 2002 (CKRC 2002) following the CCF process which paved the way for the NCC process. The NCC, which was a critical aspect of the constitution-making process, was carefully composed to ensure representation from various facets of the Kenyan society. It was made up of 629 delegates: all members of the CKRC (who were not allowed to vote), all the members of Parliament, representatives from all the registered political parties, women organisations, religious organisations, trade unions, nongovernmental organisations, and representatives from all the districts (Saati 2015). Inevitably, this careful composition reflected various interests. As such, it was a collection of concentrated group interests with potential costs and benefits[16] to the actual representatives and to those represented. The representatives had either individually or institutionally interacted with the constitution-making process, historically (as was the case with the civil society,[17] women's groups and religious organisations[18]), professionally and politically (as was the case with members of the National Assembly), through various avenues of constitutional agitation or negotiations with existing structures of government. The NCC was also a major determinant of the issues that would be isolated for a referendum in the instance that there was no agreement, either by way of consensus or a two-thirds majority vote. The Act adopted the standard *two-thirds present and voting rule* with respect to "proposals for inclusion into the constitution,"[19] failing which any proposed issue might be presented to the people through a referendum if not resolved through a repeat vote and if elected to be referred as such by *two-thirds* of the members present at the NCC.

A critical component of the NCC membership was members of Parliament. Unfortunately, President Daniel Arap Moi dissolved Parliament in October precipitating the December 2002 general elections, thus disrupting the work of the CKRC and the convening of the NCC. Ghai thought that Moi had agreed to his request to postpone the election, which under the constitution he could delay as late as March 2003, so that the new constitution would be ready by then and the new elections could be held under it. It is unclear why he reneged on his

16 See Potters/Sloof 1996. Structural characteristics of interest groups as well as their activities influence policy. The political activities of these groups, for instance, are a "transaction cost to be borne by the interest group in order for the favourable structural attributes to be effectuated." Political activities include going to court, influencing and mobilising the public, even conducting civic education. We may consider time and expertise as a cost borne by these interests and the resulting draft provisions representing clear benefits of their engagement. These provisions would then improve the structural characteristics of the groups involved, such as enabling a critical mass of female representation in government.

17 See Mutunga 1999, and CKRC 2005, 39. The Law Society of Kenya, International Commission of Jurists, and the Kenya Human Rights Commission presented a proposal for a model constitution in 1994 sparking serious debate and negotiations on the future of constitutional reform in Kenya. The authors do not think the model constitution was much use, though most of its values were included in later documents.

18 See Cottrell/Ghai 2007, and CKRC 2005, 39. In 1994, Catholic Bishops issued a pastoral letter demanding constitutional reform.

19 CAP 3A., Section 27(5)(i).

undertaking – he did sometimes mention that the US and UK would criticise him if he did not hold the elections in December (which had become customary, rather than requisite). It is possible that his decision was partly a result of active sabotage by politicians who saw the NCC and CKRC as a threat to their interests of enlarged power. As it was, the process was interrupted until April 2003. It could have been held earlier if the new President Kibaki had not turned against a new constitution (Cotrell/Ghai 2007). The people were sceptical about government interference in the CKRC-led process. Although the CKRC and especially the chair and some commissioners were fully dedicated to its mandate, there was a tendency by the government at the time to improperly interfere in legal, electoral and public processes. For instance, the history of commissions in Kenya and their unfinished and unrevealed reports made many Kenyans suspicious of government interference in important public processes (Kenya Human Rights Commission 2000). The willingness of the public to participate in the process of enacting a new constitution was the belief that the constitution-building process would improve governance and, consequently, the lives of citizens. It was a difficult time for those who were fully committed to the process. Kenyans today appreciate the contribution of the CKRC leadership, especially the chair of the commission and certain commissioners on the team who ensured that the people's views were collected, analysed and presented to the NCC for debate.

Obtaining consensus, consistent debate and discussions at the NCC were difficult. The various represented interests had hardline positions about critical aspects of the draft constitution. The process had been designed by legislators, not economists. It, therefore, did not come with prescribed incentives and remedies to reduce or unlock political capture, negotiations gridlock and instrumental irrationality (Dixit 1996). There were numerous principal-agency complexities ranging from powerful principals to an informed electorate (Cottrell/Ghai 2007). The uncertainty of the draft constitution on the structures of power made politicians nervous about the next electoral outcomes. Their participation in this process was bounded by the unknown costs and gains of various provisions. The emerging nervousness of the date of completion of CKRC's mandate can be attributed to the information asymmetry that existed in the actual contents of the draft bill. These complexities made consensus at the NCC painstakingly difficult.

For instance, despite the inclusive formula within the NCC, its legitimacy as a "constituent body" with the mandate to adopt the draft constitution (instead of the Kenyan people) was challenged for want of mandate from the sovereign (i.e., the people). The CKRC Act empowered the NCC to adopt a draft constitution which would then be presented to the National Assembly for debate and adoption. This, in our view, would have yielded a constitution that was closer to what the people had wanted. It would have minimised political influence through referendum campaign and instead focused on civic education.

However, Reverend Timothy Njoya led a group of seven others in an application to the High Court (High Court of Kenya 2004), which challenged (a) the composition of the NCC on the basis that its members did not have the direct mandate of the people to engage in the process of constitution-making; (b) the requirement to subject the outcome of the NCC deliberations to further debate and amendment by the National Assembly; and (c) the restrictive nature of the Constitution of Kenya Review (National Constitutional Conference) (Procedure) Regulations, 2003, which restricted debate, discussions and amendments to items within the scope of the draft bill.[20]

According to the applicants, the National Assembly's constitutional mandate was limited to enacting constitutional amendments as opposed to enacting an entirely new constitution, and the people had a right to participate in the constitution-making process through a referendum despite the outcome of the NCC. Two out of three judges, Ringera J. and Kasango Ag. J., ruled that all Kenyans had the mandate to exercise their constituent power through a referendum. Consequently, the challenged provisions of the Act were declared unconstitutional. Further, the court held that even though Parliament had the power to amend, alter, repeal and reenact the law, the act of enacting a new constitution was a preserve of the people of Kenya collectively as opposed to Parliament as a single entity.[21]

The third judge, Kubo J., held that Parliament's power was not limited to amending the existing constitution but could repeal and replace it with a new one, and that the questions before the court required resolution through a legislative as opposed to a judicial process. In order for the court to determine that a referendum was mandatory, it had to be expressly provided for in the legislation.

This decision presented the first major deviation from the consensual process as promulgated by Parliament in the CAP 3A.). The case was stimulated by the Kibaki government itself, which by now had lost interest in reform. Even though this decision was made after the CKRC draft constitution had been adopted at Bomas, a referendum was now a mandatory component of the process and would mark the last stage of the constitution-building process.

During the process, attitudes towards the process kept changing. Politicians oscillated between supporting an inclusive and people-driven process to completely sabotaging the process. Shifting interests primarily contributed to this phenomenon. The opposition's intent was to displace Moi. However, because of the anticipated power take-over following Moi's exit, they were also keen to maintain unrestrained political power. It was widely believed that Kibaki's

---

20 Rule 19 provided for a general debate on the report and the draft bill in plenary sessions at the start of the process, up to ten minutes. The purpose was to "open the debate on the merits and principles contained in the Commission's Report and the Draft Bill." Section 4 of the Rule says, "When the Chairperson is satisfied that each delegate wishing to speak has had an opportunity to speak, he shall declare the general debate closed without question put," (i.e., no decision). When the discussions started in committees and finally in the conference, there were no restrictions on what amendments or new proposals could be introduced.

21 For a critique of the decision, see Cottrell/Ghai 2007, and see Juma/Okpalu 2012 for a thoughtful analysis of this and other judicial decisions on constitutional processes in Kenya.

primary objective was to establish the Kikuyu hegemony (as in the days of Jomo Kenyatta) by replacing the Kalenjin hegemony of Moi.

The process also affected people's attitudes. At its start after the fall of the Berlin Wall, there was a global wave of opposition supported by powerful states. There was pressure for the ruling government to adopt democratic and fair governance structures based on human rights. This pressure was tied to withdrawal of economic and aid benefits. At the beginning of the new millennium, there had been political alliances, and other compromises that changed various attitudes towards constitution-building. Those who were committed to values stayed true to the process while those in pursuit of political and other benefits changed position based on their interests.

The role of the media

The media was also an important tool of participation. The CKRC Act mandated the Kenya Broadcasting Corporation and other registered media broadcasting stations to provide air-space to disseminate the report of CKRC through electronic and print media.[22] CKRC also facilitated media coverage of meetings at Bomas, during the NCC and its committees, and daily interviews with the chair. The media provided enormous support to the process, facilitating information dissemination in various forms: television, radio, print and sign language (Cottrell/ Ghai 2007). At the start of the process, most Kenyans had never engaged in the process of enacting any constitution, let alone a national constitution. So it was critical to ensure that civic education was conducted in every part of the country. The media, together with CKRC, ensured that the debates, expert and ordinary opinions were widely spread through television, radio and print. Though the media was completely invested in ensuring that the people enjoyed the debates, sometimes only the "heated" aspects of those discussions and the controversial, disputed issues received prominent coverage (Ghai 2014).

The Wako draft

CKRC led deliberations at Bomas and midwifed the birth of a document popularly known as the "Bomas draft" or the "people's constitution." Kibaki's government was opposed to two critical aspects: the parliamentary system of government and devolution (whereby provinces and districts would get significant powers). So the Parliamentary Select Committee, which had been mandated to assist the National Assembly in the review following the NCC process, had a retreat in Kilifi to reconsider the Bomas draft. This process was obviously at variance with the principles contained in the CKRC Act. It was an elite-led process devoid of public participation. The resulting document, the Wako draft, disregarded principles of transparency, consensus and people's participation that had marked

---

22 CAP 3A., Section 22(2).

the CKRC process. Its principal departures from the Bomas draft were the restoration of the executive presidency and the removal of devolution, though keeping that word.

By the time the 2007 general elections came, the Moi Constitution, which people had fought against, was still in force. There was also renewed distrust of government and a campaign that was fashioned along ethnic lines, infiltrating every aspect of the society, including several former champions of constitutional reform. Public participation had been disregarded and replaced by political control and manipulation. A more than usual degree of violence was deployed by political parties, killing over 1,500 people and rendering a million and a half people homeless (abandoning their homes in what can best be described enemy territory)[23] (CIPEV 2008). At the heart of the constitution-making process was the interest of the incumbent and other political interests to consolidate power at all cost. The forthcoming general elections were doomed to be violent and chaotic. Former allies of the Moi regime had become bitter enemies, ready to use violence against the other.

National Accord and Reconciliation and Agenda 4 institutions

The events of 2007–2008 awoke the nation and the international community. The whole nation was terrified at the degree of violence. It was clear that Kenyan politicians were not capable of resolving tensions between the major ethnic groups responsible for the violence. The assistance of Kofi Annan and other eminent African leaders was organised by the African Union. It played a key role in restoring Kenyans to some sanity. The framework for dealing with critical issues was developed by Annan's team, in consultation with major political parties. The agreement required a review of the Bomas and 2005 draft constitutions by a team of experts (local and external), under the Constitution of Kenya Review Act 2008.

The Act stipulated that the process would be led by the Committee of Experts (CoE) who would spearhead the participation of various entities in various forms of consultation, thematic discussions, written memoranda and public hearings encouraging public dialogue and consensus on the contended executive, legislature and devolution aspects of the earlier draft constitutions for presentation to the National Assembly for approval and then a national referendum for the final decision.

The CoE was aided by a reference group of thirty representatives from civil society. The process was bound to conclude in twelve months. Within this time, the committee was expected to complete its mandate[24] – conduct civic education, collate views that had been raised during the 2001–2005 process and collect views on contentious issues.

23 See CIPEV 2008.
24 Section 28, CKRC Act, 2009.

Political buy-in was, however, critical. A consultative forum with political parties was held on 2 September 2009 (Kimiti/Kamondia/Kimari 2009). The essence of this consultation was to reconcile the different political views regarding the proposed draft constitutions. The various political parties had taken different stands on the proposed Bomas draft. The Kenya African National Union (KANU) party had been opposed to the adoption of a new constitution in the 1990s and 2000s. For KANU, maintaining the *status quo* was an important factor in continued power. At the CoE meeting, however, KANU firmly indicated support for the proposed draft. The CoE sought the engagement of political parties to attain political, religious and cultural consensus as well as reinforce civic education to obtain an affirmative referendum result. This phase of the process was marked by higher levels of political interference compared to the CKRC process. In consequence, the resulting document was much more of a political compromise.

The harmonised draft was launched on 17 November 2009 followed by thirty days of national dialogue. The CoE consultative process shaped various aspects of governance represented in the Harmonised Draft. CoE reported that there was an equally divided preference for a pure presidential and pure parliamentary system. However, there was a unanimous rejection of an imperial president. As a result, the Harmonised Draft adopted a "dignified stately cum semi-executive presidency with sufficient authority to oversee, unite and protect the country but without the baggage of the day to day running of Government which previously exposed the office to abuse and misuse of power" (Kamondia/Kimiti 2009). It also included provisions for the impeachment of the president and vice president and the appointment of non-politicians into the cabinet to balance between professionalism and politics. The devolved system of government was proposed to regulate regional development, and address historical injustices and marginalisation. The Senate was proposed to protect the devolved units and ensure equitable and fair distribution of resources to these units. Provincial administration unit was proposed for dissolution because its roles would overlap with the devolved units.

The Revised Harmonised Draft was then subjected to review by a Parliamentary Select Committee, Reference Group and Parliament. The symbolic implication of receiving the document on behalf of various groups signified the keen intent to ensure that the marginalised were fully represented.[25] The CoE felt obliged to accept various proposals of the Parliamentary Committee, most notably a shift to an executive presidency. After the failure of the National Assembly to agree on any amendment, it was presented to a referendum on 4 August 2010 and adopted by 68.55 percent of the registered voters. It was promulgated on 27 August 2010.

---

25 Fatuma Gathoga received the draft on behalf of the women, Peter Mwaura received a braille copy on behalf of persons with disability, George Muchai received it on behalf of workers, Billy Phillip and James Itone received it on behalf of the youth, Rehal Baldip on behalf of the Sikh community, Chitnis received a copy on behalf of the Hindu Faith, Abdulahhi Abdi on behalf of the Muslim faith, while Arch Bishop Zacheaus Okoth on behalf of the Christian faith, Bishop Sulumeti on behalf of the Reference Group, Musalia Mudavadi for the Parliamentary Select Committee and the Clerk of the National Assembly received Parliament's copy.

Conclusion

Based on these processes, we draw several conclusions:

(a) Constitution-making often follows periods of oppression or dictatorship. As in Kenya, the end of the cold war prompted calls for constitutional, institutional and legal reforms in a number of African countries, including Uganda, South Africa and Ethiopia. Nevertheless, the initiatives as well as the process were largely driven by local groups (despite the brief but critical intervention in Kenya by the African Union through the Kofi Annan team). These processes were value-driven. Public participation reinforced the ownership of these values.

(b) The change in attitudes towards reform resulted from the length of time taken to complete the process, prompted by intervening factors: political party defections, boycotts of the process, political interference to slow down the process, constitutional challenges to the process, and regime change; the Constitution of Kenya, 2010, was indeed the result of a laborious process, overcoming many obstacles spanning over three decades.

(c) A process controlled by politicians and political interests ends up with a political compromise which does not prioritise the views of the public. The CKRC-led process was multi-interest and multi-sectoral compared to the CoE process. The CKRC process was more participatory. Politicians wanted to drive the process from the onset. Opposition leaders took on constitutional reform as a way of ousting President Moi's dictatorship. However, civil society largely neutralised political hijacking of the process by insisting that the process had to be people-driven and centred. Although sometimes, some of their leaders also became compromised. The infusion of people's views into the CKRC process culminated in a document that not only considered the interests of the political elite but those of women, the youth, persons with disability, marginalised (and forgotten) communities and other diverse interests. The result was a draft constitution that contained provisions acknowledging the role of marginalised groups (including women) in governance and politics, rights and obligations. It may be safe to assume that had political interests purely taken centre stage during the CKRC process, certain aspects would have taken more prominence at the expense of others.

(d) The process educated people in democracy. There were various interests at play throughout the constitution-building process. All through participation and civic education, the public was engaged in critical lessons on democracy: about rights, duties, values and norms associated with democratic governance. The resulting Constitution of Kenya, 2010, is an embodiment of the people's aspirations and persistence.[26] As we have demonstrated, participation is also a form of understanding, cooperation and reconciliation.

(e) The strength of the impact of participation upon democracy was aptly captured by Mutunga CJ (Supreme Court of Kenya 2012, as he then was) thus:

---

26 Article 10 of the Constitution of Kenya, 2010, lays out these values and principles of democratic governance.

There is no doubt that the constitution is a radical document that looks to a future that is very different from our past, in its values and practices. It seeks to make a fundamental change from the 68 years of colonialism, and 50 years of independence. In their wisdom, the Kenyan people decreed that past to reflect a status quo that was unacceptable and unsustainable, through: provisions on the democratization and decentralization of the Executive; devolution; the strengthening of institutions; the creation of institutions that provide democratic checks and balances; decreeing values in the public service; giving ultimate authority to the people of Kenya which they delegate to institutions that must serve them, and not enslave them; prioritizing integrity in public leadership; a modern Bill of Rights that provides for economic, social and cultural rights to reinforce the political and civil rights, giving the whole gamut of human rights the power to radically mitigate the status quo and signal the creation of a human-rights State in Kenya; mitigating the status quo in land that has been the country's Achilles heel in its economic and democratic development. These instances, among others, reflect the will and deep commitment of Kenyans, reflected in fundamental and radical changes, through the implementation of the constitution.

References

CIPEV (2008). "Report of the Commission of Inquiry into Post Election Violence" (CIPEV) Nairobi: Government Printer, 2008.

CKRC (2002). "The People's Choice: Report of the Constitution of Kenya Commission," September 2002.

CKRC (2003). "Report of the Constitution of Kenya Review Commission." Reprinted with technical additions and approved for issue at a special meeting of the Commission held on 4th March 2003. http://katibainstitute.org/Archives/images/VOLUME%20 1%20-%20Main%20Report%20_Orange%20Book.pdf.

CKRC (2005). "Final Report of the Constitution of Kenya Review Commission." Approved for issue at 95th Plenary Meeting of the Constitution of Kenya Review Commission on 10 February 2005. Online: http://katibainstitute.org/Archives/images/ CKRC%20Final%20Report.pdf.

Collier, P. (2009). *Wars, Guns and Votes: Democracy in Dangerous Places*, London: Bodley Head.

Collier, P., and Rohner, D. (2008). "Democracy, Development and Conflict," *Journal of the European Economic Association*, 6 (2–3) 531–40.

Cottrell, J., and Ghai, Y.P. (2007). "Constitution Making and Democratisation in Kenya, 2000–2005," *Democratisation*, 14 (1) 1–25.

Dixit, A.K. (1996). *The Making of Economic Policy: A Transaction-Cost Politics Perspective*, The MIT Press. Cambridge, Massachusetts.

Ghai, Y.P. (2014). "Civil Society, Participation and the Making of Kenya's Constitution," in Commission for the Implementation of the Constitution, Effective Citizens' Participation, Kenya Literature Bureau, Nairobi, 11–38.

Ghai, Y.P., and McAuslan, J.P.W.B. (1970). "Transition and Interlude: From Lancaster House to the Republic," in *Public Law and Political Change*, Nairobi: Oxford University Press.

High Court of Kenya (2004). "Republic of Kenya in the High Court of Kenya at Nairobi," miscellaneous civil application No. 82 of 2004 in the matter of the constitution of Kenya: *Reverend Dr. Timothy M. Njoya and 6 Others versus Honourable Attorney General and Another* Miscellaneous Civil Application No. 82 of 2004 (OS) [2004] eKLR) http://kenyalaw.org/caselaw/cases/view/9775/.

International Relations and Security Network (ISN) (2016). "Wind of Change: Speech by British Prime Minister Maurice Harold MacMillan," online: www.isn.ethz.ch.

Juma, L., and Okpalu, C. (2012). "Judicial Intervention in Kenya's Constitutional Process," *Washington University Global Studies Law Review*: Vol. 11, 287–364.

Kamondia, J., and Kimiti, A. (eds.) (2009). *Hansard Proceedings of the Launching of the Harmonised Draft Constitution by the Committee of Experts on Constitutional Review*, 17th November 2009. KICC Plenary Hall, Nairobi.

Kenya Human Rights Commission (2000). *The Forgotten People Revisited: Human Rights Abuses in Moyale and Marsabit Districts*. Nairobi, Kenya.

Kimiti, S., and Kimari, H. (eds.) (2009). *Hansard Proceedings of the Committee of Experts on Constitutional Review Consultative Forum with Political Parties*, 2 September 2009. Leisure Lodge Resort, Mombasa.

Kimiti, S., Kamondia, J. and Kimari, H. (eds.) (2009). "Hansard Proceedings of the Committee of Experts on Constitutional Review Consultative Forum with Political Parties," 2 September 2009. Leisure Lodge Resort, Mombasa.

Mati, J.M. (2012). *The Power and Limits of Social Movements in Promoting Political and Constitutional Change: The Case of the Ufungamano Initiative in Kenya (1999–2005)*. PhD thesis, University of Witwatersrand, online: http://wiredspace.wits.ac.za/bitstream/handle/10539/11720/Jacob%20Mwathi%20Mati%20PhD%20Thesis.%20The%20power%20and%20limits%20of%20social.pdf?sequence=2.

Maxon, R.M. (2011). *Kenya's Independence Constitution: Constitution Making and the End of Empire*, Fairleigh Dickinson University Press.

Mutunga, W. (1999). *Constitution Making from the Middle: Civil Society and Transition Politics in Kenya, 1992–1997*, Mwengo, Harare.

Ogot, B.A. and Ochieng, W.R. (eds.) (1995). "Decolonization and Independence (1940–1993)," *Eastern African Studies*, E.A.E.P, Ohio University Press, Nairobi.

Okoth-Ogendo, H.W.O. (1972). "The Politics of Constitutional Change in Kenya Since Independence," *African Affairs*, 71(282), 24–26.

Potters, J., and Sloof, R. (1996). "Interest Groups: A Survey of Empirical Models That Try to Assess Their Influence," *European Journal of Political Economy*, 12, 403–42.

Saati, A. (2015). *The Participation Myth: Outcomes of Participatory Constitution Building Processes on Democracy*, Department of Political Science, Umea University, Sweden.

Supreme Court of Kenya (2012). *Jasbir Singh Rai and 3 Others versus Tarlochan Singh Rai and Others*, Supreme Court Petition No. 2 of 2012. At para 89.

7 The francophone paradox

Participation in Senegal and in Central African Republic

Leopoldine Croce

Introduction

The present paper assesses public participation in recent constitutional reform processes in Senegal and in the Central African Republic (CAR).

The choice of case studies straddles francophone Africa's perhaps most and least stable democracies. Yet, both processes involved similar institutional devices, such as geographically stratified consultation, popular assemblies, appointed constitution drafting committees, constitutional court opinions, and blanket adoption by referendum.

The paper ultimately encounters a paradox: very different actors initiated and drove public participation in CAR and in Senegal. But despite unprecedented actual citizen participation in both countries, neither of the two adopted constitutional texts prescribes increased citizen participation for future constitution making and building processes.[1]

Colonial commonalities and disparities

In the early 1900s, the territory of today's CAR was subsumed into French Equatorial Africa, while Senegal was folded into French West Africa. Senegal had been Islamized in the 11th century, and Sufi brotherhoods underpin its civil society until today. CAR, in turn, remained animist until the arrival of Christian missionaries in the late 19th century.

Contrary to many African nations, both Senegal and CAR use a widespread national vernacular – *Wolof* and *Sango*, respectively – since both countries' borders align with topography. Their linguistic homogeneity and geographic contiguity, hence, would lend itself to nation building – and by extension to constitution building (Federation of the Free States of Africa 2017).

But while peanut farming dominated Senegal's colonial economy, mining drove CAR's: Sizable uranium lodes were confirmed there in 1956, followed by the discovery of some of Africa's richest deposits of diamonds, gold, and oil.

---

1 This is except for the introduction of universal standing before CAR's Constitutional Court in matters of unconstitutionality (article 98 of CAR's 2016 Constitution).

DOI: 10.4324/9781315180540-10

Their former colonizer's economic stakes in granting CAR and Senegal respective self-determination thus diverged considerably between the two territories (Kanisani 2011).

Founding fathers

Prior to decolonization, Léopold Sédar Senghor and Barthelémy Boganda represented Senegal and CAR respectively in France's Union Assembly, which also served as the Constituent Assembly for France's Fourth Republic. In 1946, then head-of-government Charles de Gaulle advocated for a bicameral presidential system. But the elected Constituent Assembly – itself a legislature – favored the parliamentary system. De Gaulle resigned, and the constitution was narrowly rejected by referendum. Fresh parliamentary elections were held – with Senghor and Boganda reelected. The new assembly revised its draft, retaining the parliamentary system, albeit with two chambers. This time, the text was narrowly adopted by referendum.

Senghor and Boganda thus served as elected constitution-makers of the French Fourth Republic, and witnessed its parliamentary system grapple with the Algerian War. In 1958, Senghor, but not Boganda, was invited to negotiate the optional clause that framed the colonies' independence under the draft constitution for France's Fifth Republic[2] – which simultaneously ushered in presidentialism.[3]

Both Senghor and Boganda subsequently played key roles in delivering the vote of their respective overseas constituencies to ensure passage of de Gaulle's convoluted referendum package. Copies of the 1958 Constitution were printed and distributed across the French-African territories (Simonis 2008). The bulk of the electorate, however, couldn't unbundle the nuance between a "no" vote, entailing immediate, unconditional independence, versus a "yes" vote, comporting membership in the French *communauté*, which preemptively fettered the colonies' impending sovereignty.

Adequate propaganda was hence put in place to ensure strong participation, as well as "results to meet the expectation of government" (Simonis 2008, 63). By universal suffrage, Oubangui-Chari (today's CAR) voted 98.5 percent, and Senegal 97.55 percent in favor of de Gaulle's presidentialism/*communauté* package (African Elections Database 2011).[4] In hindsight, the rushed 1958 plebiscite – with its overseas outcome a foregone conclusion – set a fateful precedent for public participation in francophone Africa's constituent processes ever since (Fall 2014).

Once the 1958 community framework entered into force, Senghor proclaimed Senegal's independence, while Boganda sealed that of CAR.[5] When designing

---

2 Along with Félix Houphouet Boigny and Lamine Gueye in Simonis 2008, 66.

3 Political system choice remains relevant in this paper in terms of the right to initiate constitutional reform. The 1958 Constitution initially stipulated indirect presidential election. The text was submitted to a popular referendum across the union, both in France and in its overseas territories. Four years later, de Gaulle introduced the directly elected presidency, also by referendum.

4 Only Guinée rejected the referendum, opting for immediate independence – without ties to the proposed *communauté*.

5 Both states became members of the United Nations in 1960.

respective national constitutions, Boganda embraced presidentialism from the outset, whereas Senghor opted for a three-year experiment with the parliamentary system. Initially, neither constitution was submitted to referendum, although Senegal's subsequent 1963 conversion to presidentialism was approved by 99.45 percent of its electorate.

Constitutional evolution

Senegal's 1963 Constitution survived 38 years without abrogation, among Africa's longest-lived – perhaps because it was amended 37 times (Fall 2007a). Limited multi-party democracy was introduced in 1974 and consolidated in 1981 (Fall 2007b). But Senghor's socialist party ruled for 40 years until its electoral defeat by Wade's PDS. The year 2000 marks Senegal's first democratic change of power, followed by its second in 2012 with the election of current President Macky Sall.

Since independence, Senegal thus witnessed only three constitutions – and no military coup. By regional comparison, the Senegalese have thus collected a rare dividend on upholding their social contract – political stability and social peace. And even if many of Senegal's constitutional amendments deconsolidated balance and separation of powers, electoral multi-party democracy was ultimately preserved and gradually refined (Fall 2011; European Union Election Observation Mission 2012).

In contrast, upon CAR's independence, its mineral riches attract suitors from outside the *communauté*, sending the nascent republic's constitution making on a turbulent tailspin: In 1959, Boganda opens channels to China, and weeks later, dies in a plane crash, depriving the fledgling nation of its founding father. Daniel Dacko is elected president the same year. He dissolves Boganda's political party, stripping CAR of ideological cohesion.[6]

In 1966, Colonel Bokassa overthrows Dacko in a military coup, abrogating the 1959 Constitution. Bokassa rules by decree until adopting his imperial constitution in 1976, followed by his notorious coronation ceremony.[7] Three years later, Bokassa is himself overthrown in a counter coup in 1979, and Dacko is reinstalled. A national conference is convened to draft a new republican constitution, which is adopted by referendum.

But in 1981, General André Kolingba overthrows Dacko, abrogates multi-party democracy, rules by constitutional declaration, and holds a 1986 plebiscite on CAR's fourth constitution, the approval of which automatically extends his presidential mandate for another six years (Association Manassé 2017).

In 1992, Kolingba holds and loses elections, but annuls results, and in 1993, Ange-Félix Patassé is ultimately elected, and France intervenes to foil attempted coups against him in 1996 (Bissengue 2017). Then Patassé is reelected in 1998, but overthrown in a coup by François Bozizé, who suspends Patassé's 1995 Constitution and rules by constitutional declaration. He submits

6 Mouvement pour l'Evolution de l'Afrique Centrale (MEDAC).
7 For an extensive overview please access Unmondepygmee 2011.

a new constitution to referendum in 2004 and is reelected in 2005, but then deposed by Michael Djotodia, a northern Muslim, in a 2012 coup, which abrogates Bozizé's 2004 Constitution.

France deploys military forces in response to sectarian mass killings in the wake of the coup, and motions the United Nations Security Council to authorize a peacekeeping mission under the Chapter VII mandate (Ministère de la Défense 2016; United Nations 2017).

Constitutionalism today

Disparities in respective political economies may have instilled a deeper sense of constitutionalism in Senegal – including in its army – than in CAR, where coup leaders have repeatedly legitimized unconstitutional power grabs by submitting new constitutions to referenda. Such abuses of process spawned *pro forma* constitutions that lacked popular buy-in, provoked counter-coups, and embroiled CAR in a vicious cycle.

The opposite applies to Senegal: While successive presidents opportunistically and frequently refashioned constitutions, no Senegalese constitution ever succumbed to an unconstitutional overthrow (Kanté 1989, 145). Malleable as they were, Senegal's more resilient constitutions framed two peaceful alternations of power – in line with the republican calendar they enshrined (Fall 2014, 7).

It follows that CAR's citizenry came to accord less relevance to its short-lived constitutions and to constitutionalism than Senegal's. CAR's political power flowed from the gun, while in Senegal it was won by elections – and pursuant to the constitution. Despite this disparity, it will be shown here that both populations came to associate constitutions with the whim of their respective presidential framers, rather than with the free expression of the will of the people.

Recent constitutional reform triggers

The two countries' regimes that preceded most recent constitutional reforms further reflect Senegal's stability vis-à-vis CAR's volatility: Senegal's Abdoulaye Wade was elected in credible and competitive elections, whereas CAR's François Bozizé seized power in a coup. Yet, Senegal's and CAR's 2015–16 constitutional reform cycles share several key precursors.

From the outset, both presidents framed their rule with their *personal* constitutional projects. Neither president sought adoption through the legislature, but rather submitted their project directly to referenda.[8] But later in their terms, both presidents realized that their personal ambitions outgrew the limits of their self-made constitutions. Respectively in 2008 and 2010, both Wade and Bozizé hence began chipping away at constitutional fetters on their presidential terms and mandates (Le Citoyen 2010).

Since their political parties now held supermajorities in respective legislatures, and perhaps also because their personal electoral popularity had waned,

---

8 Article 112 of CAR's 2004 Constitution.

both presidents shifted to parliamentary amendment procedures, even though they initially had their constitutions legitimized by referendum only (Elgie 2010; Bolle 2010).

Allegations of unconstitutionality arose, since both texts seemed to entrench presidential term-limits by referendum.[9] Senegalese and Central African oppositions thus decried parliamentary amendment procedures as subverting letter and spirit of the constitution, thereby undermining popular sovereignty (Bolle 2010). Constitutionalism seemed to germinate.

Presidential hubris

Furthermore, Wade and Bozizé committed the type of overreach prone to alienate even their innermost circles: They groomed their sons for succession. Wade entrusted four concurrent ministerial portfolios to his son Karim, while Bozizé appointed his son Jean-Francis as minister of defense (Duhem 2016a). In 2011, Wade proposed to introduce the vice presidency – an obvious device to shoehorn Karim into the presidency without facing elections (Bolle 2008a).

Wade's tactical choice of the parliamentary procedure to achieve this goal sparked the popular uprising of June 23, which inspired the citizen slogan "Don't touch my constitution" (Bolle no date; own translation).[10] Overnight, the Senegalese Constitution had become a fetish (Kamto 1997, 177). The Senegalese claimed ownership of the very constitution that was hitherto monopolized by its presidential framer. Thousands of protesters besieged Parliament, so that MPs ultimately dropped Wade's amendment (SeneNews Actu 2011). Wade abandoned the bill the following day (L'express 2011).[11] In Senegal, constitutionalism had prevailed – by way of the street.

Insufficient checks and balances

Deferential judicial interpretation of constitutions further fueled perceptions of presidential subterfuge in both countries, while it also frustrated attempts at public participation in constitutional processes.[12] Senegal's 2001 constitution had retained the French model of the constitutional council, and its particular variant even allowed the president to single-handedly pick the full bench. At the same time, it denied direct citizen standing to challenge unconstitutional executive, legislative or administrative action.[13]

---

9 See articles 108 of CAR's 2004 and 127 of Senegal's 2001 constitutions.
10 RADDHO (Rencontre Africaine pour les Droits de l'Homme), please view: Leral.net (2011).
11 In this context, distinction of optional and mandatory referendum becomes relevant: Both countries' successive presidents had hitherto used only *optional* referenda, the timing of which they controlled. So far, neither country had triggered *mandatory* referenda, in order to comply with constitutional entrenchment, such as Senegal's article 27. Senegal's 2016 referendum was to depart from this historical pattern.
12 Les Décisions et Avis du Conseil Constitutionnel du Sénégal, Rassemblés et commentés sous la direction de Ismaïla Madior Fall, Credila, 2008; therefore, see also Fall 2014, 8.
13 Articles 89–94 of Senegal's 2001 Constitution.

Moreover, the Senegalese council's own jurisprudence abdicated its competence outside the remit the constitution *expressly* attributed to it (*Journal Officiel du Senegal* 2003). Its hands-off approach thus deprived Senegalese citizens of a safety valve with *general* constitutional jurisdiction – short of referrals by the Supreme Court. But in 15 years, the council heard only six such referrals.[14] The council's repeated recusal ultimately instilled a sense of abandonment in citizens (Le Conseil Constitutionnel 1998). And it fed presidential hubris, with Wade proclaiming that *his* 2001 Constitution cannot be amended (or applied) without his assent (Bolle 2009).

Then, in the wake of the 2011 popular uprising, the Senegalese constitutional council delivered two highly controversial decisions. It authorized the octogenarian President Wade to stand for a third term in office, while it disqualified three independent candidates from contesting the 2012 presidential election (Le Conseil Constitutionnel 2012a; 2012b). Citizens again took to the streets to enforce *their* constitution, forcing the constitutional council to move to an undisclosed location.

CAR has a formally more independent constitutional *court* than Senegal's *council*, but CAR's court gave its blessing to a controversial extension of Bozizé's term as well (Bolle 2010). And it later abdicated its jurisdiction to hear impeachment petitions against him on grounds of unconstitutional conflicts of interest (Assingambi 2008).[15] Both countries' courts hence tended to resolve constitutional crises in favor of respective heads-of-state.

While some of CAR's earlier political transitions involved atrocities, the 2013 rupture degenerated into religious genocide. But unlike in Senegal, legal necessity for a new constitution arose from the coup's abrogation of the predecessor instrument, rather than from genuine grassroots demand for constitutional reform.

Formal frameworks

CAR's constitutional vacuum required adoption of an entirely new constitution *prior* to electing a new president. In contrast, Senegal's sitting president introduced a bundle of 15 amendments to its existing 2001 constitution, without labeling the measure a new constitution. The two countries' procedural frameworks diverge along this semantic distinction, but also along the respective role – or absence – of a dominant framer.

Senegal's constitution-making framework

Senegal's 2001 Constitution offers three avenues for constitutional amendment: the parliamentary route, the referendum route, and a combination of both. President Sall had recently disbanded the Senate in his first and only other constitutional amendment.[16] Lack of the upper house now thwarted a joint sitting of both chambers, eliminating the parliamentary route. Opting for

14 Les Décisions et Avis du Conseil Constitutionnel du Sénégal, Rassemblés et commentés sous la direction de Ismaïla Madior Fall, Credila, 2008; see also Fall 2014, 8.
15 CAR's court has, however, gone up against Bozizé on the issue of judicial independence (Bolle 2008c).
16 Loi constitutionnelle n°2012-16 du 28 septembre portant révision de la Constitution.

the article 103 procedure would have hence required adoption by referendum *in addition* to a vote in the lower house.

> Article 103: The initiative of the revision of the Constitution belongs concurrently to the President of the Republic and to the Deputies. The Prime Minister can propose to the President of the Republic a revision of the Constitution. The bill or the proposal of revision of the Constitution must be adopted by the assemblies following the procedure of Article 71.[17] The revision is definitive after having been approved by referendum. However, the bill or the proposal is not presented to referendum when the President of the Republic decides to present them to the Parliament convoked in Congress. In this case, the bill or the proposal is only approved if it meets the majority of three-fifths (3/5) of the suffrage expressed.[18]

Elected through a modern mixed system in 2012, President Sall's lower house majority hinged on a diverse ideological coalition of splinter groups (SeneNews Actu 2017). And at 42.7 percent, Senegal's lower house seats the second highest proportion of women in Africa and the sixth highest in the world (Inter-Parliamentary Union 2017). In terms of political spectrum and gender equality, the Senegalese Parliament could hence be seen as a highly representative surrogate of the general public.[19]

But from the executive's point of view, selected items in the reform bundle incurred risk of parliamentary defiance, especially those that strengthened the president's hand vis-à-vis the legislature. Nor could a popular referendum majority be taken for granted – especially if it were further eroded by parliamentary divisions. But the alternative article 51 referendum procedure bypasses Parliament entirely, depriving MPs of the opportunity to propose amendments, or even to seek their constituents' views on the reform package.

> Article 51: The President of the Republic can, after having received the opinion of the President of the National Assembly, of the President of the Senate and of the Constitutional Council, submit any bill of constitutional law to referendum. He can, on the proposal of the Prime Minister and having received the opinion of the authorities indicated above, submit any bill of law to referendum. The Courts and Tribunals see to the regularity of the operations of referendum. The Constitutional Council proclaims the results of it.

---

17 Article 71: *Après son adoption par l'Assemblée nationale, la loi est transmise sans délai au Président de la République pour promulgation.*
18 English translation by The Constitute Project (Constitute 2009).
19 President Wade had used article 103 procedures – controversially without referendum – to extend terms from five to seven years. Restoring the entrenched presidential term back to five years formed the centerpiece of Senegal's reform package, and President Sall aimed to distance his choice of procedure from that used by his predecessor (*Journal Officiel du Senegal* 2009; Le Conseil Constitutionnel 2006).

President Sall ultimately opted for article 51, outflanking Parliament entirely. The choice falls outside contemporary regional practice,[20] with the sole recent exception of the Republic of Congo (Bocas 2015). In Burundi, Parliament recently even rejected a presidential initiative to amend the constitution (RFI Afrique 2014). Ironically, the choice emulates Wade's tactic in submitting his 2001 Constitution directly to a referendum without consulting Parliament – a loophole left untouched by the 2016 reform package.[21]

CAR's constitution-making framework

Also inspired by France's Fifth Republic, CAR's 2004 Constitution offered similar amendment options as Senegal's 2001 text. But since CAR's 2004 instrument had been abrogated, it fell upon the 2013 interim charter to establish drafting and adoption procedures for CAR's new permanent constitution.

CAR's interim charter's preamble also incorporates by reference ECCAS (Economic Community of Central African States) brokered political agreements. United Nations Security Council resolutions also deferred constitution-making guidance to the ECCAS roadmap, even though the political component of the UN peacekeeping mission directly provided technical assistance to constitution drafting and consultation processes (United Nations 2014a).

Early into CAR's transition, the international community aimed to curb powers of coup leader and interim President Michel Djotodia. To that end, it instituted the National Council of the Transition (CNT), and tasked it to draft the interim charter (Darlan 2013). The CNT thus vested itself with the power to draw up and adopt CAR's new *permanent* constitution.

The international community[22] hence acquiesced to entrusting CNT with broad constituent powers, relegating CAR's interim president to proposing amendments. The set-up is remarkable because ECCAS, which drew up the roadmap underlying the CNT, gathers some of Africa's longest-serving autocrats.[23] CAR thus expected a constituent process unshackled from an overpowering head of state.

---

20 See, for instance, parliamentary consultation for constitutional amendments in Cote d'Ivoire (Duhem 2016b); although the Ivorian Parliament has not produced meaningful publicly aired debate either: Jeune Afrique 2016.

21 As an aside, article 27, which requires the referendum to amend presidential terms, converts the *optional* referendum into a *mandatory* exercise. The 2016 reform thus marks the first time a Senegalese president submitted to a *mandatory* referendum requirement, perhaps another constitutionalism milestone. Article 27: "The duration of the mandate of the President of the Republic is seven years; this modification does not apply to the mandate of the President of the Republic in office at the moment of its adoption. The mandate is renewable one sole time. This provision may only be revised by a referendum law".
For the distinction of optional and mandatory referenda, see IDEA's direct democracy database (International Institute for Democracy and Electoral Assistance (IDEA) 2017).

22 Acting under Chapter VII of the UN Charter.

23 Angola, Burundi, Cameroon, Central African Republic, Chad, Republic of Congo, Democratic Republic of Congo, Equatorial Guinea, Gabon, Rwanda, and Sao Tomé and Principe.

Article 49: The legislative and constitutive power of the Central African Republic lies with the National Council of the Transition.

Article 50: The National Council of the Transition is composed of one hundred and thirty-five (135) members representing the different political and socio-professional categories of the country.

Article 53: For the adoption of the Constitution and other framework texts of the Transition, decisions are taken within the National Council of the Transition by consensus. After exhaustion of means seeking to reach a consensus, decisions are taken by a two-thirds majority (2/3) of attending National Councilors. For all other texts, decisions are taken by a majority of attending National Councilors.

Article 55: The National Council of the Transition is in charge amongst other things of: Electing the Head of State of the Transition and the Bureau of the National Council of the Transition; Drafting and adopting the Constitutional Charter of the Transition; Drafting and adopting a draft Constitution to be submitted to the people by way of referendum.

Article 65: The initiative of submitting the Central African Republic's new Constitution to referendum belongs to the National Council of the Transition. The preliminary draft of the new Constitution is submitted to the government for its advice and amendments. The new draft incorporating the government's amendments is then subject to a national workshop (atelier) to enrich it, and organized in coordination with the National Council of the Transition. The resulting draft is presented to the Constitutional Court for its opinion and amended if applicable by the National Council of the Transition to take into account the Constitutional Court's opinion. The final draft of the Constitution adopted by the National Council of the Transition is then submitted to the people by referendum. [24]

The above provisions leave it uncertain whether CNT was bound to accept input and amendment by government, constitutional court, and the *atelier d'enrichissement*, or whether finalizing the draft for referendum submission fell back under the CNT's sole discretion. CAR's framework hence suffered some of the same gaps as Senegal's, leaving, for instance, unresolved whether the court's *avis* bound the constituent power or not (Fall 2014, 20).

Senegal's 2001 Constitution, as well as CAR's 2013 interim charter, vest sovereignty in the people. But neither framework expressly stipulates whether the referendum outcome is binding, nor what a Plan B would entail if the electorate were to reject the draft. Furthermore, neither framework requires a qualified majority or turnout threshold, which minimizes risk of rejection, but also lowers the bar for public participation. Emphasis on *passage*, rather than on *process*, perpetuates France's top-down plebiscital logic.

24 Official translation by Constitute 2013.

Constitution-making steps

Regional consultations and popular assemblies

The Senegalese Constitution limits the right to initiate constitutional amendments to president, prime minister, and members of Parliament. However, only five of Senegal's 50 constitutional amendments were so far initiated in Parliament, and only the president can submit an entirely new constitution to referendum.[25] Lacking the formal avenues for citizen initiatives of, for instance, Burkina Faso,[26] Senegal's 2016 constitutional reform process hatched informally, at the grassroots.

Senegal's Assises Nationales

Perhaps inspired by the French Revolution's *états généraux* and propelled by proliferating social media, Senegal's civil society and segments of the political opposition converged in a self-styled popular assembly in 2008 – the *Assises Nationales*. The nationwide conference aimed to deliver a citizen-driven appraisal of Senegal's state of affairs at the 50th anniversary of its independence. Without official mandate or international funding, the *Assises* set out to diagnose Senegal's chronic political and social ills.[27]

The *Assises* aimed for social inclusivity and united 69 umbrella CSOs, as well as trade unions, chambers of commerce, political parties, retiree organizations, women, youth, academics, and artists (Assises Nationales au Sénégal 2017b). The popular assembly adopted a decentralized structure, headed by a steering committee that oversaw an executive board, three crosscutting and seven thematic committees, and one for each of Senegal's administrative units, as well as one representing the diaspora. Its code of conduct was guided by five core values: neutrality, respect, responsibility, exemplarity, and volunteerism (Assises Nationales au Sénégal 2017c).

In the wake of President Wade's contested reelection in 2007, the *Assises* justified their initiative with the breakdown of political dialogue between the political class and vested popular interests, such as trade unions (Assises Nationales au Sénégal 2017d). In their manifesto, the *Assises* also denounced lack of transparency in public financial management.

Over the course of one year, *Assises* working groups roamed Senegal, holding town hall hearings with cross sections of society. Each region reported back to the central conference (Assises Nationales au Sénégal 2017e). Based on regional input, seven thematic working groups elaborated a political and constitutional roadmap, as well as a holistic societal model, which they translated into audio files in Senegal's lingua franca *Wolof* and into its five minority languages (Assises Nationales au Sénégal 2017f; 2017g). The audio files were posted on the *Assises* homepage, and overall findings of the *Assises* were widely publicized and commented on.

---

25 Pursuant to Senegalese Constitutional Council Décision 75/2000.
26 The Constitution of Benin allows 30,000 registered voters to initiate constitutional amendments.
27 See the internal regulations of the *Assises* (Assises Nationales au Sénégal 2017).

CAR's Forum of Bangui

Like in Senegal, CAR's intelligentsia demanded the holding of a popular assembly in the course of its political transition, even if the interim charter had not envisioned such format. To calm CAR's post-conflict volatility, the internationally coordinated peace process programmed a popular assembly through the Brazzaville Ceasefire Agreement in 2014 (United Nations 2014b).

The political declaration annexed to the agreement promised reconciliation through provincial consultations across CAR's 16 regions, as well as debate of relevant findings at a popular conference, the *Forum of Bangui* (RFI Afrique 2015a). The forum was to be underwritten by international donors and co-organized by international and regional organizations. But like the interim charter, the Brazzaville Agreement draws no formal or binding link between constituent processes and *Forum of Bangui* consultations (United Nations 2015a).

In contrast to Senegal's nationally sovereign *Assises*, the US State Department supported CAR's provincial consultations on the subject of reconciliation through the American Bar Association Rule-of-Law Initiative (ABA RoLI), which also assisted civic education on the constituent process. A total of 28 facilitators were trained.[28]

Each *Forum of Bangui* consultation team counted 10–15 members drawn from so-called national *forces vives* composed of 30 national civil society organizations, as well as from the international community. The teams held three-day sessions in each province (American Bar Association 2017). Some consultation teams required protection by UN peacekeeping escorts, and only 12 of CAR's 16 regions were ultimately reached. Grassroots consultations were also held in neighboring countries that harbored Central African refugees, as well as in Paris (Ministère de la Reconciliation Nationale 2015).

Like the *Assises*, CAR's regional consultations yielded sensible reform recommendations, even though CAR's security environment rendered access to the population infinitely more perilous than Senegal's. Regional consultations recommended, for instance, the right to free education and the right to compensation for civil war victims, both of which CNT included in the draft constitution.

With the assistance of UNDP and the United Nations Peacekeeping Mission to CAR (MINUSCA), the Ministry of Reconciliation consolidated provincial consultation findings in a national report (United Nations 2015b).[29] Final documents were presented to the interim president, government, civil society, the organizational committee of the *Forum of Bangui*,[30] and most importantly, to CNT – acting as constituent assembly.

---

28 According to interviews with Richard Mulengule, chief-of-party of ABA-RoLI's assistance project.
29 According to an August 16, 2016 email by ABA-RoLI Country Director Richard Mulengule.
30 The Bangui forum brings together some 580 representatives of political parties, militias, civil society, and religions, as well as emissaries from neighboring countries, the African Union, France, and the United Nations (Lamba and Kokpakpa 2015; own translation).

The bulk of consultation recommendations, however, was not taken into account by CNT drafters, such as: more equitable natural resource revenue distribution; directly elected local government; armed forces and intelligence services reform to prevent future coups; timely transitional justice; greater transparency in public administration; regional power sharing through a system of a rotating presidency limited to a single term; and stronger separation and balance of power, as well as independence of the judiciary (which also the subsequent *atelier* recommended).

Held from May 4–11, 2015, with the assistance and presence of MINUSCA, UNDP, and of the international donor community,[31] the *Forum of Bangui* subdivided its 600 participants[32] – including armed rebel leaders – into four thematic working groups (RFI Afrique 2015b): Peace and Security, Governance, Justice and Reconciliation, and Social and Economic Development (Moulougnatho 2015).

Thematic committee submissions followed one and a half hours of open debate: The peace committee suggested creation of a reconciliation commission, reduction of the number of political parties, and compulsory military service. The security committee recommended confinement of security forces to barracks, standard criteria for army recruitment, and modernization of military hardware to defend CAR's borders (Ngalangou 2015). The international community had also made known its own priorities (République du Congo and Union Africaine 2015).

The forum adopted a *pacte*, which calls for participative and inclusive democracy and gender equality, while rejecting amnesty for war crimes. Since the popular assembly enjoyed much broader attendance than the subsequent *atelier d'enrichissement*, forum participants were later adamant that its recommendations be taken into the account by the *Atelier*, as well as by CNT – even if those demands lacked formal constitution-making footing (Akandji-Kombé 2015).

Senegal's National Commission for Institutional Reform (CNRI)

In the wake of his presidential election in March 2012, Macky Sall reaffirmed his commitment to constitutional reform, which had been initiated at the grassroots by the *Assises* four years earlier. In November of the same year, President Sall solicited Amadou Makhtar Mbow,[33] former president of the *Assises*, to head a National Commission for Institutional Reform (CNRI).

Abdoulaye Wade, President Sall's predecessor, had also convened a commission of experts to draft his 2001 Constitution, albeit one that worked under his direct supervision and that did not involve public participation (Diop 2011;

---

31 Le Groupe international de contact sur la République centrafricaine (GIC-RCA) Afrique du Sud, Allemagne, Angola, Australie, Burundi, Cameroun, Canada, RCA, République du Congo, RDC, Egypte, Etats Unis d'Amérique, France, Gabon, Japon, Luxembourg, Nigéria, Norvège, Ouganda, Royaume Uni, Russie, Rwanda, Soudan, Tchad, Turque, Zimbabwe, BAD, Banque mondiale, CEEAC, CICR, OIF, OCI, Nations unies et Union Européen.
32 Revised to reflect a broader consensus: RFI Afrique 2015c.
33 Former general director of UNESCO.

Demba 2007, 5). In 2012, Wade even professed that he alone had authored the 2001 Constitution, so that commentators noted a "personalization of the constituent process" (Mbodj 2012; Fall 2007a, 95). For Senegal, creation of the formally and factually independent CNRI hence marked a significant advance in terms of officially sanctioned public participation.

In his letter, President Sall tasked CNRI to hold nationwide consultations and make recommendations on a wide range of issues (M'bow 2012).[34] President Sall also demanded "ensuring institutional stability", a criterion that later justified his rejection of the bulk of CNRI's proposals (Kitane 2015).

In May 2013, President Sall instituted CNRI by decree.[35] CNRI then set out its working methodology to trace evolution and effectiveness of each of Senegal's constitutionalized institutions since independence.[36] CNRI consultations built upon the *Assises* approach. But with more than a million dollars in government funding, the commission availed of far greater financial means (Gbaya 2013). Consultations were held at three levels: political and civil society stakeholder fora, town-hall-type citizen panels in each of Senegal's *départements*, and online and paper-based questionnaires.

Prior to on-site consultations, CNRI conducted nationwide media outreach, explaining its mandate and methodology. Under the slogan "my country's institutions matter, so I participate", CNRI messages were broadcast by television, community radio, and social media, as well as through national and local print media.

Panel participants were selected to represent gender, class, geography, and age. Town halls were moderated along a standard interactive manual (*guide d'entretien*). CNRI translated consultation tools into Senegal's six official languages, as well as into Arabic. In June 2013, CNRI held a political party forum, in which 87 of the over 200 registered political parties participated. A CNRI civil society forum attracted 30 CSO coalitions. CNRI also visited 10 notable Senegalese religious authorities.

In September 2013, CNRI held 45 countrywide town hall consultations with the support of Senegal's largest CSO forum,[37] attracting 4,400 participants and soliciting feedback through paper questionnaires from each participant. A CNRI web-space yielded 215 completed online questionnaires. Of over 1,000 paper-based feedback forms returned in addition to those collected at town halls, 175 were found usable.[38]

34 Refocusing the state on its cardinal role; consolidating the rule of law; balancing executive, legislative, and judicial powers; enhancing independence of the judiciary; deepening representative and participatory democracy; reinforcing protection of fundamental freedoms; reinforcing decentralization and devolution; and promoting good governance, transparency, and ethics in public affairs and in accountability. Décret n°2013-682 en date du 17 mai 2013.
35 Décret n°2013-730 du 28 mai 2013 (*Journal Officiel* 2013).
36 The original source was accessed on August 16, 2016, and is no longer available: http://cnri.sn/media/pdfs/1392807779.pdf.
37 Plateform des Acteurs Non-étatiques (PFAnE).
38 The original source was accessed on August 16, 2016, and due to deactivation, the website is no longer available: http://cnri.sn/media/pdfs/1395401196.pdf. For further interest, the documents have been archived at http://congad.org/.

A separate questionnaire was fielded to political party and civil society stakeholders, seeking targeted feedback on what types of constitutional provisions should be entrenched against amendment.[39] CNRI published respective approval ratings issue-by-issue; 74 percent of respondents approved of the right of citizens to initiate constitutional amendments – a demand ultimately not taken up in the final text submitted to referendum.

Even though President Sall had vested CNRI only with consultative and not deliberative constituent powers, it delivered a full constitutional text that reflected the findings of its consultations (Ndiaye 2012). President Sall's legal adviser subsequently faulted CNRI with overstepping its institutional mandate.

Participation in the drafting processes

CAR's appointed constituent assembly

At the initiative of ECCAS heads of state, the *Conseil National de Transition* (CNT) replaced the coup's *Conseil Supérieur de Transition* on April 6, 2013 (Bozizé and Djotodia 2013; Xinhua 2013). CNT initially seated 105 members. Its composition emerged by political consensus at an internationally facilitated meeting, which attributed 38 seats to political parties, 17 seats to representatives of CAR's 16 regions and the capital Bangui, 42 seats to civil society, six seats to religious authorities, and two seats to the expatriate community. Women took 27 CNT seats.

CNT adopted its unpublished *réglement intérieur* only in December 2014, on the basis of which it designated a 30-member constitution drafting committee (Ligangue 2014). The drafting committee was composed of two members of each of its permanent committees, and chaired by the president of its legislative standing committee.[40] The drafting committee neither circulated its work among other members of CNT,[41] nor among the public, until a draft was first voted on by the CNT plenary in May 2015.[42]

CNT's initial 126-article text departed only slightly from CAR's abrogated 112-article 2004 Constitution:[43] It introduced, for instance, a Senate and it imposed modest constraints on presidential overreach. The core of the draft's innovations hence reflected self-interests of its *legislative* framers,[44] rather than

---

39 Same here – the original link is not available any longer: http://cnri.sn/media/pdfs/1393060877.pdf .
40 According to the author's onsite conversations with Me Blaise Fleury Hotto, who chaired the committee.
41 According to the author's interviews with CNT member Béatrice Épayé in Bangui in June 2015.
42 For the initial CNT draft of May 2015 please view: Le Conseil National de Transition 2015.
43 The May draft also added some provisions on presidential conflicts of interest and additional safeguards on term limits, as well as asset declaration not only at the beginning, but also at the end of the term. Further, it required the president to submit natural resource concessions to Parliament and to publish adopted contracts (article 49).
44 The interim charter barred, for instance, the president of CNT from standing for elected office at the transitional elections, but not from subsequent appointment or election to a newly created upper house.

a holistic reform project in line with *Forum of Bangui* recommendations. CNT's May draft also lacked measures fostering participatory democracy.[45]

Pursuant to the interim charter, the preliminary draft went to government for its advice and amendments.[46] The interim cabinet reworked CNT's initial draft, emphasizing that its input reflected *Forum de Bangui* recommendations, i.e., that it took public participation and consultation into account.[47]

In June 2015, cabinet returned the amended draft to the CNT – with its amendments highlighted – to serve as a working basis for the *atelier d'enrichissment* (Poussou 2015). None of cabinet's amendments enhanced public participation in future constitution making or amending processes. Nor did the cabinet draft fetter presidential prerogatives to submit a new constitution, or to amend the one in force.[48] Like the May draft, the 146-article June draft was not made accessible to the wider public.

CAR's atelier d'enrichissement

Pursuant to the interim charter, CNT and cabinet appointed a joint committee to organize an enrichment *atelier*. The committee drew up a list of 110 invitees, selected to represent "various shades of CAR's society", including religious leaders, CSOs representing women, persons with disabilities, the professional classes, and unions. At the urging of the international community, it integrated armed groups (Taka Parler 2015).

Starting in March 2015, ABA RoLI had conducted trainings for representatives of 24 CSOs in preparation for the *atelier*. The ABA initiative reached more than 1,000 individuals in traditionally underserved communities. Some of the ABA-coached CSOs ultimately participated in the *atelier* (American Bar Association 2015).

In July 2015, the two-day *atelier d'enrichissement* went through the cabinet draft article-by-article and, with advice of international experts, formulated a preliminary list of comments.[49] A condensed list of recommendations was compiled by the joint committee, and approved by acclamation at the *atelier*'s closing ceremony. Many recommendations echoed demands already made by *Forum of Bangui* participants, such as stronger separation and balance of powers.

---

45 Even if it preserves Parliament's legislative ambit over the right of petition – a power it never acted upon.
46 Article 65 of the Charter.
47 MINUSCA had at this point embedded Professor Frédéric Joel Aivo to assist government with the draft.
48 The 146-article version, however, can be considered overall to consolidate, rather than deconsolidate democracy. They introduce, upon behind-the-scenes lobbying of the international community, an anti-corruption commission, a broader framework for local government and for the armed forces, and a more complete bill of rights, even if it opportunistically grants a life-term seat on the constitutional court of former *transitional* heads-of-state.
49 MINUSCA, OIF, ABA RoLI, and IFES.

The *atelier* draft reduced the cabinet draft back to 140 articles. It also brought the *atelier* rejection of a Senate in conflict with CNT's vested interest to create a second chamber.[50]

Per the interim charter, the joint CNT/cabinet committee that moderated the *atelier* submitted the July draft to the transitional constitutional court for its opinion. The court found that the submitted draft fell short of taking into account all amendments adopted by the *atelier's* plenary, and gave notice of its opinion to CNT and to the government.[51] The court's opinion was published in the *Official Journal*, but the July draft was not made public beyond hardcopies distributed to *atelier* participants.

Certain *atelier* recommendations that the court's opinion had found missing were ultimately not taken into account in the final, 159-article text, which CNT submitted to the referendum – perhaps because CNT took the position that it was neither bound by the court's opinion, nor by the *atelier's* input.[52]

Presidential drafting in Senegal

CNRI had submitted its findings and draft constitution to President Sall in May 2014.[53] In January 2015, President Sall reaffirmed his plans to submit constitutional reform to a referendum. But he already distanced himself from the draft proposed by CNRI (Xibaaru 2015). The deliberative process inside the presidency unfolded behind closed doors. Meanwhile, the thorny issue of reducing the current presidential mandate distracted the public from substantive questions surrounding overall scope and nature of reform. Senegal's constitution making was again *personalized* (Thiam and Mané 2015).

The Senegalese public first gleaned the substance of President Sall's reform agenda when a package of 15 amendments was published a year later, on January 17, 2016 (Seneweb.com 2016a). At that point, substantive debate on *how far* the document reflected CNRI's popular consultation findings was further diluted by controversy surrounding President Sall's choice of article 51 procedures, which bypassed Parliament (Nguer 2016).

In February 2016, President Sall submitted the draft amendment to the constitutional council for its opinion. The council controversially held that President Sall's current term could not be shortened *retrospectively*, applying the very device with which the council had allowed Wade to stand for a third term. Ambiguities in Senegal's normative framework raised polemic over whether the council's opinion (*avis*) bound the president, which would free him from his campaign

---

50 Inter alia, the Senate was removed, but the National Election Commission was constitutionalized, and the entrenchment provision was tightened.
51 Avis 001/CCT/15 du 04 août 2015.
52 Most importantly, separation of powers between the head of state and the Conseil Supérieur de la Magistrature.
53 The original source was accessed on August 16, 2016, and is no longer available: http://cnri.sn/les-grands-dossiers-presse.php?id_presse=41.

promise (Bocoum 2015). At this stage, procedural preoccupations had entirely drowned out substantive debate on the other 14 amendments, and on what had gone amiss in terms of *Assises* and CNRI recommendations.

While the initially confidential opinion of the constitutional council appeared in the *Official Gazette* after the referendum, the opinion of the president of the lower house – who had to be consulted per article 51 as well – has still not been published (Mane 2016). After the referendum, some of President Sall's coalition MPs felt they had misread some of the proposed reform's intricacies, because they were excluded from deliberation and drafting processes. In fact, the explanatory memorandum seems to overstate the effect of at least one amendment.

It could thus be argued that the public would have obtained more meaningful deliberation, debate, clarification, and perhaps appropriation of the reform package had it been submitted to Parliament, rather than only to an ill-prepared electorate (Thiam 2007, 151).

In hindsight, it appears that Senegal's article 51 procedures are deliberately engineered to allow the head of state to override Parliament.[54] Yet, both case studies' epic history of opportunistic constitutional amendments exposes the risk of tempting heads of state to modify – or to introduce wholly new constitutions – by direct submission to referendum. Some critics wonder how a constitution could *premeditate its own demise* without parliamentary debate and consent, while others labeled Wade's earlier 2001 avoidance of Parliament a *fraud upon the constitution* (Fall 2014, 19; Mbodj 2007).

Constitution-building frameworks and practice

Senegal's referendum framework

Senegal's electoral code lacks procedural provisions for conducting referenda (Ministère de l'Intérieur de la Sécurité Publique 2017). Other electoral codes in the region suffer the same gap, which begs the question whether the omission is due to oversight or a deliberate effort to preserve executive discretion.[55]

Like in 2001, the Senegalese government adopted 2016 referendum procedures by decree, circumventing the legislature (*Journal Officiel du Sénégal* 2016a). The decree announced the referendum date barely a month before polling (*Journal Officiel du Sénégal* 2016b). If one regards referenda as elections, Senegal's timeline breaches the ECOWAS Protocol on Democracy, which bars changing electoral frameworks later than six months before polling.[56]

Senegal's decree stipulated that the "administration prints and brings the constitutional amendment text to the voters' knowledge" (*Journal Officiel du*

---

54 Wade's 2001 Constitution widened its ambit of article 46 of the 1963 Constitution, to ensure that it covers constitutional amendments, and even fresh constitutions.
55 See for instance that of DRC: *Journal Officiel de la République Démocratique du Congo* (2015).
56 Article 2(1) ECOWAS 2001.

Sénégal 2016b).[57] Furthermore, President Sall personally demanded "a vast national and international publicity campaign to ensure appropriation of the strategic importance of the proposed reform" (Agence de Presse Sénégalaise 2016). Three weeks before polling, President Sall issued a second decree to task the ministries of justice and of the interior to implement the campaign "by all appropriate means" (*Journal Officiel du Sénégal* 2016c).

But while online media published a preliminary version of the amendment text and its explanatory memorandum in January 2016,[58] *Official Gazette* publication of the final, slightly revised package appeared only on February 29, 2016 (*Journal Officiel du Sénégal* 2016c). Online and newspaper reprint of the official text followed on March 2, 2016 (Seneweb.com 2016b; Revue de Presse du Sénégal 2016). Lack of a minimum legal timeframe between publication of the final text and polling thus compressed the period of public absorption to 20 days (*Journal Officiel du Sénégal* 2016a). Even political insiders had not fully grasped the impact of the reform – for instance, regarding parliamentary representation of the diaspora, or to reform of appointment powers to the constitutional council (Diatta 2016).

Lack of a stable legal framework for referenda can also distort the campaign playing field (Metrodakar.net 2016). Senegal's relevant decree thus referred to the electoral code's provisions on equitable distribution of airtime (*Journal Officiel du Sénégal* 2016b).[59] But in reality, the "yes" campaign dwarfed the "no" campaign in terms of billboard surface, stoking perception of unilateral use of public resources.[60] The referendum campaign, however, invited and sparked free and pluralistic debate across the media and the political spectrum (Ndiaye 2016).

CAR's referendum framework

CAR had framed referendum procedures in its permanent electoral code, thereby constraining executive discretion and ensuring legal certainty and stability. CAR's code also provides for participatory rights, such as citizen standing to challenge referendum results before the constitutional court, as does Senegal's organic law on the constitutional council.[61]

A late amendment of CAR's code, however, reduced the timeframe between announcement of the referendum date and polling from 60 to 30 days.[62] The amendment also cut the official referendum campaign period from 14 to 10 days (République Centrafricaine and Presidence de la République no date, Art. 163).

---

57 Article 2 ECOWAS 2001.
58 Some modifications were made between the January and the final official text, notably removing the immutable clause on *laïcité*.
59 Articles 6 and 7.
60 Ministry of interior-issued billboards encouraged turnout, but were also criticized as biased in favor of the "yes" vote (Mbaye 2016).
61 As does Senegal's organic law on the constitutional council.
62 CAR is a member or ECCAS, and not of ECOWAS, and thus not bound by the ECOWAS Protocol on Democracy.

And it compressed the referendum results appeals period from 10 to two days – all measures narrowing opportunities for public participation or intervention (République Centrafricaine and Presidence de la République no date, Art. 175).

For the referendum campaign, CAR's framework ensures – in theory – a level playing field between the "yes" and "no" camps, also when it comes to billboard space (République Centrafricaine and Presidence de la République no date, Arts. 164–68). CAR's code tasks the independent media commission to equally distribute airtime between opposing campaigns. CAR's code even designates the media commission to organize televised campaign debates. But while Senegal benefitted from an animated but peaceful pro-and-contra debate, CAR's "no" campaign was marred by armed violence (Ousmane 2015). During the campaign period, one rebel leader even declared secession of an independent state in protest of the proposed constitution (Dembassa-Kette 2015).

The international community played a key role in CAR's civic education and voter information efforts. ABA RoLI held a series of public awareness campaigns the week before polling, reaching around 25,000 citizens. The NGO had trained 172 community leaders to educate the population through participatory theater, radio programs, comedy sketches, leaflets, and traditional music and songs to explain the draft constitution. The US Department of State's Bureau of Democracy, Human Rights and Labor funded the project (American Bar Association 2016).

The week before the referendum, UNDP printed 2,500 copies of the final 159-article version of the constitution (Deutsche Welle 2015). Already in September, the homepage of the EU-funded Centre for Humanitarian Dialogue had published a bilingual French/Sango translation of the final version.[63] Yet, conflicting versions of the final text still circulated shortly before polling. In November 2015, CNT's president unveiled a "final" text with only 126 articles – seemingly the version CNT had initially proposed in May 2015 – before cabinet, the *atelier*, and the constitutional court brought their amendments (Martin-White 2015). CAR's voters were hence deprived of legal certainty of what text they were asked to vote on.

Referendum participation

CAR's 2015 vote marks its sixth constitutional referendum in as many decades, adopting its seventh constitution. But this time, religious resentment caused bitter controversy over enfranchising mainly Muslim refugees. The election commission and other stakeholders insisted that refugees had no treaty-based international right to vote.[64] For the sake of inclusivity and reconciliation, international donors

63 The original source was accessed on April 15, 2016, and is no longer available: http://www.hdcentre.org/fileadmin/user_upload/Our_work/Peacemaking/Central_African_Republic_2015/Supporting_documents/CAR-Bilingual-Constitution-Project.pdf.
64 With the exception of the International Convention on the Rights of Migrant Workers and Their Families, to which CAR is not a state party.

and the UN ultimately prevailed in registering CAR's refugees to vote. A UN report, however, states that only 27 percent of 198,000 eligible refugees ultimately signed up. In-country polling days were extended in insecure areas where two persons were killed and 20 wounded on referendum day (AFP Yahoo News 2015).

CAR's 2016 constitutional referendum turnout reached 741,056 valid votes cast, or 38 percent of 1,954,433 registered voters (Sangonet.com 2015). By comparison, 888,374 valid votes had been cast at CAR's 2004 constitutional referendum (African Elections Database 2011a). Paradoxically, 2015 voter registration kept up with demographic growth, but actual referendum turnout dropped, which bodes ill as a measure of constitutionalism.

The 2016 vote marked Senegal's fourth referendum since independence (Thiam 2016). Its 1963 referendum turned out 94,3 percent, while in 2001 only 65 percent, and in 2016 only 38,6 percent of registered voters participated (African Elections Database 2012). But absolute turnout counted 2,163,000 votes cast in 2016, compared to 1,685,162 votes cast at the 2001 referendum. Over 20,000 votes were cast out of country. Senegal's referendum participation has hence kept pace with its population growth.

When it comes to voter choice offered by referendum frameworks, both Senegal and CAR have not yet emerged from the plebiscite logic (République Centrafricaine and Presidence de la République no date, Art. 173). The 2016 reform proposed 15 distinct amendments, which could have allowed an *à la carte* ballot, as was used in nearby Liberia in 2011. Liberian voters seemed to have been sufficiently informed, as a popular majority rejected one of four offered amendments. Only one proposition ultimately passed, because the other three fell short of the required two-thirds majority (African Elections Database 2011b).

And while CAR voters mark a single ballot paper, Senegal clings to French-style, nontraceable multiple ballot papers and envelopes, which invite vote buying and ballot box stuffing, while saddling taxpayers with avoidable costs.

Referendum results

While CAR's 93 percent referendum approval follows the foregone conclusion pattern, Senegal's 800,000 "no" votes in 2016 mark an eight-fold increase of the 2001 referendum's 99,000 "no" votes – perhaps an indicator of surging constitutionalism. Majorities in three of Senegal's 50 *départements* even rejected the reform package. The 2016 event hence marks Senegal's first *competitive* referendum.

Access to the text

Neither CAR's, nor Senegal's framework stipulate reasonably timely publication of the proposed, as well as of the final, constitutional text, which introduces legal uncertainty, deprives voters of an informed choice, and ultimately starves constitutionalism.

Senegal has still not published a consolidated text of its amended constitution now in force. The site of the *Official Gazette* instead provides an obsolete version of the 2001 text (*Journal Officiel du Sénégal* 2017).[65] And CAR leaves citizens in doubt as to what version of the constitutional project was actually adopted by referendum. In April 2016, the newly elected Parliament posted only the 126-article version on its homepage. CAR's constitution was promulgated during the swearing in of its new president on March 30, 2016, but the official 159-article version still cannot be accessed online (Koena 2016).

Envisioned and actual participation

Senegal's permanent participation framework does not contemplate public consultation beyond holding a yes/no vote by universal suffrage.[66] But above and beyond casting referendum votes, the Senegalese popular participation *and initiative* far exceeded what its constitution envisions. Senegal's normative participation framework thus lags far behind popular demand.

In contrast, CAR's interim participation framework filled a constitutional void and aimed to mitigate armed conflict, rather than cater to grassroots demand. CAR's framework involved a modest stakeholder *atelier*, and as was the case in Senegal, it expanded *ad hoc* to accommodate wider consultations through a national *forum*. Both events were well attended by national elites and international advisers. But unlike Senegal, CAR has not seen grassroots participation overtake top-down supply.

Overall, both nations perpetuate the habit of polling citizens on complex and insufficiently published and debated constitutional texts – an arguably anachronistic paradox, especially since imposed texts themselves have not appreciably opened up government to more participatory democracy.

But actual, formative citizen experience accrued along the way defies anachronistic normative frameworks: Senegal's *Assises* have recently declared their intention to reconstitute (Dakaractu 2016).

References

African Elections Database (2011a): Elections in the Central African Republic – December 5, 2004, Constitutional Referendum. Online: http://africanelections.tripod.com/cf.html.

African Elections Database (2011b): Elections in Liberia – August 23, 2011, Referendum. Online: http://africanelections.tripod.com/lr.html#2011_Referendum.

African Elections Database (2012): Elections in Senegal. Online: http://africanelections.tripod.com/sn.html.

AFP Yahoo News (2015): Central African Republic Constitution Vote Extended Amid Violence. In: ConstitutionNet. Online: http://www.constitutionnet.org/news/central-african-republic-constitution-vote-extended-amid-violence.

65 The original source was accessed on August 16, 2016, and is no longer available: http://www.gouv.sn/IMG/article_PDF/rubrique_17.pdf.
66 As do, for instance, referendum frameworks in Thailand, Italy, the Philippines, and Switzerland.

Akandji-Kombé, J.-F. (2015): Centrafrique: Pour savoir si enrichissement de la Constitution il y a bien eu. . . Online: https://jfakiblog.com/2015/07/08/centrafrique-pour-savoir-si-enrichissement-de-la-constitution-il-y-a-bien-eu/.

American Bar Association (2015): Workshop Raises Community Awareness and Engagement in Constitution Drafting. Online: http://www.americanbar.org/advocacy/rule_of_law/where_we_work/africa/central-african-republic/news/news-car-workshop-on-constitution-drafting-0915.html.

American Bar Association (2016): Public Awareness Campaigns Prepare Central African Republic Citizens for Constitutional Referendum. Online: http://www.americanbar.org/advocacy/rule_of_law/where_we_work/africa/central-african-republic/news/news-car-campaigns-prepare-citizens-for-constitutional-referendum-0116.html.

American Bar Association (2017): *Central African Republic | Rule of Law Initiative*. Online: http://www.americanbar.org/advocacy/rule_of_law/where_we_work/africa/central-african-republic.html.

Agence de Presse Sénégalaise (2016): Le project de loi portant revision de la constitution adopté en conseil des ministers. Online: http://www.aps.sn/actualites/politique/article/le-projet-de-loi-portant-revision-de-la-constitution-adopte-en-conseil-des-ministres.

Assingambi, Zarambaud (2008): Memoire Apliatif – Plaise à la cour. Online: http://ddata.over-blog.com/xxxyyy/1/35/48/78/Centrafrique/memoire_Me_Zarambaud.pdf.

Assises Nationales au Sénégal (2017a): Reglement interieur. Online: http://assises nationales.org/?ans=his&his=231167.

Assises Nationales au Sénégal (2017b): Liste des Participants aux Assises Nationales. Online: http://assisesnationales.org/?ans=org&org=231187.

Assises Nationales au Sénégal (2017c): Code de Conduite des Assises Nationales. Online: http://assisesnationales.org/?ans=his&his=231166.

Assises Nationales au Sénégal (2017d): Pourquoi les Assises Nationales? Online: http://assisesnationales.org/?ans=his&his=231168.

Assises Nationales au Sénégal (2017e): Rapport des Consultations citoyennes, tenues à Fatick les 15 et 16 novembre 2008. Online: http://assisesnationales.org/index.php?ans=doc&doc=8.

Assises Nationales au Sénégal (2017f): Charte de Gouvernance Democratique. Online: http://assisesnationales.org/?ans=doc&doc=32.

Assises Nationales au Sénégal (2017g): Charte de Gouvernance Democratique – Audio. Online: http://assisesnationales.org/?ans=med&med=audio&audio=6.

Association Manassé (2017): Histoire de la République Centralafricaine. Online: http://manasse.asso-web.com/36+histoire-de-la-republique-centrafricaine.html.

Bissengue, V. (2017): Histoire de la République Centralafricaine. Online: http://www.sangonet.com/afriqg/PAFF/Dic/HistoireC.html.

Bocas, L. (2015): Promulgation de la nouvelle constitution de Sassou Nguesso: Une Constitution au Forceps. *DAC Presse*. Online: http://www.dac-presse.com/actualites/a-la-une/politique/2750-une-constitution-au-forceps.html.

Bocoum, T. (2015): Réduction du mandat présidentiel: Le conseil constitutionnel ne peut constituer une bouée de sauvetage. In: Dakaractu. Online: http://www.dakaractu.com/Reduction-du-mandat-presidentiel-Le-conseil-constitutionnel-ne-peut-constituer-une-bouee-de-sauvetage-Par-Thierno-Bocoum_a93832.html.

Bolle, S. (2008a): Quand Wade fait réviser sa Constitution. *La Constitution en Afrique*. Online: http://www.la-constitution-en-afrique.org/tag/centrafrique/.

Bolle, S. (2008b): L'étrange régime des règlements des assemblées (suite et fin). *La Constitution en Afrique.* Online: http://www.la-constitution-en-afrique.org/tag/centrafrique/.

Bolle, S. (2008c): La Cour constitutionnelle désavoue le Président et vice versa (II). *La Constitution en Afrique.* Online: http://www.la-constitution-en-afrique.org/tag/centrafrique/.

Bolle, S. (2010): Mandats à durée indéterminée. *La Constitution en Afrique.* Online: http://www.la-constitution-en-afrique.org/tag/centrafrique/.

Bolle, S. (2012): Le programme constitutionnel du Président. *La Constitution en Afrique.* Online: http://www.la-constitution-en-afrique.org/tag/centrafrique/.

Bolle, S. (No date): Touche pas à ma constitution. Online: http://ddata.over-blog.com/1/35/48/78/S-n-gal/SENEGAL-RETRAIT-PROJET-REVISION.doc.

Bozizé, F. and Djotodia, M. (2013): Centrafrique: à peine créé, le CNT déjà contesté. In: RFI Afrique. Online: http://www.rfi.fr/afrique/20130417-centrafrique-peine-cree-le-cnt-deja-conteste-djotodia.

Centrafrique Presse Info (2017): Online: http://www.centrafrique-presse.info/site/.

Centre for Humanitarian Dialogue (2015): Pacte républicain pour la paix, la réconciliation nationale et la reconstruction en République centrafricaine. Online: https://www.hdcentre.org/wp-content/uploads/2016/06/The-Republican-Pact-May-2015.pdf.

Commission Nationale de Réforme des Institutions (CNRI) (2013): Rapport de la Commission de Reforme des Institutions au President de la Republique du Senegal. Online: http://www.congad.org/rapports/RAPPORT%20DE%20LA%20COMMISSION%20NATIONALE%20DE%20REFORME%20DES%20INSTITUTIONS.pdf.

Constitute (2009): Senegal 2001 (rev. 2009). Online: https://www.constituteproject.org/constitution/Senegal_2009?lang=en.

Constitute (2013): Central African Republic. Online: https://www.constituteproject.org/constitution/Central_African_Republic_2013?lang=en.

Dakaractu (2016): Echanges vifs entre pro et anti Macky Sall, "le tombé du car rapide de Abdoulaye Wade". Online: http://www.dakaractu.com/Echanges-vifs-entre-pro-et-anti-Macky-Macky-Sall-le-tombe-du-car-rapide-de-Abdoulaye-Wade_a114142.html.

Darlan, D. (2013): La charte constitutionnelle de transition du 18 juillet 2013 – un compromis pour la paix en Republique Centralafricaine. Online: http://www.journaldebangui.com/files/communiques/439.pdf.

Demba, S. (2007): L'élaboration de la Constitution du 22 janvier 2001. In: *Annales Africaines*, CREDILA, Université Cheikh Anta Diop, Dakar.

Dembassa-Kette, C. (2015): Rebel Declares Autonomous State in Central African Republic. In: Reuters, World News. Online: http://uk.reuters.com/article/uk-central africa-politics-idUKKBN0TY1FO20151215.

Deutsche Welle (2015): Heavy Fighting Breaks Out in Central African Republic on Day of Constitutional Referendum Over Presidential and Parliamentary Powers. In: ConstitutionNet, online: http://www.constitutionnet.org/news/heavy-fighting-breaks-out-central-african-republic-day-constitutional-referendum-over.

Diatta, J. M. (2016): Le Referendum "Viole". In: SudQuotien, online: http://mobile.sudonline.sn/le-referendum-viole_m_30687.htm.

Diop, A. S. (2011): Pr Babacar Guèye, un des rédacteurs de la Constitution du Sénégal invalide la candidature de Wade. Online: http://www.leral.net/Pr-Babacar-Gueye-un-des-redacteurs-de-la-Constitution-du-Senegal-invalide-la-candidature-de-Wade_a18679.html#.

Duhem, V. (2016a): Centrafrique: pourquoi Jean-Francis Bozizé s'est-il risqué à rentrer à Bangui? *Jeune Afrique*. Online: http://www.jeuneafrique.com/mag/349217/politique/centrafrique-jean-francis-bozize-sest-risque-a-rentrer-a-bangui/?utm_source=Newsletter_JA_Actu&utm_medium=Email&utm_campaign=Newsletter_JA_Actu_22_08_16.

Duhem, V. (2016b): Côte d'Ivoire: extraits choisis du discours d'Alassane Ouattara devant l'Assemblée nationale. *Jeune Afrique*. Online: http://www.jeuneafrique.com/362906/politique/cote-divoire-extraits-choisis-discours-dalassane-ouattara-devant-lassemblee-nationale/?utm_source=Newsletter_JA_Actu&utm_medium=Email&utm_campaign=Newsletter_JA_Actu_06_10_16.

ECOWAS (2001): Protocol A/SP1/12/01 on Democracy and Good Governance Supplementary to the Protocol relating to the Mechanism for Conflict Prevention, Management, Resolution, Peacekeeping and Security. In: International Democracy Watch. Online: http://www.internationaldemocracywatch.org/index.php/economic-community-of-west-african-states-treaties-and-protocols/350-protocol-on-democracy-and-good-governance-2001.

Elgie, R. (2010): CAR – Constitutional amendment regulating elections. *The semi-presidential one*. Online: http://www.semipresidentialism.com/?p=452.

European Union Election Observation Mission Reports, 2012. Online: https://eeas.europa.eu/headquarters/headquarters-homepage/24366/eu-election-observation-mission-senegal-2012_en.

Fall, I. M. (2007a): *Evolution constitutionnelle du Sénégal de la veille de l'indépendance aux élections de 2007*, Crepos: Karthala.

Fall, I. M. (2007b): *Textes Constitutionnels du Sénégal du 24 janvier 1959 au 15 mai 2007* Collection du Credila, XXIII.

Fall, I. M. (2011): *Les révisions constitutionnelles au Sénégal. Révisions consolidantes et révisions déconsolidantes de la démocratie sénégalaise*. Dakar: Credila.

Fall, I. M. (2014): *La révision de la Constitution au Sénégal*. Online: http://afrilex.u-bordeaux4.fr/sites/afrilex/IMG/pdf/La_revision_de_la_Constitution_au_Senegal_Ismaila.pdf, pp. 1–46.

Federation of the Free States of Africa (2017): African Nations and Territory Identity. Online: http://www.africafederation.net/Berlin_1885.htm.

Gbaya, D. (2013): Tout ce que les Assises ont adopté est encore valable. *Enquete*. Online: http://www.enqueteplus.com/content/commission-nationale-de-reforme-des-institutions-%C2%ABtout-ce-que-les-assises-ont-adopt%C3%A9-est.

Gomis, N. C. (2016a): Macky, a l'epreuve de senghor et wade! In: SudOnLine. Online: http://www.sudonline.sn/macky-a-l-epreuve-de-senghor-et-wade-_a_28769.html.

Gomis, N. C. (2016b): "Nous n'avons pas été vigilants". In: SudQuotidien. Online: http://www.sudonline.sn/nous-n-avons-pas-ete-vigilants_a_30685.html.

International Institute for Democracy and Electoral Assistance (IDEA) (2017): Search. Online: http://www.idea.int/elections/dd/search.cfm.

Inter-parliamentary Union (2017): *Women in Parliaments: World Classification*. Online: http://www.ipu.org/wmn-e/classif.htm.

Jeune Afrique (2016): Côte d'Ivoire: l'Assemblée adopte le projet de nouvelle Constitution. Online: http://www.jeuneafrique.com/364663/politique/cote-divoire-lassemblee-adopte-projet-de-nouvelle-constitution/?utm_source=Newsletter_JA_Actu&utm_medium=Email&utm_campaign=Newsletter_JA_Actu_12_10_16.

Journal Officiel de la République Démocratique du Congo (2015): No. special 17 février 2015. Online: http://www.droitcongolais.info/files/1.16.42.-Loi-du-12-fevrier-2015_loi-electorale-du-9-mars-2006_Modifications.pdf.

Journal Officiel du Sénégal (2003): DECISION n° 1-C-2003 du 11 juin 2003. Online: http://www.jo.gouv.sn/spip.php?article1011.

Journal Officiel du Sénégal (2009): Affaire n° 2-C-2009 du 18 juin 2009. Online: http://ddata.over-blog.com/xxxyyy/1/35/48/78/S-n-gal/CC-senegal-2009-sur-LC-VP.doc.

Journal Officiel du Sénégal (2013): Décret n° 2013-730 du 28 mai 2013. Online: http://www.jo.gouv.sn/spip.php?article9775.

Journal Officiel du Sénégal (2016a): Décret n° 2016-261 du 18 février 2016. Online: http://www.jo.gouv.sn/spip.php?article10658.

Journal Officiel du Sénégal (2016b): Décret n° 2016-262 du 19 février 2016. Online: http://www.jo.gouv.sn/spip.php?article10659.

Journal Officiel du Sénégal (2016c): Décret n° 2016-306 du 29 février 2016. Online: http://www.jo.gouv.sn/spip.php?article10657.

Journal Officiel du Sénégal (2017): Constitution du Sénégal. Online: http://www.jo.gouv.sn/spip.php?article36.

Kamto, M. (1997): Les Conférences nationales ou la création révolutionnaire des Constitutions. In: D. Darbon et J. Du Bois de Gaudusson (eds.): *La création du droit en Afrique*, Paris: Karthala.

Kanisani, L. (2011): The Servitude of the Colonial Pact. *Leo Kanisani*. Online: http://leo-kanisani.blogspot.de/2011/01/servitude-of-colonial-pact.html.

Kanté, B. (1989): *Le Sénégal: un exemple de continuité et d'instabilité constitutionnelle*, Revue juridique politique et économique du Maroc.

Koena, J. F. (2016): Centrafrique: Désiré Dominique Herenon, un constitutionnaliste propose une révision de la constitution du 30 mars 2016. In: Centrafrique Réseau des Journalistes pour les Droits de l'Homme. Online: http://rjdh.org/centrafrique-desire-dominique-herenon-constitutionnaliste-propose-revision-de-constitution-30-mars-2016/.

Kitane, A. K. (2015): La gouvernance Macky Sall: La grande éclipse de la démocratie sénégalaise. In: Leral.net. Online: http://www.leral.net/La-gouvernance-Macky-Sall-La-grande-eclipse-de-la-democratie-senegalaise_a161441.html#.

L'express (2011): Sénégal: Wade renonce à réviser la Constitution. Online: http://www.lexpress.fr/actualite/monde/afrique/senegal-wade-renonce-a-reviser-la-constitution_1005728.html.

Lamba, S. and Kokpakpa, S. L. (2015): Les débats et les éclats du Forum de Bangui 4–11 mai 2015 (Spécial). Online: https://www.sangonet.com/afriqg/PAFF/Dic/actuC/debats-forum-B2015/les-debats-du-forum-de-bangui-mai2015.html.

Le Citoyen (2010): Loi Constitutionnelle No 10.005 modifiant et completant certaines dispositions de la constitutions du 27 decembre 2004. Online: http://ddata.over-blog.com/1/35/48/78/Centrafrique/RCA-Loi-constitutionnelle-mai-2010.pdf.

Le Conseil Constitutionnel (1998): DECISION n°9-C-1998 du 9 octobre 1998. Online: http://ddata.over-blog.com/xxxyyy/1/35/48/78/S-n-gal/CC-Senegal-1998-incomptence-loi-de-revision.pdf.

Le Conseil Constitutionnel (2006): DECISION du 18 janvier 2006, Affaire 3/C/2005. Online: http://ddata.over-blog.com/xxxyyy/1/35/48/78/S-n-gal/CC-Senegal-2006-confirmation-incompetence-revision.pdf.

Le Conseil Constitutionnel (2012a): DECISION du 29 janvier 2012. Online: http://ddata.over-blog.com/1/35/48/78/S-n-gal/SENEGAL-CC-29.01.2012-validite-candidature-Wade.pdf.

Le Conseil Constitutionnel (2012b): DECISION du 29 janvier 2012 – Reclamation de Abdourahmane Sarr Youssou Ndour Keba Keinde C/Le rejet de leur candidature à l'éléction presidentielle. Online: http://ddata.over-blog.com/1/35/48/78/S-n-gal/CC-Senegla-29.01.2012-irrecevabilites-reclamations-Youssou.doc.

Le Conseil National de Transition (2015): Proposition de Constitution de la Republique Centrafricaine. Online: http://www.assembleenationale-rca.org/wp-content/uploads/2016/04/projet-constitution-RCA-adopte-par-CNT-2015.pdf.

Leral.net (2011): Touche pas à ma démocratie! Online: http://www.leral.net/Touche-pas-a-ma-democratie-_a16977.html#.

Ligangue, D. (2014): Centrafrique – tentative manquee de modification du reglement interieur du conseil national de transition. In: Centrafrique Libre. Online: http://www.centrafriquelibre.info/?p=15883.

Mane, R. (2016): Qu'en est-il de l'avis de Moustapha NiASSE sur le mandat du président Macky SALL? In: Koldanews. Online: https://www.koldanews.com/2016/02/17/quen-est-il-de-lavis-de-moustapha-niasse-sur-le-mandat-du-president-macky-sall-a505919.html.

Martin-White, S. (2015): Centrafrique: La proposition du texte de la Constitution (intégralité) – Analysis. In: La Nouvelle Centrafrique. Online: http://www.lanouvelle centrafrique.info/2015/11/11/centrafrique-la-proposition-du-texte-de-la-constitution-integralite-analyse/.

Mbaye, A. L. (2016): Référendum: L'affiche publicitaire du ministère de l'intérieur devient la risée de la toile. In: SeneNews Actu. Online: https://www.senenews.com/2016/03/09/referendum-laffiche-publicitaire-du-ministere-de-linterieur-devient-la-risee-de-la-toile_150500.html.

Mbodj, E. (2012): Contribution : "La Constitution, c'est moi qui l'ai rédigée!" Il faut alors l'assumer! (El Hadj Mbodj). Dakaractu.com. Online: http://www.dakaractu.com/Contribution-La-Constitution-c-est-moi-qui-l-ai-redigee--Il-faut- alors-l-assumer--El-Hadj-Mbodj_a11612.html.

Mbodj, E. (2007): Preface of his Textes constitutionnels du Sénégal de 1959 à 2007. Dakar, Credila.

M'bow, A.M. (2012): Objet: Concertation nationale sur les réformes institutionnelle. Online: http://www.congad.org/rapports/LETTRE%20DU%20PRESIDENT%20DE%20LA%20REPUBLIQUE%20A%20AMADOU%20MACKTAR%20MBOW.pdf.

Metrodakar.net (2016): "On vote OUI" Le nouveau single pour la campagne du référendum du président Macky SALL. Online: http://www.metrodakar.net/on-vote-oui-nouveau-single-campagne-referendum-president-macky-sall/.

Ministère de la Défense (2016): *Opération Sangaris*. Ministère de la Défense, pp. 1–68. Online: http://www.defense.gouv.fr/operations/operations/centrafrique/dossier-de-presentation-de-l-operation-sangaris/operation-sangaris.

Ministère de la Reconciliation Nationale (2015): Rapport des consultation populaires à la base en Republique Centralafricaine. Online: https://jfakiblog.files.wordpress.com/2016/05/rapport-consultations-populaires.pdf.

Ministère de l'Intérieur de la Sécurité Publique (2017) : Code électoral. Online : http://www.interieur.gouv.sn/elections/code-electoral/.

Moulougnatho, M. (2015): Forum de Bangui: les participants repartis en commission et des thématiques présentées. Bangui.com. Online: http://news.abangui.com/h/26295.html.

Ndiaye, A. K. (2012): La CNRI ou la suite logique des Assises Nationales. In: Blog de Nioxor Tine. Online: http://www.nioxor.com/pages/LA_CNRI_OU_LA_SUITE_LOGIQUE_DES_ASSISES_NATIONALES-8726197.html.

Ndiaye, B. J. (2016): Quelle campagne référendaire pour le Président Macky Sall? In: Dakaractu. Online: http://www.dakaractu.com/Quelle-campagne-referendaire-pour-le-President-Macky-Sall%C2%A0-Par-Babacar-Justin-Ndiaye_a107681.html.

Ngalangou, V. (2015): *Centrafrique/Forum de Bangui: Des propositions de paix et sécurité se dessinent.* Sangonet.com. Online: https://www.sangonet.com/afriqg/PAFF/Dic/actuC/debats-forum-B2015/centr-forum-B-proposit-paix-secur-dess.html.

Nguer, A. B. (2016): Note: Project de loi au referendum, constitution de la Republique et conseil constitutionnel. In: Dakaractu. Online: http://www.dakaractu.com/NOTE-PROJET-DE-LOI-AU-REFERENDUM-CONSTITUTION-DE-LA-REPUBLIQUE-ET-CONSEIL-CONSTITUTIONNEL-Abdoulaye-Ba-NGUER-Maitre-en_a106008. html.

Ousmane, B. (2015): La campagne référendaire perturbée à Ndele. In: Centrafrique Réseau des Journalistes pour les Droits de l'Homme (RJDH). Online: http://rjdh.org/la-campagne-referendaire-perturbee-a-ndele/.

Poussou, G. A. (2015): Communiqué de presse N°002 de la primature. In: centrafrique-presse.com, 28 Mai 2015. Online: http://centrafrique-presse.over-blog.com/2015/05/communique-de-presse-n-002-de-la-primature.html.

République du Congo and Union Africaine (2015): 8ième Réunion du groupe international de contact sur la république centrafricaina (GIC_RCA) – Conclusion. Addis Ababa, pp.1–6. Online: http://www.peaceau.org/uploads/cua-conclusions-8y-me-gic-rca-27-7-2015.pdf.

République Centrafricaine and Presidence de la République (no date): Code electoral. Online: http://www.sangonet.com/afriqg/PAFF/Dic/actuC/ActuC13/code_electoral_republique_centrafricaine.pdf.

Revue de Presse du Sénégal (2016): Rp du Mercredi 03. Mars 2016. Online: http://revuedepressedusenegal.over-blog.com/2016/03/rp-du-mercredi-03-mars-2016.html.

RFI Afrique (2014): Burundi: le projet de révision de la Constitution retoqué au Parlement. Online: http://www.rfi.fr/afrique/20140321-burundi-le-projet-revision-constitution-retoque-assemblee-nationale.

RFI Afrique (2015a): Processus de réconciliation en RCA: début des consultations populaires. Online: http://www.rfi.fr/afrique/20150119-processus-reconciliation-rca-debut-consultations-populaires-forum-bangui/.

RFI Afrique (2015b): RCA: les entités participant au Forum attendent les quotas. Online: http://www.rfi.fr/afrique/20150416-rca-centrafrique-entites-milice-balaka-seleka-forum-bangui-quotas-comite-technique-samba-panza/.

RFI Afrique (2015c): RCA: consensus sur le choix des organisateurs du Forum de Bangui. Online: http://www.rfi.fr/afrique/20150416-rca-consensus-trouve-organisateurs-forum-bangui-seleka-balaka-cnt-mahamat-kamoun-reconciliation/.

Sangonet.com (2015): Résultat du référendum constitutionnel de la RCA (93% de OUI), un test en grandeur nature avant la présidentielle et les législatives. Online: http://www.sangonet.com/afriqg/PAFF/Dic/actuC/ActuC21/resultat-referendum-constitution-2015RCA.html.

SeneNews Actu (2011): 23 juin. Online: https://www.senenews.com/tag/23-juin.

SeneNews Actu (2017): Archives par mot-clé: benno bokk yakaar. Online: https://www.senenews.com/tag/benno-bokk-yakaar.

Seneweb.com (2016a): Document: L'intégralité de la révision Constitutionnelle proposée par Macky Sall. Online: http://www.seneweb.com/news/Politique/document-l-integralite-de-la-revision-co_n_172150.html.

Seneweb.com (2016b): Sénégal – Le texte définitif du Référendum. Online: http://www.sencms.com/news/Politique/senegal-le-texte-definitif-du-referendum_n_175557.html.

Simonis, F. (2008): L'administration coloniale et le référendum du 28 septembre 1958 dans les fédérations d'AOF et AEF, *Outre-mers*, 85(358), pp. 59–73.

Taka Parler (2015): La Constitution: une préoccupation de la société civile. Online: http://takaparlenews.over-blog.com/2015/06/la-constitution-une-preoccupation-de-la-societe-civile.html.

Thiam, A. (2007): Une Constitution, ça se révise! Relativisme constitutionnel et État de droit au Sénégal, In: *Politique Africaine*, 4/108, p. 145–53.

Thiam, A. and Mané, B. D. (2015): Reduction du mandate, saisine des cinq sages, referendum ou demission. . .le PR pape demba sy calrifie le jeu. In: SudOnLine. Online: http://www.sudonline.sn/index.php/politique/item/images/img/logo/le-pr-pape-demba-sy-clarifie-le-jeu_a_25363.html.

Thiam, Elhadji I. (2016): Le Sénégal, une tradition référendaire. In: Le Soleil Online. Online: http://www.lesoleil.sn/2016-03-22-23-17-43/item/47948-le-senegal-une-tradition-referendaire.html.

Unmondepygmee (2011): Mon ami l'empereur Bokassa 1er.wmv. In: Youtube. Online: https://www.youtube.com/watch?v=yHmI9d-yPiY.

United Nations (2014a): *United Nations Security Council Resolution (2149)*. United Nations, pp. 1–14. Online: http://www.un.org/en/ga/search/view_doc.asp?symbol=S/RES/2149(2014).

United Nations (2014b): Accord de cessation des hostilites en Republique Centralafricaine. *MINUSCA*. Online: http://peacemaker.un.org/sites/peacemaker.un.org/files/CAF_140723_Accord-cessation-hostilites.pdf.

United Nations (2015a): *United Nations Security Council Report of the Secretary-General on the situation in the Central African Republic*. United Nations, pp. 1–19. Online: http://www.un.org/ga/search/view_doc.asp?symbol=S/2015/576.

United Nations (2015b): Central African Republic holds constitutional referendum. UNDP. Online: http://www.undp.org/content/undp/en/home/presscenter/articles/2015/12/14/une-nouvelle-constitution-en-centrafrique.html.

United Nations (2017): *MINUSCA Mandate – United Nations Multidimensional Integrated Stabilization Mission in the Central African Republic (MINUSCA)*. United Nations. Online: http://www.un.org/en/peacekeeping/missions/minusca/mandate.shtml.

Xibaaru (2015): Macky veut un référendum pour 2016: Il revise la constitution sans la CNRI. Online: http://xibaaru.com/exclusivites/le-palais-annonce-un-referendum-pour-2016-macky-revise-la-constitution-sans-le-cnri/.

Xinhua (2013): Centrafrique: le Conseil supérieur de transition remplacé par le Conseil national de transition. In: Tchadinfos.com. Online: http://tchadinfos.com/afrique/centrafrique-conseil-suprieur-de-transition-remplac-conseil-national-de-transition/.

8 People and constitutions

The case of Zambia

Boniface Cheembe

Introduction

In 1964, Zambia gained independence from the British who had colonised the country in the late 1800s. Since independence, the country has promulgated five different constitutions: namely, the independence Constitution of 1964;[1] the Constitution of 1973, adopted during the period of one-party rule; the Constitution of 1991, which celebrated the reintroduction of democracy and established a multi-party system of governance based on the Westminster model; the 1996 "amended" Constitution;[2] and the amended Constitution No. 2 of 2016. Not all of these constitutions were new constitutional texts, but rather designed as constitutional amendments – so extensive in form, however, so as to be perceived as new constitutions. Moreover, they were all adopted under the auspices of adopting new constitutions. The processes which brought them into existence will therefore be considered constitution-making processes. Remarkably, all of these processes have not received widespread support from the various stakeholders involved. This result appears somehow paradoxical if we consider that all these processes have been undertaken with the objective to allow the people to participate in constitution-making equally and the record of citizens' participation has been rather impressive and commendable. Since the start of the reform processes, the people of Zambia have not felt like they have obtained a people-driven constitution (Munalula 2016).

With regard to the recently conducted reform process that started in 2011, this procedural difference between the promulgation of a new constitution and the amendment of an existing one is of particular importance. It has not been apparent from the outset in which direction the Zambian venture would develop.

1 There was another major constitutional amendment in 1969 which is not considered here.
2 The 1996 constitutional "amendment" can genuinely be considered a "new" constitution. As Ndulo and Kent (1996, 275) write, "Every part of the 1991 Constitution was repealed and replaced, except Part III, which governs Protection of Fundamental Rights and Freedom of the Individual. Having rejected the Mwanakatwe Commission's recommendation for ratification by a Constituent Assembly [. . .], the government in effect created a new Constitution through an act of Parliament made possible by its overwhelming majority obtained nearly five years earlier and not renewed since that time".

DOI: 10.4324/9781315180540-11

The process started with the Patriotic Front's (PF) campaign promise to "draft and present a constitution which will reflect the will and aspirations of the people" (Patriotic Front 2011, 42) and with announcements made by the president to "deliver a *new people-driven constitution*[3] within 90 days" (Africa Review 2011). With the course of time, however, the government commitment shifted towards preferring a constitutional amendment with limited public influence as well as putting forward a sequential adoption process that envisaged only the Bill of Rights to be put to a popular referendum. At the poll in August 2016, however, the required 50 percent threshold of eligible voters was not reached. This chapter argues that following either pathway would have had distinct implications for the legitimation of the process as well as the drafting bodies involved.[4] For this reason, the chapter takes a close look at the dynamics that unfolded in the reform process. It is argued that the initial enthusiasm started to fade soon and that in the end the endeavour suffered a similar fate as its predecessors. It exhibited a lack of legitimacy as well as transparency that can inter alia be traced back to the absence of a precise legal framework. Moreover, the process in its later stages can be characterised as highly politicised, being driven by partisan interests and being (re)captured by the political elite. Furthermore, it is the conviction of the author that the government's reluctance to encourage a break from the norm (old constitutions) has prevented Zambia from installing transformative constitutions.

Short history of Zambia's post-independence constitution-making processes

One of the most contentious issues in Zambia's constitution-making process is the question whether the document can be classified as "people-driven". Most constitutions that have been brought into being since independence have failed to meet this criterion. However, what does "people-driven" precisely mean? For this purpose, one could turn to an approach developed by Abrak Saati (2015, 57ff), which classifies distinct participatory constitution-making processes into four categories: false, symbolic, limited and consultative/substantial participation (each assessing four key variables). Previous processes in Zambia have exhibited certain features typical for Saati's (2015) category of "false participation" (also compare Saati's chapter in this volume).

Historically, Zambia's leaders have always promised constitutional reform that is to be driven by the desires or wishes of the people. It is noteworthy that in all four constitutional reform processes since 1990, each president has designed his own agenda responding to public demands (Munalula 2016). When it came to

---

3 Emphasis added by the author.
4 One might consider the following distinction: whereas the former would require for a drafting body outside the separated branches of government activating the *pouvoir constituent*, the latter envisages the institution of the people – or the legislative as representing the will of the people – to be involved in line with the *pouvoir constitué*.

the realisation of people's submissions in supreme law, however, national elites regularly usurped the procedure and induced modifications according to their own partisan interests (van Vliet 2009, 39, 41–42; Simutanyi 2013; Ndulo 2016). Even earlier, when Zambia underwent a process of post-independence constitutional change that led to the adoption of the 1973 Constitution, people rejected the transformation from a multi-party democracy to a one-party participatory democracy;[5] however, the government ignored public opinion and established a single-party system nonetheless.

When the Mwanakatwe Constitution Review Commission (CRC)[6] concluded its work to amend the 1996 constitution, the people were consulted on what they wanted to see reflected in a new constitution. Government representatives, however, ignored these expectations and decided independently on what to include and what not. The people, for instance, advocated a majoritarian electoral formula for electing the head of state. Nevertheless, the government opted to settle for the first-past-the-post electoral formula. In total, at least two-thirds of all recommendations made by the CRC were rejected by government by invoking the Inquiries Act[7] (van Vliet 2009, 43; Munalula 2016).

Similarly, when the Mung'omba Constitution Review Commission[8] concluded its work in 2005, the Movement for Multi-Party Democracy Government through the National Constitutional Conference (NCC) decided which proposals to pick and which ones to drop (Munalula 2016). Among the clauses that were left out – contrary to public interest – was the election of the Republican president on the basis of the majoritarian electoral formula of 50 percent plus one. The passage entered the final draft constitution, but was rejected before Parliament, and Zambia was hereby back to square one on matters pertaining to meaningful participative constitution-making. The repeated parliamentary interference was heavily criticised by civil society organisations. The OASIS Forum,[9] for instance, recommended that for further processes the constitution should be withdrawn from legislative's access and, in turn, a committee of experts should be installed in order to redraft the constitution (Green 2013, 421). In the run-up to the 2011 tripartite elections, one of the biggest issues on the campaign trail was – again – the enactment of a "new people-driven constitution", and here the promise was

5 Public opinion was gathered by the Chona Constitution Review Commission.
6 The body was named after its chairman. On 22 November 1993, the commission was appointed under Statutory Instrument No. 151 of 1993 as amended by Statutory Instrument No. 173 of 1993 with the mandate to recommend a revised (constitutional) system for Zambia (Ndulo and Kent 1996, 271).
7 The Inquiries Act, which grants extensive authority and oversight functions to the president, has been applied in all constitutional review phases since 1964 in order to appoint constitutional review commissions (Motsamai 2014, 2). The government reserves the right to accept or reject all recommendations that are proposed by the commission allowing it to simply override wishes of the people (Motsamai 2014, 3). President Kaunda already applied the Inquiries Act in previous constitutional revisions in order to alter the final text according to his personal preferences.
8 The commission, named after Wila Mung'omba, was set up during Zambia's fourth constitutional review process that was initiated by President Levy Mwanawasa in 2003.
9 An umbrella group composed of diverse civil society organisations.

made by the then biggest opposition political party, the Patriotic Front, that this would be done within 90 days of being elected into office (Africa Review 2011; Lumina 2016b; Munalula 2016; Panos Institute Southern Africa (PSAf) 2016, 4).

It can be justifiably pointed out that all previous constitution-making processes, which in parts incorporated substantial elements of involving the public, fell short of producing a "new people-driven constitution". To put it differently, how can a country conduct various constitution-making processes that involve the people and yet never deliver a people-driven constitution? This paradox will continue to be the subject of the next section that addresses the most recent revision process.

The ping-pong saga of 2011–16 constitution-making process in Zambia

Compared to previous failures to revise the country's supreme law, Zambia's recent constitution-making process started optimistically in late 2011 when the Republican President, Mr Michael Chilufya Sata, appointed a 20-member Technical Committee on Drafting the Zambian Constitution (TCDZC) with the objective to draft a "new people-driven constitution". It was announced that the country would have the new document within 90 days (Africa Review 2011; Lumina 2016b; Munalula 2016; PSAf 2016, 4). Therefore, one can assume that at this point, most Zambians were convinced the newly elected Patriotic Front (PF) would deliver on their campaign's promise of enacting a "new people-driven constitution" within this timeframe. Moreover, the Patriotic Front *Manifesto 2011–2016* (2011, 42),[10] as well as the Constitution Consultative Process Guidelines (2012, 12), had envisaged the constitution to be submitted to national referendum and to be subsequently approved by the National Assembly (PASf 2016, 4; Motsamai 2014, 6). Such proceedings were indicative of the fact that a general consensus on the constitution being enacted via referendum existed throughout the nation and that the people of Zambia would, in the end, actively endorse their own constitution. It needs to be pointed out, however, that in contrast to other recent constitution-making processes – for instance, as unfolding in Zimbabwe [2013] and Tanzania [in progress][11] – Zambia's process apparently lacked a clearly defined legal framework or roadmap with regard to the adoption of the constitution. These could have provided guidance, structured the process and reduced ambiguity, for instance with regard to timeframes or the mode of adoption.[12]

---

10 It said the PF Government shall "[e]stablish in consultation with stakeholders a Committee of Experts to review the recommendations of all previous Constitutional Review Commissions in order to draft and present a constitution which will reflect the will and aspirations of the people for submission to a referendum and subsequent enactment only, by the National Assembly" (Partriotic Front 2011, 42).

11 Zimbabwe's constitution-making process was guided by the Global Political Agreement of 2006, which was signed by rivalling political factions. Tanzania's constitutional reform process was formally conducted under the Constitutional Review Act of 2011.

12 The government had rejected the need of a legal framework in order to reduce the probability of political manipulation on the grounds that other successful constitution-making processes did not have one either (Motsamai 2014, 6).

The president, in accordance with Article 2(1) of the Inquiries Act, appointed the 20 members of the TCDZC.[13] This procedure was highly disputed, for considerable authority was thereby vested in the president with exclusive appointing powers to veto or annul certain recommendations made by the commission. The mandate of the TCDZC included reviewing all the works of previous Constitution Review Commissions (CRCs) that preceding presidents had appointed. These included the Mwanakatwe Commission of 1996, appointed by late President Frederick Chiluba and the Mung'omba Commission of 2003 that was appointed by late President Levy Patrick Mwanawasa. According to the 2011 TCDZC's Terms of Reference (ToR), the Mung'omba draft constitution of 2005 was to be reviewed and used "as a basis on which to develop the new National Constitution" (Terms of Reference for TCDZC 2011, 4.1(b)). Again, this terminology implies the objective of striving for a replacement of Zambia's old Constitution. Once all the CRC reports were reviewed, the TCDZC was supposed to draft a document taking into account what the people of Zambia had addressed in all previous consultation phases.

In fulfilling its mandate, on 30 April 2012, the TCDZC prepared a first draft constitution that then served as the basis for a subsequent consultative process, and which stipulated that nationwide forums be established at communal and district level as well as conventions at province and national level (Munalula 2016; ToR for TCDZC 2011, 4.1(c)). The community consultative forums were self-organised and accessible to everybody who was willing to participate.[14] The district consultative forums, the provincial conventions as well as the National and Sector Groups Convention were more restrictive and assembled with chosen representatives at each level.[15] Thereupon, the TCDZC began to host three-day forums in the 72 districts of Zambia at which various

13 "The President may issue a commission appointing one or more commissioners to inquire into any matter in which an inquiry would, in the opinion of the President, be for the public welfare" (Inquiries Act, 2(1)).

14 These forums could be organised by various stakeholders: (a) church groups; (b) traditional councils; (c) political party structures; (d) neighbourhoods; (e) residence development committees; (f) social clubs; (g) school clubs; (h) associations; (i) neighbourhood health committees; (j) community-based organisations; (k) work places; (l) learning institutions; (m) civil society facilitator; and (n) any other institution or organisation based and operating in that community (The Constitution Consultative Process Guidelines 2012, Part II, 6(3)).

15 Representatives at district and provincial levels were either to be elected or nominated by their respective organisations/institutions or by the district and provincial facilitator, respectively, in the case of an institutional allegiance being lacking. (The Constitution Consultative Process Guidelines 2012, Part II, 12(1); Part III, 24(1). For the list of categories along which delegates were to be nominated see the Constitution Consultative Process Guidelines (2012, Part II, Part III). It was agreed that the National and Sector Groups Convention should consist of representatives of the executive, legislative, judiciary, public service, civil society, academia, traditional leaders, representatives of political parties and the industry, provinces, local authorities, retired public servants, and members of the Technical Committee (with no voting rights). The representative delegates were to be nominated by their respective institution or organisation, with consideration of equitable gender representation (The Constitution Consultative Process Guidelines 2012, 34(1)).

stakeholders had the opportunity to provide their view on the content of the draft constitution (Motsamai 2014, 5; YEZI 2013, 33). Starting in November 2012, and progressing until February 2013, provincial conventions further reinforced the participatory nature of the outreach phase. During these conventions, conducted by the TCDZC at district, provincial and national levels, many Zambians made comments on matters they believed required to be strengthened as well as those that needed to be newly introduced in the constitution to improve their lives (Motsamai 2014, 7).

These consultative platforms provided by the TCDZC proved capable of bringing together different stakeholders in order to make substantial recommendations on various clauses in the draft constitution. The most encouraging part about all these consultative processes, however, was that since the appointment of the TCDZC in late 2011, the ruling party had upheld a neutral stand with respect to how the people should decide on most issues. In other words, the executive and the ruling party in general had not taken any position on the content of the constitution and allowed Zambians to deliberate freely (YEZI 2013, 33–34). This approach was welcomed as it allowed the nation to contemplate constitutional matters without fearing that their views would be seen as being against the government position. This atmosphere changed, however, in later stages of the adoption process, which lacked meaningful public debate on the draft. The Situation Report by the Institute for Security Studies (Motsamai 2014, 6) highlights that "[p]articipation has been limited to the public consultations spearheaded by the government at drafting stages only" and that "[a]ttempts by civil society to engage citizens in public debate on the constitution have been met with stern warning of arrests from the Minister of Justice". This represents a major drawback in terms of the process' participatory nature, since the outreach phase was characterised by PF party dominance and in later stages the influence of the citizenry was limited.

During the review phase, the TCDZC informed Zambians that the final draft constitution would be attained by the end of June 2013. This deadline was welcomed by most of the stakeholders as they felt that it would provide enough time to complete the entire process in the same year. However, the committee requested a further extension due to the high number of submissions that were made during the national convention and the sector group conventions. The government rejected the request for an extension outright with Justice Minister Mr Wynter Kabimba, insisting that the committee should conclude its work in June and submit the report by the end of June.[16]

Political stalemate and government reversal

By October 2013, the government started to make indications that the final report and the draft constitution would not be simultaneously handed over to the public and the president, contrary to the position that had been taken by

16 Some stakeholders welcomed the stance taken by the justice minister as they thought that the TCDZC was attempting to delay the process without having a good justification.

the TCDZC earlier (Lusaka Voice 2013). Minister of Justice Wynter Kabimba asserted that the government would not allow the draft constitution to be handed over to the public at the same time at which the president receives his copies.[17] He further instructed the committee to print 10 copies only and to hand them over to the president (Lusaka Times 2013b). The TCDZC responded by indicating that the new government position was contrary to what the committee had promised the people of Zambia. It threatened not to sign the reports and the draft constitution if the government continued with their instructions in this manner. Nevertheless, the committee gave in and on 30 December 2013 announced that it would submit the constitution to the president alone, since the government refused to authorise further copies (Lusaka Times 2013c). This positioning was condemned by various stakeholders and led to some degree of confusion. By the end of 2013, the public was neither informed about the next steps to follow in the constitution-making process, nor was it aware of the content of the draft, as this remained a matter of secrecy and speculation. These developments, in sum, prompted the question to what extent government representatives intended such uncertainty.

In 2014, stalemate and uncertainty continued to characterise the constitution-making process and were reinforced by confusion about the whereabouts of the final draft.[18] This ambiguous state of affairs persisted until the Constitution Summit,[19] during which Mr Kabimba informed the nation that the final draft was at the Ministry of Justice (Tumfweko 2014). At this very summit, the government updated the nation on the impending roadmap for the further process, which included the cabinet approving the release of the final draft[20] and a public debate to be held on the matter thereafter. At that time, however, senior government officials continued stating on record that Zambia was not in a constitutional crisis and that the country had a functional and democratic constitution (Lusaka Times 2014c), thereby relativising calls for an urgent need of action. By the end of 2013, the Republican President Sata had already begun to refute these assertions when he stated that "Zambia does not need a new constitution but needs to

17 Kabimba made this comment with one of the daily newspapers, in which he further claimed that the committee had been appointed using the Inquiries Act and as such the president, as the appointing authority, was the only one due to receive the draft constitution and the report.
18 The TCDZC informed the nation that the preparation work of the final draft had been concluded and handed to the government (Lusaka Times 2014a), which, in turn, however, denied ever having received the document. In March 2014, the government – through the permanent secretary in the Ministry of Justice – requested the TCDZC to wind up their work and to have their offices closed by 31 March 2014. During this period, the government continued to insist that they had not received the final draft. Some of the media sources in the country reported that the final draft constitution had gone missing (Adamu 2014b).
19 The summit was held by the Southern African Centre for the Constructive Resolution of Disputes (SACCORD) in cooperation with the Friedrich Ebert Stiftung (FES) at Protea Hotels Arcades in Lusaka on 30 April 2014.
20 When the Constitution Summit was held in April 2014, the cabinet had not yet sat to approve the release of the final draft constitution to the public.

amend the current one" (Phiri 2013).[21] This can be considered a critical juncture in Zambia's constitution-making process, as it was the first time that President Sata's government publicly contemplated not to advance the promulgation of a *new* constitution.[22]

The dismissal of Mr Kabimba as the minister of justice on 28 August 2014, who many had perceived to be a stumbling block to enacting a new constitution, reinstilled confidence.[23] With the appointment of the new Minister of Justice and Secretary General of the ruling PF, Honourable Edgar Chagwa Lungu, new hope and optimism arose that the process would regain some momentum. And indeed, it seemed as if he could live up to these expectations. On 2 September 2014, following consultations he had held with the attorney general and secretary to the cabinet, he informed the nation that he was ready to meet with a consortium of civil society organisations and opposition political parties that belonged to an alliance called the Grand Coalition (Adamu 2014a).[24] Further, to the delight of many stakeholders, he released the much-awaited draft constitution to the public in October 2014 (Lusaka Times 2014d). The release, however, came against a backdrop of acrimony and conflict since until then the document had presumed to be either missing or stolen and the now delayed publication had come without any sufficient explanation. Moreover, scepticism persisted since a roadmap for enacting the new people-driven constitution through a referendum had not been made available (Lusaka Times 2014d).

After the death of President Sata in late 2014, Edgar Lungu was elected as the next president of the Republic of Zambia on 20 January 2015. During his inauguration speech, he reassured the nation that the government would adhere to its promise of enacting a people-driven constitution (Lusaka Times 2015). He immediately tasked the new Justice Minister, Dr Ngosa Symbyakula, to prioritise its enactment. Yet a framework to guide a participatory enactment process was not provided. Instead, the ruling party shifted its position on the mode of adoption and begun to exhibit reservations about holding a stand-alone referendum on the entire document. As pressure mounted to finally enact the new constitution, the government adopted a two-tier process that was originally proposed by the Young African Leaders Initiative (YALI) in 2015. YALI had formulated that the constitution should be approved by Parliament and the Bill of Rights should subsequently be subject to a referendum alongside the 2016

---

21 He made this statement in a public speech in Mansa on 30 November 2013, as reported by a correspondent of the Zambian Watchdog (Phiri 2013).
22 This position was later reinforced repeatedly and the president even ridiculed demands for a people-driven constitution, asking why people were insisting for a "people-driven constitution" as though they had ever seen an "animal-driven constitution" (Lusaka Times 2014b).
23 Excitement was linked to people's belief that the draft constitution had, in fact, not been released due to a personal rather than a party position.
24 This announcement came after the Grand Coalition meeting held at Lusaka Mulungushi International Conference Centre (MICC) on 30 August 2014 had resolved to undertake countrywide demonstrations.

general elections. This sequential adoption process was considered a temporal compromise by President Lungu since "[t]he bulk of the document, termed non-contentious provisions, would be enacted by Parliament and become effective immediately" (Munalula 2016). In terms of the participatory nature of the process, however, this proceeding at best met the minimal legal requirement for the public to be incorporated in the promulgation. According to Article 79 of the 1996 Constitution of the Republic of Zambia, Part III of the Constitution, which contains the Bill of Rights, can only be amended via referendum. The criteria for amendments to the Bill of Rights, as well as to the entrenched Amendment Clause itself, require 50 percent of eligible voters to participate in the referendum[25] and out of these a majority must be in favour of an amendment (Constitution of the Republic of Zambia 1996, Article 79(3)). Requiring half of the countries *eligible* instead of *registered* voters sets a relatively high threshold for referenda to be valid and then pass.[26]

During the course of 2015, the government took the final draft constitution to Parliament for amendments. This approach was contrary to the initial understanding that the whole draft constitution would be taken to referendum for endorsement without major modifications. This controversial government position was to some extent substantiated by the international community. Some members of the diplomatic corps in Zambia, such as the ambassador of the United States of America (USA), openly supported holding the referendum alongside the 2016 general elections, as it would be the most prudent financial decision (Zambia Daily Mail 2015; U.S. Embassy in Zambia 2016). Consecutively, the final draft constitution was subjected to parliamentary scrutiny. The government controversially used its legislative majority and the support of members of the opposition to reject some provisions that had been prepared by the TCDZC on the basis of popular consultations. "Notably, changes proposing a devolved system of governance through elected provincial assemblies, the mixed member representation electoral system, and the appointment of cabinet ministers from outside the National Assembly were rejected" (Lumina 2016b). Moreover, the legislative made substantial adjustments to the content of the final draft – contrary to people's proposals. The concentration of power in the executive branch was not resolved. On the contrary, competences of the presidency were rather enhanced under the new constitution (Goldring and Wahman 2016, 109; Ndulo 2016, 2, 5–7). According to some observers, this illustrates one of the inherent problems of constitutional legitimacy, because the government had the

25 This presupposes a popular census being held in order to determine the actual number of eligible voters in the first place.
26 Therefore, organisations such as YALI contended that the threshold could only be reached if the referendum was held alongside the 2016 general elections (presidential, legislative and local elections) as such an environment would spur adequate voter turnout. Another rationale was that such a proceeding would be more cost effective. However, many other stakeholders, such as the Civil Society Constitution Coalition (CSCC) and several political opposition parties, opposed the proposal of holding the referendum alongside the 2016 general elections.

authority to accept or reject recommendations that had been made by the people in the course of various consultative processes (Chigunta 2016).

The outcome of this Parliament-driven process was the amended Constitution No. 2 of 2016, which was approved by the necessary two-thirds parliamentary majority and subsequently assented into law by President Edgar Chagwa Lungu on 5 January 2016[27] (Goldring and Wahman 2016, 111; Munalula 2016), with the Bill of Rights and the adjusted Amendment Clause still to be approved via referendum later that year. Therefore, the recent process again fell short of delivering a people-owned document and instead brought into being yet another elite-amended constitution. The amended constitution was vigorously criticised by leading Zambian constitutional experts as having failed people's aspirations both in terms of content and process (Ndulo 2016).[28] Against this backdrop, the ensuing popular referendum was eagerly anticipated, bearing in mind a potential rejection as a consequence of this political intervention.

By invoking Article 79 of the 1996 amended Constitution, the adoption process proceeded and the referendum on the Bill of Rights and the entrenched Amendment Clause was held alongside the 2016 general elections on 11 August 2016.[29] Although the majority voted in favour of the amendment (71 percent), the proposal was rejected due to a low turnout that characterised the election at large (44 percent). Hence, the threshold requirement that 50 percent of the electorate cast their vote – a general criterion for constitutional referenda – was not met in the first place (Electoral Commission of Zambia 2016a; Lumina 2016a). One could elaborate a number of hypotheses explaining the failure of the referendum. At the end of the day, it could have been a coalescence of various factors. Cephas Lumina (2016a), for instance, points to the unfortunate timing of the referendum, the high statutory threshold, the lack of public education[30] as well as the low literacy rate (61.4 percent) among the Zambian population. Further potential explanations relate to voter apathy, the rather technical and two-fold formulation of the referendum question as well as the politicisation of the process.[31] As Lumina (2016a) emphasises, "Referendums tend to be successful in circumstances where there is bi-partisan support for proposed change". Another closely related aspect might have been the effect of no-campaigns by the political opposition and civil society organisations who

27 For a detailed analysis of specific provisions in the Constitution No. 2 of 2016 see Ndulo (2016).
28 Nevertheless, some of the progressive clauses entered the amended Constitution No. 2 of 2016, including the adoption of the 50 percent plus one electoral formula for electing the Republican president, presidential running mate, constitutional court, and provision for directly electing mayors and council chairpersons as well as dual citizenship (Munalula 2016).
29 For a presentation of some of the novelties in the Bill of Rights and the Amendment Clause see Lumina (2016b).
30 Attempts to educate voters regarding the content of or changes to the Bill of Rights and the Amendment Clause were insufficient. In order to respond to the uncertainty about the proposed changes, the Electoral Commission (2016b) published a comic. This comic was, however, published a month before the referendum and in English only (Lumina 2016b).
31 The electorate predominantly voted according to party affiliation.

had urged their supporters to boycott the referendum in order to fall short of the required voter turnout (Adamu 2016; Goldring and Wahman 2016, 114; Lumina 2016a). The most persuasive factor, however, might have been the "controversy surrounding the reform process" (Lumina 2016a) in general, which may have resulted in a lack of democratic legitimacy – reflected in the low turnout of the referendum. The outcome of the constitutional reform process highlights the odd situation of Zambia's legal system in which the country is left with a recently enacted constitution, but with a Bill of Rights that stems from 1991 (as even the 1996 constitution-making process maintained Part III of the constitution unaltered).

It can be argued that the entire constitution-making process has eventually been delegitimised in the eyes of the people who felt betrayed. Additionally, the opaque genesis of the document prompted stakeholders to claim that the government hijacked the constitution-making process in order to produce what some termed a "Patriotic Front (PF) driven" constitution (QFM Zambia 2015). Accordingly, the continuous confusion surrounding the adoption process needs to be seen in the light of a partisan strategy. The government manoeuvres that had led to such turmoil appeared to be driven by a hidden agenda as a means of delaying the process. It could be assumed that such a specific government blueprint was aimed at buying time in order to alter the modus of adoption as well as the content of the final constitutional draft. It is such interference by politics in Zambia that has repeatedly (re)captured the constitution-making process. It can be argued that constitution-making fails when the executive intervenes in such a manner, starting to decide which clauses to adopt and which ones to drop or alter, thereby undermining people's interests. Hence, the procedure in Zambia can be considered as being a prime example of utilised "false participation" (Saati 2015).

Furthermore, the developments in Zambia's recent constitutional reform process illustrate how the absence of a regulatory framework can affect the mode of adoption as well as the outcome. The conception of the envisaged constitution has shifted over time – from envisioning a "new people-driven constitution" towards accepting the "light version" of an amendment. The decision to allow the Bill of Rights and the Amendment Clause to be approved via referendum, whereas the vast amount of provisions was ratified by Parliament, merely reflects the minimal participatory requirement captured by the Amendment Clause of the 1996 Constitution. Recent experiences from Kenya [2005] illustrate how in similar instances the judiciary has intervened in order to expand the influence of the electorate within the ratification process[32] (compare the chapter by Ghai and Macharia in this volume). The decisive distinction, however, might be that Zambia, in the end, pursued a constitutional revision and did not work towards drafting a *new* document as it was originally envisaged.

---

32 In Kenya, the High Court has decided that a referendum is to be obligatory in the ratification of the constitution. Originally, a national referendum had not been envisaged.

Conclusions

The fact that Zambia has yet again failed to deliver a substantially people-driven constitution is particularly striking given the fact that the country has been undergoing constitution-making processes for some time, with the one initiated by the Patriotic Front (PF) being the fifth in Zambia's postcolonial history. All of these processes, however, have failed to enact a progressive constitution owned by the people – an ownership that has ever since been the prolonged desire of the populace.

It is the conviction of the author that undertaking a process of constitution-making while keeping an eye on the constitution in force, was one of the main factors that caused the recent constitution-making processes to fail. When the time came for the country to put in place a new and transformative constitution, leaders could refer to the country's already functioning constitution – as late President Sata claimed at the apex of demands for a new constitution (Lusaka Times 2014c). In other words, in the course of Zambia's constitution-making processes, difficulties have arisen, due to the country's reluctance to create either "power-sharing governments" or "interim constitutions" during the transition period. States such as Kenya [2010] and South Africa [1996], among others, have had to undergo a break from the status quo, in turn allowing them to put in place transformative constitutions.

A further drawback was that the process could not be separated from politics. Partisan interests and party considerations continued to play a decisive role in the drafting stage. The submissions by the people were not taken into account in a meaningful way as the executive yet again thought it appropriate to decide which provisions to accept and which ones to reject. This pattern has already occurred in previous constitutional reforms in which the executive intervened significantly. Therefore, Zambia will continue to be looked at as a country that has maintained the *status quo* and has failed to enact a "new people-driven constitution". This paradox will only ever be solved, it appears, if the government of the day will wholesomely embrace the submissions provided by the people of Zambia.

References

Adamu, P. (2016). "Hichilema Urges Supporters to Ignore Referendum", 20 July 2016, (https://zambiareports.com/2016/07/20/hichilema-urges-supporters-to-ignore-referendum/).

Adamu, P. (2014a). "Edgar Lungu Reaches Out to Oasis Forum", 2 September 2014, (https://zambiareports.com/2014/09/02/edgar-lungu-reaches-oasis-forum/).

Adamu, P. (2014b). "Comical: Draft Constitution Copies Go Missing", 10 April 2014, (https://zambiareports.com/2014/04/10/comical-draft-constitution-copies-go-missing/).

Africa Review (2011). "Zambia's President Sata Promises New Constitution in 90 days", (http://www.africareview.com/news/Zambias-Sata-promises-new-constitution-in-90-days/979180-1255828-se7x38z/index.html).

Chigunta, Francis (2016). "Perspectives on Zambia's 2016 Elections", paper presented PANOS and OSISA Public Forum on the 2016 general elections in Zambia at Taj Pamodzi Hotel in Lusaka, Zambia.

Constitution of the Republic of Zambia (1996). Government of the Republic of Zambia.

Constitution of the Republic of Zambia (2016). Government of the Republic of Zambia.

Electoral Commission of Zambia (2016a). 2016 Referendum, (https://elections.org.zm/results/2016_referendum).

Electoral Commission of Zambia (2016b). "Referendum Question: The Bill of Rights", (https://www.elections.org.zm/referendum_question.php).

Goldring, E., and Wahman, M. (2016). "Democracy in Reverse: The 2016 General Election in Zambia", in: *Africa Spectrum*, 51(3) 107–21.

Green, C. (2013). "Religious and Legal Pluralism in Recent African Constitutional Reform", in: *Journal of Law and Religion*, 28(2), 401–39.

Lumina, C. (2016a). "Zambia's Failed Constitutional Referendum: What Next?", 12 Speptember 2016, (www.constitutionnet.org/news/zambias-failed-constitutional-referendum-what-next).

Lumina, C. (2016b). "Zambia's Constitutional Referendum: More Rights, Questionable Legitimacy?", 10 August 2016, (http://www.constitutionnet.org/news/zambias-constitutional-referendum-more-rights-questionable-legitimacy).

Lusaka Times (2015). "President Edgar Lungu's inauguration Speech", (https://lusakatimes.com/2015/01/29/president-edgar-lungus-inauguration-speech/).

Lusaka Times (2013a). "Final Draft Constitution Will be Handed Over Simultaneously to the Republican President and General Public", (https://www.lusakatimes.com/2013/09/25/final-draft-constitution-will-be-handed-over-simultaneously-to-the-republican-president-and-general-public/).

Lusaka Times (2013b). "Refusing to Sign Draft Constitution Is Against Terms of Reference-Kabimba", (https://www.lusakatimes.com/2013/11/10/refusing-sign-draft-constitution-terms-reference-kabimba/).

Lusaka Times (2013c). "President Sata to Receive Final Draft Constitution Alone", (https://www.lusakatimes.com/2013/12/30/president-sata-receive-final-draft-constitution-alone/).

Lusaka Times (2014a). "Soft Copy of Draft Constitution was Kept at Ministry of Justice for Security", (https://www.lusakatimes.com/2014/01/24/soft-copy-draft-constitution-kept-ministry-justice-security/).

Lusaka Times (2014b). "Show Me an Animal Driven Constitution Before Demanding for a People Driven One-President Sata", (https://www.lusakatimes.com/2014/02/20/show-animal-driven-constitution-demanding-people-driven-one-president-sata/).

Lusaka Times (2014c). "Zambia Has a Functional Constitution-President Sata", (https://www.lusakatimes.com/2014/04/09/zambia-has-a-functional-constitution-president-sata/).

Lusaka Times (2014d). "Final Draft Constitution Finally Released, but No Road Map Presented", (https://www.lusakatimes.com/2014/10/23/final-draft-constitution-finally-released-road-map-presented/).

Lusaka Voice (2013). "Technical Committee U-Turns on Final Draft Constitution", (http://lusakavoice.com/2013/09/26/technical-committee-u-turns-final-draft-constitution/).

Motsamai, D. (2014). "Zambia Constitution-Making Process: Addressing the Impasse and Future Challenges", Institute for Security Studies, Situation Report, January 2014, (http://dspace.africaportal.org/jspui/bitstream/123456789/34223/1/SitRep2014_15Jan_2.pdf).

Munalula, M. M. (2016). "The 2016 Constitution of Zambia: Elusive Search for a People Driven Process", (http://www.constitutionnet.org/news/2016-constitution-zambia-elusive-search-people-driven-process).

Ndulo, M., and Kent, R. B. (1996). "Constitutionalism in Zambia: Past, Present and Future", *Cornell Law Faculty Publications*, Paper 64, 256–78.

Ndulo, M. (2016). "Zambia's Unfulfilled Struggle for a New Constitution: Comments on the 2016 Constitution", Southern African Institute for Policy and Research, Discussion Paper Series No. 1, 4 April 2016.

Panos Institute Southern Africa (PSAf) (2016). *The Quest for a People Driven Constitution in Zambia, 2011–2015*, Grand Coalition on the Campaign for a People Driven Constitution in Zambia.

Patriotic Front (2011). *Manifesto 2011–2016*, Produced by the Office of the Secretary General and approved by the Central Committee of the Party.

Phiri, D. (2013). "Zambia Does Not Need New Constitution – Says Sata", Zambian Watchdog, 30 November 2013, (https://www.zambiawatchdog.com/zambia-does-not-need-new-constitution-says-sata/).

QFM Zambia. "Zambia to Have a PF Driven Constitution?", (http://www.qfmzambia.com/2015/12/02/zambia-to-have-a-pf-driven-constitution/).

Saati, A. (2015). *The Participation Myth: Outcomes of Participatory Constitution Building Processes on Democracy*, Umeå University, Department of Political Science, Research Report 2015: 1.

Simutanyi, Neo (2012). "The Politics of Constitutional Reform in Zambia: From Executive Dominance to Public Participation?", in: D. M. Chirwa and L. Nijzink (eds.), *Accountable Government in Africa. Perspectives from Public Law and Political Studies*, United Nations University Press, Tokyo, New York, Paris, 26–42.

Terms of Reference for the Technical Committee on Drafting the Zambian Constitution (2011). (https://wiredproject316.files.wordpress.com/2011/11/terms-of-reference.pdf).

Tumfweko (2014). "Kabimba Ends Speculation on Draft Constitution 'PF Will Not Doctor Draft Constitution'", (https://tumfweko.com/2014/05/01/kabimba-ends-speculation-on-draft-constitution-pf-will-not-doctor-draft-constitution/).

U.S. Embassy in Zambia (2016). "Transcript of Ambassador Schultz and U.S. Deputy Assistant Secretary of State Haskell", Press Avail, 6 April 2016, (https://zm.usembassy.gov/ambassador-and-das-interview-after-epd/).

van Vliet, M. (2009). "The Politics of Constitutional Reform Processes in Zambia", in: *Writing Autobiographies of Nations: A Comparative Analysis of Constitutional Reform Processes*, NIMD Knowledge Centre, The Hague, The Netherlands, 38–58.

YEZI Consulting & Associates (2013). *Political Governance Study in Zambia*, Lusaka, March 2013.

Zambia Daily Mail (2015). "Referendum costly – US envoy", 28 April 2015, (https://www.daily-mail.co.zm/?p=27577).

9 Public participation under authoritarian rule

The case of Zimbabwe

Douglas Togaraseyi Mwonzora

Introduction

On 29 March 2008, President Robert Mugabe, who hitherto had dominated Zimbabwean politics since independence, lost the first round of presidential election to Morgan Tsvangirai of the Movement for Democratic Change (MDC-T).[1] The period preceding the presidential run-off election can be described as one of the bloodiest in Zimbabwe's post-independence history. State agents and militia loyal to Mugabe openly waged a violent campaign against the MDC, and in the process murdered over 300 (MDC-T) supporters (US Department of State 2009). Fearing for his life, Tsvangirai escaped to neighbouring Botswana before completely withdrawing from the race due to the violence that unfolded (McGrael 2008). Not surprisingly, the international community – in particular the Southern African Development Community (SADC) and the African Union – condemned the elections. Through the mediation of former South African President Thabo Mbeki, the international community put pressure on Mugabe to enter into a power sharing agreement with his main rivals Morgan Tsvangirai of the MDC-T and Professor Arthur Mutambara of the MDC-M.[2] This arrangement culminated in the signing of the Global Political Agreement (GPA), which led to the establishment of a Government of National Unity (GNU) on 15 September 2008. A key requirement from both MDC formations was the promulgation of a new democratic and people-driven constitution of Zimbabwe. In the inclusive government that was created as a result, Mugabe retained the presidency while Tsvangirai and Mutambara became prime minister and deputy prime minister respectively.

Although the parties shared cabinet posts equitably, the bureaucracy, the army, police and intelligence, which were hitherto made up of Mugabe's appointees, remained intact under Mugabe's control. Moreover, the president continued to assign key political positions (permanent secretaries, the reserve bank governor,

---

1 It is widely believed that the Zimbabwe Electoral Commission (ZEC), headed by a former top military officer appointed by Mugabe, had manipulated the results in order to force a presidential run-off election on 27 June 2008 (Makumbe 2009, 131; Tendi 2013).
2 After the 2005 Senate election, the MDC split into two factions. The MDC-T was led by Morgan Tsvangirai and the MDC-M by Arthur Mutambara.

DOI: 10.4324/9781315180540-12

the attorney general, provincial governors etc.) without consultation with the other parties to the Global Political Agreement (Ndulo 2010, 181). Accordingly, despite a Government of National Unity having been formed, Zimbabweans largely remained under authoritarian rule, consolidated by the predominance of the executive branch headed by Mugabe.

This politically unstable climate was moreover characterised by the state's repressive grip on the political opposition and civil society. Against this backdrop, the constitution-making process in Zimbabwe was not embedded in an environment conducive for meaningful constitutional change. This contribution aims to illustrate the challenges that diverse actors who were involved in constitution making faced throughout the process. They needed to adapt to adverse conditions, which involved anticipating impending interference. It is argued that where the authoritarian state is dragged into a constitution-making endeavour – often as a result of rising public demand – it tries to retain as much of a grip as possible on the process. Moreover, channels of interference are built in order to delay or even discredit the work of constitution makers. The incorporation of participatory elements is even more difficult given the conditions of repression. In the Zimbabwe process, the regime effectively distorted the consultation phase by orchestrating violence, supressing alternative views and by bussing Zanu (PF) supporters to various venues across the country. In spite of this interference, a sufficient degree of meaningful public input via civil society engagement could be observed. Although large stages of the process were driven by the political elite in Zimbabwe, the substantial outcome is considered to boldly reflect people's views.

The article is structured following the chronological order of events. First, a brief constitutional history of post-independence Zimbabwe is provided. In a next step, the legal framework in which the process was embedded is analysed. In the sections thereafter, attention is turned to its implementations. A focus is put on the mechanisms that were applied to ensure public participation and on the tactics of interference by the authoritarian state apparatus, paying close attention to the distinct roles of different actors. Subsequently, the drafting process, which was characterised by party bargaining as well as political stalemates during large parts of the negotiations, is illustrated and analysed. The final section is dedicated to the Second All Stakeholders Conference and the national referendum, that were both envisioned to ensure that the public has decisive influence on the outcome.

A brief constitutional history of post-independence Zimbabwe

In the years following independence in 1980, Zimbabwe was governed by the Lancaster House Constitution (LHC),[3] which was widely regarded as a ceasefire agreement that retained the political, social and economic injustices of the colonial period – especially with respect to land ownership and white predominance

---

3 The LHC was negotiated between representatives of the ceasing colonial regime and a small national political elite at Lancaster House in London from 10 September to 21 December 1979.

in general (Nyabeze 2015, 1). Most of the 18 amendments that were made to the constitution between 1980 and 2007 – no less than 11 in the first decade[4] – were designed to extend executive powers and to entrench Mugabe's rule (Sachikonye 2011, 5–7; Panfil 2012, 25). This development led to the establishment of a *de facto* one-party state in Zimbabwe. Other amendments were designed to grant the ruling elite special economic privileges, especially access to land and minerals. The most prominent examples were the abolition of minority seats in Parliament that were reserved for the white population, the dissolution of the post of the prime minister, and the Constitutional Amendment No. 17 of 2005 that aimed at redressing colonial grievances by nationalising land without compensation and without mechanisms to legally challenge the state's action in this regard (IDEA 2016).

In 1997, however, Zimbabweans represented by civic society, especially by the National Constitutional Assembly (NCA),[5] started clamouring for a new democratic and people-driven Constitution of Zimbabwe (ZESN 2013, 4). These calls for a new legal framework can be considered a reaction to the growing executive dominance vis-à-vis other government branches (Hatchard 2001, 210; Dzinesa 2012, 2–3; Panfil 2012, 25).

As a result, in 1999, President Mugabe reacted to these rising demands from civil society and launched a constitution-making process. Using his powers under the Commissions of Inquiry Act, Mugabe appointed a Constitutional Commission headed by the then Judge President of the High Court Godfrey Chidyausiku, who was also a member of his party (Hatchard 2001, 210). The commission was tasked to collect the views of the citizenry on the constitution and to present both their findings as well as the resultant draft constitution to the president himself. Despite having applied a selection mechanism that allowed for an executive-oriented composition of the Constitutional Commission and the fact that the commission had apparently been dominated by the Zanu (PF) party stance, President Mugabe was not satisfied with the presented outcome and adjusted it accordingly (Hatchard 2001, 213). Not surprisingly, in the constitutional referendum in 2000, Zimbabweans overwhelmingly rejected the commission's draft constitution.

Since society's demand for a new supreme law had not been met by the state's political elite, the struggle towards a legitimate constitution continued. The resumption of the constitution-making process began in earnest after the signing of the power sharing agreement between Zanu (PF) and the two MDC factions, following the highly contested 2008 presidential elections. A substantial part of this Global Political Agreement (GPA) was dedicated to providing a mechanism through which to reformulate the country's supreme law, with significant involvement of the citizenry.

---

4 The vast amount of fundamental constitutional amendments made to the LHC in a short period of time could hint to its limited degree of legitimacy in the eyes of the national political elite.
5 The NCA was an amalgamation of diverse civil society organisations and individual civic representatives committed to foster a transparent and people-driven constitution-making process.

It has to be noted, however, that civil society organisations (CSOs) had little influence on the process, which was highly partisan and dominated by political parties (Ndlovu-Gatsheni 2010; Panfil 2012, 27; Zembe and Masunda 2015, 35). Therefore, it can be argued that the constitution-making process was initiated by Zimbabwe's political elite (Saati 2015, 147). However, some civil society organisations raised concerns about it being a manifestly politically dominated process. Some boycotted the political-party-led initiative and ran parallel programmes aimed at kick-starting a constitution-making process of their own. In July 2009, the NCA, for instance, established the "Take Charge" initiative that advocated and developed an alternative approach towards the drafting of a new constitution for Zimbabwe (Dzinesa 2012, 6; Saati 2015, 146–47).

The constitution-making endeavour can be subdivided into four distinct stages. First, in the preparatory phase, the guiding constitutional body was set up. This Parliamentary Select Committee on the Constitution (COPAC) was made up of elected members of Parliament, appointed by their political parties on the basis of representation in the bicameral legislature (ZESN 2013, 3). Subsequently, the First All Stakeholders Conference was held, *inter alia*, to ensure the incorporation of civil society actors into the process. Subsequently, general preparations as well as funding of the programme were organised prior to initiating the public consultations. The public consultations were conducted and supervised by COPAC and constituted the second stage of the process. It encompassed all efforts to accomplish a highly representative, inclusive, open as well as transparent process with the objective of reaching out to the populace. Third, in a negotiating and drafting stage, the wide spectrum of public input was collected, evaluated, bargained and debated among political party representatives before being translated into the legal text. While the first two phases exposed a stronger integration of the citizenry, the latter can be labelled as rather expert- or elite-driven with only major political parties participating and civil society largely being excluded. Finally, the drafting stage paved the way for a newly elaborated constitution for Zimbabwe, which, however, still needed to be approved via public referendum. Thus, the final authority again vested in the hands of the people, as a public referendum was the requirement for constitutional approval.

Legal framework outlining the constitution-making process

After the Global Political Agreement was signed on 15 September 2008, it was presented to Parliament to be promulgated into law as Constitutional Amendment No. 19. Article 6 of the GPA provided for the crafting of a new constitution of Zimbabwe. It can thus be asserted that for the first time in the state's history the force of law legally consolidated the constitution-making process. With regard to the participatory nature of that process, the GPA acknowledges the "fundamental right and duty of the Zimbabwean people to make a constitution by themselves and for themselves" (GPA 2008, Article 6). Moreover, the article clearly provides that the process "must be owned and driven by the people and must be inclusive and democratic" in its nature. It further required the state to create conditions to enable the public to participate in the process. The resultant constitution should deepen "democratic values and principles and the protection of the equality of all citizens, particularly the enhancement of full citizenship and equality of women".

Concerning the involvement of constitutional bodies, Article 6 of the GPA provides for the establishment of the Parliamentary Select Committee on the Constitution (COPAC). When the committee was appointed by the House of Assembly on 12 April 2009, it counted a total of 25 members. Ten seats were assigned to Zanu (PF), 11 to MDC-T and three to MDC-M, in line with their respective representation in Parliament. The remaining seat was reserved for a representative of the Traditional Chiefs Council who was a Zanu (PF) party member (Zembe and Masunda 2015, 27). In terms of gender representation, 17 men and eight women were on the committee (Dzinesa 2012, 5; IDEA 2016).

In order to effectively conduct its programme, COPAC was empowered to establish sub-committees "as may be necessary to assist the Select Committee in performing its mandate" (GPA 2008, Article 6.1(a)(i)). Moreover, the article provides for an active involvement of civil society, especially in the form of participation in the sub-committees. Such a committee, however, could only be chaired by members of Parliament, cutting back on the influence of civil stakeholders to some degree. In practice, COPAC set up five sub-committees[6] and a total of 17 distinct thematic committees tasked to deal with different constitutional matters. These had a membership of 40 people each and simultaneously worked to prepare the public outreach programme as well as the analysis of its results. Political party delegates that also chaired these committees made up 30 percent of its members, while civil society represented 70 percent and had the deputy chair in each of these sub-committees. Further, 70 outreach teams of 16 members each travelled to the various regions of the country to conduct the consultation of the populace (Vollan 2013, 33; Zembe and Masunda 2015, 29).

With regard to the conception of the public outreach programme, COPAC was obliged by law to hold public meetings and consultations as they deemed necessary (GPA 2008, Article 6.1(a)(ii)). On this particular point, the framework was rather vague, leaving COPAC with a wide scope of interpreting the legal text. Before the commencement of the outreach programme COPAC was supposed to convene the First All Stakeholders Conference, *inter alia*, for purposes of consulting distinct stakeholders on their representation in the sub-committees. The constitution would only be drafted after the public consultation process had taken place. A Second All Stakeholders Conference would be held for purposes of verifying the degree to which the draft constitution corresponded with the views of Zimbabweans as expressed during the public consultation process. After this rigmarole, the draft constitution would be subject to a public referendum (GPA 2008, Article 6.1 (c)(viii)).

---

6 (1) Budget and Finance; (2) Human Resources; (3) Stakeholders; (4) Information and Publicity; (5) Legal (Zembe and Masunda 2015, 27).

Explicit timelines within which the process should be completed were provided by the GPA as well. Accordingly, the whole endeavour was supposed to take no longer than 20 months from the date of inception of the Government of National Unity and by 2010 Zimbabwe was supposed to have a new constitution (GPA 2008, Article 6.1(c)(viii)).

For the sake of completeness, it needs to be mentioned that the Referendum Act of 2000, chapter 2, that was originally enforced in the run-up to the 2000 constitutional referendum, regulated issues pertaining to national referendums in Zimbabwe. Furthermore, the Referendums Regulations (Statutory Instrument 26, 2013) had been passed by the Zimbabwe Electoral Commission (ZEC) with the approval of the minister of Constitutional and Parliamentary Affairs and were gazetted shortly before the 2013 Referendum, complementing the Referendums Act (ZESN 2013, 7). A simple majority of the votes cast was the requirement for a constitutional draft to pass in a referendum, which was designed in a binary fashion (Yes or No).

In sum, the GPA provided a legal framework for the incorporation of participatory mechanisms in Zimbabwe's constitution-making process. The intention of the drafters can be regarded as determined to ensure full and meaningful participation of the citizenry in all major stages of constitution making. Representatives of civil society indeed could occasionally shape and determine the events in this process despite the destructive agendas initiated by Zanu (PF).

The First All Stakeholders Conference

In accordance with regulations captured in the GPA, the First All Stakeholders Conference was scheduled for 13–14 July 2009, three months after the establishment of the Select Committee. In the run-up to the conference, massive resistance from Zanu (PF) could be observed, with party officials incomprehensibly arguing that they were not ready for it to start. When the argument for postponement was defeated in COPAC, they spoke out against the involvement of civil society representatives on the basis that civil society organisations were mainly pro-MDC. Following this logic, Zanu (PF) officials would have been "outnumbered" at the conference. Thereupon, party representatives demanded that if civil society organisations participate, some organisations like the War Veteran Association – which is regarded as a reserve army in Zimbabwe – should equally be granted participation to the conference (Mhanda 2011).

A total of 4,000 delegates, mostly representing civil society, were invited to the First All Stakeholders Conference. Although COPAC invited all principals of the GPA to the opening ceremony of the conference, only Mutambara and Tsvangirai of the two MDC factions turned up, while Mugabe refused to come. As the conference was about to start, hordes of Zanu (PF) youths bussed from the surrounding farms stormed the conference room, throwing water bottles and other missiles at COPAC members as well as other officials, completely disrupting the proceedings. They shouted that the process should not proceed because it was part of MDC-T's regime change agenda. Some of Mugabe's top ministers openly supported the disrupting mobs. The proceedings had to be abandoned (Shaw 2009). Considering the manner in which the event unfolded, it is hard to deny that Mugabe had most likely not turned up because he was aware of the impending violence.

Members of civil society, however, led by the International Socialist Organisation, refused to vacate the venue and insisted on proceeding with the conference. In the end, the meeting proceeded as scheduled the following day. Its main achievement was the formation of 17 distinct thematic committees which were important for determining the content of the constitution. In all constitution committees, 50 percent of the members had to be women. It was also resolved that in all constitutional committees, civil society representatives would constitute 70 percent of each committee while MPs would form the other 30 percent (Zembe and Masunda 2015, 28). Further, it was agreed that COPAC committees would enlist public views through a transparent public outreach process.

Considering the events in the wake of the First All Stakeholders Conference, it becomes clear that the authoritarian state embodied by Zanu (PF) was bent on hindering genuine public participation in the process. They were defeated, however, by the resolve displayed by the public represented by civil society.

The public outreach process

Succeeding the First All Stakeholders Conference, the Select Committee started the process of preparing for the public outreach phase.

Clearly the Zimbabwean state was not financially prepared for the constitution-making process. The Ministry of Finance submitted a budget of 1 million US dollars for the entire constitutional reform process, which would serve only as a fractional amount of the funding needed to set up an efficient programme (Dzinesa 2012, 6). Thus, COPAC naturally sought to engage the donor community. By opposing this proposal, Zanu (PF) found another excuse to impede the programme. Party representatives argued vehemently against a donor-funded process, insisting that it would compromise the country's sovereignty. Moreover, they argued that donor funding would open the process for manipulation by the donor community that predominantly consisted of Western nations. The other parties found nothing wrong with donor funding and the bickering went on for weeks, thus delaying the outreach programme.

The principals reacted by setting up the Management Committee, which would supervise the work of COPAC. The Management Committee was made up of government ministers who had been the key negotiators of the GPA. Through the Management Committee, it was agreed that donor funding would be sought on the condition that individual donors would contribute their resources to a basket fund administered by the United Nations Development Programme (UNDP). The donors agreed to this arrangement on the condition that a special body, known as the Project Board, was established. It was made up of representatives of the donor community, the co-chairpersons of COPAC as well as the members of the Management Committee. The Project Board would receive and approve budgets from COPAC. Moreover, they would receive progress reports from COPAC on the status of the process (UNDP 2009). In financial terms, the UNDP had offered to provide more than 20 million US dollars to fund the reform process in Zimbabwe (Dzinesa 2012, 6).

In another effort to obstruct public outreach, President Mugabe and Zanu (PF) sought to reintroduce a constitutional version that had been drafted by the representatives of the political parties on a boat on Lake Kariba in 2007. This draft had become known as the Kariba Draft.[7] The other parties argued that the reintroduction of the Kariba Draft would fall short of the provisions laid out in Article 6 of the GPA, as it would convert the process into an elitist enterprise. In the end, the Kariba Draft was rejected as official point of departure. However, Zanu (PF) would later embark on a process of coaching its members and the public to simply parrot the provisions of the Kariba Draft in an effort to reproduce it "*via the outreach*" process.

The outreach programme that was designed to enlist the views of the public eventually began in June 2010, more than a year after the establishment of COPAC.[8] A total of 70 teams – each composed of 16 multi-stakeholder representatives and technical staff – were deployed to the country's 10 provinces. Each team was co-chaired by parliamentarians from the three political parties. In sum, 4,943 public meetings were lined up throughout the country in order to collect 1,118,760 views of the people on constitutional matters (Zembe and Masunda 2015, 29). The public media, as well as locally active stakeholders such as political parties, were encouraged to publicise the meetings for the benefit of their members as well as for the public in general.

Role of the national broadcaster

In Zimbabwe, most public broadcasters are known for their pro-Zanu (PF) media policy and coverage (Dzinesa 2012, 11). At the commencement of the outreach programme, the national broadcaster – the Zimbabwe Broadcasting Corporation, which was completely controlled by Zanu (PF) – started attacking the process by labelling it a complete waste of money. Further, they insisted that it was simply part of a Western-sponsored regime change agenda. Various scholars and "experts" were given enormous airtime to denigrate the programme. Therefore, it can be considered obvious that the authoritarian regime sought to impede the programme, seeking to foster people's disapproval of the outreach process by spreading hostility. Moreover, radio contributions were designed to incite violence against COPAC. When COPAC sought to engage the services of the national broadcaster in advertising its outreach campaign, it was deliberately charged abnormally high and prohibitive rates, while the Zanu (PF) programmes denigrating the process were aired for free on the national broadcaster.

---

7 For a critical analysis of the content of the Kariba Draft see, Zimbabwe Independent 2009.
8 The GPA had envisaged a timespan of seven months after the erection of the Select Committee for the outreach phase to be completed.

In one instance, in spite of COPAC having paid the invoiced fees, exorbitant as they were, the public broadcaster failed to air the notices of public meetings in Harare, an area perceived to be an MDC stronghold. As will be illustrated below, the national broadcaster maintained its hostile stance throughout the drafting process.

Role of the security services

The security services which include the army, police and intelligence agencies – who alongside the Zanu (PF) militia had violently suppressed the opposition in the presidential run-off election – played an active but destructive role in the public outreach programme. Their teams were deployed to the countryside to intimidate local communities and to prevent them from participating actively in the process (Zembe and Masunda 2015, 34; Dzinesa 2012, 6). Moreover, they instructed communities on what to say or not to say during public meetings with the COPAC teams. In most instances, they would choose the people in advance who would then speak on behalf of the local communities during the public consultation meetings (Zembe and Masunda 2015, 34). Further, they threatened to unleash the same violence they had unleashed upon people during the presidential run-off elections, should anybody disobey them. COPAC teams were thus surprised that in a meeting attended by approximately 2,000 people, only five would speak on behalf of the entire gathering.[9]

Role of war veterans and the Zanu (PF) militia

The war veterans and the Zanu (PF) militia worked closely with the security services to suppress meaningful public participation in the public outreach program. In areas dominated by the MDC, hundreds of members of the Zanu (PF) youth brigade and war veterans would be bussed from different areas in order to "flood" the area in question and disrupt the meetings. In some cases, these groups would unleash violence on the local people with the tacit approval of the police. Thousands of Zimbabweans, mainly MDC supporters, were beaten while some were even murdered during the process, as was the case in a public meeting in Harare (Zembe and Masunda 2015, 33; Human Rights Watch 2011).

Role of the traditional leaders

In rural areas, all traditional leaders were obliged to force-march people to the outreach meetings for purposes of reinforcing what was thought to be the Zanu (PF) position. As they played a central role in the distribution of food aid as well as agricultural inputs, they threated to deny these important items to anybody who did not parrot the Zanu (PF) position (Manyukwe 2010).

9 Witnessed by the author.

Role of international actors

The violence unleashed by Zanu (PF) during the public consultation programme completely outraged SADC as well as the donor community. SADC brought diplomatic pressure to bear on Mugabe while donors, through the Project Board, threatened to withdraw their funding. Anticipating violence surrounding the Second All Stakeholders Conference, the UNDP Fund, for instance, withdrew its total funds of 2 million US dollars (Zembe and Masunda 2015, 34). Further, donors refused to pay for the services of the Zimbabwe Broadcasting Corporation. The nature of this interference demonstrates the positive role that the international donor community can play when addressing political violence. Faced with the brutality of the authoritarian regime, both COPAC and civil society devised ways to ensure more meaningful public participation throughout the process.

Role of civil society organisations

Major civil society organisations made it clear that despite the signs of constitutional reform, the process could not be left solely in the hands of political parties. Thus, they formed an umbrella body called the Independent Constitution Monitoring Project (ZZZICOMP),[10] *inter alia*, for purposes of monitoring the public outreach process.

Further, civil society organisations initiated a massive awareness programme meant to motivate Zimbabweans to participate in the consultation phase. Not surprisingly, ZZZICOMP subsequently became a target of the militia, police and the secret service – their harassment, in turn, evoking public outrage. In close cooperation with the Zimbabwe Lawyers for Human Rights (ZLHR), COPAC issued letters of authority to all civil society groups involved in the monitoring programme. In these letters, they advised law enforcement agents that ZZZICOMP and its members were part of the constitution-making process and were allowed to carry out the constitution awareness programmes.

By monitoring the public outreach process, ZZZICOMP periodically reported, *inter alia*, on the levels of violence and other malpractices in public meetings. On its part, COPAC agreed to hold weekly briefings with civil society and media representatives during the programme. Much to the chagrin of the authoritarian state, COPAC emphasised that the revelations by ZZZICOMP would be included in COPAC's report on the process and be addressed to Parliament. The presence and monitoring function of civil society, as well as its cooperation with COPAC in the course of the programme, can be considered one of the game changers in the process that challenged the authoritarian state apparatus by revealing its practices. All violence, intimidation, harassment and other malpractices that were committed by militia and state agents was exposed by civil

---

10 ZZZICOMP was initiated by separate civil society organisations, namely the Zimbabwe Lawyers for Human Rights (ZLHR), the Zimbabwe Election Support Network (ZESN), and the Zimbabwe Peace Project (ZPP).

society (Meerkotter 2012). These activities certainly acted as deterrence and ensured more meaningful public participation.

COPAC's efforts to ensure public participation

Apart from effective engagement with civil society, COPAC devised a few more methods to maximise public participation. First, COPAC embarked on a public awareness campaign that emphasised the need for public participation. Billboards were erected in major cities encouraging people of all races, ages and sexes to actively participate in the outreach programme. Additionally, COPAC sponsored drama groups to motivate people to participate. Second, in line with the inclusivity principle, COPAC ensured that in the distinct committees, all major political parties were represented and that these co-chaired the committees. This inclusiveness can be described as having had a motivational effect for the citizenry, in the sense that people saw hitherto antagonistic political parties working together on the programme. This unified process helped to alleviate fear on the part of the public.

In order to avoid the occurrence of violence in public meetings and in parallel to the monitoring function exercised by civil society organisations, COPAC instructed all meetings to be audio and video recorded. No voting was allowed at the meetings. People were rather encouraged to record their views by writing small notes which could be handed to the COPAC teams present. These "little notes" formed an integral part of the report on the meetings. Likewise, institutions including civil society were encouraged to make written submissions to COPAC on their areas of interest.

In order to reach out to a wider public, COPAC deployed alternative mechanisms to collect people's views as well. Through a special internet platform, Zimbabweans in the diaspora were able to contribute their views online. These were captured, recorded and stored. Further, because of the highly physical nature of public outreach, COPAC devised a separate outreach programme exclusively for disabled people. Special facilities were made available in order for people with disabilities to participate meaningfully in the programme. Through two additional fora, the Children's Parliament and the Children Summit, COPAC collected the views of children on the constitution. Methodologically, children were addressed in form of various game plays, in which they had to solve distinct problems. Their behaviour in distinct situations was then taken as input that helped COPAC to address and emphasise the special needs of a child in constitutional provisions (Saati 2015, 147; COPAC 2011, 4).

Considering all these efforts by COPAC, one can conclude that the committee vehemently aspired to facilitate such participatory mechanisms that accommodated the views of all groups of society. This variety of constitutional proposals assigned an inclusive and representative character to the whole process. Against this backdrop, it was very important to COPAC that all views would be recorded and stored. The committee had invested heavily in modern equipment to record and preserve all the views. According to the UNDP, a total of 4,821 public meetings to collect people's views were held. A total of about 1.2 million Zimbabweans interacted with the COPAC outreach teams, and 51 organisations made institutional submissions, while 2,397 electronic submissions were made by Zimbabweans in the diaspora. The demographic group that participated least were the youth who constituted less than 18 percent of the participants.

The drafting process

At the end of the outreach phase, COPAC found itself with a 10,000-page labyrinth of data made up of views gathered during public meetings. These included views gathered from the public consultations, including the small notes written during the public outreach meetings, institutional, diaspora and children's submissions as well as submissions from people with disabilities. Through multi-party thematic committees, this data was summarised into one document called the National Report. Based on this National Report, COPAC developed 26 constitutional principles that were to act as a moral compass in the drafting of the constitution. These addressed, *inter alia*, the recognition of the separation of powers, the rule of law, human rights, the principle of decentralisation, the devolution of power, wealth sharing, minority rights and the status of traditional leadership.[11]

Thereafter, COPAC established a committee of 15 legal experts with each party seconding five experts of its choice. The main task of this committee was to act as an advisory body to COPAC in the compilation of the documents to be used by the drafters. It soon dawned on COPAC that while it had tried to be as comprehensive as possible during the outreach phase, people generally answered the question of "*what*" they would like to see installed in a new constitution, but did not deal with the question of "*how*" to implement these proposals. COPAC agreed to use the committee of 15 multiparty-seconded experts to fill those gaps by looking at what was "*world best practice*". The resultant document would be presented to COPAC for endorsement (COPAC 2012, 5).

Through consensus within itself, and subject to the ratification of the Management Committee, COPAC appointed a team of three professional drafters. To avoid distraction by the militia and state security agents, the actual drafting process was done at a secret location. In an apparent move to put pressure on the drafters, as soon as drafting commenced, Zanu (PF) started to intensify its campaign against the constitution-making process through the national broadcaster. The state-controlled Zimbabwe Broadcasting Corporation is commonly known for their political interference overwhelmingly favouring the Zanu (PF) stance (Freedom House 2013).

After the production of the first draft constitution, serious contention erupted between Zanu (PF) and MDC representatives in COPAC over the content of the draft. MDC basically sought to defend the draft while Zanu (PF) advocated to change the draft according to their preferences, irrespective of whether it was drawn from the national data or not. Zanu (PF) sought to

11 For the list of all 26 guiding principles see The Zimbabwean (2012).

retain as many clauses of the old constitution as possible while the MDC opted for more revolutionary changes to the old constitution. After earnest negotiations, a second draft was produced in April 2012, which COPAC submitted to the political parties. Zanu (PF), however, demanded 265 changes to the draft which itself was 133 pages long. Most of these changes were designed to ensure the introduction of as many elements of the Kariba Draft as possible, triggering another round of exhaustive negotiations between the parties. This negotiation process became a serious contestation for power between the MDC formations and Zanu (PF), in which a lot of compromises were made between the political parties. For example, although the clause providing for presidential term limits was retained, it was agreed that the same should not have a retroactive effect so that it would not apply to President Mugabe. This compromise was forged despite the fact that Zimbabweans had taken a different stand according to the national data. Eventually, a final draft was produced on 18 July 2012, after another round of protracted negotiations involving the Management Committee. This draft was then referred to the Second All Stakeholders Conference for discussion.

As stated above, the negotiation process was confined only to the major political parties of the Inclusive Government. Civil society and smaller political parties, who hitherto had been part of the constitution-making process, were effectively excluded in the drafting and negotiating phase of the process. At this point it has to be stressed, however, that small and technocratic-oriented drafting bodies, which can rely on in-depth legal expertise, bear significant advantages and are considered more effective than larger drafting forums (Brandt et al. 2011, 29). Further, the political parties were, in their negotiations, well aware that the draft would still need to be taken to referendum. In this regard aware of the centrality of the land question, the MDC was careful not to be seen as opposed to expropriation of land for redistribution to the landless black majority. It thus predicated its stance on the need to provide adequate compensation and de-racialise the land issue. It is clear that this sobering thought kept the parties within certain parameters, in line with Jon Elster's (1995, 373–75) logic of a downstream constrain imposed by actors that are involved in a later stage of the process.

The Second All Stakeholders Conference (SASC) and the national referendum

The SASC was arranged in order to analyse the elaborated draft and ensure its consistency with the views of the people as summarised in the national data. It was held from 21–23 October 2012 with 1,400 civil society and political party representatives attending (Zembe and Masunda 2015, 27). The thematic committees, made up of members of civil society and members of Parliament, were reconvened for this purpose. Towards the convening of the SASC, Zanu (PF) sponsored one of its officials to seek a court interdict in order to stop COPAC from convening the conference. Within one week he took COPAC's co-chairpersons to court on three different occasions. Fortunately for the programme, his matters were dismissed by the courts. The SASC gave the draft constitution a seal of approval.

After the SASC, COPAC advocated for more time to take the document to the people before referendum. President Mugabe, however, set a date which was only three weeks from the date of publication of the final draft.[12] As usual, civil society analysed the draft and produced a summary of the constitutional content. Although they had certain misgivings, they generally certified that the constitution reflected people's views. The two major political parties, Zanu (PF) and MDC, urged their members to endorse the draft. This synergy can be regarded as an absolute novelty in the country's political history, especially when considering the political animosity that had characterised the rules of conduct between these two parties for over a decade. To everyone's surprise, the national broadcaster toned down its anti-constitution mantra and started to support the draft as well. Awaiting the referendum, representatives of COPAC toured the country in order to campaign for a "Yes" vote. COPAC in particular incorporated the use of social media to promote the draft.

It has to be noted, however, that there was some resistance against the constitutional draft as well. Civil society organisations, especially the NCA, led a "vote No" campaign, in particular criticising the short time period in advance of the referendum. According to the Zimbabwe Election Support Network (ZESN), this no-campaign had an effect of raising awareness for the referendum, thus motivating more people to cast their vote at the referendum poll (ZESN 2013, 17).

In the end, 95 percent of the voters approved the constitution. This outcome was historic in the sense that it was the first time that Zimbabweans voted "Yes" in a referendum at all. The sudden change of mind by Zanu (PF) to support the draft may be explained by the people's massive national excitement about the constitution.

Conclusion

The Zimbabwean case clearly exposes the challenges a constitution-making process faces when operating in an environment that is characterised by authoritarian structures. Precautionary measures such as the secrecy of drafting locations, the precise monitoring of all meetings, the firmness in light of repressive mechanisms as well as physical violence are tactics that need to be considered in this context when progressing towards constitutional renewal.

The Zimbabwean experience confirms that an authoritarian state would want to control and manipulate the process as far as possible. However, the provision of a sound legal framework for the constitution-making process made the process less susceptible to blatant manipulation by the state. The key stages such

---

12 The GPA had originally envisaged to hold the referendum "within 3 months of the conclusion of the debate [in Parliament]" (GPA 2009, Article 6.1(c)(viii)).

as the First All Stakeholders Conference, the outreach process, the Second All Stakeholders Conference as well as the referendum ensured meaningful public participation in the process. Although the authoritarian state had sought to manipulate the views of the people in the public meetings, its success was limited. This was predominately due to the existence of a courageous and powerful civil society that, *inter alia*, was exercising a monitoring function by making repressive actions by the authoritarian regime widely public. Further, the process illustrated that it is possible to involve the international donor community in the process at the same time without submitting oneself to external manipulation.

Though the signatories of the Global Political Agreement designed the elements of public participation in the process, thereby excluding others such as the Democratic Party or civil society actors (Zembe and Masunda 2015, 27), Zimbabweans by and large believe that they have a legitimate constitution (Tavaruva 2013). The process also made evident that despite the strong commitment to participatory processes, constitutional negotiations among smaller groups are unavoidable at some stages.

With regard to the educative aspect that a participatory process can have on society (Moehler 2008), a survey by Afrobarometer (2015), conducted approximately one year after the promulgation of the new constitution, does not provide an all-too promising outlook. It finds that 78 percent of the interviewed Zimbabweans had no or just little knowledge of the content of their new constitution. It remains to be seen how distinct state organs and political actors interpret the constitution and whether they comply with its provisions. After all, the lived constitutional practice affects the document's relevance and success as well as to some degree its legitimacy in the eyes of the people.

References

Afrobarometer (2015). "Zimbabweans Largely Ignorant of 2013 Constitution", press release, 1 April 2015, (http://afrobarometer.org/press/zimbabweans-largely-ignorant-2013-constitution).

Brandt, M., Cottrell, J., Ghai, Y., and Regan, A. (2011). *Constitution-making and Reform: Options for the Process*, Interpeace: Switzerland.

COPAC (2012). "The National and Provincial Statistical Reports", (http://www.constitutionnet.org/vl/item/national-and-provincial-statistical-reports).

COPAC (2011). "Milestones Towards a New Constitution for Zimbabwe", (http://www.constitutionnet.org/vl/item/zimbabwe-overview-constitution-making-process).

Dzinesa, G. A. (2012). "Zimbabwe's Constitutional Reform Process: Challenges and Prospects", Institute for Justice and Reconciliation: Wynberg, South Africa.

Elster, J. (1995). "Forces and Mechanisms in the Constitution-Making Process", *Duke Law Journal*, 45(2), 364–96.

Freedom House (2013). "Freedom of the Press. Report: Zimbabwe", (https://freedomhouse.org/report/freedom-press/2013/zimbabwe).

Political Agreement (GPA) (2008). "Agreement between the Zimbabwe African National Union-Patriotic Front (ZANU-PF) and the two Movement for Democratic Change

(MDC) formations, on resolving the challenges facing Zimbabwe", (http://www.constitutionnet.org/vl/item/zimbabwe-global-political-agreements-2008).

Hatchard, J. (2001). "Some Lessons on Constitution-making from Zimbabwe", *Journal of African Law*, 45(2), 210–16.

Human Rights Watch (2011). "World Report 2011: Zimbabwe", (https://www.hrw.org/world-report/2011/country-chapters/zimbabwe).

IDEA (2016). "Zimbabwe – Country Constitutional Profile", (http://www.constitutionnet.org/country/zimbabwe-country-constitutional-profile).

Makumbe, John (2009). "Theft by Numbers: ZEC's Role in the 2008 Elections", in E. V. Masunungure (ed.), *Defying the winds of change: Zimbabwe's 2008 elections*, Konrad-Adenauer-Stiftung: Harare, 119–32.

Manyukwe, C. (2010). "Elections Present Political Fix for Zim chiefs", *The Financial Gazette*, 5 November 2010, (http://www.financialgazette.co.zw/elections-present-political-fix-for-zim-chiefs/).

McGrael, Chris (2008). "This Is No Election. This Is a Brutal War", *The Guardian*, 22 June 2008.

Meerkotter, Anneke (2012). "Zimbabwe's Constitutional Process in Crisis", OSISA, 6 September 2012, (http://www.osisa.org/law/blog/zimbabwes-constitutional-process-crisis).

Mhanda, Wilfred (2011). "The Role of War Veterans in Zimbabwe's Political and Economic Process", SAPES TRUST DIALOGUE FORUM, Harare, 7 April 2011, (http://solidaritypeacetrust.org/1063/the-role-of-war-veterans/).

Moehler, D. C. (2008). *Distrusting Democrats: Outcomes of Participatory Constitution Making*, The University of Michigan Press: Ann Arbor.

Ndlovu-Gatsheni, S. J. (2010). "The Constitution and the Constitutional Process in Zimbabwe", Solidarity Peace Trust, 18 May 2010, (http://solidaritypeacetrust.org/703/the-constitution-and-the-constitutional-process-in-zimbabwe/).

Ndulo, M. (2010). "Zimbabwe's Unfulfilled Struggle for a Legitimate Constitutional Order", in L. E. Miller (ed.) with L. Aucoin, *Framing the State in Times of Transition: Case Studies in Constitution Making*, US Institute of Peace Press: Washington D.C., 176–203.

Nyabeze, T. H. (2015). "Progressive Reform in the New Constitution of Zimbabwe: A Balance between the Representative and Transformative Constitution Making Process", Konrad-Adenauer-Stiftung, Country Report, February 2015, (http://www.kas.de/wf/en/33.40484/).

Panfil, S. T. (2012). *Constitutional Development with Civil Society: Case Studies from Southern and Eastern Africa*, (http://works.bepress.com/cgi/viewcontent.cgi?article=1005&context=sylvia_panfil).

Saati, Abrak (2015). "The Participation Myth: Outcomes of Participatory Constitution Building Processes on Democracy", Department of Political Science, Research Report 2015:1, Umeå University: Umeå.

Sachikonye, L. (2011). "Zimbabwe's Constitution-Making and Electoral Reform Processes: Challenges and Opportunities", Makerere University, 30 May–1 June 2011.

Shaw, Angus (2009). "Zanu PF Loyalists Disrupt Constitution Indaba", *New Zimbabwe*, 4 March 2009, (http://www.newzimbabwe.com/news-613-Zanu+PF+disrupts+constitution+indaba/news.aspx).

Tavaruva, P. (2013). *People's Perceptions on Zimbabwe's Constitution Making Process; A Case of Glen Norah A, Harare*, Department of Sociology, University of Zimbabwe: Harare.

Tendi, B.-M. (2013). "Why Robert Mugabe Scored a Landslide Victory in Zimbabwe Elections", *The Guardian*, 5 August 2013.

158   *Douglas Togaraseyi Mwonzora*

UNDP (2009). "Terms of Reference for a Consultancy for the Project Evaluation of Support to Participatory Constitution Making in Zimbabwe".

US Department of State (2009). "2008 Human Rights report: Zimbabwe", 25 February 2009, (http://www.state.gov/j/drl/rls/hrrpt/2008/af/119032.htm).

Vollan, Kåre (2013). "The Constitutional History and the 2013 Referendum of Zimbabwe", A NORDEM Special Report 2013, Norwegian Center for Human Rights, University of Oslo: Oslo.

Zembe, Wurayayi and Masunda, Octavious Chido (2015). "The Global Political Agreement (GPA) Constitution in Zimbabwe: A New People-Driven Constitution or a Misnomer?", in J. de Visser, N. Steytler, D. Powell, and E. Durojaye (eds.) *Constitution-Building in Africa*, Law and Constitution in Africa, Volume 26, Community Law Centre, University of the Western Cape, Nomos: Baden-Baden.

The Zimbabwean (2012). "COPAC Completes Review of 18 Chapters", 10 March 2012, (http://thezimbabwean.co/2012/03/copac-completes-review-of-18/).

Zimbabwe Election Support Network (ZESN) (2013). "Zimbabwe Constitution Referendum Report and Implications for the Next Elections", 16 March 2013.

Zimbabwe Independent (2009). "Exposing the Shortcomings of the Kariba Draft Constitution", 2 July 2009, (https://www.theindependent.co.zw/2009/07/02/exposing-shortcomings-of-the-kariba-draft-constitution/).

10 The role of civil society in the Libyan constitution-making process

Omar Hammady[1]

Introduction

The emergence of a vibrant civil society could be considered as the brightest achievement of post-Qadhafi's Libya (Ramonet, 2015). Yet, despite the enthusiasm of Libyan activists for the constitutional process, their effective involvement was very limited. This relates to the very design of the process and its implementation during a full-fledged civil war without taking into consideration the constraints of peace-making. As it took place in the midst of a conflict, the stalled constitutional process in Libya should have comprised and shaped a more comprehensive peace-making process. It was, however, designed and implemented in total isolation from the latter and without the involvement of the actual political stakeholders on the ground and was, therefore, doomed to fail. It remains to be seen as to whether the lack of public participation was a substantial cause of the failure of the process. The needs of constitution-making linked to a peace-making process could, presumably, justify a limited involvement of civil society at certain stages in order to protect the peace deal to be reached, first, amongst the elite, the major warring parties.

While it would be presumptuous to assess the issue of public participation and draw final conclusions in an ongoing and highly volatile process, it is nevertheless important to evaluate the constitution-making process in Libya so far and analyze the extent to which it did – or did not – allow for meaningful public participation and draw some lessons therefrom.

This chapter will attempt to do so by providing some background to the current Libyan transition; analyzing the design of the overall transition and the design and implementation of the constitution-drafting process in relation to public participation; presenting some reflections on the nascent Libyan civil society and its role in the constitutional process; and addressing the role of international actors in promoting public participation. It will conclude with some tentative conclusions and prospective remarks.

---

1 The author would like to thank Zaid Al-Ali and Felix Van Lier for their comments on an earlier version of this chapter.

DOI: 10.4324/9781315180540-13

Background to the Libyan transition

Unlike Tunisians or Egyptians, Libyan transitional authorities could not build, in 2011, on existing state institutions or a democratic political culture, including organized political parties and an active civil society. Further, the country is one of the most conservative Arab societies, where tribes are still the most important institutions, and where the very concept of the modern state is still to be established (Obeidi, 2014). Since its independence, Libya only had a constitution for a short period of time, the eighteen years of King Idriss Sanussi's rule (Mayer, 1996). Under Qadhafi's regime, besides the Constitutional Declaration of 1969 that stayed in force only briefly, the country had no formal constitution. The very idea of having one was rejected by Qadhafi's views, explained in the *Green Book* published, first, in August 1975, and supposed to be a third world alternative to both communism and capitalism. Provisions said to have constitutional value were found in many documents, most notably the *Declaration of the Establishment of the People's Authority* adopted in 1977, *The Great Green Charter of Human Rights of the Jamahiriyan Era* of 1988, and the *Law on the Consolidation of Liberties* (1989).

The peculiar system established by Qadhafi left little room for any form of modern civil society to emerge. Political parties were criminalized and with the stringent limitations on freedom of association and of speech, only exiled opponents, most particularly Islamist groups, could organize themselves in the diaspora. Internally, tribes remained key structures in Libya's political life, serving as intermediaries between citizens and the state. Wary of their influence, Qadhafi attempted instrumentalizing them, notably by creating a National Council for tribes. During the popular uprising and throughout the subsequent civil war, they emerged as key actors in Libya's politics (Cherstich, 2014; Lacher, 2016).

With the limited room left for civil society to organize, it was no surprise that the popular uprising of 2011 originated in the eastern region of the country where tribes, largely loyal to King Sanussi, have always perceived Qadhafi as a usurper and where Islamist groups have always been perceived as strong and well organized. During this uprising, Libyan society revolted and its youth marshaled the slogans of human rights and liberty against the very regime which encroached upon rights and liberties. These protests rapidly transformed into a fully fledged rebellion and an open armed conflict, eventually bringing about the overthrow and assassination of Colonel Qadhafi on 20 October 2011. The newly established National Transitional Council, originally formed in Benghazi in February 2011, moved then to the capital Tripoli where it started to implement its plans for the transitional process.

Libyan transitional process: A problematic design

The design of the Libyan transitional process was problematic in many regards. Its shortcomings include questionable sequencing of the transition, unrealistic timelines and the exclusion of important Libyan groups. This resulted in a lack of inclusiveness of the entire process and notably the sidelining of civil society in the constitution-making process.

The transition's roadmap was spelled out in article 30 of the Interim Constitutional Declaration adopted on 3 August 2011. It envisioned the election of a General National Congress (GNC) after the liberation of Tripoli (i.e., the fall of Qadhafi) followed, one month later, by the appointment of a Constitutional Assembly. The assembly was expected to draft a new constitution for the country within just two months. The reasons for this unrealistic plan go back to the circumstances of the drafting and adoption of the Interim Constitutional Declaration. This document was drafted hastily, without any consultation whatsoever with political constituencies or local scholars or experts (Sallabi, 2011). The determining factor, back then, was the search for international recognition while the cohesion of the "revolutionaries" was taken for granted. Little to no thinking was devoted to the issues of planning the transitional process, its sequencing, timeline, institutions and involvement of the public in the process. And yet, Libya was the least prepared country in the region to hold elections, as the country had no experience with them for five decades, no experience with political parties and no state institutions or infrastructure to support the planned polls. Notwithstanding, the country held three separate elections in less than two years, which partially explains the ensuing fragmentation of the political and security landscapes.

Due to its unrealistic character, as well as to emerging dynamics of the process, including the return of the "revolutionaries" from the battle field, the Constitutional Declaration created many controversies and had to undergo several, sometimes confusing, amendments regarding the design of the transitional process, and most particularly the constitution-making.

A first amendment to the Interim Constitutional Declaration clarified, in March 2012, the composition of the Constitutional Assembly, its functioning and decision-making process. It provided that the assembly was to be composed, like the one of 1951, of 60 members, equally representative of the three main regions of the country (Cyrenaica in the east, Tripoli in the west and Fezzan in the south). By virtue of the same amendment, all decisions of this assembly ought to be taken by a majority of two-thirds plus one. While the regional concerns of the population of the eastern regions and their federalist demands can partly explain this amendment, the mere consideration of the 1951 Constitution as ideal both in terms of its drafting process and content, did also enter into the calculations that led to this amendment. Finally, the timeframe for the drafting of the constitution was extended from 60 days to 120 days, which was still unrealistic by any standards. One explanation often given by some Libyan politicians to these rushed timelines, was the willingness of transitional authorities not to be seen as trying to perpetuate their own power. Yet, the GNC was a democratically elected Parliament and could have been granted a reasonable term to effectively lay the ground for a well-designed and managed transition. It is most likely that the lack of confidence between the elite leading the process and the pressure of certain armed groups better explain both the timelines and the option for election. The same elite's unreasonable expectations further complicated matters and led to a permanent search for a fresh start whenever institutions were faced with a problem.

A second amendment, adopted in June 2012, changed the procedure for appointing members of the Constitution-Drafting Assembly (CDA): no longer were they to be appointed by the General National Congress, but to be elected in a direct and free election. After the election of the General National Congress in July 2012, the newly established Parliament came to the conclusion that organizing a direct and nationwide election would be rather complicated. It amended, once again, article 30 of the Interim Constitutional Declaration to vest itself with the power of appointing or electing members of the Constituent Assembly. However, under the pressure of several stakeholders contesting the legitimacy of the GNC to do so, a further constitutional amendment was adopted, in April 2013, confirming the election of the CDA through universal direct suffrage.

Yet, the election of CDA members through direct universal suffrage could bring about the involvement only of a limited number of Libyans in their public affairs. Several legal and de facto measures excluded important segments of the Libyan society from the overall process, including the constitutional process. A "political isolation law" (*qanun al-azl al-siyassi*), adopted on 5 May 2013, barred, for 10 years, wide categories of Libyans from holding any public office. It targeted all those who, from 1 September 1969 until 23 October 2011, held any position under Qadhafi's rule, regardless of the nature or level of the position (Eljarh, 2013; Human Rights Watch, 2013).

In addition, the overthrow of Qadhafi had already led to the de facto exclusion of his social base, which included large tribes notably in the west of Libya. The overall conflict led also to around 2 million Libyans being exiled and, therefore, excluded from the political process. Finally, some groups simply boycotted the process. This was the case of minority groups, notably Tebu and Amazigh, who found that the overall design of the transition did not take into consideration their demands of pre-agreed guarantees for their cultural rights.

CDA elections were eventually held in February 2014 amidst deep political crisis. The assembly started its work in April 2014.

The Constitution-Drafting Assembly's process and the participation of civil society

Theoretically, the Libyan constitution-drafting process was envisioned to be highly inclusive and participatory. Citizens were to be directly involved throughout the process: the Libyan people elect the constitution drafters at the beginning of the process, adopt the draft constitution in a popular referendum with a two-thirds majority and were sought to provide public input during the drafting phase. In practice, the implementation of these three forms of public involvement entailed real limitations. The CDA was elected based on an electoral framework that did not really favor inclusivity. In addition the assembly's bylaws and other acts on public participation could have been improved, their implementation, in the challenging Libyan context, proved to be problematic.

Election of the CDA

The election of the Constitution-Drafting Assembly (CDA) on 20 February 2014, reflected already a certain "democratic fatigue": voters were disillusioned with the whole political process. Only 45 percent of registered Libyans took part in the election, which amounted to 14 percent of eligible voters, or, put differently, 10 percent of the estimated total population (Eljarh, 2014(c); Carter Center, 2012). Furthermore, the electoral law did not favor inclusivity: Members of the CDA were elected in individual constituencies on a first-past-the-post basis. Since political parties and active politicians were not to stand for election, very few political figures made it to the CDA. The assembly's members enjoyed only limited legitimacy as they were generally elected by a small number of voters reflecting rather their tribal or regional affiliations. Moreover, the electoral law only provided for 10 percent of the seats to be reserved to women and another 10 percent to the three minority groups, Tebu, Amazigh and Tuareg (Democracy Reporting International, 2013). Finally, four of the assembly's seats remained vacant due to the boycott by the Amazigh and the impossibility of holding elections in the Islamist-controlled city of Derna in the eastern region (Carter Center, 2014).

The election of the CDA coincided with another dramatic development in the country's descent into chaos (Lacher, 2014; Gartenstein and Barr, 2015). Due to the growing dissatisfaction with the GNC, a new House of Representatives (HoR) was elected in June 2014. Islamist groups who significantly lost in this election contested its legitimacy, launched a military attack on the capital and claimed that the GNC was still the legitimate legislator. The newly elected House, which was internationally recognized, convened in the eastern city of Tobruq and endorsed the then in charge government. To complicate matters further, in November 2014, the Libyan Supreme Court ruled that the election of the internationally recognized Parliament was unconstitutional and ordered its dissolution (Maghur, 2014; Eljarh, 2014(b)). The court's ruling was based on the unconstitutionality of the procedure by which the amendment, which served as basis for the Parliament's election, was adopted.

The existence of two competing Parliaments left the CDA in an uncertain legal situation and complex political landscape (Hammady and Meyer-Resende, 2014). Further, the political dialogue launched under the auspices of the United Nations in January 2015 to overcome the situation of competing governments, and of which the CDA was excluded, became the focus of the political process and made the CDA lose relevance. Such focus was notably due to the deteriorating security situation which transformed into a full-fledged civil war. As a result, priorities of international community shifted from democracy promotion and supporting the inclusive drafting of a constitution to the immediate security challenges resulting from terrorism and illegal migration. It is noteworthy that the CDA itself wanted to distance itself from the political dialogue and claimed to be adopting an impossible neutrality. This helped only by keeping the members of the CDA together while making the assembly irrelevant, since the terms of the political dialogue were, by excellence, constitutional ones. The claimed neutrality was impossible to sustain and the assembly ended up mirroring the divisions of political stakeholders. Yet, when some senior members of the CDA eventually realized that their work would be pointless if disconnected from the political process, they tried to reach out to participants to the political dialogue, notably through written petitions and memoranda. Their move was not welcomed by the sponsors of the dialogue.

It could be claimed that this was the turning point where the international community and Libyan stakeholders missed an important opportunity to use the CDA which was, by then, the only democratically elected, most inclusive and unanimously accepted Libyan institution. As such, the CDA could have served as a forum to build consensus between the warring factions that were, after all, fighting over constitutional matters by excellence, including state structure, system of government, status of Islamic Shari'a, governance and distribution of natural resources, amongst others (Hammady and Meyer-Resende, 2015).

The CDA kept functioning with its many congenital defects and increasing disconnection from political realities and produced three drafts before its members were divided over the fourth one in April 2016, which led to freezing the assembly's work until April 2017.

In order to compensate the many shortcomings resulting from its design, electoral framework and the general context of the transitional process, the CDA was to build the credibility and legitimacy of its outcomes notably through effective working methods, ensuring a participatory, inclusive and transparent drafting process (Eljarh, 2014(a)).

CDA's rules of procedure and civil society participation

During its first session, held on 21 April 2014, in the eastern city of Al-Baydha, the CDA elected its presidium and adopted its rules of procedure as well as a roadmap for the constitution-drafting and a code of conduct. All these acts were accomplished within a timeframe of one week without any of them being prepared beforehand by a technical or preparatory body and without any expertise being available to the members during this session. The members thus improvised and this reflected on the quality and coherence of the adopted documents.

The roadmap was a very succinct document spread over two pages, highlighting "sources" and "references" as well as guiding principles for the drafting, and envisioned the basic structure for a constitutional draft. The document was drafted in very general and vague terms to offer concrete drafting guidance.

The rules of procedure devoted an independent chapter to "seeking assistance of experts and social outreach". It was under this heading that public participation and the role of civil society were dealt with. Different forms of public participation were considered, including interaction with citizens in public meetings and direct inputs from citizens during the drafting process. However, the CDA's rules of procedure did not provide for a plan of civic education nor was such a plan developed later on by the assembly.

The rules of procedure did provide some guidance for the information of the public on the constitution-making process – however, only with regards to the final draft constitution. More specifically, article 79 provides that the CDA must circulate the draft of the constitution or any draft section to the public. The right of citizens to be informed on the actual proceedings – and thus the public's ability to monitor the debates and voting procedures of the assembly – was practically ruled out by the decision not to air the sessions of the CDA, unless the assembly decided otherwise. Likewise, deliberations of thematic committees remained secret and could not be attended by the public except those that "they may seek for assistance such as counselors, experts, civil society and others, in coordination with the Bureau of the Assembly's Presidency". While this exception might open room for hearing sessions for civil society organizations, it was not implemented to the best of our knowledge. This secretive approach undermined the possibility for civil society organizations to monitor and report on the assembly's work. It also questions the transparency of the CDA's work as well as the accountability of constitution-drafters before citizens. Finally, the rules of procedure require the documentation of all the debates of the assembly, including plenary sessions and thematic committees' deliberations, as well as workshops, conferences, submitted petitions and legal opinions. But the same rules indicate that this documentation work is meant to be transferred to the national archives upon completion of the assembly's work rather than being released for the purpose of public information during the drafting process.

Beyond information of the public, the CDA was expected to enter into a real exchange of opinions in public discussions with citizens. Under the rules of procedure, thematic committees were tasked to establish a plan for outreach to citizens and civil society organizations. The establishment of offices (called delegations) in three different cities, one year after the CDA started its work, was meant to facilitate CDA members' interaction with the public. In practice, however, no specific plans for public outreach were developed. The assembly conducted field visits to different cities immediately after its first session. But meetings were held mostly with local notables rather than with ordinary people.

Besides, the rules of procedure provide for the establishment of a website and the use of social media to foster the interaction with citizens. The presidency of the CDA was also to establish procedures to process the petitions submitted by citizens and civil society organizations. Yet no plan was released on how citizens' inputs would be collected, let alone what mechanisms would be used to analyze and process their petitions. It is noteworthy that interaction with civil society was entrusted to a single office, staffed with only one employee who reported to the presidency rather than to thematic committees.

Yet, at least during the first year of the CDA's work, and in contrast with the general mood, some segments of the nascent Libyan civil society did show interest and sometimes enthusiasm in accompanying the drafting process. According to the assembly's most recent report, which already dates back to November 2014, 462 petitions and proposals were submitted to the CDA by civil society organizations, unions, local councils and municipalities, representatives of minority groups as well as individual experts and citizens (CDA, 2014). Many organizations had prepared themselves for years to contribute to this process.

But since the CDA did not develop a protocol or a procedure for classifying, processing, analyzing and taking into account these petitions, their content was neither discussed nor taken into consideration by thematic committees while drafting their respective chapters. Many of these petitions touched upon the most debated Libyan constitutional issues. These included the status of Islamic Shari'a, federalism, women and foreigners' rights.

A number of civil society organizations made the effort to visit the CDA's headquarters. However, such visits remained informal and their effect was limited as the operational method of the CDA was restricted to receiving petitions, listening to petitioners without engaging in interactive debates. This was explained by the willingness of members not to express their individual views on submitted petitions before they were discussed by the relevant committees. Two categories of groups were, however, an exception in this regard as they were more successful in their advocacy work: tribal groups and heavily internationally supported local NGOs. Tribal delegations could always rely on direct ties with individual members of the assembly. Their petitions generally found their way to the CDA draft, which was noticeable, for instance, in the draft chapters on decentralization. Likewise, some heavily supported NGOs had the necessary means, both in terms of logistics and substantive support, and could attend all fora where CDA members were invited, and also conducted several visits to the assembly. The absence of clear rules for engagement with civil society led to the over-empowerment of these kinds of actors. Yet, while the CDA's working methods did not facilitate the involvement of citizens and civil society organizations, this factor explains only the operational aspect of public participation. The most important limitations resulted, rather, from the general context of civil war which made it highly risky to engage in certain forms of advocacy and activism and silenced important segments of a vibrant, albeit nascent, civil society.

Independent activism on the constitutional process

One of the major features of the Libyan popular uprising and early stages of the transitional process was, without doubt, the emergence of a real public space, made up of a variety of groups, organizations and associations of citizens, meeting beyond the traditional family links and working to further shared objectives and ideas of public interest. Most of these groups' members identify themselves, above all, as citizens of the Libyan state. Going beyond the traditional economic and political spheres as strictly defined, these organizations would fall within the Tocquevillian concept of civil society. According to the Libyan National Commission for Civil Society, there were over 4,519 civil society organizations officially registered by the end of 2016 pursuing a variety of activities. By comparison, and according to a survey covering 2012–14, Libya had a greater number of members of volunteer organizations per capita than any other Maghreb country, and than Egypt (Ramonet, 2015).

As early as 2011, a variety of actors were already preparing the then upcoming constitutional process. These included networks of Libyan scholarly society, notably from Benghazi University which undertook surveys on the views of

Libyans on the constitution and on the overall transitional process (Benghazi University, 2013). They also prepared studies on options for the substantive content of the constitution based on surveys and other field work run by hundreds of youth activists. Bar associations and judges' unions as well as advocacy associations working on democracy promotion began organizing a variety of events aimed at preparing Libyans for the upcoming process. Minorities' associations, wary of their status under the upcoming fundamental text, were particularly active throughout Libya on constitutional matters. Libyans from the diaspora provided meaningful contributions, especially in the promotion of fundamental rights during the drafting process. Lawyers for Justice in Libya notably launched the "Watan Bus Tour", which consisted of a tour throughout the country run by activists of the organization holding "constitution days" in different cities. During the drafting process, the same organization assisted individual CDA members and provided detailed comments on the different drafts of the assembly. The Libyan Women's Platform for Peace designed and launched a campaign called "dastoor" (*Constitution*) with the view of making women's voices heard by the constitution-makers. Several other networks were set up and supported by international actors in order to promote the participation of specific groups. These included networks of youth and women, supported largely by the UNDP and UN-Women and which held several workshops and other meetings with CDA members.

However, Libya's civil society has evolved in a challenging context, especially since the breakout of civil war in 2014. It operated amid lack of clarity on its governing legal framework: there is no law so far on associations or civil society in post-2011 Libya. Libyan civil society activists were also targeted by kidnapping and assassination campaigns (Ramonet, 2015). This led to many being silenced and others suspending their activities when they did not simply opt for exile. This situation favored the most conservative segments of the Libyan civil society. Since civil war broke out in 2014, radical Islamists have been propagating anti-democratic discourse. Following the release of the last CDA draft, preachers at Friday prayers are more often attacking the draft constitution supposedly "imported from abroad" with "anti-Islamic provisions" (M'hawash, 2017). The very idea of having a constitution is said to be alien to Islam, according to these preaches.

Yet, the less conservative Libyan civil society could rely on the assistance of international actors supporting the constitution-making process and offering fora for debates amongst Libyans over constitutional matters as well as for direct exchange between CDA members and activists.

The role of international actors in promoting the Libyan civil society participation

Since its early days, the Libyan transitional process was marked by heavy international engagement aimed at supporting Libyans throughout the transition with a special focus on the then upcoming constitution. A United Nations Assistance Mission to Libya (UNSMIL) was established on 16 September 2011 with a mandate to "assist and support Libyan national efforts to [. . .] undertake inclusive political dialogue, promote national reconciliation, and embark upon the constitution-making and electoral process [and . . .] coordinate support that may be requested from other multilateral and bilateral actors as appropriate" (UNSCR 2009 (2011)). The support to be provided by international actors was direly needed as Libya did not have any democratic model to follow in the region. Only a limited number of local experts had real expertise in constitutional law, and even fewer had experience in democratic settings.

During the constitutional process, in addition to the UNSMIL, several governmental and nongovernmental organizations were implementing projects in support to the CDA. This support helped diffuse important ideas and concepts on constitutionalism, democracy and the rule of law. This was done amongst a relatively limited circle including mainly CDA members, Libyan experts and certain groups of activists. International actors had an undeniable impact on the quality of certain chapters of the CDA drafts and gave their Libyan partners the opportunity to interact with national, regional and international experts. They also sometimes mediated between the drafters and some civil society organizations. This exercise of interaction between drafters and local experts and activists proved very useful to both parties although it had its limitations: by the time the CDA started operating, almost all international organizations and embassies had relocated to Tunisia for security reasons. Accordingly, most events took place abroad in Tunisia, Egypt and Turkey, which made it impossible for a larger number of activists to be included and led to the emergence of a category of "permanent participants", limiting the rotation, and thus, the scope of beneficiaries. This impacted most particularly women, as the practice in Libya is that women would not travel alone. Therefore, most female participants had to ensure that a male member of the family would be available to accompany them and that the hosting organization would also cover his expenses.

Notwithstanding, international actors had to make their support fit within a framework that was partially established in a somewhat questionable manner: as mentioned above, the Libyan process design was already decided on hastily, and without consultation with national stakeholders, scholars and experts. The UN apparently did not seek to advise its Libyan partners in this regard. In the words of then Special Representative Ian Martin, the organization opted for "a light footprint" approach and sought to abide notably by the principle of "humility" (Martin, 2015). It is also likely that Libyan authorities would not have been, in that context, receptive to such advice (Al-Ali, 2017). Upon the election of the CDA, the UNSMIL sent a delegation to the newly elected assembly, in April 2014, but the little interest exhibited by the assembly left little choice to the UNSMIL but to maintain its "light footprint" approach.

After the outbreak of the civil war in summer 2014, the UN abandoned its "light footprint" approach in favor of a more intrusive one. Paradoxically, this took place while the UN-led political dialogue pushed the CDA to the sidelines. After the signature of the Skhirat agreement, in December 2015, the UN envoy, at the time Mr. Bernardino León, whose mandate was ending, started pressuring the CDA to complete its draft and put at its disposal significant logistical facilities for this purpose. Ambiguous motivations for such a move, and the very embarrassing episode of the leaked information on Mr. León's interested contacts with certain regional players, tarnished in a lasting manner the image and credibility of the UN and of the international community in Libya in general (The Guardian, 2015(a), (b)).

UNSMIL's intrusive approach towards the Libyan CDA increased further under Mr. León's successor, Mr. Martin Kobler, who took office in January 2016. Notwithstanding the continued fragmentation of the Libyan political and security landscape, Mr. Kobler maintained his predecessor's approach and kept pushing for the implementation of the agreement which was never endorsed by the internationally recognized Parliament. In a move reflecting, rather, the need for reporting some progress, the special envoy took the initiative of inviting the Libyan CDA to a plenary session in Salalah, Sultanate of Oman, between March and April 2016. He pushed, during this session, for the completion of the draft and its submission to the Parliament in order for the latter to prepare the popular referendum. The very initiative brought about further divisions in the assembly: more than 20 members of the CDA boycotted this meeting and rejected any outcomes it might lead to (Kent Think, 2016). The 33 members who took part in Salalah's meetings adopted, in April 2016, a slightly amended version of the third CDA draft, thereby following the advice of the UNSMIL (CDA members, 2016). Since the rules of procedure required the vote of two-thirds plus one majority, they amended the rules of procedure in order for this threshold to be reduced. The draft was then adopted and submitted to the House of Representatives. This was another turning point in the assembly's work since boycotting members brought the matter to court and the Administrative Chamber of the Appellate Court of Al-Baydha annulled, on 7 May 2016, the amendment of the rules of procedure and the adoption of the Salalah draft (Alwasat, 2016(a); Libya Observer, 2016(b); Hanly, 2016). Since then, the CDA's work was frozen for almost a year. In March 2017, however, both groups, Boycotters of Salalah and their counterparts, agreed finally to forming a joint "Consensus Committee" made up of 12 members in order to overcome the deadlock. This committee is reported to be close to reaching an agreement on a common draft to be submitted to a plenary session early May 2017 (Alwasat, 2017).

This episode of Salalah seems to have further undermined the credibility of the UNSMIL and its stand as an impartial partner to the CDA. Several members of the assembly and many activists went on to publicly blame the bias of the UN mission and many rule out any cooperation with it in the future (Alwasat, 2016(a)).

In reality, the UN lacks a coherent strategy to support constitution-making processes in general and its approach towards specific cases depends significantly on the preferences of individuals who happen to be in charge within field missions (Al-Ali, 2017). This would have been acceptable had the relevant staff members been chosen based on their particular expertise in the field of constitution-making and familiarity with the specific countries. But the UN recruitment's logic is famously opaque. At best, "there is some logic to the recruitment process, but it is not the type of logic that you would have liked for it to adopt" to use the words of a senior UN officer (Al-Ali, 2017). The lack of accountability and responsibility both at the institutional and individual level generates a sense of impunity amongst UN officials (Al-Ali, 2017).

While the positive contribution of some international actors was undeniable, the support provided by these organizations was merely a drop in the ocean compared to the mobilized resources and to the needs of the process. This was due to a variety of factors, some of which are related to the working methods and functioning of the CDA itself, which did not develop a clear protocol for cooperation with international actors nor for the delivery of expertise. Other factors are related to some of the perverse features of democracy promotion's "industry" which were displayed, beyond decency, in the Libyan context. Although some foreign NGOs struggled to provide the best tailored expertise, involving notably national and regional experts in addition to international ones who were familiar with the Libyan context, the general quality of expertise provided by international organizations supporting the CDA could have been improved. A very limited number of mobilized experts did speak Arabic and a majority of them had a limited understanding of local realities, culture and history. On the other hand, the mere fact of speaking Arabic was equated, sometimes, with expertise. This is not to mention that some international actors may provide only experts they could control or who are in line with their views. Further, most of these organizations were implementing pre-set projects that neither took into account beneficiaries' inputs, nor undertook an in-depth analysis of the country's needs. Their main concern remained, thus, meeting donors' requirements which are generally phrased in terms of quantity of events.

In addition, there remains in Libya a certain apprehension towards foreign intervention, especially on matters involving deep differences in terms of values and culture. As a result, international support to civil society was perceived by some, at best, as the implementation of a hidden political agenda, if not a "soft penetration" of the Libyan society (Kendir, 2014(a), (b)). Libyan scholars and organizations engaged with international partners were perceived as agents of foreign actors. Their credibility is questioned in the national debate. This is even worse with women, whose presence in the public sphere was significantly reduced in the aftermath of the 2011 uprising and whose interaction with foreigners is perceived as "inappropriate". This explains the recently established ban on women's traveling abroad and which was justified by "the negative aspects of Libyan women traveling in foreign countries" (Libya Herald, 2017).

Conclusion

Notwithstanding the emergence of an effective Libyan civil society and its willingness to actively contribute to the constitution-making process, the design of the latter and the context of war made it impossible for civil society to make a genuine difference. Rather, the best prepared and active segments of this society were silenced or pushed to exile. The already unrealistic design of the process was not reviewed in light of emerging dynamics.

There is a wealth of scholarly literature on the sequencing and tensions between constitution-making and peace-making. We will not attempt to frame a new theory here. However, few lessons can be learned from the Libyan process.

In a context of conflict or efforts aiming at ending it, constitution-making should fit, shape and reflect an overall peace process. A constitution is supposed to enshrine the consensus of a society on its shared values and foundations of a common future. It cannot be drafted when the society is severely divided and managing its differences through violence. A minimal level of stabilization and consensus is necessary to engage in constitution-drafting and for civil society's role to be effective.

Public participation and the active involvement of civil society are key to legitimizing constitutions, building consensus on their content, ensuring their local ownership and even improving their very quality. However, the sequencing of the different stages of constitution-making, especially during or after conflicts, should be carefully crafted. The entry of civil society on the scene should happen at the right sequence, when there is a momentum for it to make a real and positive difference. Priority should be given to ending violence through a deal between the actual stakeholders on the ground. Attempts to put them under pressure by mobilizing civil society too early proved to be risky for both, peace-making and civil society. One of the main reasons for the failure of the Libyan Political Agreement relates to it being signed by a large group of brilliant intellectuals and activists, while the real stakeholders on the ground were neither formally nor effectively represented. It was no surprise that both competing Parliaments rejected it.

While the Libyan process was characterized by heavy international engagement, the actual impact of international actors remains very limited and sometimes problematic. The mandated UN mission could not develop and implement a coherent approach towards the constitutional process. It confined itself to a role of coordination, which was hard to implement due to the lack of an overall strategy and of appropriate channels of communication with the relevant Libyan actors. The shift in the UNSMIL's approach, from a "light footprint" to a more intrusive one, did not stem from a proper analysis of the needs of the process. It seemed to have been justified rather by the need to meet certain objectives unilaterally determined by the UNSMIL itself. This, combined with the serious ethical questions raised by the circumstances of departure of former UN Special Envoy León, could only undermine both the process itself and the credibility of the UN.

A variety of other international organizations, most of them nongovernmental, endeavored to support Libyans in a very hostile context and their positive contribution is undeniable. They notably offered a highly needed forum for Libyan constitution-makers to directly interact with activists, experts and international counterparts. The work of these organizations was not facilitated by the very design of the process nor by the country's descent to civil war. However, some international organizations displayed, in their work in Libya, regrettable features of an "industry" operating with a free market logic. The need for meeting donors' requirements in terms of implementation, reporting and spending of funds determined more often than not the work of these organizations. This contributed to undermining the image of the international community and the field of democracy and rule of law promotion. While a coherent strategy towards the support of constitution-making processes in post-conflict countries is still to be developed by relevant actors, most notably the UN, future plans of support should learn lessons from the shortcomings and mistakes of international actors' experience with the CDA process. These should most particularly include the need for a context-based support, effectively coordinated, duly taking into account the perspective of local actors and abiding by basic ethical rules. The experience of international actors in Libya was not a success story. But it is still time to address mistakes and prepare future successes. The constitution-making process in Libya is most likely still to come.

By the time of submitting this chapter, a CDA Consensus Committee is reported to be close to agreeing on a draft to be discussed early May 2017. Yet, it remains doubtful that the current, and stalled, Libyan process is likely to be the one leading to the country's future constitution. The assembly's divisions, delays and lack of representativeness seriously call its legitimacy into question. In addition, the completion of the constitutional process will have to make space for forces that have emerged during the current civil war and are shaping the country's politics. Currently, the CDA's work remains completely disconnected from the political process and, therefore, would not reflect the views of the actual stakeholders on the ground. Most likely, once Libyan stakeholders have reached a political deal, they would then reconsider the CDA draft if not alternative options to the very assembly. Options range from a rushed process led by an *ad hoc* body to be appointed by the institutions resulting from a peace agreement, to a more sustained and credible process. The latter could be provided for in the peace agreement and, ideally, follow a period regulated by transitional constitutional arrangements building notably upon the acceptable parts of the CDA's work and of the 1951 Constitution which remains an important reference in the Libyan constitutional debate. A staged constitution-making would favor inclusiveness as the country stabilizes. It will also make it possible to manage the country's smooth transition from authoritarianism to a more competitive system of government. Under such process, Libya could definitely count on its civil society to foster legitimacy, national consensus and local ownership.

References

Al-Ali Z., "International Assistance to Arab Spring Transitions: Is There Any Order to the Chaos?", in J-P. Filiu and S. Lacroix (ed.), *Revisiting the Arab Transitions: The Politics of a Revolutionary Moment* (forthcoming, 2017)
Alwasat, "Ibtissem Ibhih calls for holding the UNSMIL accountable", 6 April 2016(a). Accessible at: http://alwasat.ly/ar/news/libya/101703/the

Ibid., "Nine CDA Members Reject the Consultation Meetings in Oman Sultanate", 21 March 2016(b). Accessible at: http://alwasat.ly/ar/news/libya/100011/

Ibid., "Badri Sherif: The Adoption of a Constitution Shall End the Transitional Phase and Overcome the Competition between Governments", 20 April 2017. Accessible at: http://www.alwasat.ly/ar/news/libya/139499/.

Benghazi University and The National Dialogue Preparatory Commission, Research and Consulting Centre, "Libyans Views Regarding the National Dialogue Survey Report", Benghazi University, 2014.

Benghazi University, Research and Consulting Centre, "Results of the National Survey on the Constitution", Benghazi University, March 2013.

Carter Center, "The General National Congress Elections in Libya", 7 July 2012, p. 5–6. Accessible at: https://www.cartercenter.org/resources/pdfs/news/peace_publications/election_reports/libya-070712-final-rpt.pdf.

Carter Center, "The 2014 Constitutional Drafting Assembly Election in Libya: Final Report", 2014. Accessible at: https://www.cartercenter.org/resources/pdfs/news/peace_publications/election_reports/libya-06112014-final-rpt.pdf.

CDA, Rules of Procedure of the CDA: www.cdalibya.org.

Ibid., Roadmap for Constitution-Drafting: www.cdalibya.org.

Ibid., CDA's Code of Conduct: www.cdalibya.org.

Ibid., "Proposals Submitted to the CDA", November 2014. Accessible at: http://www.cdalibya.org/%D9%85%D9%82%D8%AA%D8%B1%D8%AD%D8%A7%D8%AA-%D9%85%D9%82%D8%AF%D9%85%D8%A9-%D8%A5%D9%84%D9%8A-%D8%A7%D9%84%D9%87%D9%8A%D8%A7%D8%A6%D8%A9.

Ibid., CDA, Initial Proposals of the CDA. Accessible at: http://www.cdalibya.org/%D9%84%D8%AC%D8%A7%D9%86-%D8%A7%D9%84%D9%87%D9%8A%D8%A6%D8%A9.

Ibid., CDA Presidency Decision Establishing Regional Delegations, Presidency's Decision no. 17/2014. Accessible at: http://www.cdalibya.org/%D9%85%D9%86%D8%AF%D9%88%D8%A8%D9%8A%D8%A7%D8%AA-%D8%A7%D9%84%D9%87%D9%8A%D8%A6%D8%A9.

Cherstich I., "When Tribesmen do Not Act Tribal: Libyan Tribalism as Ideology (Not as Schizophrenia)", *Middle East Critique*, 23, issue 4, 5 November 2014, p. 1.

Constitution of Libya, Interim Constitutional Declaration of 3 August 2011 with Its Amendments. Accessible at: http://www.constitutionnet.org/vl/item/law172013-organisation-elections-constituent-assembly-libya.

Constitutional Amendment no. 1, of 13 March 2012.

Constitutional Amendment no. 2, of 10 June 2012.

Constitutional Amendment no. 3, of 5 July 2012 on 9 April 2013.

Constitutional Amendment no. 4, of 9 April 2013.

David R., and Mzioudet H., "Personnel Change or Personal Change? Rethinking Libya's Political Isolation Law", Brooking Doha Cente, Standford University Project on Arab Transition, Paper series no. 4, March 2014.

Davis D.J., *Libyan Politics: Tribe and Revolution*, London, IBTauris, 1987.

Democracy Reporting International, "Constituent Assembly Elections in Libya: An Assessment of the Legal Framework", September 2013. Accessible at: http://democracy-reporting.org/publications/country-reports/libya/report-september-2013.html.

Eljarh M., "Isolation Law Harms Libya's Democratic Transition", Foreign Policy, 8 May 2013. Accessible at: http://foreignpolicy.com/2013/05/08/isolation-law-harms-libyas-democratic-transition/.

Ibid., "The Libyan Assembly Needs to Ensure that the Constitution Drafting Process Is as Inclusive as Possible", 5 May 2014(a). Accessible at: http://www.constitutionnet.org/news/libyan-assembly-needs-ensure-constitution-drafting-process-inclusive-possible.

Ibid., "The Supreme Court Decision that's Ripping Libya Apart", 6 November 2014(b). Accessible at: http://foreignpolicy.com/2014/11/06/the-supreme-court-decision-thats-ripping-libya-apart/.

Ibid., "Democratic Fatigue in Libya", Foreign Policy, 26 February 2014(c). Accessible at: http://foreignpolicy.com/2014/02/26/democracy-fatigue-in-libya/.

Gartenstein D., and Barr R.N., "Dignity and Dawn: Libya's Escalating Civil War", International Centre for Counter-terrorism, The Hague, February 2015.

Gluck J., "Constitution-Building in a Political Vacuum", in International IDEA, *Annual Review of Constitution-Building Processes*: 2014, p. 44.

GNC: Law no. 17 of 20 July 2013 on the Election of the CDA.

Hammady O., and Meyer-Resende M., "Saving Libya's Constitution-making Body", Carnegie Endowment for International Peace, 18 December 2014. Accessible at: http://carnegieendowment.org/sada/57565.

Ibid., "These 56 People Have a Chance to Save Libya", Foreign Policy, 21 April 2015. Accessible at: http://foreignpolicy.com/2015/04/21/these-56-people-have-a-chance-to-save-libya/.

Hanly, K., "Libyan Court Declares New Constitution Draft Illegal", *Digital Journal*, 10 May 2016. http://www.digitaljournal.com/news/world/libyan-court-declares-new-constitution-draft-illegal/article/465065.

Human Rights Watch, "Libya: Reject Political Isolation Law", 4 Mays 2013. Accessible at: https://www.hrw.org/news/2013/05/04/libya-reject-political-isolation-law.

International Crisis Group, "The Libyan Political Agreement: Time for Reset", 4 Nov. 2016.

International IDEA, "Analysis of the Draft Constitution of Libya Thematic Committees of the Constitution Drafting Assembly Status: December 2014". Available at: http://www.constitutionnet.org/sites/default/files/2015.03.31_-_analysis_of_draft_libya_constitution_english.pdf.

International IDEA, "Libya Constitution-building Manual", Accessible at: http://www.constitutionnet.org/files/libya_constitution-building_manual.pdf.

International IDEA, "The Main Steps in the Libyan Constitution-making Process", Accessible at: http://www.constitutionnet.org/ar/vl/item/almhawr-alryysyt-fy-almlyt-aldstwryt-allybyt.

International IDEA, "The Main Steps in the Libyan Constitution-making Process". In Arabic. Available at:

Interview conducted by the author with Judge Faraj Sallabi, from the Libyan Supreme Court, one of the Interim Constitutional Declaration's three drafters (August 2011).

Interview conducted by the author with Dr. Amal Obeidi from the University of Benghazi (5 May 2014).

Interview conducted by the author with Ibrahim El-Baba, chairperson of the CDA Thematic Committee on local governance (December 2015).

Interviews conducted by the author with activists from the cities of Al-Baydha, Benghazi and Tripoli, led by Mohamed M'hawash (February 2017).

Kendir A., "Foreign Funding of Civil Society Organization and Political Agendas", Libya Al-Mustakbal, 30 April 2014(a) (in Arabic). Accessible at: http://www.libya-al-mostakbal.org/news/clicked/48859.

Kendir A., "The Soft Penetration" (in Arabic), 5 May 2014(b), The Legal Agenda.

Kent Think, "Libyan Constitutional Drafting Committee Moving to Oman", 18 March 2016. Accessible at: http://kenthink7.blogspot.de/2016/03/libyan-constitutional-drafting.html.

Lacher W., "Libya's Local Elites and the Politics of Alliance Building", *Mediterranean Politics*, 21 (2016) 1, p. 64.

Ibid., "Libyan Transition towards Collapse", *SWP Comments*, no. 25, May 2014. Accessible at: https://www.swp-berlin.org/fileadmin/contents/products/comments/2014 C25_lac.pdf.

Ibid., Supporting Stabilization in Libya: The Challenges of Finalizing and Implementing the Skhirat Agreement", *SWP Comments*, July 2015.

Libya Herald, "Nazhuri Bans Women Flying from Labraq Without Male Guardian", 19 February 2017. Accessible at: https://www.libyaherald.com/2017/02/19/nazhuri-bans-women-flying-from-labraq-without-male-guardian/.

Libya Observer, "Constituent Assembly Boycotters Rebuke UNSMIL for Meddling in Constitution Process", 12 October 2016(a). Accessible at: https://www.libyaobserver. ly/news/constituent-assembly-boycotters-rebuke-unsmil-meddling-constitution-process.

Ibid., "Al-Muwatana Hakki Movement Welcomes Al-Bayda Appeals Court's Verdict", 11 May 2016(b). Accessible at: https://www.libyaobserver.ly/news/al-muwatana-hakki-movement-welcomes-al-bayda-appeals-court%E2%80%99s-verdict.

Ibid., "CDA Boycotting Members Consider Oman and Al-Bayda Meetings Illegal", 19 April 2016(c). Accessible at: https://www.libyaobserver.ly/news/cda-boycotting-members-consider-oman-and-al-bayda-meetings-illegal.

Ibid., "Constitution-Drafting Assembly Accuse UNSMIL of Bias", 13 March 2016(d). Accessible at: https://www.libyaobserver.ly/news/constitution-drafting-assembly-member-accuses-unsmil-bias.

Libya's Channel, "Libya's Constituent Assembly Divided Over Oman Sessions", 22 March 2016. Accessible at: http://en.libyaschannel.com/2016/03/22/in-depth-libyas-consti tuent-assembly-divided-over-oman-sessions/.

Libyan Political Agreement. Accessible at: https://unsmil.unmissions.org/LinkClick.aspx? fileticket=miXuJYkQAQg%3D&tabid=3559&mid=6187&language=fr.

Maghur E., "A Legal Look into the Libyan Supreme Court Ruling", 8 December 2014. Accessible at: http://www.atlanticcouncil.org/blogs/menasource/a-legal-look-into-the-libyan-supreme-court-ruling.

Martin, I., "'The United Nations' role in the first year of the transition", in. P. Cole and B. McQuinn, *The Libyan revolution and its aftermath*, OUP, 2015, p. 129–130

Mayer A.E., "In Search of a Sacred Law: The Meandering Course of Gadhafi's Legal Policy", in Dirk Vandewalle (ed.), *Qadhafi's Libya 1969–1994*, London: Macmillan Press ltd, 1996, p. 123.

Obeidi A., "Tribe and Tribalism: An Alternative to Civil Society" Baxley, 2011.

Ramonet J-L., "Libya's Untold Story: Civil Society Amid Chaos", *Middle East Brief*, Crown Centre for Middle East Studies, No. 93, May 2015. Accessible at: https://www. brandeis.edu/crown/publications/meb/MEB93.pdf.

Report of the Secretary General on the United Nations Support Mission to Libya, S/2016/1011 of 1 December 2016.

Reuters, "Libya Faces Chaos as Top Court Rejects Elected Assembly". Accessible at: http:// www.reuters.com/article/us-libya-security-parliament-idUSKBN0IQ0YF20141106.

The Guardian, "Libyan Faction Demands Explanation from UN Over Envoy", 5 November 2015(a). Accessible at: https://www.theguardian.com/world/2015/nov/06/libyan-faction-demands-explanation-from-un-over-envoy.

Ibid., "UN Libya Envoy Accepts £1,000-a-Day Job from Backer of One Side in Civil War", 4 November 2015(b). Accessible at: https://www.theguardian.com/world/2015/nov/04/un-libya-envoy-accepts-1000-a-day-job-from-backer-of-one-side-in-civil-war.

The Libyan Political Agreement. Full text of the agreement accessible at: https://unsmil.unmissions.org/LinkClick.aspx?fileticket=miXuJYkQAQg%3D&tabid=3559&mid=6187&language=fr.

UN, Report of the Secretary General on the United Nations Support Mission to Libya, S/2016/1011 of 1 December 2016, §29–30.

UN, UNSCR 2009 (2011), 16 September 2011, §12-b and f.

Vandewalle D., "After Qadhafi: The Surprising Success of Libya", *Foreign Affairs*, Vol. 91, No. 6 (Nov./Dec. 2012), p. 8.

11 Public participation and elite capture

A yet incomplete struggle towards a new constitution in Tanzania[*]

Philipp Michaelis

Introduction

As is the reality for most African countries, Tanzania suffered immensely under colonialism,[1] with the repercussions and its post-colonial component still being felt today. *Inter alia*, due to these experienced developments, the country can look back on a rather brief history with regard to constitutionalism, let alone people-driven processes of shaping one's constitution. One needs to acknowledge, though, that such participatory dynamics have only recently started to emerge globally and yet have been turned into some kind of "cure-all recipe". Like most erstwhile British colonies, Tanganyika, after gaining its independence in 1961, inherited a constitutional system that was developed and installed by the former colonial administration without any effective and meaningful exertion of influence by the citizenry in form of some kind of participative device (Roschmann, Wendoh and Ogolla 2013, 155).[2] With the end of colonialism in 1961, a new constitution based on the Westminster system was drafted by Tanganyika nationalists in close cooperation with the former colonial power Great Britain and installed Queen Elizabeth II as the formal head of state (IDEA 2014). Paradoxically, "colonial sponsored written constitutions embodying idealist rules which were hardly practiced under colonialism" (East African Centre for Constitutional Development (EACCD) 2013, 7) were tailored for many newly founded or liberated African states. The constitutional history of Tanzania can therefore be regarded as rather young, and its supreme law can be seen as a prime example of what H.W.O. Okoth-Ogendo (1993) paraphrased as "constitutions without constitutionalism".

---

[*] This chapter is based to a significant degree on first-hand information drawn from the Blog of Humphrey Polepole (2015) who was involved in the Tanzanian constitution-making process and who was a member of the Constitutional Review Commission (CRC) from April 2012 to March 2014.

1 From 1891 onwards, Tanganyika was officially part of the former colony German East Africa, before it became a British protectorate by the end of World War I. After World War II and with the end of colonial rule, Tanganyika gained its independence in 1961. It soon merged with the former British Protectorate Zanzibar in 1964, which had become independent the year before. Zanzibar has formerly been an Oman-Arab Sultanate since the 17th century.

2 This procedure was typical of the Lancaster House negotiations, which forged the independence constitutions of the former British colonies.

DOI: 10.4324/9781315180540-14

It is all the more remarkable that in 2011, Tanzania launched a constitutional review process that for the first time in the country's constitutional history incorporated substantial participatory elements.[3] Although the impetus came from Jakaya Mrisho Kikwete, the then president of Tanzania, the situation has to be seen in the light of a rising societal demand to draw up a constitution which is more in line with the needs of the time and better reflects people's wishes and daily concerns (Polepole 2015). As it has been argued, "[t]he goal was to draft a more legitimate and nationally owned constitution" (IDEA 2014).

This chapter puts its focus precisely on the participatory element within the constitutional reform process. It is structured to follow the chronological order of events, which can be subdivided into four distinct phases. In a first step, an overview of the legal framework is provided for each of the four distinct periods, before subsequently contrasting the framework with its factual implementation. In a second step, particular dimensions of the process are scrutinized with regard to their participative nature and people-driven impact. It is argued that although the constitution-making process in Tanzania provided the public with a great opportunity to (re)shape the constitution according to their individual preferences, the manner in which the process unfolded can be regarded as a prime example of elite-capture. Even though the citizenry participated vividly during the public outreach as well as in the review phase and saw their contributions reflected in a draft constitution, their expectations were not met with regard to the content of the revised proposed constitution. Compared to the 1977 Constitution, which is currently in force, all recently formulated versions include progressive propositions and improvements to the Bill of Rights and can at large be regarded as significant milestones. However, the final document that has been prepared by the constituent body on the basis of these drafts is more conservative and can be identified as being the closest to the *status quo*. At the time of writing, the reform process in Tanzania is in limbo and the appraisal of the final document via popular referendum – initially scheduled for October 2015 – has been adjourned *sine die*.

Brief constitutional history of Tanzania

Following the end of British colonial rule, Tanzania adopted the Westminster Constitution and a constitutional monarchy was put in place. This laid the groundwork for multi-party democracy, without, however, including a Bill of Rights. The legal document was soon replaced by the Republican Constitution of 1962 that installed a presidential system with a dominant executive compiled of the then ruling party, the Tanganyika African National Union (TANU).

3 In fact, in 1991 the Tanzanian government reacted to societal demands for constitutional reform and created the Nyalali commission that would conduct public opinion polls on the national political system. Furthermore, the government issued the White Paper No. 1 of 1998, asking the public to respond to a list of different constitutional issues (Nyirabu 2002, 102–103; Hydén 1999: 147). These two reform initiatives are not considered here since the agenda-setting function remained with the government – later appeared to utilize public input to legitimize its own preferences (Nyirabu 2002, 107–8).

In 1964, when Tanganyika merged with Zanzibar to form the United Republic of Tanzania, the constitution was revised a second time and replaced by an interim constitution. In this context, the two-tier government structure was reformed to accommodate a union government and a semi-autonomous government for Zanzibar (IDEA 2014). Various adjustments were made to the interim constitution, such as in 1965 when a single-party political system led by the TANU government was formally consolidated for mainland Tanzania.[4] The interim constitution was in force until 1977 when the ruling party Chama Cha Mapinduzi (CCM), which had emerged out of a fusion of TANU and Zanzibar's ruling Afro-Shirazi Party (ASP) and was spear-headed by President Julius Nyerere, gave impetus to revise the document. In this process of revision, Tanzania promulgated the 1977 Constitution, which was the first permanent constitution and is *de jure* still the officially valid document for the country. Since the constitution came to force in 1977, it has been amended several times, including in 1992 when Tanzania returned to a multi-party political system and in 1984 when a Bill of Rights was added (IDEA 2014; Masabo and Wanitzek 2015, 334). The last constitutional modification has since been made in 2005. The institutional architecture of the 1977 Constitution places a strong emphasis on the executive branch. Under the presidential system, extensive competences are deployed to the head of state. The formal state is based on a two-tier government structure with a national government responsible for union matters as well as for mainland Tanzania, and a semi-autonomous government for Zanzibar. The highest juridical organ under the 1977 Constitution is the Court of Appeal.[5]

Zanzibar, after gaining its independence in 1963, passed an independence constitution the same year. This constitution became subject to diverse executive decrees, before Zanzibar and Tanganyika were eventually united under union law, and Zanzibar's constitution was incorporated separately in a chapter attached to the union constitution. In 1979, a separate constitution was endorsed for Zanzibar (Revolutionary Government of Zanzibar (RGoZ) 2013).[6] The current constitution of Zanzibar was adopted in 1984 and has been amended several times since. Matters regarding the United Republic of Tanzania remain settled by the 1977 Constitution of Tanzania. Recent constitutional debates have been strongly defined by the Zanzibari political context and the political reconciliation process within the semi-autonomous region. In a referendum that was held prior to the general elections in 2010, Zanzibari citizens voted for the formation of a proportionally based Government of National Unity (GNU)[7], *inter alia*, in order to avoid post-election unrest that had overshadowed previous polls (RGoZ 2013). The overarching national constitutional reform process can be regarded as an integral part to that reconciliation process (Olsen 2014, 5–6).

---

4 In Zanzibar, the Afro-Shirazi Party (ASP) remained the dominant political party.
5 For an in-depth analysis of the major aspects of the 1977 Constitution in comparison to the two versions prepared by the Constitutional Review Commission and the Constituent Assembly see (Masabo and Wanitzek 2015; IDEA 2014).
6 Not interfering with matters regarding the United Republic of Tanzania.
7 Between Zanzibar's two main political parties, the CCM and the Civic United Front (CUF).

In this nationwide context, a constitutional review process was kick-started by then President of the United Republic of Tanzania Jakaya Kikwete, who in a public speech by the end of 2011 declared that the time had come to initiate a process leading to a new constitution. This announcement came as a surprise to many, as it was originally not on the CCM agenda. It can also be assumed that the rationale behind the initiative was to tone down demands by the political opposition (Babeiya 2016, 79).

A constitution in the making: Legal framework and its implementation

The Constitutional Review Act (CRA) of 2011, Chapter 83 (amended in 2012 and twice in 2013) provides the legal framework for the constitution-making process. It outlines the course of action, rules, and procedures; sets out which legal bodies and actor groupings will partake; and defines forms of envisaged citizen involvement. In particular, sections 9, 18, 22, and 25 are of special interest to this contribution since these refer to the composition and mandate of the involved constitution-making bodies as well as to regulations regarding the set up and work of constitutional review fora. The second legal document that structures the process is the Referendum Act of 2013 which, coupled with the CRA, constitutes the juridical foundation of the process. The legal text outlines a fourfold procedure that should ultimately pave the way for a new constitution, co-created and owned by the people of Tanzania. First, a Constitutional Review Commission (CRC) shall be responsible for the collection of public opinion and shall ensure that outcomes are reasonable products of citizen involvement. On the basis of public input, a first draft constitution will be prepared which, in a second step, will be subject to a revision by civil society in so-called constitutional review fora. This consultative phase shall culminate in a report and a second draft constitution. Third, a Constituent Assembly (CA) shall discuss and review the draft elaborated by the commission and produce a final version that, in turn, requires the approval by a two-thirds majority in the CA. Fourth, this document will then be subject to a vote in a popular referendum that requires a 50 percent majority of all casted votes in mainland Tanzania as well as in Zanzibar. While the first two stages, that most clearly entail participatory elements, should be guided by the CRC, the third stage is supposed to be conducted by the CA. The institution empowered in the final stage is the citizenry, whose approval is required to seal the ratification process.[8] For the sake of completeness, three major amendments need to be mentioned that were made regarding the legal provisions in the CRA. These should serve to increase the participation of key stakeholders as well as citizens in the process (EACCD 2013, 26).[9]

---

8 For a detailed actor analysis see (Babeiya 2016).

9 The first amendment, passed by Parliament on 10 February 2012, made four decisive changes concerning the composition of CRC and CA, the appointment as well as drafting procedures, and the respective powers of the two presidents (referring to the competences of the presidents of Tanzania and Zanzibar, for instance when appointing members to the CA). In September 2013,

Collecting people's views (Stage I)

The process officially started on 30 November 2011, when the Constitutional Review Act was enacted by Parliament, designed to outline the rules and procedures that should serve as a regulatory framework in the constitution-making process. In order to provide a device intended to reach out to the people, in a first step, a Constitutional Review Commission was to be established. The legal provisions that authorize the president of the Republic[10] to appoint delegates to the CRC were captured in Sections 5 and 6 of the Constitutional Review Act of 2011. The commission consisted of 32 members, 15 nominated from Tanzania mainland and 15 from Zanzibar, chosen from a pool of 550 people that had been proposed by different stakeholders such as religious organizations, civil society organizations (CSOs), and political parties (CRA 2011, Section 6(6)). Members of the commission were appointed to their posts on 6 April 2012 and two additional members – the chairperson[11] and the vice chairperson[12] – were designated to provide guidance and leadership.[13] The equal representation of mainland Tanzania and Zanzibar within the commission can be regarded as an impulse to guarantee inclusiveness, independence, and sovereignty (EACCD 2013, 20). The CRA empowers the commission with the followings tasks and provides distinct tools for their accomplishment:

First, the CRC was mandated to conduct a public outreach program. The program was designed to collect citizens' opinions regarding the content of the constitution – i.e., what kind of provisions they would like to see installed in the legal document. Second, the CRC was asked to transform the information gathered in the course of the public outreach program into a first draft constitution. This tentative document was due to be handed to the vice president for a revision. Precisely referring to its functions, Chapter 83, Section 9 of the CRA determines that:

> The functions of the Commission shall be to: (a) co-ordinate and collect public opinions; (b) examine and analyse the consistency and compatibility of the constitutional provisions in relation to the sovereignty of the people, political systems, democracy, rule of law and good governance; (c) make recommendations on each term of reference; and (d) prepare and submit a report.

This section, however, leaves some room for interpretation as Section 9(1) (b) is rather vaguely formulated and does not specify precisely what is meant

---

several other amendments were made with regard to the CA's composition, its order of operations as well as the considered dissolution of the CRC after completion of their work. The third and last amendment to the CRA increased the total number of non-parliamentarian members of the CA from 166 to 201. Other changes were made with regard to certain text passages concerning the referendum and matters of voting in the CA (Polepole 2015).

10 In agreement with the president of Zanzibar.
11 The former Attorney General and Prime Minister Joseph Warioba was named president.
12 This post was conferred to former Chief Justice Augustino Ramadhani.
13 Nominations to the CRC should take into account the diversity of the country in terms of gender, geography, social groups, etc. (See Section 6(3)(a),(b),(c) of the CRA of 2011).

by "consistency" and "compatibility" in relation to the identified aspects that are enumerated (Enonchong 2012). Nevertheless, the scope of the mandate provided the people of Tanzania with a first-time opportunity to interact with constitution-makers. This participatory nature, which allowed people to freely utter their opinion on matters such as the powers of the executive, was a novelty in the Republic's history. Matters such as the structure of the union, amongst others, were hitherto thought to be sacred and out of citizens' direct influence (Polepole 2015). The scope of people's competences is stated in Section 9, Subsection (3), which clearly manifests their influence and strengthens their role in providing views in public. Here it reads, "[t]he commission shall afford the people an opportunity to freely express their opinions with a view to further enrich those matters".

In terms of *de facto* participation, Tanzanians seized the occasion and grabbed their chance of contributing actively. Public meetings that were organized by the CRC were characterized by lively debate. To widen its actual outreach, the CRC provided awareness programs and subsequently divided itself into several groups that could simultaneously visit different parts of the country in order to collect citizens' views. The East African Centre for Constitutional Development (EACCD 2013, 21) speaks of a total number of 1,773 held meetings in all constituencies, with a total of approximately 1,400,000 (1.4 mil.) people attending those meetings. Thereof, more than 350,000 people made use of the opportunity to express their opinion within such meetings (Polepole 2015) and around 60,000 of them in form of direct contributions and presentations (EACCD 2013, 21–22). In addition to the collection of orally given contributions, the commission provided special forms in which people could express their views in a written manner. These forms could then be handed in at centres on a municipal level. Noteworthy concerning the documents, however, was that these required detailed personal information such as full name, gender, address, profession, etc., which potentially fuelled a reluctance or cautiousness to freely express one's views. In sum, a total of 300,000 people provided their opinions in this manner between July and December 2012 (EACCD 2013, 22). The commission additionally gathered people's proposals via telephone calls, blogs, e-mails, and social network contributions (IDEA 2014). This incorporation of predominantly digital sources in the process of opinion gathering was criticized, however, with the argument that it led to the exclusion of numerous Tanzanian citizens who are not equipped with digital devices (Katundu and Kumburu 2015). In terms of gender equality, it can be noted that women participated actively in the organized meetings as well. In Zanzibar, for instance, 42 percent of all contributions collected by the commission came from women (Olsen 2014, 6)[14].

In January 2013, another institutionalized mechanism was designed in order to reach out to the wider public. The commission had special meetings with different stakeholders such as CSOs, NGOs, religious groups, political parties, and others, wherein the different actors were asked to provide their opinions on

---

14 Referring to statistics provided by the CRC.

the new constitution, an opportunity that was made use of extensively and had considerable influence on constitutional proposals that found their way into the first draft constitution (EACCD 2013, 22; Polepole 2015). All that input was then assessed, analysed, and evaluated and, after four months, integrated into the first draft constitution that was presented to the vice president and prime minister on 3 June 2013.

The outreach phase can be considered a once-in-a-lifetime opportunity for the Tanzanian people that was made use of actively, as many people freely gave their opinions on distinct constitutional modules and models. The whole program was a major success and its scope was unique in terms of displaying a participatory dimension that has never before been reached by any kind of public consultation on constitutional matters (Polepole 2015).

Constitutional review (Stage II)

During the second stage, designed to review the first draft constitution, special constitutional fora – the so-called *barazas* – were installed in order to provide a platform for mutual exchange of standpoints on the constitutional draft. Based on the input gathered in citizen constitutional fora, as well as in special institutional fora, the commission was tasked with elaborating a second draft. Concerning the legal provisions of the second stage, Chapter 83, Section 18 of the Constitutional Review Act calls for the establishment of these forums and defines the manner in which they are to function. The text says that "[t]he fora for constitutional review shall provide public opinions on the Draft Constitution through meetings organized by the Commission" and further, that they shall "be formed on ad hoc basis [. . .] based on geographical diversity of the United Republic and shall involve and bring together representatives of various groups of people within the communities." In addition, the CRA states that "the Commission may allow organizations, associations or groups of persons to convene meetings in order to afford opportunity to its members to air their views on the Draft Constitution and forward such views to the Commission". It has to be pointed out that these fora were exclusively reserved for Tanzanian citizens. This aspect can be regarded as an attempt to lower the influence of external actors. Given these ample opportunities to exert influence on the constitutional text, it can be noted that the CRA entailed significant potential for the promotion of a people-driven document. The commission was furthermore provided with a sufficient mandate in terms of its geographical and societal representation. All social groups were given the opportunity to influence the draft constitution according to their preferences and to lobby for their interests. But, how were these provisions realized in practice?

With the mandate to organize the second stage, the CRC, referring to Section 18(3), convened a total number of 177 constitutional fora within the Republic of Tanzania, one for every district (EACCD 2013, 22; Polepole 2015). Additionally, two separate fora for people with disabilities were assembled in mainland Tanzania and another one for Zanzibar. All these fora were set up by the citizens of Tanzania at village or street level, in rural or urban areas, respectively. Each forum consisted of five representatives, of which one of the five was a member of the local government authority. Citizens, in turn, would elect additional candidates to represent the following: the youth, the elderly, women, as well as a representative in one additional category – for instance persons with disabilities (Polepole 2015). The CRC was divided into 14 groups that were sent to hold constitutional fora, staying at least three days at each location before moving to the next district. Typically in each district, the draft constitution was first introduced and then subjected to discussions and revisions in special working groups. Finally, the draft was discussed openly in a plenary session (EACCD 2013, 22). A total of 18,000 people attended these meetings across Tanzania and Zanzibar. In the run-up to the meetings, the commission was supposed to publish the preliminary version of the draft constitution in the *Gazette* and other local newspapers, therefore giving the public the chance to further enrich the proposed articles, taking into account the outcome of the debates in the distinct forums.

Another way in which proposals could be submitted to the CRC was through so-called independent forums, in line with Section 18(6) of Chapter 83 of the CRA. With this mechanism, organizations, institutions, and associations were given the opportunity to organize independent forums throughout the country. Institutions were requested to apply to the commission and, in case of approval, could submit their views on the constitution. In sum, 500 institutions, which dispatched a total of 614 submissions in this manner, were approved by the commission to form such an institutional forum (EACCD 2013, 22). According to information provided to the commission, all institutions taken together could reach out to more than six million people through these independent forums (Polepole 2015). The outcome was manifested in the second draft constitution, which was submitted to the president of the union on 30 September 2013 with the duty to publicize it in the *Gazette*. In addition, a report was formulated by the commission and also handed to the president.

Considering the manner in which the participatory dimension was implemented in practice, as well as the enormous effort made by the CRC to reach the public, the whole program can be regarded as a major success. Propositions concerning presidential powers, the structure of the union, or legislative oversight mechanisms, just to name a few, found their way into the draft and were based on numerous contributions made by the society. The revision and translation of these contributions into legally binding text were the subsequent steps of the process that begun with the establishment of the CA. Despite all accomplishments, a drawback regarding the independence of the forums as well as the representativeness of people's remarks has to be mentioned in this context. It was reported that the *barazas* were occasionally characterized by a dominance of the ruling political party, the CCM (Toniatti 2014, 97–98). While acknowledging the fact that the CCM had a majority in Parliament at the time, it could nevertheless also be regarded as an indicator for inadequate representation and a lack of inclusivity. Furthermore, individuals and CSOs that intended to conduct awareness programs were required to disclose their sources of funds (CRA 2011, 17(9)(b)(ii)), thereby somehow impeding privately organized consultation formats. A breach of these regulations constituted an offence that could be punished by financial fines or even imprisonment. This procedure can be regarded as controversial and a hindrance to free expression, since these criminalizing regulations served to create fear among the citizenry (EACCD 2013, 25).

A process captured by national elites (Stage III)

After the finalization of the second draft constitution that was submitted to the president of the Republic by the end of December 2013, the constitution-making process turned to its third phase. At this stage, the Constituent Assembly was to be composed. "The design for finally adopting a constitution is of critical importance to its legitimacy. From the background, it has been shown that the ideal design is for a representative body to debate a draft and promulgate the constitution" (EACCD 2013, 25). From the chairman of the CRC, the CA received the second draft constitution that was to serve as a point of departure for the further procedure.

The mandate and the precise powers of the CA were highly debated among the diverse political actors within the constitution-making process (Ackson 2015; Masabo and Wanitzek 2015, 339–40; Polepole 2015). It seems that the Constitutional Review Act leaves some room for interpretation when it states that:

> The Constituent Assembly shall have and exercise powers to make provisions for the New Constitution of the United Republic of Tanzania and to make consequential and transitional provisions to the enactment of such Constitution and to make such other provisions as the Constituent Assembly may find necessary (CRA 2011, 25(1)).

This subsection outlines two major functions of the body, namely to make provisions for a new constitution and to furnish consequential and transitional provisions concerning the process that should ultimately lead to the enactment of a new constitution. This paragraph, and especially the passage "such other provisions as the Constituent Assembly may find necessary", was subject to wide-ranging discussions regarding its interpretation and implementation. A controversy arose around the ambiguous mandate of the CA concerning its actual right to alter and remove entire passages entailed in the draft constitution, which had been stipulated in Section 25(1) of the CRA (Polepole 2015). The debate, in turn, had far-reaching implications in relation to the content and perceived legitimacy of the final outcome, in particular with regard to the degree to which people-induced provisions were to be kept in the final draft.

With regard to the composition of the CA, Section 22 and 23 of the CRA provide the legal groundwork for its configuration. The CA should be composed of all delegates from the National Assembly of the United Republic of Tanzania,[15]

---

15 Of the 355 members of Parliament, 262 belonged to the government party (CCM) and 92 to the opposition plus the attorney general. Among these, 70 were from Zanzibar (Ackson 2015, 370).

the members of the House of Representatives of Zanzibar,[16] and 201 members that were "appointed by the President in agreement with the President of Zanzibar" (CRA 2011, Section 22(1)). Out of these 201 members, a third should be from Zanzibar and two thirds from mainland Tanzania. There were special quotas according to which the president was supposed to nominate the additional candidates. A certain number[17] was to be nominated from among lists provided by each of the following groups: NGOs (20), faith-based organizations (20), political parties (42), learning institutions (20), people with disabilities (20), trade union organizations (19), agricultural associations (20), fishery associations (10), livestock keepers (10), and other interest groups made up by persons having a common interest (20). Considering this selection mechanism by which the delegates were drawn from distinct lists submitted by different civil society actors, the composition of the CA could be regarded as more representative than that of the CRC. One could argue that in terms of legitimacy, the body was made to be more accessible and transparent in comparison to the rather exclusive nature of the CRC.[18] Nevertheless, the body could also be considered as rather limited when it comes to people's direct influence, as it was not directly bound to citizens' inputs (as subsequent events will illustrate). Regarding the fact that the president was more or less given sole authority over the additional nominations to the CA, and the fact that the CCM ruling party had an almost indisputable supermajority,[19] the presence of the opposition appeared to be a mere rubber-stamp. In addition, the fact that the CA was predominantly composed of members of Parliament (MPs), a situation was induced in which politicians, having partisan and individual interests, voted on their own political future "act[ing] as judge in their own case" (Brandt et al. 2011, 235) – for example when proposals affected legislative term-limits, expenses, or other payouts.

Turning to the implementation phase of the legal framework, it can be noted that the process by which the 201 additional members of the CA were nominated to the body was initiated by the Government Notice No. 443 of 13 December 2013, by which the distinct interest groups were asked to submit their lists of candidates for the posts. In sum, the total number of candidates came to 628, the two Attorney Generals from mainland Tanzania and Zanzibar included (Ackson 2015) – out of which 409 were from mainland Tanzania and 219 from Zanzibar. The CA officially started its work on 18 February 2014 when the body was sworn in. The assembly was at the time divided into 20 committees that would work on different issues at the same time.

16 Of the 82 members, 48 represented the CCM, and 33 the Civic United Front plus the attorney general of Zanzibar (ibid. 370).

17 As indicated by the number in brackets below.

18 This aspect is also taken up by Tulia Ackson (2015, 385), when referring to the court case *Saed Kubenea versus The Attorney General*, Misc. Civil Application No. 29 of 2014, High Court of Tanzania at Dar es Salaam (arising from Misc. Civil Cause No. 28 of 2014).

19 From a government perspective, just a few out of the 201 delegates needed to be won over in order for the proposed constitution to be passed with a two-thirds majority. See Tulia Ackson (2015, 383–85) for a detailed analysis of the vote configuration.

After the appointment of the 201 delegates, people's reactions towards the installation of the CA were mixed. On the one hand, some people were looking forward to the process finally setting off now that the composition of the CA had been completed. Others, to the contrary, were afraid of a polarization within the institution, due to the fact that the majority of members in the CA were affiliated with the ruling political party (CCM). The argument was that the need for consensus-building surrounding contentious issues was hereby minimized (Polepole 2015). As a matter of fact, calls for decision-making based on unanimity, bargaining, and consensus-seeking were *de facto* ignored by the majority of the CA members, who predominantly stuck to their party line, thus making no effort to overcome the divisions that characterized the state of affairs in the assembly (Polepole 2015). Moreover, instances of bribery were reported, allegedly aimed at securing the support of assembly members for the government-line (Babeiya 2016, 82). This tense atmosphere became even worse when abusive language entered the assembly sessions (Babeiya 2016, 83; Polepole 2015). Another highly contested matter in this context were the voting procedure preferences in the CA, a matter on which members were divided along party lines. While most associates of the ruling party preferred an open ballot, large parts of the opposition plead for a secret ballot – some say so as not to be seen as deviating from the party line (Babeiya 2016, 85). It needs to be stressed in this context that a significant number of MPs belonging to the CCM – who were privately supporting the second draft submitted by the commission – would have voted in favour of that draft had there been a secret ballot.[20]

Among other factors, this divided nature of the constituent body led to the formation of two opposing factions within the CA. The first camp, mainly composed of CCM cadres and those with close ties to the ruling party, labelled themselves as *Tanzania Kwanza* – meaning as much as "putting national interests first". The second block, labelled UKAWA,[21] was spear-headed by a coalition of the major opposition parties Chadema, CUF, and NCCR-Mageuzi. It became clear during negotiations that the CA was not dependent on the votes of the opposition with regard to effective decision-making. Consequently, large parts of the opposition left negotiations, indicating that reaching a consensus had from the start not been the aim of the parties involved. This "walk-out" on 16 April 2014 can be regarded as a multi-causal outcome of the factors mentioned above. The reluctance to aim for a procedure characterized by the negotiation of preferences, to include minority opinions, and to seek for consensus, can be considered as a major drawback in terms of the inclusiveness as well as representativeness of the process. After more than 200 delegates had left the assembly sessions one might have expected the CA leadership to postpone its work and to call for an emergency consensus meeting. Instead the vice-chair holder of the assembly asked the secretaries to inquire whether the threshold for

20 Informal statements of members of Parliament made in the presence of Polepole (2015).
21 An acronym of *Umoja wa Katiba ya Wananchi* referring to a coalition in favor of a people-centered constitution.

a quorum was reached, before continuing the sessions (Polepole 2015). As an outcome of the subsequent negotiations, the proposed constitution was drafted by the incomplete assembly and – in fulfilling its mandate[22] – handed to the president of Tanzania on 2 October 2014. When evaluating the procedure by which the proposed constitution was drafted, it becomes evident that the process was highly controversial. The proceedings become even more interesting if one considers the argument of some authors that those constitutions, which are produced by a rather consensus-oriented procedure, tend to be more stable, representative, and democratic (Okodi 2005; Brandt et al. 2011, 87; Ghai and Galli 2006, 10, 15; Samuels 2006, 667–69). Since there is not enough evidence, however, to conclude that an actual link exists between a consensus-based promulgation and a more consolidated constitution, it remains to be seen how durable the new constitution will be in case it is adopted. Its promulgation, however, lies in the hands of the public, for an obligatory approval via popular referendum is still to come.

In terms of content, the proposed constitution deviates significantly from the two preceding draft constitutions. As illustrated by Humphrey Polepole (2015), crucial changes have been made with regard to substantive issues such as the structure of the union, presidential powers, the size of government and Parliament, term limits and by-elections for MPs, and the separation of powers, to name only a few. During the outreach program a large number of people articulated the wish to curb the extensive powers of the presidency, in particular with regard to appointing powers. People suggested that major political appointments, such as judges to the Supreme Court, should be subject to legislative approval so as to lower presidential influence. Passages in favour for such a decrease in executive competence – which had been captured in the draft constitution – were dropped in the proposed constitution, thus maintaining the *status quo* according to the 1977 Constitution. Another crucial claim raised by citizens pertained to the horizontal architecture of state institutions. A broadening of checks and balances in the form of more oversight, greater autonomy, and increasing competences for the Parliament vis-à-vis the executive was called for. Likewise, it was the view that the separation of government and Parliament should be advanced, including that ministerial posts should no longer be occupied by MPs. Additionally, the president should no longer be allowed to resolve the Parliament on the grounds that it has repeatedly rejected government bills for improvement. The CA in the proposed constitution rejected all of these proposals, which were aimed at strengthening the separation of powers. The document also falls short of directly addressing the issue of gender inequality within society – for instance in government institutions such as Parliament – leaving the enforcement mechanism to legislation (Allen 2014, 20; Kibamba 2016a).[23]

22 In line with Section 28A(1) of the CRA 2011.
23 The second draft constitution intended for the introduction of two-member constituencies (male and female representatives), which would have assured gender parity in Parliament. The proposed constitution calls for gender equality, but is silent on the procedure (Allen 2014, 20).

The perhaps most controversially discussed aspect was the envisaged structure of the union. The CRC had proposed a three-tier federal government structure, adding a further jurisdiction solely for union matters. This proposition was built on claims from the public. Some Tanzanian scholars have, in turn, however, questioned precisely the translational mechanism that was used by the CRC to convert people's input into a legal frame (Ackson 2015, 386–87; Katundu and Kumburu 2015). Referring to statistics provided by the CRC, it is argued that on the basis of people's articulations, the commission could have equally put forth a different scheme of government structure. While in mainland Tanzania 61.3 percent were in favour for a federal structure with three authorities (compared to 1.0 percent for confederation), in Zanzibar a majority of 60.2 percent plead for a confederation with only 5.0 percent in favour of a federation. Hence, the favoured schemes in Zanzibar and mainland Tanzania display two distinct extremes, which could have induced the commission to prefer a more consensus-oriented government design. A two-tier government structure, for example, was supported by 34.6 percent in Zanzibar and 24.3 percent in mainland Tanzania. However, acknowledging the fact that merely 14 percent of all casted opinions even referred to the union structure, the representativeness of such results can be regarded as questionable. Above all, this example vividly illustrates the dilemma of how to transfer citizen's inputs into constitutional modules and it prompts the question whether the tools required for an effective and reliable translation even exist.

Other proposals that were later dropped in the legal text pertained to a reduction of Parliament size, legislative term limits,[24] motions of no confidence against parliamentarians, innovative provisions facilitating new sources of government revenue, an ethical code for public servants, and the constitutional manifestation of national core values such as dignity, patriotism, unity, integrity, and transparency (Polepole 2015). At first glance, it is striking that many proposals aimed at constraining parliamentarians were rejected. It nevertheless becomes less surprising when one considers that the CA is predominantly composed of members of Parliament. Further recommendations that aimed to ensure a decrease in executive powers were rejected as well. The outcome therefore somewhat reflects the individual preferences of the actors involved. The proposed constitution, which had been approved by a two-thirds majority in the CA, should ultimately be subject to a people's referendum.

The people as the final authority (Stage IV)

The proposed constitution was supposed to be taken to referendum, paralleling the general election scheduled for October 2015, but it was postponed *sine die*. According to the Referendum Act of 2013, Section 36(1), the referendum was to be conducted, supervised, and analysed by the National Electoral Commission

---

24 The CRC proposed a term period of five years that is renewable twice at the most. The CA changed it back to the possibility of being MP for life.

(NEC) in close cooperation with the Zanzibar Electoral Commission. The CA made one constitutional version public and only the constitution as a whole awaited citizens' approval. The threshold for the proposed constitution to pass was set at 50 percent of the votes cast in Tanzania mainland and those cast in Zanzibar, without providing additional requirements.[25] Hence, the final authority vests in the hands of the Tanzanian people, as they are provided with the function and power of a veto player in the institutional architecture of the constitution-making process. This capacity has been referred to by Jon Elster (1995, 373–75) as a type of "downstream constrain" that is imposed on actors or institutions in an upward (upstream) position within that process, such as the CRC or the CA. Considering the fact that this constrain was neglected or not anticipated – in the sense that a bulk of proposals based on people's input was overthrown by the CA – it will be interesting to observe the forthcoming reaction of the citizenry.

Recent experiences from other African countries have demonstrated that once the public has been involved in the process of drafting a constitution and has been empowered to exercise considerable influence, they want to see this influence reflected in the legal outcome. In Zimbabwe [2000] and Kenya [2005] for instance, the population had been equipped with the function of a veto player, and was given the final say on the elaborated constitution in the form of a popular referendum. In Zimbabwe [2000] the draft constitution, which was formulated under close consideration of citizens' proposals, was later amended to a great extent by the president before putting it to the vote. In consequence, the proposed constitution was rejected by the people in a referendum by absolute majority in February 2000.[26] Developments in Kenya [2005] unfolded in similar fashion. For the first time in the country's constitutional history, the population was provided with participatory tools to channel their interests with respect to a constitutional design. The Constitution of Kenya Review Commission (CKRC) was set up in order to prepare a preliminary draft constitution based to some extent on public input. The draft was revised by the National Constitutional Conference (NCC) that was composed of MPs, political party representatives, and different civic society stakeholders. The resulting draft, however, was changed again, this time by Parliament on behalf of the government. Shortly before, the High Court had deemed a referendum to be necessary, even though such a mechanism was originally not envisaged.[27] The final draft to be voted on

25 In case the constitution is rejected by more than half of the votes in either constituency, there are several steps laid down by the Referendum Act. First, another date would need to be set in order to repeat the referendum within 60 days. Second, more sensitization on the referendum should be conducted. And third, if there is sufficient time, the president should reconvene the CA in order to consider people's views and opinions anew. If the constitution should be rejected for a second time, the 1977 Constitution would remain in force (Referendum Act 2013, Section 35).

26 For a detailed illustration of the Zimbabwean constitution-making process [2000] see John Hatchard (2001). For an examination of Zimbabwe's recent constitution-making process [2013] see the contribution of Douglas T. Mwonzora in this volume.

27 Earlier provisions saw the Parliament as the final institution in the promulgation process (Konrad-Adenauer-Stiftung (KAS) 2012, 43–46).

departed significantly from the earlier version. In a situation that became highly politicized, the people of Kenya finally rejected the constitution. With regard to motive, people were said to have repudiated the document due to a general dissatisfaction with the ruling party, ethnic considerations, but foremost because they had preferred the earlier draft (Brandt et al. 2011, 340–41).

These two examples illustrate that where national elites are reluctant to respond to an actively involved citizenry and to consider their wishes, people tend to make use of their veto power. Against this backdrop, it remains to be seen to what extent the Tanzanian people realize the opportunity to shape their legal future, the possible socio-legal outcome being a people-owned constitution. Further, it will be interesting to see whether or to what degree the referendum – assuming that there will be a vote after all – will be politicized or linked to diverse partisan interests (as was the case in Kenya for example).

Concluding remarks

In terms of envisaged and implemented modes of participation, the entire constitutional reform process was conceptualized in a fashion that left ample room for participatory elements and the Tanzanian people, in fact, vividly took these up. The endeavour in itself can be regarded as pivotal for the county, for the Tanzanian people were at the centre of such a domestic process, which provided the potential for ownership of a new constitution and for fostering its legitimacy. The first and second draft constitution as well as the proposed constitution can jointly be considered landmarks in the constitutional history of Tanzania, especially when compared to the 1977 Constitution, which remains supreme law until it is amended or replaced. These three latest versions share a lot of common provisions with regard to their proposed content. Nevertheless, there are a few progressive aspects considered to be valuable for a new constitution that were neglected or altered by the CA, in particular with regard to the structure of the union, presidential powers, separation of powers, and checks and balances (Masabo and Wanitzek 2015, 341, 368). This political interference by the ruling elite, which in the course of the process unilaterally decided to alter or drop several public proposals, needs to be assessed as deficient in terms of popular ownership.

In addition, it can be argued that experiences from other recent constitution-building processes in near geographical surroundings (Kenya [2005], [2010]; Uganda [1995]), as well as from other parts of the world, were only marginally taken into account when elaborating the design of the reform process. The neglected downstream constrain function of the populace, for instance, could have been anticipated considering other recent constitution-making processes. Similarly, the restrictiveness of partaking constitution-making bodies, the evasion of a consensus-oriented drafting mode, or the politicization of the process could have been contemplated from the outset. This rather limited recognition of other procedural blueprints could be considered a shortcoming of the process.

Finally, the question remains as to what exactly the purpose of designing a process is, one that envisages participatory elements as being inherently central, when the outcome of that same process is, in turn, not adequately taken into account. When citizens are incorporated as an institution within the process, they subsequently want to see their contributions reflected in the outcome – the constitution. One can hardly imagine that the adjustments that the CA made to the draft constitution did not discourage people's confidence in a "people-driven" or "people-owned" legal document. Maybe time is of crucial relevance here, supposing that the farer the referendum moves from its scheduled date, the likelier it is that the line between political interest and constitutional content becomes blurred. Therefore, a further politicization of the process to come needs to be anticipated. Moreover, a "no" vote in a referendum could be a blessing, too, as a veto by the people, having been educated in constitutional matters, could be another lesson learnt for elite constitution-makers in the future. It remains to be seen whether the people make use of their veto-function, assigned to them by the Referendum Act 2013, and thus maintain their struggle in search of a new constitution. Lately, however, renewed calls for the constitutional review phase to be restarted came up and views in favour of a modification of the legal text closer to that of the draft constitution have gained momentum (Kibamba 2016b, Kibamba 2016c). Therefore, one can only eagerly wait to see how future events unfold.

References

Ackson, T. (2015). "Winnowing Tanzania's Proposed Constitution: The Legitimacy Question", *VRÜ Verfassung und Recht in Übersee*, 48(3), 369–89.

Allen, M. (2014). "Women and Constitution-Building in 2014", *Annual Review of Constitution-Building Processes: 2014*, International IDEA, 17–41.

Babeiya, E. (2016). "New Constitution-Making in Tanzania: An Examination of Actors' Roles and Influence", *African Journal of Political Science and International Relations*, 10(5), 74–88.

Brandt, M., Cottrell J., Ghai, Y., and Regan, A. (2011). *Constitution-making and Reform: Options for the Process*, Interpeace, Switzerland.

Constitutional Review Act (2011). *Constitutional Review Act, 2011, Cap. 83*, revised edition of 2014, The United Republic of Tanzania, Dar es Salaam, 6 February 2014, (http://www.constitutionnet.org/vl/item/tanzania-constitutional-review-act-2014).

East African Centre for Constitutional Development (2013). *Report of East African Consultative Theme on the Tanzania Constitutional Review Process*, Report of Kito Cha Katiba, East African Centre for Constitutional Development.

Elster, J. (1995). "Forces and Mechanisms in the Constitution-Making Process", *Duke Law Journal*, 45(2), 364–96.

Enonchong, L.-S. (2012). "Tanzania's Constitutional Review: A New Era for the Union?", 7 February 2012, (http://www.comparativeconstitutions.org/2012/07/tanzanias-constitutional-review-new-era.html).

Ghai, Y., and Galli, G. (2006). *Constitution Building and Democratization*, International IDEA, Stockholm.

Hatchard, J. (2001). "Some Lessons on Constitution-Making from Zimbabwe", *Journal of African Law*, 45(2), 210–16.

Hydén, G. (1999). "Top-Down Democratization in Tanzania", *Journal of Democracy*, 10(4), 142–55.

IDEA (2014). "Tanzania – Country Constitutional Profile", (http://www.constitutionnet. org/country/tanzania-country-constitutional-profile).

Katundu, M. A., and Kumburu, N. P. (2015). "Tanzania's Constitutional Reform Predicament and the Survival of the Tanganyika and Zanzibar Union", *The Journal of Pan African Studies*, 8(3), August 2015, 104–18.

Kibamba, D. (2016a). "Talking Point: Proposed Constitution Falls Short of Guaranteeing Gender Parity", *The Citizen*, 12 October 2016.

Kibamba, D. (2016b). "Talking Point: Why Ultimate Power Ought to Be Vested in the People", *The Citizen*, 28 September 2016.

Kibamba, D. (2016c). "Tanzania: How Verdict On Bageni Jump-Started the Katiba Debate", *The Citizen*, 21 September 2016.

Konrad-Adenauer-Stiftung (KAS) (2012). *History of Constitution Making in Kenya*, Media Development Association and Konrad Adenauer Foundation, Kenya.

Masabo J., and Wanitzek U. (2015). "Constitutional Reform in Tanzania", *VRÜ Verfassung und Recht in Übersee*, 48(3), 329–68.

Nyirabu, M. (2002). "The Multiparty Reform Process in Tanzania: The Dominance of the Ruling Party", *African Journal of Political Science/Revue Africaine de Science Politique*, 7(2), 99–112.

Okodi, B. J. (2005). *The Search for a National Consensus: The Making of the 1995 Uganda Constitution*, Fountain Publishers, Kampala.

Okoth-Ogendo, H.W.O. (1993). "Constitutions Without Constitutionalism: Reflections on an African Political Paradox", in D. Greenberg, S. N. Katz, M. B. Oliviero, and S. C. Wheatley, *Constitutionalism and Democracy*, Oxford University Press, New York, 65–84.

Olsen, E. F. (2014). *Women in Politics: A Case Study on Women's Engagement in the Reconciliation and Constitution Review Processes in Zanzibar*, ILPI Report, International Law and Policy Institute (ILPI), Oslo.

Polepole, H. (2015). "Making the New Constitution for Tanzania: Challenges and Opportunities", Humphrey Polepole Blog, 12 March 2015, (http://hpolepole.blogspot. de/2015/03/making-new-constitution-for-tanzania.html).

Referendum Act (2013). The United Republic of Tanzania, 30 December 2013.

Revolutionary Government of Zanzibar (RGoZ) (2013). "Historical Background of Zanzibar", (http://zanzibar.go.tz/index.php?rgo=history#).

Roschmann, C., Wendoh, P., and Ogolla, S. (2013). "Kenya's Constitutional Review Experience and Lessons to be Learned for the Constitution-Making Process in Tanzania", in J. Döveling, K. Gastorn, and U. Wanitzek (eds.), *Constitutional Reform Processes and Integration in East Africa*, Dar es Salaam University Press, Dar es Salaam, 155–81.

Samuels, K. (2006). "Post-Conflict Peace-Building and Constitution-Making", *Chicago Journal of International Law*, 6(2), 663–82.

Toniatti, R. (2014). "Federalism and Regionalism", *Annual Review of Constitution-Building Processes: 2014*, International IDEA, 87–103.

12 Mission impossible?

Opportunities and limitations of public participation in constitution-making in a failed state – the case of Somalia

Jan Amilcar Schmidt

Introduction

After the collapse of central government institutions in 1991 and decades of anarchy and political turmoil, constitution making became an important tool for the Somali peace and state-building process. Given the unique Somali situation and political culture, constitution making was considered to bring the Somali people together in order to agree on the basic features of a new Somali state (Schmidt 2011, 119). For this purpose, public participation was considered instrumental for the success of the overall process (UNDP 2008, 1). However, the two transitional constitutions adopted in 2000 (Transitional National Charter) and 2004 (Transitional Federal Charter) were not publicly consulted. The 2012 adopted provisional constitution was consulted upon, but the outcomes of these consultations were hardly taken into account, rendering this consultation process to be largely ineffective. Given these shortcomings, the provisional constitution envisaged a constitutional review process involving national dialogue and extensive public consultation, which, however, never unfolded.

For the only time in 16 years (2000–16), the publication of a consultative draft constitution in 2010 and the organization of an extensive public consultation process from 2010–11 gave reason to believe that this aspect would indeed be taken seriously. However, due to the difficult security situation, the process of public consultation faced many challenges, and, in the end, internationally empowered political elites finalized the constitutional process through political negotiations without taking the results of the public consultation process into account (Efendija 2016, 3). This article argues that the political fragmentation, the high number of small but powerful political elites following total state collapse, and the lack of political reconciliation did not allow the outcomes of the public consultation exercise to translate into actual constitutional text and thus rendered an already limited national dialogue and public participation process in Somalia to be largely ineffective. Given the importance of such public participation in the Somali context, this has a significant negative effect on the Somali peace and state-building as such.

DOI: 10.4324/9781315180540-15

Background

The constitutional process in Somalia was to be undertaken in a country which had been in a state of civil war and violent conflict for more than two decades. The Somali people had seriously suffered from high levels of violence and were torn by inter-clan conflicts, warlord struggles for control, and ongoing smaller violent conflicts over resources or land (Samuels 2008, 600). In addition to power struggles between various factions, there remain serious divisions and potential conflict points resulting from unaddressed war crimes, stolen property, occupied territory, refugees, and internally displaced peoples resulting from the ongoing conflicts since the 1980s (Menkhaus 2006/07, 81).

Furthermore, the constitutional process was to be undertaken in a country whose only experience of a state was through colonial occupation, followed by a short period of nine years of tentative democracy and then enduring the repressive and corrupt dictatorship of General Siyad Barre for decades (Samuels 2008, 601).

This was then followed by state collapse, and from 1991, Somalis have lived without a national government. The former British protectorate in the north-west, Somaliland, proclaimed its independence in 1991 and although it has not received international recognition as a separate state, has succeeded in establishing a minimalist but democratic and politically stable state in the territory of the former British protectorate (Schmidt 2013, paras. 24–26). Similarly, in the North-East, the autonomous region of Puntland has also begun developing its own governmental structures, although it has not sought to secede from Somalia (Schmidt 2013, para. 27). Also, other regional entities providing for the exercise of governmental functions have been established (Galmudug, Xeman and Xeeb and others), but so far have not proven their capabilities to provide political stability and basic governmental services in the long run (NDI 2015, 11).

Somalis' longing for improved security, rule of law, and predictability embraced by businessmen, professionals, and neighborhood groups has resulted in important home-grown developments even within the remainder of Somalia. Local governance structures, which are inherently endogenous and have a high degree of local ownership, have evolved, such as the coalition of clan elders, intellectuals, businessmen, and Muslim clergy to oversee, finance, and administer Sharia courts to provide some security and rule of law. Some municipalities have also been able to offer some basic services, operate piped water, regulate marketplaces, and collect some taxes and user fees, often in collaboration with various NGOs (Menkhaus 2014, 3). In fact, the private sector in Somalia has been quite innovative in finding ways to compensate for the lack of effective government. Again, often in collaboration with various foreign-funded NGOs, the private sector is the only provider for such services as health care, education, and local electric and water pipe grids (Menkhaus 2006/07, 90).

However, the legacy of the civil war was profound and included unaddressed war crimes, deep inter-clan grievances over atrocities committed, stolen land, and unresolved property disputes (Menkhaus 2006/07, 81). Only after more than 14 failed attempts by the international community to assist Somalia to achieve peace and rebuild itself as a state, significant progress was made with the adoption of the Transitional Federal Charter of 2004 (TFC) (Schmidt 2013, para. 30). The TFC established the Transitional Federal Government as a transitional national government with the mandate to reestablish Somalia as a federal state through a constitutional process developing a new federal constitution for the country (Schmidt 2011, 130).

Meanwhile, in 2001, Somaliland organized a public referendum adopting a new constitution, establishing Somaliland as an independent Republic. The constitution was adopted with an overwhelming majority (97.9 percent) and ever since, the government of Somaliland refused to take part in any constitutional or state-building processes in South and Central Somalia (Bradbury 2008, 133).

Legal framework for the constitutional process under the Transitional Federal Charter

The constitution-making process in Somalia was a requirement of the TFC. Article 71 No. 1 and No. 9 TFC provided that within two and a half years of the formation of the Transitional Federal Government, a new (federal) constitution was to be prepared and adopted by popular referendum within three years. The TFC provided that the new constitution was to be prepared by an Independent Federal Constitutional Commission (IFCC) and to be based on the TFC mandate to establish a federation within the same time frame of two and half years (see Articles 11 No. 5, 8 (3a) TFC). The commissioners of the IFCC were to be nominated by the Council of Ministers and by the president (see Article 11, No. 5 TFC). The details of the mandate and competences of the IFCC were to be provided by an Act of Parliament (see Article 11 No. 6 TFC), which was enacted on 15 June 2006.[1] § 5 (3) of the IFCC law confirmed the mandate of the IFCC as an independent commission to prepare the draft constitution for approval by a public referendum. According to § 1 of the IFCC law, the IFCC comprised 15 commissioners of whom 13 were to be appointed according to the 4.5 clan formula[2] and another two according to their qualifications. By the end of June 2006, the IFCC was appointed and commenced its work.

Despite Somaliland's claims for independence, the IFCC, according to the adopted 4.5 clan formula, also comprised members representing the clans residing in Somaliland. Indirectly, therefore, Somaliland was involved in the process (in fact, a member hailing from the Gadabursi clan from Somaliland even became the chairperson of the IFCC in 2010). However, officially the Government of Somaliland denounced any partaking in the process and never permitted the IFCC any engagement in Somaliland territory.

---

1 IFCC law, Reference No.: RS-TS-OP/395/2006 (on file with the author).
2 The 4.5 clan formula was first applied for the Mbagathi peace conference and grants the four major clan families within the Somali clan system (Darod, Digil Mirifle, Dir, and Hawyie) an equal share of representation and the minority clans half of that share.

Furthermore, the TFC established a Ministry for Federal and Constitutional Affairs to oversee the implementation of the federal and constitutional tasks and mandates of the Transitional Federal Government (Article 11 Nr. 7 TFC). Within the Transitional Federal Parliament, a Parliamentary Constitutional Commission (PCC) was established with the same objective. In case the Transitional Federal Government would not fulfill its mandate to federalize the country and develop a new federal constitution within two and a half years after establishing the IFCC, the TFC regulated for the possibility of a vote of no confidence and the possible replacement of the government by the Transitional Federal Parliament (Article 11 Nr. 9 TFC). According to Article 11 No. 10 TFC, a newly elected government would have had another year to fulfill its mandate to federalize the country and develop a new federal constitution before another vote of no confidence was possible.

The TFC provided that an internationally supervised National Referendum should be organized to approve the new constitution (Article 11 No. 3 (b) TFC). Article 3 (c) TFC further provided that the Transitional Federal Government would request the international community to provide both technical and financial support.

The constitutional process

The main objective of the constitutional process in Somalia was to help the country to move peacefully from a post-conflict situation and to lay the foundation for a stable and secure future. More specifically, the objectives were to promote reconciliation, peace, and stability in Somalia through a consultative constitution-making process at the national level. Expected outputs, thus, were the preparation of a context-appropriate constitution and the development of a framework for its implementation, accompanied by targeted consultative meetings on the constitution-making process, in which the public is informed and public views are heard and incorporated in the constitution to the extent possible (UNDP 2012, 2). The international donor community invested heavily in this process and through its national and international implementing partners facilitated and promoted the design of a participatory constitutional process by the relevant constitution-making bodies of the Transitional Federal Government, i.e., IFCC, PCC, and Ministry of Constitution and Federal Affairs.

However, Somalia embarked on this constitution-making process in a very challenging security context, including the increasing presence of the terrorist group Al Shabaab and continuing clan-based political conflict. Under these circumstances it was exceptionally difficult to ensure that the constitution-making process was inclusive and effective, and that it indeed promoted national unity, a sense of shared history, and a common destiny. Given a legacy of failed governance and numerous unsuccessful attempts to revive the state, the Somali citizens were quite skeptical of this process. Political crises within the Transitional Federal Government leadership led to successive changes in the executive during the constitutional process, which led to changes in policy, to which the process had to be continually realigned (UNDP 2012, 3). For instance, from February 2009 to August 2012, there have been three councils of ministers headed by three different prime ministers, each with different approaches to the constitutional process. In early 2010 a new president was elected, who insisted to have his influence on the composition of the IFCC as well – eventually leading to the increase of the IFCC from 15 to 30 commissioners. The timelines for the conclusion of the process and, thus, the term of the Transitional Federal Government institutions were extended numerous times (Schmidt 2011, 134).

While the working relationship between the three Somali institutions responsible for the constitutional process, i.e., IFCC, PCC, and the Ministry for Constitution and Federal Affairs, remained unclear and contested throughout the whole process, the international support to the constitutional process also faced some considerable challenges including competition among the international agencies involved. Originally, in 2008, upon request from the Transitional Federal Government and the Inter-Governmental Authority for Development (IGAD), a constitutional consortium was established to provide for the necessary support to the process. This constitutional consortium comprised the United Nations Development Program (UNDP), the United Nations Political Office for Somalia (UNPOS), the National Democratic Institute (NDI), the Association of Western European Parliamentarians for Africa (AWEPA), the Max Planck Institute for Comparative Public Law and International Law (MPIL), Interpeace, and Oxfam. The consortium partners were expected to support the process according to their respective experience and expertise. The constitutional consortium was expected to be coordinated and provided with technical and financial support by UNDP and to provide the necessary support to the relevant Somali institutions, i.e., the IFCC, the PCC, and the Ministry for Federal and Constitutional Affairs. However, along the process numerous consortium partners dropped out of the process or were sidelined, leaving UNDP as the main driving force within the consortium.

The IFCC was appointed and became operational in 2006. Given the difficult security situation within Somalia, a first capacity-building workshop for the IFCC was conducted by MPIL in Yemen in July 2007. Again, due to the political stalemates and pertaining security challenges, not earlier than from August 2008 onwards, the MPIL was able to carry out a series of workshops in comparative constitutional law aimed at informing the IFCC commissioners about the constitutional options available to them.

In early 2010, the IFCC was extended by 15 additional commissioners appointed by the newly elected President Sheikh Sharif. Soon after this extension, in March 2010, the IFCC became fully operational as UNDP provided stipends and other allowances to the 30 IFCC commissioners, their secretariat, and consultants. The IFCC and the then Minister of Constitution and Federal Affairs decided to start working on a first draft of the Constitution in Djibouti. It was decided to proceed and prepare a draft constitution, which would facilitate a broader civic education and public consultation to commence after publishing this Consultative Draft Constitution (CDC). While Djibouti offered the advantage that international and Somali experts could more easily come to work with the IFCC, this decision caused multiple challenges, including significant organizational and financial challenges, but also perceptional implications (see below).

a) The public consultation process

In the view of IFCC commissioners it was considered to be essential that the people of Somalia understand why and how a new constitution is made, if the constitution is to reflect their views and values, and if they are to participate in the process in a meaningful way (IFCC 2011, 2). Given the years of conflict and the lack of any experience of a positive effect of national government structures, it was considered even more important that the people of Somalia had the opportunity to understand basic constitutional concepts, such as what a state can provide, issues of human rights protection and electoral processes, and also be introduced to common notions that will be central to the debate, such as federalism (IFCC 2010, 13). Without a broad civic education program, any consultation process was considered to be meaningless, and the final referendum considered very risky as the people voting would not understand what they are voting on.

The civic education program was expected to be overseen by the IFCC but to be undertaken by and with the support of international actors. Once the civic education program had been rolled out, the IFCC was expected to undertake a broad consultative process and initiate national debate on key issues. Such a process was considered to increase the legitimacy of the constitution (IFCC 2010, 15).

Making use of existing communication systems most frequently used in the Somali context, i.e., telecommunication, radio, and internet, the IFCC (through UNDP) contracted a number of media partners to conduct civic education initiatives.[3] The selected partners were: BBC Media Action (formerly BBC World Service Trust), Star FM, Universal TV, and Souktel. The media outreach campaigns received many comments and recommendations relating to the draft constitution through phone calls and personal follow-up meetings, information sessions, and workshops, which were recorded and shared with the IFCC. The phone-ins and text messages received were compiled by Souktel and BBC Media Action and given to the IFCC secretariat and analysis unit which transcribed all the submissions, analyzed, summarized, and cross referenced them to the relevant CDC provisions and thematic headings. The website www.dastuur.org continued throughout 2011 to allow people to vote on polls regarding the CDC content and give personalized comments and feedback on the IFCC blog. The website was administered by KenyaWeb, UNDP ICT, and the media partners who also monitored the monthly clicks and visits to the website (UNDP 2012, 6).

With support from NDI, the IFCC conducted public consultation activities on the content of the draft constitution and process in all 16 districts of

---

3 During the late 1990s and early 2000s, local businessmen have developed one of the most advanced telecommunication systems around the globe in Somalia – see de Waal 2015, 120.

Mogadishu, in the towns of Galkayo, Abudwaq, Adado, Baladweyne, Dollow, Afgoye, Baidoa, Gedo, Luuq, and Liboi as well as in Nairobi, London, Oslo, Minneapolis, and Ohio. In total, the IFCC engaged with over 1,000 people from 11 regions in south central Somalia and in the diaspora. In these consultations, the IFCC held presentations on the CDC followed by open floor discussions on its contents (IFCC/CoE 2012, 7–8).

The most interesting points of the feedback the IFCC received from its consultations were maybe the following:

Constitution making

The question was raised of whether the constitution-making process as such was a genuine Somali exercise. Especially the timing for the constitutional processes was largely perceived as premature in the Somali context of conflict and pre-determined by the international community rather than Somali-owned and Somali-driven (IFCC/CoE 2012, 2).

Shari'ah

There was a universal view that a Somali Constitution should be based on the principles of Islam and grounded in the Shari'ah. Participants were united in calling for a constitution that is Shari'ah-compliant and in expressing their support for a constitution that is subject to the authority of the Koran (IFCC/CoE 2012, 2).

Citizenship

Citizenship emerged as one of the more sensitive matters discussed during the public consultation process. Participants often expressed their concerns on how the CDC addressed Somali citizenship, i.e., allowing for dual citizenship, granting citizenship to children born to parents of Somali origin (without defining that origin), and any child of unknown origin and below the age of eight found in the Somali Republic (Articles 11 and 12 of the CDC). An often-raised opinion was that the CDC provisions defining eligibility for citizenship were insufficiently rigorous and would grant the rights associated with citizenship, including the right to hold a position of leadership in governance, far too easily (IFCC/CoE 2012, 3).

Federalism

The vast majority of participants consulted actually opposed the idea of a federal Somalia. Somalia was considered to be one nation with one religion and one language. Because of that, federalism was largely perceived as an inappropriate system of governance for Somalia seen as potentially divisive, further entrenching clanism (IFCC/CoE 2012, 4). Some participants, however, seemed to have indicated that they might support a federal Somalia if they had more information and clarity on what the federalization process would look like and how Somalia would be organized as a federal state. There was a suggestion that federalism may lie in Somalia's future, once peace would be established and Somalis would be in a better position to properly negotiate the details of a federal state organization (IFCC/CoE 2012, 4).

Women

Participants expressed general support for the participation of women in institutions of governance. Especially, the proposal of the Garowe II Principles (see below) that women should be guaranteed a quota of 30 percent of seats in the National Constituent Assembly and new Federal Parliament received broad support (IFCC/CoE 2012, 5).

Youth

At some consultations, participants expressed a sense that the constitution ultimately should be for the benefit of future generations of Somalis, thus particularly for the youth. Therefore, there was a suggestion presented that youth be included as part of decision-making processes and that a certain percentage of parliamentary seats be reserved for youth representatives, similar to the reserved quota of seats for women (IFCC/CoE 2012, 5).

Status of Mogadishu

Most participants in the public consultations supported the idea to retain Mogadishu as the Somali capital. Concerning the capital's status within a future federal system, a majority expressed support for the capital having the status of a regional state in order to maintain its independence and prevent it from any influence from the regional state in which it is geographically situated (IFCC/CoE 2012, 6).

The territory of the Somali Republic

Some participants commented on the absence of a definition of Somalia's territory in the CDC and indeed the CDC's lack of definition of Somali territory was seen as a key omission from the constitutional draft by many participants (IFCC/CoE 2012, 7). It was understood that the intention of the drafters was to avoid any statement on Somaliland's independence claims. However, many participants were convinced that the people of Somaliland would happily reunite with south and central Somalia once these regions had been pacified and stabilized and a truly federal constitution was adopted (UNDP/UNPOS JCU 2012, 37).

As a result of this broad public consultation campaign, reinforced by civic education programs, large segments of the Somali population in south central Somalia and beyond were aware of the constitution process, although the security situation did not allow for many to directly participate in the process. The major shortcoming of this public consultation process at a later stage, however, was that the political roadmap process of ending the transition superseded these efforts.

b) *The political process*

After another political conflict between the president, prime minister and the Transitional Federal Parliament, the Kampala Accord signed in July 2011 provided for the extension of the Transitional Federal Government institutions for one final additional year until August 2012. As part of the deal, it was agreed that the office of the prime minister was changed one last time and the new prime minister and Council of Ministers would be given the chance to finalize the preparations for the elections of a new Parliament in August 2012.[4] The Kampala Accord was complemented by the adoption of the "roadmap for ending the transition" in Mogadishu in September 2011 by the so-called Roadmap Signatories comprised of the president, the prime mister, the speaker of the Transitional Federal Parliament, the president of the autonomous region of Puntland, the president of the regional administration of Galmudug, the chairman of the Sufi-Militia Ahlu-Sunnah wal Jamaah, and the special representative of the secretary general for Somalia (SRSG). This roadmap was a turning point by ultimately linking the political process of ending the transition with the technical process of finalizing the constitution. In fact, the constitutional process was envisaged to become the vehicle for the political process of ending the transition, providing for new governmental structures in the post-transition era (Security Council 2011, para. 3).

However, the Roadmap Signatories considered the CDC as an inadequate basis for the political process of negotiating the new constitution for Somalia. They considered the CDC to be a blueprint of a constitution, not a reflection of Somali realities and peculiarities and which was mainly drafted outside the country. In order to "Somali-ize" the constitution, the Roadmap Signatories agreed to establish a new Committee of (Somali) Experts (CoE) to develop recommendations and advise the roadmap signatories on a draft constitution that more adequately reflected the Somali context.[5]

The establishment of the CoE, legally formalized by an Executive Order in January 2012,[6] was largely perceived as disempowering the constitutionally mandated IFCC and heavily criticized as unconstitutional and illegal. This situation proved to be even unacceptable for the Somali experts constituting the CoE. Thus, after undertaking significant mediation efforts, IFCC and CoE agreed to work collaboratively together on a joint draft constitution to be submitted to the Roadmap Signatories.[7] Unfortunately, however, this joint approach caused another rift between the CoE and the Minister of Constitutional Affairs and Reconciliation in charge of the constitutional process on behalf of the Transitional Federal Government and thus the roadmap signatories, ultimately leading to the sidelining of both the IFCC and the CoE.

---

4 See Article 4 of the Kampala Accord (document on file with the author).
5 See Roadmap (document on file with the author).
6 See Executive Order XRW/LT/00.125/01/12 (document on file with the author).
7 See Agreement on Working Relationship between Committee of Experts and Independent Federal Constitution Commission, dated 17 January 2012 (document on file with the author).

The constitutional process thus became a political process of negotiations and bargaining among the small group of national and regional leaders constituting the Roadmap Signatories. These negotiations were facilitated through the organization of a number of constitutional conferences and Roadmap Signatories meetings. The first of these constitutional conferences took place in Garowe, the capital of the autonomous region of Puntland, later to be known as the Garowe I Conference. The Garowe I Conference, which took place in December 2011, clarified the provisional adoption of the new constitution by a National Constituent Assembly by May 2012 at the latest (as the timely conduct of a public referendum to adopt the new constitution as was provided for by the TFC was perceived as practically impossible) and the structure, size, and selection criteria for a new federal Parliament under the new federal constitution (Security Council 2012a, para. 5). As a result of the Garowe I Conference, the so-called "Garowe Principles" were produced, providing further guidance on the finalization of the draft constitution and the process of ending the transition.[8]

After the Garowe I Conference, an International Constitutional Expert Forum was organized in January 2012. The Expert Forum provided the stakeholders with an opportunity to study and discuss key contentious issues in the CDC, including the federalization process and institutional set-up, distribution of competences and fiscal federalism issues, system of government (presidential, parliamentary, and mixed systems), electoral system, and transitional provisions pending elections. Over 150 participants attended the five-day-long conference organized in Djibouti. Among the participants were representatives from the Roadmap Sigantories, other representatives from the Transitional Federal Government and Parliament, Puntland, Galmudug, Ahlu Sunnah wal Jamaah (ASWJ), and civil society, IFCC, PCC, CoE, Ministry of Constitutional Affairs and Reconciliation (MoC), and Consortium Partner Organizations (UNDP, UNPOS, COSPE, IIDA, AWEPA, MPIL, NDI, IDLO). Divided into four working groups, the Expert Forum developed recommendations, which later informed the substantial decisions on the final draft provisional constitution.[9]

In February 2012, another constitutional conference was organized in Garowe (Garowe II Conference), which provided further details on the model of indirect elections and accommodated some of the Constitutional Expert Forum working groups' recommendations in the form of a political agreement. The Garowe II Communiqué adopted the so-called Garowe II Principles, providing for further guidance on the applicable criteria for the formation of federal member states (at least two of the former administrative regions to merge based on a voluntary decision). They called for the establishment of a parliamentary system of government, a bicameral federal legislature, and provided for further guidance and details on the operationalization of the roadmap, including the appointment of

8 See Garowe I Communiqué (document on file with the author).
9 See Constitutional Expert Forum – Working Group Recommendations (document on file with the author).

members of the National Constituent Assembly and the new federal Parliament by traditional elders on the basis of the 4.5 clan formula.[10]

The Garowe II Conference was followed by a Civil Society Forum organized in Entebbe in March 2012. The Civil Society Forum brought together representatives from numerous civil society groups from all parts of Somalia – including Somaliland – to deliberate on the Constitutional Expert Forum working groups' recommendations from the perspective of the Somali civil society. The final communiqué of the Civil Society Forum endorsed the political decisions reached by the Roadmap Signatories at the Garowe I and II Conferences. It also developed recommendations for strengthening political participation and engagement of Somali civil society in the political end of transition and constitutional processes with the aim of enhancing democratic procedures and the overall transparency of the process.[11]

However, in March 2012, a meeting among the Roadmap Signatories organized in Galkayo, the capital of the Galmudug regional administration, resulted in the adoption of the so-called Galkayo Accord. The Galkayo Accord was an attempt to accelerate the process of ending the transition and operationalizing the principles agreed upon at the Garowe I and II Conferences.[12] The Galkayo Accord was criticized for neglecting the Civil Society Forum Communiqué and the therein-articulated recommendations of the civil society and largely considered as an attempt by the Roadmap Signatories to secure the supremacy of the political negotiations process, thereby (over-)emphasizing their own role as political leaders and chief negotiators (Menkhaus 2012, 171). And indeed, the Galkayo meeting can be seen as a turning point in the political end of transition and the constitutional process as it vested all responsibilities and authority to manage the process of ending the transition, including the constitutional process, in the Roadmap Signatories, which were also to serve as a final dispute resolution mechanism.[13]

The Roadmap Signatories took full advantage of the powers they vested in themselves. With full support and even urged by the international community, the constitutional order provided by the TFC since 2004 was abolished by side-lining the Transitional Federal Parliament, which in a desperate attempt to prevent itself from becoming irrelevant, had elected a new speaker and thereby opposed the roadmap process and the implied empowerment of the Roadmap Signatories, and providing for themselves the necessary legislative framework in the form of presidential decrees (conveniently ignoring that even presidential decrees required endorsement by Parliament according to the 1960 Constitution, which served as the legal basis of this approach).

Consequently, the Roadmap Signatories also took over the constitutional process. In April 2012 IFCC and CoE submitted their consolidated draft constitution to the Roadmap Signatories for their review and feedback. Instead of providing such feedback, during another political meeting in Addis Ababa,

---

10 See Garowe II Communiqué (document on file with the author).
11 See Civil Society Forum Communiqué (document on file with the author).
12 See Galkayo Accord (document on file with the author).
13 See Paragraph 7 of the Galkayo Accord (document on file with the author).

organized in May 2012, the Roadmap Signatories submitted the draft constitution prepared by IFCC and CoE to a Technical Review Committee comprised of handpicked legal experts, which started a parallel process of constitutional drafting (TCIR 2012, 5). The Technical Review Committee according to the Protocol Establishing the Technical Facilitation Committee adopted by Presidential Decree JS/XM/217/06/2012 of 23 June 2012 became the Technical Facilitation Committee, which, comprised of hand picked representatives of the Roadmap Signatories, was tasked with finalizing the draft provisional constitution for final submission to the National Constituent Assembly.[14] The Presidential Decree JS/XM/217/06/2012 of 23 June 2012 also adopted the necessary amendments to the TFC to allow for the adoption of the new federal constitution by a National Constituent Assembly. This assembly comprised of 825 representatives from all sections of society to be appointed by the traditional leaders of the Somali clans and a number of protocols aimed at "legalizing" the establishment of the National Constituent Assembly and the appointment of members of the new federal Parliament by the traditional leaders of the Somali clans based on the 4.5 clan formula. However, due to the fact that the president did not have any such powers under the TFC, under which he was elected and empowered, certainly such legality could not be provided for in the end.

The Technical Facilitation Committee, tasked with the preparation of the draft provisional constitution, finalized the constitutional document as instructed by the Roadmap Signatories and the feedback from the public outreach and consultations campaign was largely ignored. The constitution was not ratified through popular referendum as envisaged in the TFC but instead provisionally adopted on 2 August 2012 by 96 percent of the votes of the 825-member National Constituent Assembly (Security Council 2012b, para. 8). The new House of the People of the Federal Parliament was appointed and sworn into office on 20 August 2012. Ironically, the establishment of the Upper House of the Federal Parliament was postponed until such a time that all federal member states were being formed (Article 138 (2) of the Provisional Constitution) even though all roadmap agreements had envisaged for this House to be established no later than August 2012. The Upper House even today is yet to be established as not all federal member states have been formed.

c) The results

The last drafting stage of the provisional constitution has been especially heavily criticized and not really been accepted by the Somali people (Efendija 2016, 3). Many perceive the constitution as a result of political maneuvering and manipulation rather than a social compact agreed upon by genuine political leaders or representatives (UNDPA/UNDP 2013, 2).

14 See Presidential Decree JS/XM/217/06/2012 (the decree as well as the Protocol Establishing the Technical Facilitation Committee are on file with the author).

The provisional constitution is most advanced in providing an extensive human rights catalogue, which, however, appears to be rather ambitious and it remains to be seen if future Somali governments will indeed be able to implement these provisions to their full extent or if they will need to be readjusted (see, for example, only the rights to free health care and full social security provided in Article 27). Most problematically, perhaps, was the heavy influence external advisers played in the design of this human rights catalogue, which led for example to a provision like Article 15 (4) of the provisional constitution prohibiting female circumcision in a country where this is still a widely accepted practice exercised on more than 95 percent of the women.[15]

Moreover, due to a rather partisan negotiation among the Roadmap Signatories, they were not able to sort out the rather ambiguous and contentious political relationship between the president and the prime minister that had haunted Somalia during the years of transition. The provisional constitution provides for a semi-presidential system with a rather ceremonial president as head of state (see Article 87) and a prime minister as head of government (see Article 97). However, due to the power of the president to appoint the prime minister and the applied power sharing formula, which so far saw every president hail from either the Darod or the Hawyie clan and the prime minister from the opposite clan, no president so far could afford to play a ceremonial role only but would take on a political leadership role as much as possible.

Maybe even worse, the results of the extensive public outreach and consultations campaign did not translate into the content of the final constitution, which certainly did not serve its legitimacy and acceptance. Just taking a look at the points of feedback the IFCC received and reported on as presented above illustrates this:

1   Despite concerns raised, the constitution-making process was pushed through and finalized by summer 2012 even though fundamental questions of state building and future governance structures remained unaddressed.
2   The only point that was fully recognized was the requirement for the constitution to be in compliance with the Shari'ah and its general principles (see Articles 3 (1) and 4 (1) of the provisional constitution.
3   The eligibility criteria for citizenship were not tightened up. Instead, the provisional constitution provides for an incoherent and flawed regulation of Somali citizenship in its Article 8.
4   Despite major resentments against the idea of federalizing Somalia in large parts of the country, the provisional constitution declared the Somali Republic as Federal Republic and provided for further federalization of the country, while offering only insufficient and flawed regulation of most of the details of such a federal system. Major shortcomings were, for example, the following: calling for the merger of at least two former administrative regions to become a federal member state based on a voluntary decision,

---

15 See latest figures of the World Health Organisation, available at: http://www.who.int/reproductive health/topics/fgm/prevalence/en/.

without specifying how such a voluntary decision is to be taken in light of actual political realities; providing for an unworkable representation formula for the members of the Upper House representing the federal member states in the federal Parliament; and not defining basic powers and competences of the different levels of government within the federation but instead subjecting this important matter to future negotiations between the federal government and federal member states.

5 Even though the Roadmap Signatories had agreed on a 30 percent quota for women in all government institutions at the Garowe II Conference (see above), which had received broad support during the public consultation process of the IFCC, such a quota did not make it into the final constitutional text.

6 The calls for special political participation and representation rights for the youth were not attended to and no such regulations can be found in the provisional constitution.

7 While Mogadishu is declared to be the capital of the Federal Republic of Somalia in Article 9 of the provisional constitution, the status of the capital within the federal state structure has not been defined but instead subjected to further regulation by ordinary legislation.

8 The territory of the Federal Republic of Somalia is defined in Article 7 of the provisional constitution, but again, in such an incoherent and flawed way (by defining borders in one paragraph only to refer back to the 1960 Constitution in another paragraph, which deliberately left the border issues undefined) that the regulation became quite meaningless in the end.

Conclusion

The process of public consultations on the CDC that took place in Somalia from 2010–12 is evidence enough that it was indeed not impossible to conduct such a process in a meaningful and effective way despite all the challenges provided for by a difficult security situation and politically charged context. However, the political realities did not allow for the results of this public consultation process to be taken into account properly and to matter in the end.

In light of considerable fragmentation of the political arena in Somalia and the absence of clearly identifiable political elites, the international community involved in Somalia conveniently empowered a small group of political negotiators, which took decisions on behalf of the Somali people on the contents of their constitution, which in the end did not provide for the necessary public buy-in and backing. After having invested heavily in the constitutional process, the international donor community engaged in Somalia apparently had lost patience and was in urgent need to see results (Menkhaus 2012, 170). In order to guide and influence the political process, the SRSG was even made a Roadmap Signatory himself, who, in fact, proved to be quite skillful in keeping the political process on track. This, however, was managed quite clearly at the expense of an inclusive and participatory constitutional process allowing for the development of viable solutions for the Somali state-building process.

On the other hand, the question arises whether such political elites and representatives, which could confidently speak on behalf of the Somali people, can be identified at all. The Somali political culture is one that has been described as uncentralized rather than decentralized (Lewis 1999, 3), meaning, Somalis don't like to be represented politically but rather want to make decisions by themselves. Because of this most liberal, almost anarchic mind-set of the Somali people, which does not allow for a clear separation of people governed and those governing, it has even been suggested that any attempt to establish a Western style of representative democracy will not work in the Somali context (Van Notten 2005, 9). While this may be a discussion best undertaken by the Somalis during the constitutional process, this, in my view, makes participatory constitution making in Somalia an imperative, but it also provides for the biggest challenge for such a participatory approach. Even within a small population of approximately 10 million people (Schmidt 2013, para. 1), it will be very difficult to design a process where all these people will have a meaningful say on the content of their constitution. Who, on the other hand, can be identified to speak on behalf of the Somali people? Even the numerous clans currently dominating the political arena in Somalia are divided into hundreds of sub-clans and even smaller affiliated groups and groupings. The main issue of constitution making in Somalia in the long run, thus, will be to find mechanisms that will give all relevant political groups of Somalia the chance to contribute meaningfully to the constitutional process.

The provisional constitution of 2012 envisages a comprehensive constitutional review process to take place during the first term of the Somali Federal Parliament from 2012–16. Rightfully, this constitutional review process was expected to involve the Somali people and be again largely transparent and participatory (see Article 133 (8) of the provisional constitution). However, this process was not able to unfold. Not surprisingly, the main challenge was to identify mechanisms for a meaningful public outreach and political engagement campaign (Efendija 2016, 6). Currently, it seems as if the constitutional review and thereby the ongoing constitution-making process will be deferred to the second term of the Somali Federal Parliament from 2016–20. Certainly, also during this period the main challenge will be to organize a meaningful national dialogue of the Somali people on their future constitution and its contents.

References

Bradbury, Mark. *Becoming Somaliland, African Issues*, Indiana University Press, 2008 (Bradbury 2008).

Efendija, Edmond. "The Implementation of the Provisional Constitution of Somalia from 2012–2016 – A Critical Assessment", report on file with the author (Efendija 2016).

Independent Federal Constitution Commission. "Final Report on the Consultative Draft Constitution", 2010, report on file with the author (IFCC 2010).

Independent Federal Constitution Commission. "Monthly Progress Report", January 2011, report on file with the author (IFCC 2011).

Independent Federal Constitution Commission/Committee of Experts. "Report on Public Consultations", 2012, report on file with the author (IFCC/CoE 2012).

Lewis, I.M. *A Pastoral Democracy – A Study of Pastoralism and Politics among the Northern Somali of the Horn of Africa*, Reprint, James Currey Publishers, 1999 (Lewis 1999).

Menkhaus, Ken. "Governance without Government in Somalia", in: *International Security* No. 31, 2006/07, 74–106 (Menkhaus 2006/07).

Menkhaus, Ken. "Somalia at the Tipping Point", in: *Current History*, May 2012, 169–74 (Menkhaus 2012).

Menkhaus, Ken. "If Mayors Ruled Somalia", in: *Nordiska Afrikainstitutet* Policy Note No. 2 (2014) (Menkhaus 2014).

National Democratic Institute. "Federalism in Somalia – Considerations and Lessons Learned for the Establishment of Subnational Administrations", 2015, report on file with the author (NDI 2015).

Samuels, Kirsti. "Constitution-Building During the War on Terror – The Challenge of Somalia", in: *NYU Journal for International Law and Politics* No. 40 (2008), 597–614 (Samuels 2008).

Schmidt, Jan Amilcar. "Somalia unter der Übergangsverfassung von 2004", in: Peter Scholz/Naseef Naeem (eds.) *Jahrbuch für Verfassung, Recht und Staat im islamischen Kontext* No. 1 (2011), 105–36 (Schmidt 2011).

Schmidt, Jan Amilcar. "Somalia, Conflict", in: *Max Planck Encyclopedia of Public International Law*, last updated July 2013 (Schmidt 2013).

Security Council. "Report of the Secretary-General on Somalia", S/2011/759, available at: http://www.un.org/ga/search/view_doc.asp?symbol=S/2011/759 (Security Council 2011).

Security Council. "Report of the Secretary-General on Somalia", S/2012/74, available at: http://www.un.org/ga/search/view_doc.asp?symbol=S/2012/783 (Security Council 2012a).

Security Council. "Report of the Secretary-General on Somalia", S/2012/643, available at: http://www.un.org/ga/search/view_doc.asp?symbol=S/2012/643 (Security Council 2012b).

Technical Committee on the Implementation of the Roadmap. "Third Progress Report", 31 May 2012, report on file with the author (TCIR 2012).

United Nations Development Program. "Outcome of the Strategic Discussions on the Somali Constitution", Kampala, Uganda, 24–29 May 2008, report on file with the author (UNDP 2008).

United Nations Development Program. "Somalia Constitution-Making Support Project 2009–2012 – Final Report", 2, report on file with the author (UNDP 2012).

United Nations Development Program/United Nations Political Office for Somalia – Joint Constitution Unit. "Report on Public Consultations to Support the Constitution Building Process in Somalia", 2012, report on file with the author (UNDP/UNPOS JCU 2012).

United Nations Department of Political Affairs/United Nations Development Program. "Somalia Constitutional Assessment Visit – Final Report", 2013, report on file with the author (UNDPA/UNDP, 2013).

Van Notten, Michael. *The Law of the Somalis*, The Red Sea Press, 2005 (Van Notten 2005).

de Waal, Alex. *The Real Politics of the Horn of Africa – Money, War and the Business of Power*, Polity Press, 2015 (de Waal 2015).

13 The process of drafting a citizen-driven constitution in South Sudan

Which role for the public?

Katrin Seidel[1]

Introductory remarks

When walking through the capital of South Sudan in 2013, huge billboards were posted at main roads promoting, 'And now our Constitution – let us shape our destiny – be part of the process'. These announcements were part of a campaign called 'Towards the Constitution of *Zol Meskin*' [common people], launched by South Sudanese civil society organizations (CSOs)[2] a few months after the declaration of independence. Distrusting the ruling elites to implement the 'permanent constitution process'[3] stipulated in the Transitional Constitution of the Republic of South Sudan of 2011 (TCRSS)[4] in the envisioned inclusive manner, civil society actors created their own citizens' constitution-making forums with the desire of participating in the official negotiations.

The constitution-making efforts since 2011 have shown that the CSOs' apprehension has become reality. The constitution-making process itself seems to threaten the idea of a citizen driven constitution as not only promoted by international actors and stipulated in the TCRSS but also demanded by many civil society actors, who are mostly excluded from the *de jure* constitution making. The making of the 'permanent' constitution has been continued in an exclusive manner similar to the drafting of the interim arrangements. Accordingly, neither the 'top-down' revisions of the Interim Constitution of Southern Sudan of 2005 (ICSS), nor current efforts to draft a 'permanent' constitution by only revising the TCRSS could establish or consolidate state actors' legitimacy and identity of the emerging state.

It must be considered that the emerging state of South Sudan currently appears to be 'only slightly more than a geographical factum' (Jok 2012: 58–59). The political actors' constellations are still changing during the ongoing political

---

1 Max Planck Institute for Social Anthropology, Dept., Law & Anthropology; Fellow at Käte Hamburger Kolleg / Centre for Global Cooperation Research (2015/16), kseidel@eth.mpg.de
2 The term CSOs is used here to refer to local (national or sub-national) nongovernmental associations concerned with issues of governance, rule of law, and constitution making.
3 Art. 202f TCRSS.
4 The TCRSS is based on the Interim National Constitution for the Republic of Sudan 2005 whose substance was largely predetermined through the Comprehensive Peace Agreement (see Dann and Al-Ali 2006: 447–49).

DOI: 10.4324/9781315180540-16

and military negotiations of statehood.[5] The negotiation processes are not institutionalized as stable procedures, within clearly defined spaces of action among well-defined bodies of participating actors.

Thus, constitution making has become a key element in political transition. It revolves around the construction of sovereignty in an attempt to control territorial borders, to more clearly define a 'national' interior and convince the people that this interior does exist. The highly fragmented political and military actors are in constant quarrel over the issue of who is at or absent from the negotiation table.

This study takes a closer look at the 'realities' of constitution making through the lenses of proclaimed public participation. This highly dynamic process is difficult to interpret and to ultimately predict the outcome. Therefore, this study can only serve as a snapshot (covering the timeframe of the process from 2011 until 2017). Furthermore, this chapter sheds light on the resulting dilemma between the attempt of quickly producing a 'permanent' constitution out of predefined international models[6] and the idea of deriving 'its authority from the will of the people',[7] implying the existence of a certain societal consensus in emerging South Sudan. Since the different elements to be included in the constitution (such as the vertical separation of power, the executive legislative relationship, legal pluralism, etc.) are contested by multiple actors with different normative claims, constitution making has become a bargaining chip of state formation. As will be further demonstrated, not only the process of the constitution making itself, but also the TCRSS of 2011 has already served as 'a handmaiden of the party in power, as a means to the retention of power', relating Yash Ghai's (1972: 406) much earlier assessment on constitutions in general also to interim constitutional arrangements.

The only few national actors involved in the official constitution making negotiate within predetermined international frames. Nowadays, international governance institutions design and provide the frames for constitution making in war-torn settings (Wolfrum 2005: 649; Chesterman 2004). Thereby, external influence is 'increasingly becoming an object of international law [which] add[s] a new dimension to the traditional concept of constitution-making' (Dann et al. 2006: 424). A key feature of these frames is public participation as part of the international discourse on 'local ownership'. The concept of 'ownership' has emerged as a lesson learned in the general debate on what is known as 'aid' or 'development' assistance. Ownership is considered crucial for enhancing the

---

5 The major violent conflict spreading at the end of 2013 has already caused about 50,000 deaths, more than one million displaced people and a situation in which almost two-thirds of the population depend on external food aid (see UNHCR 2017, Weber 2016). It began as a political power struggle within the ruling party Sudan People's Liberation Movement (SPLM) and disputes on the party's constitution making that escalated in December 2013 and set in motion a still ongoing violent conflict spiral.

6 Models can be understood as 'analytical representations of particular aspects of reality created as apparatus of protocol for interventions to shape this reality for certain purposes' (see Rottenburg 2009; Behrends et al. 2014).

7 Art. 3(1) TCRSS.

process's legitimacy and effectiveness (see Bargués-Pedreny 2015; Chesterman 2007; Ginsberg 2008). Accordingly, 'the common people in war-torn societies are [. . .] expected to participate, to be consulted and have their say on the formulation of new constitutional frameworks' (Sannerholm 2012: 124). These participatory frames applied in South Sudan by international actors[8] are highly contested. As Simeon (2009: 242) mentioned, 'constitution-making is in large part about making bets about the future'. These *bets* are challenged by various actors at and away from the negotiation table since these extrapolations are very much connected with critical questions about values and the distribution of power but also embedded in specific constitutional historical settings. One has to bear in mind, public participation in constitution making is a new phenomenon in the (Southern) Sudanese context. Since the 1950s, there has been a belief in a state-driven (or ruling party) constitution making rather than one that requires citizens' engagement, which is reflected in the 'traditional' constitution making throughout history. This mind-set seems to be replicated in the South Sudan context (Yakani 10 June 2015). The ongoing constitution making has shown that ruling elites have utilized the international concept of 'local ownership', with its participatory ideas as a tool of gaining and enhancing their legitimacy. This study demonstrates that *de facto* the well-intended international 'technical assistance' and models on how to produce a citizen-driven constitution co-regulates South Sudan's constitution making in a way that rather impends the chances of integrating ideas and interests of the highly segmented society.

However, South Sudan's constitution making enterprise *de facto* has been put on ice due to the ongoing (2017) uncertain political and military renegotiations and reshuffling of the governmental actors since the still-lasting disastrous political crisis has erupted in 2013. As will be demonstrated, it has slowed down the too ambitiously envisioned process. This could open space for addressing and renegotiating the tensions inherently arising out of the chosen design and process of constitution making: on the one hand the pre-modelled process, and on the other hand the idea of a citizen-driven constitution making. The focus of analysis is on these tensions.

Models supposed to be followed: Public participation envisaged in the making

The Transitional Constitution of 2011 lays out the design for the making of the 'permanent' constitution that is supposed to derive 'its authority from the will of the people'.[9] The constitution-making design follows the internationally widespread applied stages of constitution making. The supporting 2009 guidance note on United Nations assistance to constitution-making processes with its attached template of a to-be process (Ki-moon 2009) promotes an inclusive

---

8 The vague term 'international actors' comprise individual activists and academics, individual and groupings of states, (supra-)regional institutions, nonlocal NGOs, commercial enterprises, research institutions/think tanks, etc.

9 Art. 3(1) TCRSS.

participatory process. This guidance note echoes the 'standard': drafting, consultation, deliberation, adoption, and ratification to be followed.

Accordingly, the drafting of the permanent constitution has been delegated to a 'constitutional commission' (Ki-moon 2009): the National Constitutional Review Commission (NCRC).[10] Even though the UN guidance note does not address the modus of 'establishing' the constitutional commission, the TCRSS specifies that the NCRC 'shall be established by the President'.[11] It is interesting to note that only ad hoc commissions shall be appointed by the president, whereby 'independent commissions' shall be 'established' by the president.[12] The NCRC seems to be perceived as an 'ad hoc' commission, since all 54 members are presidentially appointed.[13] Moreover, the NCRC was supposed to be established with 'due regard for gender, political, social and regional diversity of South Sudan in recognition of the need for inclusiveness, transparency and equitable participation'.[14] Following the UN suggestion of 'consultation', the commission shall 'collect views and suggestions from all the stakeholders regarding any changes that may need to be introduced to the constitutional system of governance'.[15] The NCRC is further mandated to reconcile traditions, social values, and local laws with the state laws and principles of international law (Kulluel 2012). This goal seems to be in tension with the commission's general mandate of only 'reviewing' the TCRSS.[16] This stipulation has limited the NCRC's scope to only adjusting the TCRSS instead of revisiting and drafting a constitutional document from scratch; just like the Interim Constitution of 2005 that was only reviewed by a presidentially appointed Technical Committee in 2011.

The timeframe for producing a permanent constitution was obviously over-ambitiously set. Originally, the NCRC was supposed to draft a constitution within one year of its establishment.[17] Already two constitutional amendments[18] have extended the commission's life span. Beginning of 2015 the NCRC requested a second extension of its mandate 'for a period of not less than three years' (NCRC 2015).

The National Constitutional Conference (NCC) was envisioned to be the second official negotiation table to deliberate on the NCRC draft, to gather public input as well as to approve and pass a draft constitutional text within six months. The NCC was designed to be a 'constitutional convention' as one type of representative forum suggested by the UN guidance note. It shall represent political parties, civil society organizations, women organizations, youth

10 Art. 202 TCRSS.
11 Art. 202(1) TCRSS.
12 Art. 101(f, j) TCRSS.
13 Presidential Decrees RSS/PD/J/02/2012; RSS/PD/J/03/2012; RSS/PD/J/09/20212; RSS/PD/J/36/2012.
14 Art.202(5) TCRSS.
15 Art. 202(6) TCRSS.
16 Art. 202(6) TCRSS.
17 Art. 202(4) TCRSS.
18 TCRSS (Amendment Act 2013); TCRSS (Amendment Act 2015).

organizations, faith-based organizations, people with special needs, traditional leaders, war widows, veterans, war wounded, business leaders, trade unions, professional associations, academia, etc.[19]

Subsequently, the national legislature has to deliberate and adopt the draft constitutional text within three months.[20] Finally, the president is supposed to ratify the constitution.[21] A constitutional referendum was requested by CSOs, but is not envisioned in the TCRSS.

According to the TCRSS, the tenure of the national and state legislatures together with the president were supposed to terminate by 9 July 2015 for the purpose of national elections. In March 2015 the South Sudan National Legislative Assembly (NLA) passed the Constitutional Amendment Bill 2015, extending its own tenure and the tenure of the president until 9 July 2018, and the mandate of the NCRC until 31 December 2018.[22] The opposition criticised the amendment as 'unilateral[ly] lacking the consensus of the people'.[23] When taking a closer look at the current composition of the Parliament – which is supposed to represent the people – it shows that the overall majority belong to the ruling party Sudan People's Liberation Movement (SPLM)[24] and almost half of its members are presidentially appointed.[25]

Even though public participation is envisioned at the stages of NCRC and NCC, one can identify an inherent contradiction in the process: The project design is an impediment to a citizens-driven constitution 'since governmental actors debate rather among themselves not only in the NCRC' (Yakani 10 June 2015). Due to the current political constellations in the emerging state, any input from the citizens will occur during the NCC; ultimately the results will be decided afterwards in the partly presidentially appointed Parliament by SPLM dominated politicians. However, this constellation might change due to the constitutional amendment of 2015 in case the envisioned national elections will be held in 2018. Then, a new elected legislature in another composition without comprising presidential appointees might deliberate and adopt a 'permanent' constitution.

Local translation dynamics in response to international participatory models

The South Sudanese public have received the Transitional Constitution of 2011 with mixed feelings since the draft had been produced without the participation of many (An-Na'im 3 April 2011; Adiebo and Lubang 6 April 2011). Criticisms

---

19 Art. 203(1,3) TCRSS.
20 Art. 203(7) TCRSS.
21 Art. 203(8) TCRSS.
22 TCRSS (Amendment Act 2015).
23 Lam Akol Ajawin, www.southsudannewsagency.com/opiunbion/analyses/ca-a-democratic-government -extend-its-own-life. . . ., 24 February 2015.
24 The ruling party SPLM is the civil wing of the Sudan People's Liberation Army (SPLA).
25 Out of the 332 members, only 170 are elected, whereas 162 members are presidentially appointed.

were, for instance, directed towards the two-thirds dominance of the ruling SPLM within the Technical Committee to Review the Interim Constitution of Southern Sudan of 2005 (Seidel and Moritz 2011). The presidentially hand-picked committee quickly reviewed the already predefined Interim Constitution of Southern Sudan (ICSS) that was part of the Comprehensive Peace Agreement (CPA).[26] It was a quick 'top down' exercise and largely informed by the CPA/ICSS[27] that again emerged without a participatory process. Moreover, the Technical Commission granted 'hyper-powers' to the president[28] behind closed doors as a governance tool to deal with war-torn political and military fragmentation. The remaining committee members perceived their participation as being reduced to a 'rubber stamp' function (Aciek 14 April 2013) in light of a two-thirds majority vote system.[29] Additionally, 'no public consultation on the nature of the constitution' (Yakani 10 June 2015) took place as it did not happen during the drafting of the Interim Constitution.

Certainly, besides a lack of political will, the reviewing process was very much motivated by (international) political pressure and time constraints, since the document was supposed to enter into effect upon South Sudan's declaration of independence. The adoption of the TCRSS by the Parliament was pushed through only a few days before 9 July 2011 even though crucial issues regarding the political order, such as government structure, the distribution of state functions, and distribution of powers between the federal and state governments[30] remained unresolved. During a last legislative debate, many members of Parliament (MPs) complained about the lack of participation. Concerned MPs were reassured that full participation and discussions of all contentious issues would be constitutionally guaranteed during the making of the 'permanent' constitution.

The political reality since 2012 has shown that the president used his constitutionally granted excessive power. He dismissed his vice president twice, his entire cabinet, the majority of state governors and appointed 'caretakers' intensifying political tensions and triggering severe political and military renegotiations. Moreover, as mentioned before, the constitutional amendments of the TCRSS are used to extend the tenures of the executive and the legislature.[31] Accordingly, the president got the authority to use the TCRSS as a power instrument handed

---

26 The Comprehensive Peace Agreement (CPA) paved the way for the declaration of independence. The attached Interim Constitution 2005 can be seen as starting point of South Sudanese constitution making (see Johnson 2011; Wassara 2009; Grawert 2010). This paper's scope is limited to the post-2011 constitution making.

27 Southern Sudan Legislative Assembly. "The Transitional Constitution of South Sudan. Ordinary Sitting no. 25, Second Session on 6 July 2011," Juba [recording provided by NLA on 2 May 2013].

28 See Art. 101 TCRSS.

29 Art. 10(1) NCRC Internal Rules of Procedure.

30 Southern Sudan Legislative Assembly. Presentation of the Transitional Constitution of the Republic of South Sudan, 2011 by H.E. J. L. Jok, Minister of Legal Affairs and Constitutional Development Ordinary Sitting no. 18, 7 May 2011, Juba [recordings provided by NLA on 2 May 2013].

31 TCRSS (Amendment Act 2015).

over by the Parliament and prepared by the Technical Committee. Numerous contested issues already inscribed in the TCRSS are not only postponing further negotiation to the constitution, but also limiting the space of negotiations on the fundamental choices regarding the political design.

The NCRC was mandated to be the forum for drafting a 'permanent' constitution. The commission was constitutionally supposed to be inclusive and to 'conduct nation-wide public information programme and civic education on constitutional issues'.[32] Public participation and integration of legal pluralities have become crucial elements in sustainable constitution making as lessons learned from other constitution-making experiences. In South Africa, for example, public participation (in form of mass demonstrations, conferences, local public forums) became institutionalized through the elected Constitutional Assembly (CA) and its six theme committees. In an extensive public participation programme, they collected ideas from the public and held workshops involving both CA and CSOs (Kramer 1997: 477; Klug 2011: 60). Deriving from this experience, it seems to be the ethos of participation serving as process of integration through which the imagination of all parties steadily evolves towards potential sustainability, rather than as a significant source of legal ideas (Klug 2011: 70–71).

In South Sudan, already a closer look at the composition of the appointed NCRC reveals that the constitutional stipulation of establishing an inclusive commission with 'due regard for gender, political, social and regional diversity of South Sudan' is not followed. Forty-three of its fifty-four members represent political parties while twenty-six were appointed by the SPLM.[33] Only six representatives of CSOs were appointed as part-time members. This choice has implications on public trust in the official constitution-making institution (Mabor 24 May 2015). As it was the case for the TCRSS drafting, the ruling political party and its alliances carved out a privileged position for negotiating the political space necessary to assert significant control over the constitution making.

When taking a closer look at the activities of the NCRC, its 'Action Plan 2013/14', for instance, follows the mentioned 2009 UN guidance note and the attached example of a process regarding structure, activities, and timeline. Three components are involved in the sequencing: (1) civic education and public consultation proceedings (of about six months); (2) constitutional review proceedings; 3) NCRC deliverables. Accordingly, the plan ingrained the idea of 'popular ownership' envisioned in the TCRSS.[34]

The NCRC formed six thematic committees.[35] Following the schedule, the NCRC launched a civic education programme to involve the public in the regional states in the constitution making (Aniaito 29 May 2015). Despite internal disputes about the significance of public participation at this stage of constitution making, the NCRC civic education sub-committee had started to collect views from different stakeholders comprising local administrators,

32 Art. 202(8) TCRSS.
33 Presidential Decree RSS/PD/J/03/2012.
34 Art. 3(1) TCRSS.
35 Art. 4 NCRC Internal Rules of Procedure.

community leaders, clerics, women, academia, military, and police personnel in various regional states. Consulted people complained about the unsolved issue of 'federalism at different levels'. This concern is connected to inter-state disputes, the powers of the president, the centralized judiciary and police, etc. Moreover, the surveyed people addressed the legally unsolved relationship between state law and customary law. Different normative logics and approaches become visible in dealing with issues such as early marriage but also with land and property rights (Aniaito 29 May 2015). To enhance public participation, a few workshops have been conducted in the capital. While internationally designed plans and intentions exist, the development of an interactive NCRC website to gather public submissions, the creation of information and education materials as well as the establishment of consultation forums and conduction of public hearings in any county have not been implemented. Ideas of utilizing e-technologies, social networking, and phone-in mechanisms for public opinions and the design of a database to document public submission have also stagnated in the planning stages (Aniaito 29 May 2015).

Both the continuous dearth of key resources (such as financial means and logistical limitations) and the December 2013 'political crisis' have restricted the NCRC's ability to continue its civic education and public consultation campaign due to severe security concerns (IDEA 2014). Particularly, the latter has slowed down the scheduled constitution making. The circumstances forced the NCRC to step out of the tight timeframes setting in motion new discussion dynamics. Even though the commission has not been able to conclude the civic engagement campaign yet, the already gathered public input seemed to have become direct sources for legal ideas and has opened the space beyond the symbolic dimension of public participation. The NCRC judiciary sub-committee has started to redesign the judiciary (Mabor 28 May 2015), for instance, as response to the public critique of the unsatisfactory status of the centralized judiciary with its challenges of lack of manpower and backlogs, of 'escaping and delaying justice' (Aniatio, 29 May 2015).

It remains to be seen what effects the established Transitional Government of Unity[36] – including the governmental reshuffling in this context – will have. The latest Agreement on the Resolution of the Conflict in the Republic of South Sudan (ARCRSS), which was negotiated and signed by the warring factions in August 2015 under pressure from the East African Community (EAC), the Intergovernmental Authority on Development (IGAD) and the international community modified their previous approach to constitution making. However, the ARCRSS's reach is limited due to the ongoing military re-negotiations. In the amended roadmap, the guiding principles are expected to be local

36 The Intergovernmental Authority on Development (IGAD) including the AU, UN, EU, the Troika (US, UK, and Norway), China, and the IGAD Partners Forum brokered seven ceasefire agreements that included the formation of a Transitional Government of National Unity between main warring factions of South Sudan's political leadership. Since May 2016 South Sudanese leadership negotiate the implementation of the 'Agreement on the Resolution of the Conflict in the Republic of South Sudan of 17.08.2015 (ARCRSS).

ownership and a comprehensive popular participation.[37] Basic open questions are: Will the constitution-making process design be renegotiated, and if so how will the NCRC continue its work, what will an amended action plan look like, and how will the raised challenges be further discussed and considered.

Despite the efforts of the NCRC, many informants have expressed their dissatisfaction with the constitution building thus far (Aciek 14 April 2013; Lorna 16 April 2013, 15 May 2015; Gideon 24 May 2015; Yakani 10 June 2015; Swaka Joseph 10 April 2013), including members of the SPLM political leadership (Thiik 8 August 2013; Mijak 10 April 2013). It is interesting to note that the late NCRC chairperson self-reflected his previously expressed notion of 'we draft for the people' (Tier 2013) as well of involving the common people at this early production stage are too time-consuming and would cause confusion (Tier, 3 April 2013). In 2015, he admitted, 'constitution making is not a switch on switch off operation' (NCRC 2014). He emphasized the significance of civic engagement, questioned the chosen constitution-making design, and wondered whether it would be more conducive to start with a National Constitutional Conference to agree first on constitutive elements of a South Sudanese Constitution (Tier 3 May 2015). Parallel to these reflections, other options for redesigning the process were discussed during the IGAD (Plus)-led peace mediation in 2014/15. At this negotiation table, opinions ranged from reforming the SPLM-led NCRC (including the nomination procedure) to fundamentally 'scrapping' the NCRC and restarting the process by nominating a 10-member drafting technical committee. At this external negotiation, ideas arose to shift from constitutional drafting 'through the NLA' to a 'through referendum' deliberation and adoption to guarantee a consultative process (Gideon 24 May 2015; Yakani 10 June 2015).

Being relegated to a second tier of negotiations, civil society actors constantly formed various citizens' constitution-making fora (Lorna 4 April 2013, 1 May 2013, 15 May 2015; Manyuon 11 April 2013). The South Sudan Civil Society Alliance, an umbrella organization of about 200 civil society organizations, for instance, successfully fought for a voice in the NCRC (Swaka Joseph 10 April 2013; Lorna 16 April 2013).[38] However, the few appointed NCRC members representing civil society had a rather observatory status than being full members (Yakani 10 June 2015). Their influence seemed to be reduced again to a 'rubber stamp', with their signatures becoming a formality in light of the majority voting system[39] and a presidentially designed 'veto' structure (Yakani 10 June 2015). This situation only serves to increase tensions, as many actors feel increasingly marginalized despite all the efforts made to win a place at the negotiation table (see Seidel and Sureau 2015). As was the case for the TCRSS drafting process, the ruling political party attempts to keep control over the constitution making.

Anticipating that the actual 'permanent' constitution process will be conducted in a rather exclusive manner similar to how it had been conducted during

37 See Ch. VI ARCRSS.
38 Presidential Decree RSS/PD/J/36/2012.
39 NCRC Internal Rules of Procedure.

the TCRSS drafting, civil society actors are prepared partially to fill the gap by promoting a comprehensive dialogue. The above-mentioned civil society actors' campaign 'Towards the Constitution of *Zol Meskin*' was supposed to 'contribute towards a constitution that reflects the will of the people' (SSLS 2014). For example, they had already collected views in all former 10 states for inclusion in the constitution in 2012–13. About 1,200 citizens were consulted via focus groups – traditional authorities, women's groups, youth groups, civil society, state assemblies, religious groups, MPs, and local government actors (Manyuon, 3 April 2013, 11 April 2013). These categories are similar to those one can find in the TCRSS when it comes to the composition of the National Constitutional Conference.[40] The data were evaluated by the coordinating South Sudan Law Society and subsequently passed on to the NCRC mid-2013, before the NCRC started its own civic consultation programme. The key findings reflect plural views on the elements to be inscribed in the constitution such as political system, democratic governance, call for federal political structure, human rights, peace and security, distribution of power, term limits, elections, and regulation of gender relations (Manyuon, 3 April 2013, 11 April 2013). Additionally, civil society actors collected women's views from the regional states. In 2013 women civic groups, CSOs, academia, politicians, government officials, and 'ordinary' citizens held a women's constitutional conference. This forum sought to 'advocate for provisions that enhance gender-sensitive legislation, democratic practices, accountability, culture of the rule of law and inclusive decision-making': The constitution shall guarantee women's social, economic, and political empowerment at all societal levels. They plead for affirmative action such as including women's quota in the constitutional document and reviewing of local laws including the property and inheritance rights systems (National Women Conference South Sudan 2013). Additionally, the South Sudan National Youth Forum for Dialogue and International IDEA jointly organized another meeting in 2013, to work out effective strategies for civil society contributions to the permanent constitution (IDEA 2013). The Sudan Council of Churches also participated in 'awareness creation and training on constitutional review process and collected some issues which will need to be acted upon by the NCRC' (SCC 2013).

As these examples have shown, civil society actors have set up their own fora hoping to substantially contribute to and have their specific group demands be considered in the constitution making. Plural views gathered from an eclectic stratum of society in the regional states have been handed over to the NCRC. However, this campaign cannot be perceived as a comprehensive outreach, since the campaign had only been concentrated in the municipalities (Mabor 24 May 2015). Moreover, when collecting the views, normative tools such as selected focus groups, moderator guidelines, questionnaire templates as well as pre-defined legal categories were utilized to channel the plural views (Manyuon 3 April 2013). Despite being bound to the 'technical game' (Rottenburg 2009: 142), the spaces of negotiations and range of participants

---

40 Art. 203(1) TRCSS.

are broadened and less bound to governmental actors. These efforts open space for discussion among the population beyond the participants at the official negotiation table.

How toolboxes of the international community shape public participation

The appointed South Sudanese actors have been joined by several international actors at the NCRC negotiation table. The extensive assistance of international actors in war-torn settings such as South Sudan has become part of peace building (for example, Ludsin 2011; Hay 2014; Turner 2015; Wolfrum 2005; Chesterman 2004; Bogdandy et al. 2005; Choudhry 2005). Thereby, constitution making is used as a common normative tool within the context of the broader rule of law framework (May 2014; Humphreys 2010; Costa et al. 2007; Carothers 1998; Kendall 2013). Technical support and legal advisory services to predominantly government actors come with a range of normative international benchmarks and conflict-resolution mechanisms (for example, Eriksson and Kostić 2013; Sannerholm 2012; Humphreys 2010). Drafters are not only prone to apply model constitutional frameworks but also create 'procedural objectivities' through supporting guidelines and activity plans. In this way, 'ostensibly neutral, elementary procedures are introduced, which are supposed to correspond to an unproblematic reality of facts and data' (Rottenburg 2009: 137, 140).

In South Sudan, the TCRSS stipulated that 'the commission [NCRC] may seek the assistance of other experts'.[41] The competition among the international actors seemed to be specifically regulated by a presidential order: the '[NCRC] secretariat may seek technical assistance from international partner organizations such as IDLO [International Development Law Organization], PILPG [Public International Law & Policy Group], UNMISS [United Nations Mission in the Republic of South Sudan] or any other organization as necessary'.[42] Moreover, IDLO's legal experts obtained a seat at the NCRC negotiation table and provided wide-ranged well-intended assistance, as an IDLO 'briefing note' (IDLO 2012) demonstrates:

- prepared the step to be taken in the constitution making;
- drafting the decree to establish the NCRC;
- preparing memo to the MoJ to give the president his strategy for the constitution process;
- concept notes on involving of CSOs, public participation;
- preparing talking points for the president's speech at swearing in NCRC at the request of the president's office;
- providing support to the development of Rules and Procedures for the NCRC;
- developing of NCRC Action Plan.

41 Art. 202(7) TCRSS.
42 Presidential Decree RSS/PD/J/02/2012.

Accordingly, the Internal Rules of Procedure of 2012 that the NCRC was constitutionally required to set up[43] were taken from the international toolbox, designed and provided by international actors. The procedural rules, that seem to be the amended Technical Committee internal procedural rules, follow the majority vote system as well.[44]

Another well-intentioned provided tool is the above mentioned 2009 guidance note on 'United Nations assistance to constitution-making processes' which states:

> Certain elements of a constitution-making process require careful early advance planning to be carried out successfully in an inclusive, participatory and transparent fashion. The UN should advise national actors of these requirements and assist them to begin the process in a timely fashion, taking into account the country-specific circumstances [. . .].

> In particular, the creation and implementation of public education and consultation campaigns [. . .] require advance planning. [. . .] The process should than be followed by a structured national dialogue or consultation process that feeds back the views of the people to the decision makers involved in the drafting and debating of the constitution.

> Attached to this guidance note is an example of a constitution-making process timeline.

This guideline reflecting the 'local ownership' discourse whereby the concept of ownership includes both, in the narrow sense, the national government and its institutions and, in the broader sense, a form of popular participation (Sannerholm 2012: 121f).

The 2013–14 NCRC Action Plan follows the 2009 UN guidance note and the attached example of a process, determining what actions are viewed as necessary to achieve the goals, as well as the conditions, timing, and personnel involved, since the plan ingrains the idea of 'national ownership', 'responsible actors', and 'implementing actors' are defined. In general, the NCRC was defined as the responsible actor whereas the international partners were supposed to be *de jure* implementing actors. However, activities relating to technical assistance and to special expertise are constructed conversely, e.g., international actors such as IDLO and IFES (International Foundation for Electoral Systems) are responsible for creating public submission databases and online public submission forms, providing thematic research, recruiting short-term thematic experts for contextualized research on South Sudan, producing comparative studies, recruiting constitution drafting experts, etc. Within the context of this division of labour, the question of who actually *owns* the process arises. Even though it is the NCRC that officially *owns* the process as part of the national elites – as they are accountable for its outcome – strategic key (procedural) activities such as 'recruiting, establishing, drafting, and finalizing' are carried out by international partners.

---

43 Art. 202(9) TCRSS.
44 NCRC Internal Rules of Procedure.

Even though 'experts' are appreciated to share experiences (Yakani 10 June 2015), the massive influx of 'foreign' experts has been criticized, since 'the assistance that was given goes back. The money brought in is taken back' (Aniatio 29 May 2015). This perspective reflects the previously criticized phenomenon in the 'development' cooperation arena, in which funds are circulated back to benefit the markets (labour and material) of the donating countries. The financial incentives prove to be not very productive to the recipient countries. Additionally, international partners promised to create 'online public submission forms' to gather public input (NCRC 2013). This well-intended participatory tool belongs to 'best practices' tested, for instance, during South Africa's and Kenya's constitution making. The concept of 'best practice' in policy discourses, however, is based on a fatal underlying assumption: that production and management processes are uniform enough that a 'best practice' can be identified and then adopted more or less 'as is' by another entity. 'Good' and 'best' practices become a standardization tool that allows different settings to be compared and measured against one another. In the end, they become strategic representations and an advocacy device for those whose interests 'best practices' serve. Accordingly, the applicability of those tools is quite questionable in the South Sudanese setting because they do not take into account the conditions of the context. There is only very sporadic Internet access in this war-torn country, even in the major cities. Hence, Internet-based tools such as databases cannot live up to their promise. They need to be adapted to the local circumstances. James Aniaito, chairperson of NCRC's civic education sub-committee, commented on these 'online public submission forms', noting that they are better suited to encouraging diaspora engagement by getting opinions 'even from outside, from the diaspora in different parts of the world' (Aniaito 29 May 2015).

This brings us to the issue of 'popular ownership' mentioned in the 2009 UN guidance note as well as to the constitutionally enshrined goal of an inclusive constitution making. The NCRC timeframe foresaw civic engagement campaigns of six months. As demonstrated above, it is generally questionable whether in the tight timeframe available, such civic education and public consultation tools go beyond a mere awareness campaign on the constitution-making process of the (inter-)national elites. A conceptual dilemma exists between the public consultation process and the application of the project management tools as, for example, the timetable was not open and flexible enough for the introduction and reevaluation of ideas that might arise within the public consultation process. Accordingly, one could ask how the NCRC should deal with the idea of popular ownership while following the convincing logic of the procedures of objectivity. As demonstrated above, the political crises force the NCRC to step out of tight timeframes and the international market place situation, opening space for the commission to deal with the dilemma.

Concluding remarks

As seen above, the actual constitution drafting is mainly in the hands of the ruling national elites and international actors. Different 'models', including participatory and inclusive templates and guidelines of how a permanent constitution should be produced have been brought in by the international community. Unfortunately, these well-intended internationally designed tools themselves are too often based on the false premise that South Sudan is a 'reconstruction state', i.e., assuming that the 'state' exists, instead of starting from the reality of being a 'construction state'. In the emerging state, no societal consensus has been reached (yet) on key elements to be inscribed in the constitution such as on common values, on the governmental structure, division of power, or the polity. The participatory international models are not flexible enough to take the emerging nature of the state as a starting point where the political actors' constellations are changing during negotiations. They do not much take into account the specific dynamic plural political and military constellation and its manifold normative contestations.

Moreover, the international 'models' create desires, 'because it mentors the mind-set of governmental actors towards something that is not existing within the present state' (Yakani 10 June 2015). The national actors involved are prone toward applying constitutional frameworks, creating procedural objectivities, and utilizing procedures such as guidelines and templates to enhance their (international) legitimacy. Even though participation is envisioned in the constitution making, in practice, local ownership of the process seems to be an expression of the end result, 'while during the actual process ownership is curtailed through notions of shared ownership or by external supervision' (Narten 2008: 254). Thereby, public ownership with its participatory ideas seems to have been reduced to a tool for gaining (internal) legitimacy. Dominant national actors take the international tools for their own purposes and benefits. The reality on the ground again shows that what local actors accept, adopt, and appropriate from the international tools very much depends on whether the offers strengthen their own positions. Accordingly, the international tools, the constitution-making process itself as well the contested issues inscribed in the Transitional Constitution have already become powerful weapons in the hand of a few dominant local actors whereby local ownership becomes a legitimizing tool fuelling the political struggle as well as the violent (re-)negotiation. Thus, the translation process demonstrates that the localization dynamics are controlled by local politics whereby the translation results seem to be contrary to intended public participation.

Side-lined civil society actors are pushing for an inclusive approach. They have developed their own methods for engagements and foster negotiation forums to integrate fragmented social forces with the desire of participating in the official state formation. The plurality of ideas demonstrates the processual dynamic character of ongoing negotiations with no definite societal consensus on crucial issues such as governmental structure. Accordingly, without radically reevaluating the so far chosen path of constitution making, legitimacy of a constitution which is produced in such a way seems to be hardly given. In order to become accepted and appropriated by the norm addressees as 'supreme law of the land', the constitution needs to rather arise out of a dialogue and an open public debate on fundamental issues.

Thus, transforming interim and transitional arrangements directly into 'a supreme law of the land' does not seem to be an appropriate path. A slowing down of the constitution making and a rather processual solution without any claims to consent or specific substance seems to be a step forward and a more sensible approach.

The current political renegotiations can be seen as opportunity for rethinking the constitution-making endeavour and for getting CSOs on the table: The impact of the post-2013 'political crisis' has forced the actors at the official NCRC negotiation table to step out of the predefined constitution-making route. The National Dialogue recently launched by the President (PD RSS/RO/J/08/2017) could be a chance for a more inclusive approach, if there is a genuine political will to break the vicious cycle of exclusion. It provides the chance to open up the constitution-making process and to integrate the so far gathered public input. These dynamics have the potential of going beyond a 'false' public participation. It could become more than an information campaign on the constitution making of the (inter-) national actors and might lead to an inclusive consensus production of the key elements to be inscribed in the future constitution.

References

Aciek, G.N. (14 April 2013). Interviewed by author, Juba, South Sudan.

Adiebo, K.A. and Lubang, S.M. (6 April 2011). Interviewed by author, Juba, South Sudan.

Aniatio, J. (29 May 2015). Interviewed by author, Juba, South Sudan.

An-Na'im, B. (3 April 2011). Interviewed by author, Khartoum, Sudan.

Behrends, A., Sung-Joon Park, and Rottenburg, R. (eds.) (2014). *Travelling Models in African Conflict Management: Translating Technologies of Social Ordering*, Brill, Boston.

Bargués-Pedreny, P. (2015). 'Conceptualising Local Ownership as Reflexive Cooperation: The Deferral of Self-Government to Protect "Unequal" Humans?', *Global Cooperation Research Papers* 11.

Bogdandy, A. v. et al. (2005). 'State-Building, Nation-Building and Constitutional Politics of Post-Conflict Situations', *Max Planck UNYB* 9, 579–613.

Carothers, T. (1998). 'The Rule of Law Revival', *Foreign Affairs* 77, 95–106.

Chesterman, S. (2007). 'Ownership in Theory and in Practice: Transfer of Authority in UN Statebuilding Operations', *Journal of Intervention and Statebuilding* 1(1), 3–26.

Chesterman, S. (2004). *You, the People: The United Nations, Transitional Administration, and State-Building*, Oxford.

Choudhry, S. (2005). 'Old Imperial Dilemmas and the New Nation Building: Constitutive Constitutional Politics in Multinational Polities', *Connecticut Law Review* 37, 933–45.

Costa, P. et al. (eds.) (2007). *Rule of Law. History, Theory and Criticism*, Springer.

Dann, P. and Al-Ali, Z. (2006). 'The Internationalized Pouvoir Constituant: Constitution-Making Under External Influence in Iraq, Sudan and East Timor', *Max Planck UNYB* 10, 423–63.

Eriksson, M. and Kostić, R. (eds.) (2013). 'Peacemaking and Peacebuilding: Two Ends of a Tail', in *Mediation and Liberal Peacebuilding: Peace from the Ashes of War?*, Routledge, New York, 5–21.

Ghai, Y. P. (1972). 'Constitutions and the Political Order in East Africa', *The International and Comparative Law Quarterly* 21(3), 403–34.

Ginsberg, T. et al. (2008). 'The Citizen as Founder: Public Participation in Constitutional Approval', *Temple Law Review* 81(2), 361–82.

Government of South Sudan (2011). *The Transitional Constitution of the Republic of South Sudan*, Juba.

Government of South Sudan [GoSS] (2012). Presidential Decrees (RSS/PD/J/02/2012, January 21, 2012; RSS/PD/J/03/2012, January 9, 2012; RSS/PD/J/09/2012, February 29, 2012; RSS/PD/J/36/2012, May 28, 2012), Juba.

—— (2013). The Transitional Constitution of the Republic of South Sudan (TCRSS), Amendment Act 2013, Juba.

—— (2015). The Transitional Constitution of the Republic of South Sudan (TCRSS), Amendment Act 2015, Juba.

Government of Sudan (2005). Interim Constitution of Southern Sudan, Khartoum.

Grawert, E. (2010). *After the Comprehensive Peace Agreement in Sudan*. Currey.

Hay, E. (2014). 'International(ized) Constitutions and Peacebuilding', *Leiden Journal of International Law* 24, 141–68.

Humphreys, S. (2010). *Theatre of the Rule of Law: Transnational Legal Intervention in Theory and Practice*. Cambridge University Press, Cambridge.

IDEA (2014). 'Amid Conflict and Crisis, What Future for the South Sudan's Permanent Constitution Project?', (http://www.constitutionnet.org/news/amid-war-and-crisis-what-future-south-sudans-permanent-constitution-project).

IDEA (2013). 'Symposium: Civil Society Contribution to the Constitution of South Sudan', August 28, (http://www.idea.int/africa/symposium-civil-society-contribution-to-the-constitution-of-south-sudan.cfm).

IDLO (2012). 'Strengthening Constitutionalism and Rule of Law in South Sudan, Project Briefing Notes', [unpubl.]

Johnson, H. (2011). *Waging Peace in Sudan: The Inside Story of the Negotiations That Ended Africa's Longest Civil War*. Sussex Academic Press.

Jok, J.M. (2012). 'South Sudan: Building a Diverse Nation, in Sudan after Separation: New Approaches to a New Region', *Publication Series on Democracy* 28, edited by Heinrich Böll Stiftung and T. Weis, 58–67, (http://www.boell.de/downloads/Sudan_after_Separation_kommentierbar.pdf).

Kiir Mayadit, S. (2016). 'Speech of His Excellency the President Announcing the Commencement of National Dialogue', Juba 14 December 2016.

Ki-moon, B. (2009). 'Guidance Note of the Secretary-General: United Nations Assistance to Constitution-Making Processes', (http://www.unrol.org/doc.aspx?n=Guidance_Note_United_Nations_Assistance_to_Constitution-making_Processes_FINAL.pdf.).

Kendall, S. (2013). 'Constitutional Technicity: Displacing Politics through Expert Knowledge', *Law, Culture and the Humanities*, 1–15.

Klug, H. (2011). 'South Africa's Experience in Constitution-Building', in Morris, C. et al. (eds.) *Reconstituting the Constitution*, Springer, Heidelberg, 51–81.

Kramer, J. and Schneider, H.P. (1997). 'Das Fundament des Regenbogens. Ein Zeugnis der Verständigung – die Verfassung des neuen Südafrikas', *Kritische Justiz* 4, 475–90.

Kulluel, A. (2012). 'Kiir Names Constitution Review Team', *The New Nation*, 12 January 2012, (www.thenewnation.net/news/34-news/293-kiir-names-constitutional-review-team.html).

Ludsin, H. (2011). 'Peacemaking and Constitution Drafting: A Dysfunctional Marriage', *University of Pennsylvania Journal of International Law* 33(1), 239–311.

Lorna, M. (4 April 2013, 16 April 2013, 1 May 2013, 15 May 2015). Interviewed by author, Juba, South Sudan.

Mabor, B.G. (24 May 2015). Interviewed by author, Rumbek, South Sudan.

Mabor, J.A. (28 May 2015). Interviewed by author, Juba, South Sudan.

Manyuon, P.G. (3 April 2013, 11 April 2013). Interviewed by author, Juba, South Sudan.

May, C. (2014). *The Rule of Law: The Common Sense of Global Politics*. Edward Elgar, Cheltenham.

Mijak, D.B. (10 April 2013). Interviewed by author, Juba, South Sudan.

Narten, J. (2008). 'Post-Conflict Peacebuilding and Local Ownership: Dynamics of External–Local Interaction in Kosovo under United Nations Administration', *Journal of Intervention and Statebuilding* 2, 369–90.

National Women Conference South Sudan. (2013). 'South Sudan National Women Conference on Constitution Making Process Resolution, 6–10 May 2013'. (https://nationalwomenconferencesouthsudan.wordpress.com/).

NCRC (2015). 'Timelines for Constitutional Review Entities in Other Countries" Juba, March 23 [unpubl.]

NCRC (2014). 'Update on the Activities of the Commission and Request for Extension the Mandate' (RSS/NCRC/LT/No. 108/2014), Juba, December 19 [unpubl.]

Sannerholm, R.Z. (2012). *Rule of Law after War and Crisis: Ideologies, Norms and Methods*, Series on Transitional Justice 7, Intersentia, Cambridge.

Schauer, F. (2004). 'On the Migration of Constitutional Ideas', *Connecticut Law Review* 37, 901ff.

Seidel, K. and Sureau, T. (eds.) (2015). 'Introduction: Peace and Constitution Making in Emerging South Sudan On and Beyond the Negotiation Tables', Special collection: Emerging South Sudan: Negotiating Statehood, *Journal of Eastern African Studies* 9(4), 612–33.

Seidel, K. (2015). 'State Formation through Constitution Making in Emerging South Sudan: Unveiling the Technicity of the Rule of Law', *Recht in Africa – Law in Africa – Droit en Afrique* 18, 3–16.

Seidel, K. and Moritz, J. (2011). 'The Transitional Constitution of the Republic of South Sudan. Ein Kontroverses Dokument des jüngsten Mitglieds der Staatengemeinschaft.' *GAIR-Mitteilungen (Journal of the Association for Arabic and Islamic Law)* 3, 92–98.

Simeon, R. (2009). 'Constitutional Design and Change in Federal Systems: Issues and Questions', *The Journal of Federalism* 39(2), 241–61.

South Sudan Law Society (2014). 'Constitutional Development', (http://www.sslawsociety.org/programs_const_dev.html).

SPLM/A and GOS. (2005). 'The Comprehensive Peace Agreement Between the Government of the Republic of the Sudan and the Sudan People's Liberation Movement/Sudan People's Liberation Army'.

Sudan Council of Churches (SCC). (2013). 'Pastoral Letter on the National Constitutional Review of the Transitional Constitution of the Republic of South Sudan', Catholic Peacebuilding Network, (http://cpn.nd.edu/).

Swaka Joseph, H. (10 April 2013). Interviewed by author, Juba, South Sudan.

Thiik, A.R. (8 August 2013). Interviewed by author, Juba, South Sudan.

Tier, A.M. (3 April 2013, 3 May 2013, 3 May 2015, 14 May 2015, 26 May 2015). Interviewed by author, Juba, South Sudan.

Tier, A.M. (2013). Juba Lecture Series on 'Building the Constitution in South Sudan', University of Juba, Juba, 06.03.2013 [recoding provided by Rift Valley Institute].

Tier, A. M. (14 May 2015, 26 May 2015). Interviewed by author, Juba, South Sudan.

Turner, C. et al. (2015). 'Constitution Making in Post Conflict Reconstruction', in Saul, M. (ed.) *International Law and Post Conflict Reconstruction Policy*, Routledge.

Wassara, S. (2009). 'The Comprehensive Peace Agreement in the Sudan. Institutional Developments and Political Trends in Focus Areas', *Chr. Michelsen Institute, Sudan Working Paper SWP*, Berlin.

Weber, A. (2016). 'Wieder zurück auf Los. Der Konflikt im Südsudan flammt wieder auf', SWP-Aktuell A46, (www.swp-berlin.org/fileadmin/contents/products/aktuell/2016 A46_ web.pdf July 2016).

Wolfrum, R. (2005). 'International Administration in Post-Conflict Situations by the United Nations and Other International Actors', *Max Planck UNYB* 9, 649–96.

Yakani, E. (10 June 2015). Interviewed by author, Juba, South Sudan.

Part III

Participation in context

Does it make a difference?

14 Wanjiku's constitution

Women's participation and their impact in Kenya's constitution-building processes

Jill Cottrell

It all started with Moi asking the question: "What does Wanjiku [a common, Kikuyu (woman's) name] know about constitution making?" In answering Moi, and mainly popularized by the brilliant cartoonist, Gado, Wanjiku has displayed all the great qualities of the ordinary Kenyan. . . . She remains a beacon of the hope that a just Kenya and a just world are still possible.

— Willy Mutunga, Chief Justice of Kenya
(Shitemi and Kamaara 2014, preface)

Historical overview

Kenya became independent of the UK in 1963. It was unusual among African colonies in that there was an armed independence movement – Mau Mau – during the 1950s, in which women were prominent. Indeed, the British government believed they were "far more rabid and fanatical than the males" (Presley 1988, 504 op. cit).[1] One colonial strategy to get support among the people was to involve women in social service activities, especially through *Maendeleo ya Wanawake* (Progress among Women) clubs. The clubs were also seen as a way of involving women in public life to some extent (Presley 1988, 521), and have been identified as a factor in the development of a Kenyan Women's Movement (Kabira/Kimani 2012, 843).

The 1963 Constitution was a fairly standard British decolonisation model, but with special provisions, including a degree of federalism, and provisions on land and citizenship, to protect the resident white population. It was made by a standard British process, involving negotiations in London between Kenyan politicians and the British government, negotiations in which only one woman was involved.[2]

Though the Bill of Rights recognised that certain rights were to be enjoyed regardless of sex, the prohibition of discriminatory legislation did not cover sex

---

1 Presley C.A. quoting Kenya National Archives (KNA), Native Affairs Department (NAD), *Annual Report* (AR) *1953*, 2. See also, Kinyatti (2008).
2 Maxon (2011) describes the negotiations. The woman was Priscilla Obwonya, see Kabira 2012, 54.

DOI: 10.4324/9781315180540-18

discrimination. In addition, a foreign woman married to a Kenyan had a right to become a citizen, but not a man married to a Kenyan.

Soon after independence a trend towards authoritarianism set in, and for a while the country was legally a one-party state. Amendments made little difference to the situation for women, except that the prohibition on discriminatory legislation did come, in 1997, to include sex.[3] But an exception for personal law (meaning customary or Islamic law applying to matters like marriage and family) continued. A provision was introduced that 12 extra MPs, nominated by parties, would "represent special interests" taking "into account the principle of gender equality".[4]

During the 1990s, the head of steam in society for constitutional change built up, culminating in 2000 with the president's acceptance that something must be done and the appointment of a commission to review the constitution. That commission produced a draft constitution that was adopted, with changes, by a national constitutional conference in 2004. But the government disliked some aspects, and took it to Parliament proposing amendments. The revised draft was submitted to a referendum in 2005 and rejected (for reasons mainly concerned with generalised support for or opposition to the president though opposition to women's rights to land was a factor for some). Part of the settlement following serious post-election violence in 2007–8 was a revived constitutional process. This led to the adoption of a new constitution in 2010.

Gender dimensions of the run-up to the formal process

One writer comments that the 1985 Nairobi World Conference on Women "(m)arked the beginning of the awakening of Kenyan society to the fact that the issue of women's empowerment was central to the triple goals of equality, development and peace" (Kihiu 2010, 162). Women's groups campaigned to have the government translate conference commitments into reality (ibid. 175).

But, generally speaking, progress in the development of a women's movement is traced to 1992. Previously, women's organisations "had to limit their 'women's agenda', strictly to social welfare provisioning, promoting the role of women as homemakers and mobilizing and organising women at grassroots level into women's groups to support agendas of male political elites" (Nzomo 2014). In 1992 a major women's conference took place in Nairobi where a central focus was getting women into leadership positions (Kabira/Kimani 2012, 843; Kabira 2012, 19). In 1997 a failed attempt to get the law changed to require parties to have at least one-third women candidates spurred the establishment of the Women's Political Caucus which "rejected the role of merely saying prayers, making tea and dancing for politicians during meetings" (Kabira/Kimani 2012, 843; Kabira 2012, 20–25).

In 1994 civil society organisations had produced a model constitution, including a directive to the state to pursue "concrete measures" to ensure the rights of

3 Art. 82 of the Constitution of Kenya 1969 (as amended in 1997).
4 Art. 33 of the Constitution of Kenya 1969 (as amended in 1997).

women,[5] and a directive to the state to ensure women the equal opportunity to participate in development (clause 17(3)). Citizenship was to pass through either parent (clause 3), and any spouse of a Kenyan would have a right to be a citizen (clause 5). There was an extensive clause (26) on a gender commission. Names for the election commission were to be put forward by civil society, including women's organisations (clause 59).

By 1996 women were raising more radical suggestions – not necessarily for the constitution – including on female genital mutilation, affirmative action to ensure gender parity in decision-making positions, and public funding for candidates, particularly women (Mutunga 1999, 433–40).

A stop-start process involving various meetings of parties, alone or with civil society participation (Kabira 2012, 32–36), vacillation on the part of the president, and a separate civil society "People's Commission" to draft a constitution, culminated in an Act to set up an official process, and a merger of the official and the people's commissions in 2001. Women played a major part in this whole process, and the Act required the bodies involved to ensure that the review process accommodated "the diversity of the Kenyan people including (. . .) gender (. . .)", that the process was guided by the principle of gender equity,[6] that the formation of the Constitution of Kenya Review Commission (CKRC) respect the principle of gender equity,[7] and one of the three vice-chairs to be a woman. On substance, the commission was to "examine and review the right to citizenship and recommend improvements that will, in particular, ensure gender parity in the conferment of the right", and "examine and review the socio-cultural obstacles that promote various forms of discrimination and recommend improvements to secure equal rights for all". In addition, there were provisions for the National Constitutional Conference that was to consider the CKRC's draft, to have significant women representation. The government set up a mixed politician/civil society committee to draft the legislation for the constitutional review. Kabira says "[w]omen [six of the 14 members] attended these sessions religiously and strategised at every stage" (Kabira 2012, 34).

The mechanisms

This kind of strategizing ensured a significant proportion of women on the constitutional commission. The merged civil society/government commission had 29 members (including the secretary and the attorney general) of whom seven (or just fewer than 25 percent) were women. Most had strong feminist credentials, notably Phoebe Asiyo who entered Parliament in 1979, Nancy Baraza, former chair of FIDA (International Federation of Women Lawyers), Wanjiku Kabira, founding secretary of the Women's Political Caucus, and Salome Muigai, gender and disability activist.

---

5 Clause 8. The draft is in Mutunga (1999) 323ff.
6 Constitution of Kenya Review Act, section 5.
7 Constitution of Kenya Review Act, section 6(5)(b).

The draft constitution and report of the CKRC went to a National Constitutional Conference, comprising 629 members: 222 of these were MPs (17 women), three from each district, of whom one had to be a woman, totalling 222, 41 from parties, and the rest the CKRC commissioners, and representatives from various organizations, including women's as well as special interests including business. In the event, 148 (23.5 percent) were women.

The final special body was the Committee of Experts, responsible for the post-2008 constitution-making phase. Its Act required "gender equality" in nominating its nine members (six Kenyan and three foreign). One third of the members (or actually 27 percent if one includes in the total the attorney general and the secretary, non-voting ex officio members) were women: Njoki N'dungu (former nominated MP, architect of the 2006 Sexual Offences Act), Atsango Chesoni (co-author of the World Bank *Kenyan Strategic Country Gender Assessment 2003*) and Christina Murray (Professor of Law, University of Cape Town).

Methodology and strategies in the process

The CKRC itself prepared for its task not only by public consultations, but by a series of seminars. Some focussed on gender, including culture and gender, Islam and women's rights, on women and constitution making in Uganda and South Africa, as well as on the more familiar issues of women and the constitution, with overseas speakers and prominent Kenyan women, academic and political.[8]

Civic education on constitutional matters through civil society preceded the CKRC. It developed a curriculum for civic education for accredited organisations. And its booklet of "Issues and Questions" for Kenyans to consider included the citizenship of spouses of Kenyan citizens, who could pass citizenship to children, how the electoral process could be designed to increase the participation of women in Parliament and local authorities, and whether men and women should have equal access to land, and, if so, how.

In its many public hearings women contributors were active, if rather less than men. The commission did organise, in some places, hearings for women only, with women commissioners hearing the views submitted. It was thought particularly desirable to do this in places with Muslim communities.[9]

Women's organisations were prominent among the many that made written submissions to the commission. The Women's Political Alliance submission was typical.[10] It was not limited to "women's issues" but, for example, recommended a fully presidential system of government. Specifically in relation to women it focussed on: representation in elected and other public bodies

8 These papers were published by the CKRC in Part Two of Vol. 5 of its 2003 report, Technical Appendices.
9 See Kabira (2012, 95–191) on submissions at meetings around the country, including some women only (e.g., 145 and 154). Many summaries and verbatim accounts are available on the Katiba Institute website at http://katibainstitute.org/Archives/.
10 Submitted January 21, 2002 (on file with author). See also Kabira (2012, 196–205) for summaries of women's organisations' submissions.

(interestingly, an early appearance of the idea of putting a minimum for both sexes); public funding for women candidates (citing Zambia); limits on campaign expenditure; permitting independent candidates; whether a presidential running mate must be of the opposite gender to the presidential candidate; affirmative action policies in education and ensuring the one-third rule in appointments; employment and other spheres; a gender commission; enshrining women's rights in the Bill of Rights; a right to be free from violence; citizenship issues; equal access to land for men and women; and protection of rights of widows and widowers.

While not very detailed or sophisticated, this submission raises most of the issues that were to preoccupy the commission. Notably absent is any mention of abortion (or reproductive health generally). This is not to say that abortion is not a significant issue in Kenya. The current law is very restrictive; about 465,000 women annually have induced abortions, there are perhaps 266 deaths for every 100,000 unsafe abortions while 120,000 seek treatment for post-abortion complications (Ministry of Health 2013, 17, 24). It might have been difficult for the WPA to get agreement on any particular position.

It was not women's groups alone that raised women's issues. For example, a major political party's oral submission to the CKRC included:[11]

> NAC feels that our outdated constitution, statutes, laws, customary laws and cultural practices have been used to rationalize the oppression and exploitation of women and to deny them their basic rights including the right to political participation. (. . .) The new constitution should also provide that as a general rule, at least one third of all civil service and all elective positions in any organization in Kenya, from village to national level, be held by women.

The commission responded by including most of the points raised by the WPA. The women were pushing at an open door so far as the chair was concerned, and while some male members were sceptical, others were supportive,[12] and the women members were very effective.[13]

The next hurdle for the women was the NCC. The women's movement geared up to defend the "gains" in the CKRC draft. Four organisations in particular worked together: Kenya Human Rights Commission (an NGO), Federation of Women Lawyers (Kenya), Institute of Education in Democracy, and the League of Kenya Women Voters. They

> spent months analysing the draft constitution, identifying the provisions that safeguarded democracy, transparency, accountability and the people's participation in government and highlighting principles of social justice, gender

11 Verbatim Report of Public Hearing, National Alliance for Change Held at Charter Hall, Nairobi on 07.03.02, presented by Kiraitu Murungi, later minister for justice in the government elected late in 2002.
12 Kabira (2012, 49–50) identifies Dr Ooki Ombaka and Prof. Okoth-Ogendo.
13 Personal information from the Chair.

equality and gender mainstreaming. (. . .) We developed three guiding principles for our work and targeted 29 provisions of the Draft Constitution for which we have suggested alternative language that would clarify and strengthen these principles, which reflect the wishes of the Kenyan people.[14]

They continued,

We have compiled several materials that contain these principles, suggestions and position papers that are published in three handbooks: a training manual, a delegates' manual that contains a simplified version of the conference rules and procedures and a parliamentary handbook. (. . .) We have provided training to provincial delegates and conducted a survey of delegate's views on certain issues. We received a warm reception from provincial delegates.[15]

The women MPs, they reported, were less responsive.
Wanjiku Kabira has written of the NCC.

[T]he women delegates took the baton and ran their part of the relay race. The women at the conference met every Tuesday and Thursday (. . .) to share what was happening in the various committees, to educate themselves on particular issues, such as, Mixed Member Proportional Representation (MMPR), Devolution, Affirmative Action, among other issues. They mapped strategies at various committees and also gave feedback shared with other women.

The venue, Bomas, was a cultural centre, and tents were erected for various groups to meet, and the women's tent was the most consistently active.[16]
How they fared is perhaps best explained by looking at a few concrete examples.

Two-thirds gender rule[17]

From the beginning, drafts have included something on the lines of "the State shall implement the principle that one-third of the members of all elective and appointive bodies shall be women".[18] But concrete measures to achieve this have varied.

Focussing on elected bodies: the CKRC draft included Art. 105 "At least one-third of the members of each House shall be women" – a provision that would have presented the country with the precise dilemma it faces now (see below). Concretely, CKRC proposed a new electoral system (mixed-member proportional)

---

14 Information from a paid media advertisement.
15 Reproduced in "Kenya's Regime Change and Constitutional Review Process: Prospects for Women's Solidarity Across Religious Difference and Increased Political Participation", compiled by Athena Makau (on file with author).
16 Personal information from the Chair.
17 Kabira (2012) includes detailed accounts of this aspect.
18 From the National Values Article of the CKRC Draft (Art. 14(13)).

with 210 constituencies and 90 list members. Party lists must "begin with a woman and alternate between women and men in the priority of the nominees".

The CKRC also included measures designed to propel political parties towards being more democratic and women friendly, including public funding for parties, with an element in distribution being "the number of women candidates elected to represent each party" (Art. 92(4)(b)).

The electoral proposals ran into opposition in the NCC, and women's groups quite rightly pointed out that the CKRC proposals would not guarantee one-third women.[19] The KHRC/FIDA group proposed that the lists be required to be 80 percent women (and at the top of the lists). In the event the NCC discarded MMP,[20] and opted for something derived from the constitutions of neighbouring countries, Uganda and Rwanda: in addition to the regular constituencies (for which anyone could stand), there should be separate constituencies for women candidates only. These would be the administrative districts. There being at the time about 74 districts, the house would have had at least 74 women, and – if the regular constituencies had remained at 212 – the worst-case scenario would have been 25.9 percent women.

The CoE was bolder and in its second draft introduced a top-up list system: enough members would be elected on the basis of party lists to ensure that not more than two-thirds of the house were men. This, of course, left the size of the house uncertain.

The CoE draft went to a parliamentary committee, which reverted essentially to the NCC draft (while adding more regular constituencies). And the CoE, since this was a highly political matter, felt unable to reject this change. The special seats for women were reduced to 47 (because the number of sub-national units in the devolved system of government was reduced). And 12 members now come from party lists to represent special interest groups like persons with disability. Of these 12, between four and eight will be women. So in the worst-case scenario of no women elected to regular constituencies, there would be 51 women and 298 men (or 14.6 percent women).

The CoE retained the essentially CKRC provision about implementing "the principle that not more than two-thirds of the members of elective or appointive bodies shall be of the same gender" but in the Bill of Rights.

It is only fair to note that the CoE "top-up" provisions survived for the lower level of government; thus, every county has one-third women (none having elected as many as one-third for local constituencies).

Land rights

Women's land rights were not specifically addressed – though arguably implied – in the 1994 civil society draft constitution. But by the end of the 1990s property

19 As few as about 50 of the list seats might have been held by women. If no more than 12 of the constituencies elected women members that would have been 62 out of 300, or 20 percent.
20 See Kabira (2012, 235) on the fate of MMP at Bomas.

rights were on the women's agenda,[21] and by the time an official process got under way, an NGO (Kenya Land Alliance, KLA) had been working on the ingredients of a national land policy. Its work had considerable influence on the CKRC. In a submission to the CKRC in 2002, the KLA said,[22]

> Many local cultures do not guarantee a wife's rights to inherit her husband's property. Widows are often dispossessed by their in-laws and rendered homeless. Even when they have taken care of their parents, brothers often evict sisters when parents die. Since many wives have little control over income during marital discord, many women are sent away with little if any means of survival.
>
> (. . .) African customs support patrilineal inheritance and male control of decision-making that exclude females from land ownership. Women are regarded as neither belonging to their natal nor their marital clans. Male family members take advantage of the adjudication and land titling process to deny women their share in family land.

The CKRC draft responded by providing: "Women and men have an equal right to inherit, have access to and control property" (Art. 34(3)). It required law protecting dependants of deceased persons including the interests of spouses in actual occupation of land, the protection of matrimonial property and, in particular, the matrimonial home (Art. 227(4)(a)). The provisions were intended to tackle particularly the customary law rules. The second provision looked to developments in other countries that prevent widows and children being left without a home, and prevent one spouse (usually the husband) from selling or mortgaging the family home without the awareness of the other.

The NCC added a more specific provision about succession: "A surviving spouse shall not be deprived of a reasonable provision out of the estate of a deceased spouse whether or not the spouse died having made a will." By the time the CoE began its work, the country had adopted a National Land Policy drawing heavily on the work of the KLA and reflecting the decisions in the NCC on women and land. So, although reports suggested that women's land rights were something of a factor in the 2005 referendum, the CoE did not categorise it as a contentious issue (Mbatiah 2010; United Nations 2007).

Abortion

The CKRC draft provided only "[e]veryone has the right to life"; indeed, one commissioner said, "I don't think the Commission was able to arrive at any

21 E.g., Achieng (1998) "Women Campaign for Constitutional Changes", reporting plans for the 1998 "16 days of activism campaign" by various women's groups including on "ownership of property laws that discriminate on the basis of sex".
22 "Land, Environment and Natural Resources: Submission to the Constitution of Kenya Review Commission" from the Kenya Land Alliance July 2002 (on file with author).

decision about abortion".[23] It also provided, "Every person has the right to health, which includes the right to health care services, including reproductive health care (Art. 56(1)) (derived from the South African Constitution). The future argument is foreshadowed by this remark from an NCC delegate before the conference even began: "There are a lot of things in reproductive health care and this Draft seems to be silent about abortion. Probably I would like it to be said very clearly the issue of abortion, can somebody introduce abortion . . .?" Another (male) commissioner said, "So we are trying to secure that in Article 32, Right to life as 'life starts at conception'".

Things got tougher at the NCC. The committee on the Bill of Rights proposed

(1) The right to life is protected.
(2) In relation to unborn child, Parliament shall enact legislation that recognizes the sanctity of life and ensures-

    (a) the safety of the pregnant woman; and
    (b) the safety of the unborn child.[24]

As a controversial issue, it had been referred to a group within the conference mandated to try to reach consensus. But, when the chair tried to present its recommendation to the plenary, his words, "the Consensus Group (. . .) after very lengthy debate said that there should be no reference to the conception of life and there should no reference to abortion which is already taken care of in the criminal law of the country", induced "uproar" according to the record (Constitution of Kenya Review Commission 2004). At the same session, a Catholic priest moved the inclusion of "[e]very person has a right to life from conception" and "abortion is not allowed unless on the medical advice where the life of the mother is in danger". This was basically adopted.

An attempt to remove "reproductive health" from the right to health – on the basis that it brought abortion back in – was defeated, particularly by a concise intervention by a (male) CKRC commissioner, and current attorney general.

The CoE wrestled again with the issues, and tried to pare it back to the minimum:

(1) Every person has the right to life.
(2) A person shall not be arbitrarily deprived of life.

But the committee of parliamentarians reverted to the NCC draft.[25] The CoE was reluctantly persuaded by the parliamentary committee that the life begins at conception provision was a deal breaker as far as the Catholic Church was concerned (Committee of Experts on Constitutional Review 2010, 111). But they modified

---

23 Charles Maranga, see Constitution of Kenya Review Commission (2002).
24 As stated by Millie Odhiambo, see Constitution of Kenya Review Commission, National Constitutional Conference (2004).
25 Kabira (2012, 399–402), includes a memo reacting to the committee changes; abortion is at page 401.

the other provision to read, "Abortion is not permitted unless, in the opinion of a trained health professional, there is need for emergency treatment, or the life or health of the mother is in danger, or if permitted by any other written law".

The CoE Final Report relates this episode (ibid. 10–11):

> [T]he clergy appears to have prevailed upon the Parliamentary Select Committee to enlarge the life clause with the inclusion of the words "life begins at conception until natural death". This provoked strong objections from the medical fraternity, gender groups and many other Kenyans.
>
> The Committee struggled to rephrase the clause so as to accommodate all competing interests and this is why the clause appears the way it does in the Constitution. But the clergy remained adamant and refused to budge despite the inclusion of the words "abortion is not permitted".

During the referendum campaign in 2010, the abortion provision was consistently misrepresented as freely permitting abortion by opponents of the draft constitution (whose real reason for opposing was something else, probably land).

Abortion, while important, did not loom large in submissions, but obsessed particularly some Americans, who became convinced that the US government was funding pro-abortion campaigns in Kenya.[26] It is interesting that Wanjiku Kabira does not identify foreign hands in the Kenyan debate. She comments, "It was amazing how this debate on abortion by men of the cloth demonstrated their desire and obsession with the woman's body" (Kabira 2012, 286).[27]

Since the constitution

Failure to respect provisions about diversity, including gender diversity, in recruitment to the police accounted for the decision of the courts to cancel a major recruitment exercise (*Attorney General & 2 others v Independent Policing Oversight Authority & another* [2015] eKLR). This can be directly traced to the constitution. But other provisions have proved less clear, and less effective. A court challenge to the make-up of the Supreme Court (five men and two women) failed, on the basis that it was necessary to wait until legislation was passed (*Federation of Women Lawyers Kenya (FIDA-K) & 5 others v Attorney General & another* [2011] eKLR). However, a challenge to the composition of the cabinet (under 25 percent women) was successful. The judge held that it was unconstitutional, but suspended the effect of his decision until after the election due in a few months' time (*Marilyn Muthoni Kamuru & 2 others v Attorney General & another* 2016).

On the two-thirds gender rule, the electoral management body, before the 2013 elections, proposed a quota system (grouping four constituencies within which in rotation only women could stand for one) which was rejected by the

<hr/>

26 See e.g., Smith (2010): Smith is a member of the US House of Representatives. For another view see Sheppard (2011).
27 In a section on abortion and the church see Kabira 2012, 284–86.

Cabinet and MPs. The Supreme Court held that, if the houses of Parliament did not meet the two-thirds rule, Parliament would not be unconstitutionally constituted (*In The Matter of the Principle of Gender Representation in the National Assembly and the Senate* [2012]eKLR). But it gave a deadline of mid-2015 for law on the subject. By late 2016, despite intense debate,[28] no legislative provision or constitutional amendment had been passed – MPs seem to have avoided forming a quorum for the subject.[29] However, another High Court decision, a few months before the 2017 election, ordered that law be passed to ensure satisfaction of the gender rule (*Centre for Rights Education and Awareness & 2 others v Speaker the National Assembly & 6 others* [2017] eKLR).

There are significant numbers of court claims to family land by women, though it is not clear how far the poorer members of society benefit. Recent land legislation has not fully reflected the constitution. For example, new law on matrimonial property, passed in 2013, defines such property (other than the matrimonial home) as property "jointly owned and acquired" excluding property in the name of one spouse only (Matrimonial Property Act 2013, s. 6.). However, it does provide that matrimonial property may not be sold, mortgaged, etc. without the consent of both spouses (ibid. s.12(1)).

Abortion remains controversial. Kenya ratified the Maputo Protocol to the African Charter and Human and People's Rights, on the rights of women, with a reservation on the abortion issue, in 2010. Although the Ministry of Health developed some quite reasonable guidelines on when abortion might be permitted, in 2013 they withdrew them. The issue has been raised in litigation by FIDA, which is asking for guidelines to be reintroduced and for safe abortion training to be instituted (Center for Reproductive Rights 2015).

Reflections

Women's issues do not necessarily receive a very sympathetic hearing in Kenya (as elsewhere). A typical experience is that of the KHRC/FIDA group who were invited to a conference but "[e]xperts speaking on a variety of issues were well received, but unfortunately our expert speakers on gender were ridiculed and hardly had an opportunity to make their presentation". The KHRC/FIDA alliance was not successful in removing the phrase "natural maternal role" (they wanted the word natural removed), in a provision about protection of women.

The 2010 Constitution did achieve many significant advances for women. This paper has focussed on three issues, but other gains are: prohibitions of discrimination on the grounds of sex, and pregnancy and marital status. And during the NCC "dress" was added in response to a particular incident of women being victimised because of their form of dress. There is a general duty on the part of

---

28 The attorney general set up a working group to make proposals; it covers all the reasonable possibilities (report on file with author).

29 Most recently on 16 November 2016, when it seems that even the 47 women county members were not present – see National Assembly (2016) "Official Proceedings".

public officers to address needs of vulnerable groups including women, a general obligation to take affirmative actions to redress past discrimination, the right to be free from violence, various specific provisions on the need to have women in public bodies, including equality in the public service, and the duty of political parties to respect and promote gender equality and equity, the provision that treaties form part of Kenyan law, and the inclusion of justiciable socioeconomic rights including housing and water, as well as reproductive rights, in the Bill of Rights.[30]

Certain lessons about constitution-making processes, and for women, may be perhaps, if tentatively, drawn from the Kenyan story.

The first is that it seems to help to have a history of consciousness and organisation. By the time the constitution-making process began, there was a core of women with considerable experience of public life and organising on women's issues. This showed in the way they were able to present their case especially to the NCC. A corollary of this depth of experience was almost certainly that foreign donors, including UN agencies, already disposed towards supporting women's issues, were able to find effective women's groups to fund.

While undoubtedly international trends were important, most of the impetus was home-grown. Again, while some foreign interference was undoubtedly present over the abortion issue, foreigners were far less interested in electoral systems and social justice. And the process itself was locally designed. Indeed, it seems likely that without genuine local support and initiative, any major developments in constitution making will be doomed to fail, whether they concern women or not. Women's participation and planning did, in reality, prove to be a significant factor in achieving gains for women.

Foreign experiences can provide inspiration, or warning, and concrete ideas. The experiences of Uganda and South Africa played a part, each having achieved a new constitution through participatory processes a few years before Kenya began its own. Specifically, in relation to women, the electoral system owes something to Uganda. South Africa and Rwanda were also sources of inspiration.

Kenya's experience also shows that women's groups can be effective even in rather hostile environments. The two-thirds principle and the land provisions are examples of this. There is still a good deal of resistance to these ideas, and yet they did not change radically during the whole process.

But the abortion issue is rather different. It is suggested that Kenya demonstrates at least two points. First, especially when emotions may be involved, it may be easier to persuade smaller, more technically minded groups of a position than a big popularly elected assembly – even if there are a reasonable number of women in the latter. The CKRC, and the CoE, the Technical Committee of the NCC, and the consensus group found it easier either to accept positive positions on abortion, or to take a hands-off approach. It is suggested that this may be because in a smaller group people are more willing to express an opinion that goes counter to mass opinions, and because an in-depth discussion is simply more possible.

---

30 Kabira (2012, 294–96) highlights the gains from the final constitution.

The second dimension of the abortion issue is that when religion is involved women are likely to be more divided, have stronger views, and perhaps even to take the more conservative view. Arguably, women would have a greater reluctance to speak out in public against a majority, especially a religiously held, view.

From the two-thirds gender saga it seems the main lesson to be learned is the unwisdom of putting into a constitution any provision which is likely to arouse opposition, and for which no legislative or other approach that is likely to be acceptable is apparent. What this also suggests is the importance of taking seriously the technical side of constitution making.

Kabira suggests that working with political parties was a strategy that payed off (2012, 350–51). Yet the history shows how women's causes can often be undermined by politicians – as with the 2010 Parliamentary Select Committee's changes to the CoE draft, and the post-constitution developments, or lack thereof, on the two-thirds issue. Kabira also comments that sometimes women's issues were subordinated to ethnic claims – the bane of Kenyan politics (ibid. 335).

A final general reflection relates to how quite radical ideas may still manage to get into a constitution despite a reality of underlying opposition. It is suggested, by way of a hypothesis rather than conclusion, that where there is a very substantial groundswell of support for generally quite radical change, a range of changes may be swept along on the general tide of desire for change even if they go beyond what has popular support. But this will not last forever, and tradition and vested interests will begin to reassert themselves.

References

Achieng, J. (1998). "Women Campaign for Constitutional Changes". InterPress Third World News Agency (IPS), Hartford Web Publishing, online: http://www.hartford-hwp.com/archives/36/196.html.

Attorney General & 2 others v Independent Policing Oversight Authority & another [2015] eKLR.

Center for Reproductive Rights (2015). "Kenyan Women Denied Safe, Legal Abortion Services – Center for Reproductive Rights Files Case Against Ministry of Health in High Court of Kenya". Press Release 06.09.2015, online: https://www.reproductiverights.org/press-room/kenyan-women-denied-safe-legal-abortion-services.

Centre for Rights Education and Awareness & 2 others v Speaker the National Assembly & 6 others [2017] eKLR Petition No. 371 of 2016, online: http://kenyalaw.org/caselaw/cases/view/133439/

Committee of Experts on Constitutional Review (2010). "Final Report of the Committee of Experts on Constitutional Review", online: https://katibaculturalrights.files.wordpress.com/2016/04/coe_final_report-2.pdf.

Constitution of Kenya Review Commission, (2002). "Verbatim Report of the National Constitutional Conference, Briefings for District Men Delegates (Algak)", held at KCCT Mbagathi on 23rd October 2002.

Constitution of Kenya Review Commission, National Constitutional Conference (2004). "Verbatim Report of Plenary Proceedings on Decisions on Draft Bill by the Committee of the Whole Conference Held at the Plenary Hall". Bomas of Kenya, 9 March 2004.

Federation of Women Lawyers Kenya (FIDA-K) & 5 others v Attorney General & another [2011] eKLR.

In the Matter of the Principle of Gender Representation in the National Assembly and the Senate, Advisory Opinion No. 2 of 2012 [2012] eKLR, online: http://kenyalaw.org/caselaw/cases/view/85286/

Kabira, W.M. (2012). *Time for Harvest: Women and Constitution Making in Kenya.* University of Nairobi Press, Nairobi.

Kabira, W.M. and Kimani, E.N. (2012). "The Historical Journey of Women's Leadership in Kenya". *Journal of Emerging Trends in Educational Research and Policy Studies (JETERAPS)*, 3(6): 842–49.

Kihiu, F. (2010). *Women as Agents of Democratisation: The Role of Women's Organisations in Kenya (1990–2007)*. Lit Verlag Dr W. Hopf, Berlin.

Kinyatti, M.W. (2008). *History of Resistance in Kenya 1884–2002*. Nairobi: Mau Mau Research Centre, 2008, pp. 211–23.

Marilyn Muthoni Kamuru & 2 others v Attorney General & another [2016] eKLR Petition 566 of 2012, online: http://kenyalaw.org/caselaw/cases/view/129670/.

Maxon, R.M. (2011). *Kenya's Independence Constitution: Constitution Making and the End of Empire.* Fairleigh Dickinson University Press.

Mbatiah, S. (2010). "KENYA: A Brand New Constitution, But Can Women Enjoy Land Rights?" Global Issues, Inter Press Service, online: http://www.globalissues.org/news/2010/11/23/7719.

Ministry of Health (2013). *Incidence and Complications of Unsafe Abortion in Kenya: Key Findings of a National Study*, online: http://aphrc.org/archives/publications/incidence-and-complications-of-unsafe-abortion-in-kenya-key-findings-of-a-national-study.

Mutunga, W. (1999). *Constitution-Making from the Middle: Civil Society and Transition Politics in Kenya, 1992–1997.* Harare, Mwengo.

National Assembly (2016). "Official Proceedings", 16 November 2016, online: http://www.parliament.go.ke/the-national-assembly/house-business/hansard?start=60.

Nzomo, M. (2014). "Women in Political Leadership in Kenya: Access, Agenda Setting & Accountability", University of Nairobi, online: https://ke.boell.org/sites/default/files/uploads/2014/01/women_in_political_leadership_in_kenya-_access_influence-.pdf.

Presley, C.A. (1988). "The Mau Mau Rebellion, Kikuyu Women, and Social Change". *Canadian Journal of African Studies*, Special Issue: Current Research on African Women, 22(3): 502–27.

Sheppard, K. (2011). "Chris Smith's African Abortion Adventure: The New Jersey Republican Spent Part of Last Week Meddling in Kenya's Abortion Politics—and Taxpayers Footed the Bill". *Mother Jones*, online: http://www.motherjones.com/politics/2011/03/chris-smith-kenya-abortion-constitution.

Shitemi, N.L. and Kamaara, E.K. (2014). *Wanjiku. A Kenyan Sociopolitical Discourse.* In: Contact Zones NRB, Vol. 11, Goethe-Institut Kenya and Native Intelligence, in cooperation with Ford Foundation.

Smith, C. (2010). "U.S. Taxpayer Funding for Kenyan Referendum Soars to $23 Million", online: http://chrissmith.house.gov/news/documentsingle.aspx?DocumentID=198790.

United Nations (2007). "Anti-Discrimination Committee Urges Kenya to Continue Pursuing Gender Equality Despite Referendum's Rejection of Women-Friendly Draft Constitution". Chamber B, 799th and 800th Meetings, online: http://www.un.org/press/en/2007/wom1644.doc.htm.

15 Societal engagement, democratic transition, and constitutional implementation in Malawi

Matteo Nicolini and Martina Trettel[1]

The durable path towards democracy in Malawi

Over the last three decades, new winds of democratic change have been blowing over African constitutionalism (Oloka-Onyango 2001; Manga Fombad 2007; Manga Fombad and Murray 2010). These winds have stimulated the transition of several states from authoritarian rule to a democratic regime, and therefore have favoured the adoption of new constitutions in many emerging African democracies.[2] The details of this assumption need not detain us here: suffice it to say that transitions also concerned the former English colonies, in general, and the Anglophone commonwealth countries of eastern and southern Africa (ESA states),[3] in particular.

The purpose of this chapter is not to assess the multifaceted features that democratisation has taken on throughout Anglophone Africa since the inception of this democratisation wave in the early 1990s. Nor will it focus on how African countries underwent democratic transition: in-depth analyses have been already dedicated to this topic.[4]

Instead, it will focus on the case of Malawi, an ESA state that experienced a remarkable constitution-making process. We contend that, when drafting its

---

1 While this chapter was discussed jointly by both authors, sections 1, 2, and 6 were written by Matteo Nicolini, and sections 3, 4, and 5 by Martina Trettel.

2 For more on these new winds of change, see Slinn 1991; Ghai 1991; Richard 1997. For Francophone Africa, see Reyntjens 1991, 44; Gaynor 2010. For Anglophone Africa, see Hatchard et al. 2010, 22–23. For a critical assessment, see Green 1989, 47. Botswana was the only country that retained a democratic constitutional context in the aftermath of decolonisation: see Cook and Sarkin 2001.

3 See Hatchard et al. 2010, 2–4, and 3 note 7, where Mozambique is omitted from the ESA states because it is 'a Lusophone country with a radically different constitutional tradition'.

4 See Huntington 1991. Although scholars mainly focus on South Africa (Sachs 1991; Wing 2000; Asmal 2007), all ESA states – with the major exception of Zimbabwe – have experienced a transition to democracy, including Kenya, Lesotho, Malawi, Tanzania, and Zambia. See Hatchard et al. 2010, 22 and 28ff. This is apparent as regards Namibia: see Cottrell 1991 and the seminal judgment in *S v Van Wyk* 1992(1) SACR 147 (Nm. SC), at 172–73: 'Throughout the preamble and [. . .] the Namibian Constitution there is one golden and unbroken thread – an abiding "revulsion" of racism and apartheid. [. . .] I know of no other Constitution in the world which seeks to identify a legal ethos against apartheid with greater vigour and intensity.'

DOI: 10.4324/9781315180540-19

constitution, Malawi blazed innovative trails to democracy in the process of transition. On the one hand, leaders and political movements that promoted democratic transition resorted to constituent assemblies and constitutional commissions. On the other hand, as they were 'seeking the people's views' (Hatchard et al. 2010, 29), they adopted innovative constitution-making mechanisms. To this extent, constituent assemblies were complemented by mechanisms of both direct democracy and citizens' participation, such as commissions of inquiry or constitutional commissions that toured the countries in question to hold public meetings.[5]

The choice to involve the populace reveals a fallacy in the current Western narrative on Africa's transition to democracy. Instead of merely mimicking the Western legal tradition (Banda 2009), African constitutionalism proved to be innovative and far-sighted. Indeed, although American and European scholars have been examining civic and public participation since the second half of the 20th century (Kaufman 1969; Auerbach 1972; Hart 1972), the most developed countries have been drawing on participatory mechanisms in constitution-making processes only since the first decade of the 21st century, as the cases of Iceland, Ireland, and, at the subnational level, Canada and Italy, show (Tushnet 2014, 19ff; Suteu 2015; Trettel 2015).

This blazing of innovative trails towards constitutional democracy allows us to propose an alternative reading of African constitutionalism. Societal inclusion in constitution-making processes has proven to render durable the transition to democracy and therefore the new constitutional designs that have been developed: since the early 1990s, legacies of transition have continued to shape African constitutionalism. Such durability is apparent when we consider how 'most of the post-1990 [. . .] African constitutions attempt [. . .] to place some limits and restrictions on the powers of governments to amend the constitution' (Manga Fombad 2013, 383). Legacies of the democratic shift are still present, as the numerous new democratic constitutions, recently approved in Kenya (2010), Zimbabwe (2013), and Zambia (2016), demonstrate (Stacey 2010; Chizuda 2014). Finally, durability has also been embedded in democratic constitutions, and societal engagement now governs the implementation of these durable constitutions.

This also holds true for Malawi, a small developing country in southern Africa, bordered by Mozambique, Tanzania, and Zambia (Patel et al. 2007, 2–4). To this extent, the chapter is aimed at examining public and democratic participation in Malawi's constitutional environment by focusing on the following questions: (1) how participation was really envisaged in the drafting process of the constitution enacted under the auspices of the democratic winds of change in the 1990s; (2) how the international community and foreign countries affected public participation in the constitution-making process; (3) whether the Malawian Constitution and legislation translated into practice its participatory spirit or not – and, if the latter were the case, which are

5 For a comprehensive overview, see Hatchard et al. 2010, 29ff.

the relevant discrepancies between the forms of participation embedded in the black-letter constitution and their effective implementation.

As for the role of participation in the drafting process of the constitution and in its implementation, suffice here to say that public participation effectively complemented the work of the 1994 constituent assembly; furthermore, the 1995 Constitution explicitly refers to societal participation in decision-making processes, in general, and in the implementation of governmental activities, in particular. There are indeed several participatory mechanisms that allow civil society to engage in parliamentary activities, including 'advocacy and direct lobbying, developing position papers [. . .] civic education and networking' (Hussein 2005, 88–90).

In this respect, we may say that participation pervades the entire spectrum of constitutionally entrenched decision-making processes, and represents a strong critical voice that has proven to be a contrast to attempts, in the last two decades, to turn Malawi into an authoritarian democracy. This is particularly apparent as far as decision-making at the local level of government is concerned: there public participation is really relevant, although the flaw between the black-letter law and its effective implementation gives rise to some issues that will be addressed in paragraph 6.

Setting the scene: The colonial legacy and Malawi's participatory spirit

In order to shed light on the role of public participation in both Malawi's democratic transition and constitutional implementation, we will first provide a brief overview of the socioeconomic, historical, and political scenario that characterises this southern African country.[6]

With about 15 million inhabitants, Malawi is one of the world's poorest countries, and with more than half its population living in poverty, Malawi 'has ranked consistently as one of world's least developed countries and relies heavily on concessionary development aid' and donations coming from foreign countries, especially the United States and the United Kingdom (Scholz 2008, 1). Thus, Malawi is a 'small heavily donor-dependent nation [. . .] subject to the preferences of donors' (Anderson 2016, 1).

This means that the international community and foreign countries have always played a relevant role in Malawi's constitutional history, in general, and in shaping public participation in the constitution-making process, in particular.

When it comes to considering its constitutional history, we may note that Malawi tried to sever its relations with its former colonial rulers. As soon as it gained independence from the United Kingdom in 1964 (on the colonial period, see Rotberg 1965), it promptly relinquished the Westminster model. The Queen, who originally remained as head of state represented by a governor-general under the 1964 Constitution (see Section 28: Roberts 1964), was replaced in 1966 by

6 On Malawi's constitutional development, see Kapindu 2014.

an elected president. Nevertheless, colonial legacies contributed to rendering Malawi a closed society, which indeed had its roots in the English Protectorate of Nyasaland (1891–1961)[7] and in the Constitution of the Federation of Rhodesia and Nyasaland in 1953.

This closed society was then secured by the authoritarian dictatorship of Hastings Kamuzu Banda, which lasted more than 30 years (1961–93) until 1994, i.e., when the country moved in the direction of multi-party democracy (Chirwa 2014, 3). Indeed, from 1961 to 1993, Banda presided over Malawi's one-party state, which was characterised by autocratic and oppressive rule. This, however, did not prevent the regime from adopting an authoritarian constitution in 1966. According to Section 4 of the 1966 Constitution, the Malawi Congress Party (MCP) was the only legally acknowledged political movement in the country, and Section 9 declared Banda president for life (Kanyongolo 2012, 3; Nkhata 2016). Moreover, Section 2(1) codified unity, loyalty, obedience and discipline, and party slogans as the four cornerstones of the government and the nation (Chimimba 2012, 40).

The same holds true for the role of foreign countries: donors also contributed to the preservation of Malawi's closed society. Because of Banda's anti-communist politics, the regime benefited from strong support among Western powers. As a consequence, 'Malawi was the only African state which maintained full and cordial diplomatic relations with the apartheid government of South Africa' (Patel et al. 2007, 7).

The authoritarian regime lasted for about 30 years until the 'winds of change began to blow across the globe, also engulfing the continent, and change became imminent' in Southern Africa (Patel et al. 2007, 7).

This means that Malawi's closed society started opening up and experiencing democratic participation after the end of the Cold War and the collapse of the Soviet Union in the late 1980s. Again, international donors triggered the path towards an open society. Various domestic and international actors exerted pressure on the authoritarian regime in order to open up Malawi's closed sociopolitical context.[8] Banda's authoritarian government thus agreed to hold a national referendum in order to directly involve the population in the decision regarding what kind of political structure Malawi would adopt.

This referendum may undoubtedly be considered the starting point for comprehensive reflection on societal participation in Malawi's constitutional democratic rule: participation was really envisaged in the drafting process of the constitution. In fact, direct democracy represented the first stage of the whole constitution-making process, through which Malawi also devised its own

---

7 See Africa Order-in-Council 1889, followed by the British Central Africa Order-in-Council 1902 (as amended in 1907 and 1912). See Chimimba 2012, 23, notes 19 and 26.

8 See Patel et al. 2007, 7–8, which provides examples of events and actors pushing for the democratic transition. Among them, we can mention the 1992 pastoral letter issued by eight Catholic bishops against the regime, worker demonstrations and riots, the return from exile of opposition and trade union leader Chakufwa Chihana, and the creation of new political groups. As for external pressure, in 1992 the World Bank Consultative Group 'froze all aid to Malawi, citing the Banda government's poor human rights record and widespread political repression'. See Meinhardt 2001, 223ff; Chikaya-Banda 2012, 9.

constitutional conception of popular participation. Societal involvement must then 'take into account the concerns of the widest possible segment of the population, must be transparent in its work, and to make such consultations meaningful, must properly structure its methods of consultation' (Hatchard et al. 2009, 34).

This is what we call 'participatory spirit': not only does it still pervade Malawi's Constitution, but it has also played a role in contrasting shifts towards authoritarianism. In fact, several constitutional amendments passed between 2000 and 2004 were aimed at subverting Malawi's constitutional democracy and therefore at satisfying 'the personal short-term interests of those wielding governmental powers'.[9] Nonetheless, '[t]hese and similar moves prompted civil society to keep a close watch on the government, making it more a watchdog than a partner in the governance process' (Patel et al. 2007, 20).

When devising the evolution of public participation in Malawi, we thus cannot limit our study to the period of the constituent process. We also have to take into account how public participation has evolved in the last 20 years of democratic rule. First, the voices of citizens have been heard through many channels during the development of a democratic Malawi. Second, participation adopted both an institutional (i.e., top-down) approach, as well as a bottom-up perspective.[10] Put differently, public participation at the constitutional level was conductive to the development of participatory mechanisms at the sub-national level, especially through local entities.

In this regard, with its 23 chapters and 214 sections, the constitution covers every conceivable area of Malawi's economic, political, and social life (Mutharika 1996, 205), as well as public participation. On the one hand, Section 40(1)(c) explicitly states that every person must have the right 'to participate in peaceful political activity intended to influence the composition and policies of the Government'. On the other hand, Section 146(2)(c) does the same with regard to local government, which has the responsibility for 'the consolidation and promotion of local democratic institutions and democratic participation'. Finally, Section 212 of the 1994 Constitution provided for the consultation of Malawian society when reforming the same constitution – and national legislation conveys alternative forms of popular participation, thus integrating bottom up claims for participation into manifold decision-making mechanisms.

Popular participation in the constitution-making process (1994–95)

We have already referred to the external and domestic actors that promoted Malawi's transition to democracy. In this respect, both international donors and

---

9 Patel et al. (2007, 19–20) highlight how these amendments included the repeal of the section on the Senate, the amendment to Section 65 dealing with floor-crossing by members of Parliament, and the attempt to extend the presidential term of office.
10 Both features usually complement analyses of Malawi's evolution towards constitutional, participatory democracy. For an assessment of popular participation from an institutional perspective, see Wiseman 2014. On the bottom-up approach, see Chihana 2008.

a popular movement acted as variables pushing for the introduction of a new democratic design, and therefore led to seeking the people's views through the means of direct democracy. Hence, a referendum was held in 1993, and voters were asked to choose whether they preferred Malawi to remain a one-party state or to become a multi-party democracy.

Although 'President Banda was confident that Malawians would vote to retain the status quo – a one party system with him as head of state' (Chikaya-Banda 2012, 9; see also Nkhata 2013), the referendum demonstrated Malawi's mature democratic and participatory spirit. The referendum saw a very high degree of voter participation, in African terms, with a 69 per cent turnout. About 67 per cent of all those who voted chose multi-party democracy, while 33 per cent were in favour of preserving a one-party system (Dzimbiri 1994).

The constitution-making process started at the beginning of 1994, right after the referendum was held. The National Assembly eventually passed the provisional constitutional provision for the Republic of Malawi (Constitution), Act No. 20 of 1994. However, the pivotal decision to transform Malawi into a plural-democratic system was complemented by a traditional constitution-making process, as the constitutional assembly acted without any proper and broad-based societal consultation.

In this regard, the responsibility for drafting the new constitution was entrusted to a National Consultative Council (NCC), which was established by the National Consultative Council Act No. 20 of 1993 (Chimimba 2012, 47). However, 'none of [its] members [. . .] were such by virtue of any popular elections; they did not have any direct mandate from the people to determine even the most basic framework of the Constitution' (Hara 2007).

Furthermore, there was a 'significant influence of the "international experts" in the drafting process [. . .] of the Constitution' and '[s]ome of the recommendations of the international experts seem to reflect the Western Donors' views of the Constitution to be created' (Hara 2007). In addition, the NCC delegated the constitution-making process to a team of five Malawian experts with a British lawyer acting as an advisor (Chikaya-Banda 2012, 9; Kanyongolo 2012, 7; Nkhata 2013, 234).

It should also be noted that the NCC started drafting the constitutional text at a time when many other activities were taking place, especially the organisation of the first general and democratic elections after 30 years of authoritarian rule.

The lack of democratic legitimacy, however, did not affect Malawi's democratic spirit. In this regard, it should be noted that the 1994 Constitution was an *interim constitution* that was to enter into force only for a one-year provisional period. In fact, Section 212 of the 1994 Constitution provided for the review of the constitution during its provisional application by foreseeing the three following activities:

(a) national civic education and consultation, during which the Committee would be involved in matters of public awareness and consultation on the Constitution; (b) the holding of a national conference 'fully representative of Malawian society'; and (c) the consideration of the constitutional proposals by the National Assembly.

(Chimimba 2012, 50)

The National Assembly (Malawi's legislative body) appointed an internal Parliamentary Constitutional Committee, which was entrusted with the examination of the interim constitution in order to propose amendments that could make it a permanent constitutional text. The committee was also charged with the organisation of a popular consultation (the so-called Constitutional Review Conference): via public participation, citizens and representatives of all segments of Malawian society were thus given an opportunity to propose constitutional amendments. The committee conducted hearings in the 24 administrative districts of Malawi, and every citizen could attend and make proposals. A national constitutional conference was then organised in February 1995: it was attended by 274 delegates from political parties and civil society organisations and lasted five days (Hara 2007).

Despite the efforts to involve the populace in the revision process, the conference was considered inadequate: it was capable neither of exerting a real influence on the drafting of the permanent constitution nor did it create a strong link with the population.[11] This is apparent if only we consider that, when Parliament voted on the final constitutional text, it disregarded the two recommendations explicitly framed during the conference: one regarded 'the suspension of a provision for a senate', and the other 'the repeal of the recall provision' (Chikaya-Banda 2012, 10).

Even in the absence of tangible popular involvement in the process, the permanent constitution became the Constitution of Malawi Act No. 7 of 1995, which was passed by the National Assembly on 11 May 1995 and assented to by the president on 17 May 1995.

What is the best form of participation for Malawi's constitutional democracy? From elections to the Law Commission

Even if popular involvement was relatively scarce throughout the constituent process, since 1993 Malawians have had the possibility to take part in parliamentary and presidential elections, and therefore to democratically express their will.

It should be noted that the concept of participation takes different forms and often serves different functions according to both the constitutional context and the subject matter it applies to. When applied to mature democracies,[12] citizen participation usually encompasses a decision-making process that goes beyond representative democracy. As the latter is currently undergoing a profound structural crisis, Western countries usually complement representative institutions with democratic participation, i.e., with mechanisms that enable citizens to be directly involved in policy-making processes (Ank 2011; Sintomer et al. 2012).

---

11 Indeed, two years later, 'few people reportedly had "any idea what a constitution is"'. See Brown 2008. See also Nkhata 2013, 236.
12 Mature democracies encompass those legal systems in which constitutions are fully developed, operational, and guaranteed. See Dahl 1992.

However, it is indisputable that, in modern and contemporary constitutional history, the concept of participation has always been theoretically related to representative democracy, to which, in more recent times, it has added elements carved out from deliberative and direct democracy (Frankenberg 2012). The representative character of the liberal democratic system thus influences the same degree of institutional innovation. This holds true as far as participatory and deliberative democracies are concerned. Under constitutional democracy, liberal democracy governs the relations between different kinds of democracy (Wampler 2008, 70). Representative democracy is related to deliberative democracy, which presupposes a model in which deliberation, through argumentation and persuasion, gives way to the broadest consent possible in public decisions. Evidently, when applied to representative democracy, *deliberation* aims to establish qualified majorities, not only in constitutional legislation or reform but also in the basic laws of local autonomies (Nicolini 2015, 440).

This also holds true when we apply the concept of participation to emerging democracies; indeed, the concept in question allows us to examine their institutional developments from a very broad constitutional perspective that includes direct, deliberative, and representative mechanisms of public participation.

These theoretical reflections also match Malawi's empirical experience, where political participation through free and equal elections has contributed to the development of the democratic features of the new institutional system. Furthermore, the interrelations between the concept of participation and representation are particularly apparent in Malawi; indeed, '[a]lternative definitions and forms of democracy were not discussed in Malawi, and a liberal democracy with the principle of separation of powers with adequate checks and balances among the three arms of government was thus the essence of the constitution making [process]' (Patel et al. 2007, 9). Together with the popular commitment to democracy, the trust placed in the traditional democratic decision-making process is empirically demonstrated by the extremely high turnout in the 1994 and 1999 elections, which reached 80 per cent and 94 per cent, respectively.

Electoral participation, which played and still plays a pivotal role in the development of Malawi's constitutional democracy, is complemented by additional channels of popular involvement, which support a viable and durable democratic evolution of Malawi's institutional context.

We refer to the activity of the Law Commission, as it is laid down in Section 135 of the Constitution, which reviews Malawi's laws in order to ensure that they comply with constitutional and international law. On the one hand, this independent body was conceived of as a means for guaranteeing the coherence of the legal system by amending and removing all pieces of legislation that were inconsistent with the democratic constitutional provisions.[13] On the other hand, it has the power to review and make recommendations regarding any

---

13 For more information regarding the Law Commission and its composition, see http://www.sdnp. org.mw/lawcom/index.htm?http%3A//www.sdnp.org.mw/lawcom/personnel.htm.

matter pertaining to the constitution: to this extent, and pursuant to these powers, two public conferences were organised in 2006 and 2007. As stated by a former member of the Law Commission:

> The Law Commission receives submissions calling for changes in the law from individual and institutional sources both private and public. [. . .] Submissions are assigned to law reform officers. They then conduct research to identify potential problem areas with the topic. These are set out in an 'issue paper' which announces the inception and scope of the review.
> (Chikaya-Banda, 2012, 11)

In order to strengthen citizen participation, the commission decided to establish special and provisional law committees, which were entrusted with reviewing legislation related to specific and technical topics. We can detect a strong participatory feature in the approach to the committees, as their composition included representatives of different segments and the interests of civil society. Commissioners could indeed be professionals, such as judges and lawyers, traditional leaders, or members of associations and organisations (Chikaya-Banda 2012, 11).

Since its establishment in 1998, public stakeholders have engaged the Law Commission in order to undertake a comprehensive review of the constitution. The commission was persuaded that such a review had to rely on broad popular engagement, contrary to what happened in the process of the adoption of the 1995 Constitution. Therefore, the commission decided in 2004 to establish a nationwide, highly publicised consultation that would last one year and take place through specific focus groups, discussions with traditional authorities, and informal consultation panels (Chikaya-Banda 2012, 16).

Finally, it should be observed that Malawi's Constitution has been amended many times, without recurring to participatory procedures. These changes have been of various kinds, from very narrow to very broad amendments. The most extensive changes occurred in 1995, 1997, 1998, 1999, 2001, and 2010 regarding mainly the form of government and the local decentralisation system (Chirwa 2014, 5).

Spreading the participatory spirit in Malawi: Public access to policymaking and local government

As we have already said, the participatory spirit enshrined in the constitution pervades not only constitutional and law-making processes, it also shapes governmental action: (a) civil society organisations may be granted a permanent seat on the governing boards of state institutions or parastatal organisations; (b) the executive may allow non-governmental organisations to take part in the development of public policies; and (c) the executive has embraced a participatory approach to budget-making procedures. During budget-making sessions, the minister of finance organises workshops and breakfast meetings on a merely consultative basis; civil society organisations, universities, and the private sector are thus involved in the budgetary process (Chirwa 2014, 9).[14]

Furthermore, citizens participate in the design and implementation of state legislation and public policies at the local level. Pursuant to Sections 3 and 6(1)(b) of the Local Government Act 1998, local government must promote the participation of the people in decision-making processes and consolidate local democratic institutions and participation (see Patel et al. 2007, 61ff.). Indeed, a high degree of subnational and local decentralisation offers 'many opportunities to look for new ways of increasing citizen participation' (Sommermann 2015). In Malawi, the decentralisation process traces back to the colonial rule (Chasukwa et al. 2013, 3ff.). After the democratic transition, it has been very weak because of the absence of a clear political project regarding local entities and the failure to hold local elections that should have taken place the year after the general elections (1994).[15] Only in 1998 was the government of Malawi able to pass a law on local government (the above-mentioned Local Government Act 1998) which was subsequently amended by the 2010 Local Government (Amendment) Bill. The act established local entities and approved the National Decentralisation Policy (NDP). Thereafter, local elections were finally held in 2000, though with a very low turnout of only 14 per cent.

The pendulum swung back towards recentralisation in 2005. As local government mandates came to an end, assemblies were dissolved and eventually suspended. The details of the suspension of Malawi's local government need not detain us here; suffice it to say that, while framing a new NDP, the executive identified in the lack of popular awareness and local participation one possible reason for this political failure (Chihana 2008, 61).[16]

However, budgetary and political issues regarding the further development of local government structures remained unresolved, and local elections were postponed until 2014, when the presidential, parliamentary, and local elections were all held simultaneously for the first time in the country's history (Patel and Wahman 2015, 80). In order to support the development of a stronger local level of government, a pilot participatory experience was established in February 2006 in three Malawian districts. This was implemented through the method of open space technology, a participatory approach invented by Harrison Owen in 1992 (Owen 2008) and examined how civil society should contribute in the development of local districts. The experiment had a positive effect and showed that it would be possible to strengthen local government by opening up space for

---

14 This approach to the budget-making process is akin to participatory budgeting. See Sintomer et al. 2012; Wampler 2012. For a broad comparative overview, see Dias 2012.
15 On local government, see Section 146(2) of the Constitution.
16 From 2005 to 2014 local government elections were not held for different reasons. Among them Chasukwa et al. 2013, 3, refer to 'lack of financial resources, famine that meant diverting funds meant for local government elections to buy food stuffs, fear by the ruling party of losing the majority of the seats, therefore implying loss of control over local politics, and an unfavourable legal framework.'

citizens to be directly involved in policymaking processes.[17] This methodology in fact increases the legitimacy of representative institutions, which comply with their legislative and executive decisions (Chihana 2008, 61).

Does the participatory spirit really work? The light and the shadow of Malawi's democratic constitutional framework

Unlike other African countries, Malawi resolved the political, ethnic, and religious conflicts that arose during its transition towards democracy through institutional solutions instead of resorting to violent armed conflicts. This was possible because the participatory spirit enshrined in the 1995 Constitution helped in developing Malawi's democratic governmental framework. To this extent, the examination of how public and democratic participation really works in Malawi's constitutional environment upholds that participation was really envisaged in the drafting process of the constitution; it also highlights the penetrant role of international donors in the constitution-making process.

We come now to consider whether Malawian Constitution and legislation has translated into practice this participatory spirit. To this extent, the constitution was aimed at promoting and safeguarding multi-party democracy, separation of powers, as well as the civil, political, and social rights of all Malawians (Chikaya-Banda 2012, 6). However, it has been argued that, using Roscoe Pound's legal taxonomies, Malawi's Constitution has probably remained more 'law in books' rather than becoming 'law in action' (Pound 1910, 12–15); the failure of the constitution 'to facilitate democracy and development is attributed mainly to dysfunctions in its interpretation, application and enforcement, and not to its fundamental premises' (Kanyongolo 2012, 2).

Whereas the fundamental principles and rules foreseen in the constitution grant Malawi the basis for establishing a real multi-party democracy, as well as civic and political participation, the subsequent evolution of the political, economic, and social reality has led to a misuse of the constitutional rules, as the saga of the approval of several amendments and of the suspension of local government clearly demonstrates.

From this, however, it does not follow that no lessons can be drawn from how Malawi articulated public participation. If we compare Malawi to many other African countries, we can positively evaluate the role played by the participatory spirit entrenched in the constitution. As already mentioned, this spirit helped avoid violent conflicts during the transition to democracy. In addition, it ensured broad public participation in the constitution-making process and allowed the populace to take part in the implementation of the constitution, in general, and

---

17 Indeed, Owen states that 'the outcome of the OST pilot projects in Rumphi, Mchinji, Zomba and Mangochi shows an unprecedented increase in self-organised groups, irrigation farmers and linkages between service providers ranging from public to civil society. It seems that the approach is the right step towards the integration of implementation at district level and towards planning frameworks both at district and national level'. See Chihana 2008, 63.

in legislative and governmental policymaking processes and actions, in particular. In other words, 'the [c]ountry has a popularly accepted constitution that enjoys broad-based legitimacy, established institutions for democratic governance and adequate mechanisms and opportunities for the promotion of popular participation in politics' (Chirwa 2014, 30).

This is not to deny the frequent problems that affect the transition to democracy and the establishment of constitutional democracy in Malawi. The high levels of aid dependency and indebtedness, the conditional use of donors' funds, the high degree of corruption in politics, the absence of strong guarantees ensuring the application of the constitution, and the failure of the decentralisation process made it possible to challenge and progressively reduce the room left for popular participation.

Thus, tensions and contradictions remain. On the one hand, there is the black-letter constitution with its provisions regarding democracy, civil and social rights, citizenship and participation; on the other hand, there are political and cultural legacies, such as the role of traditional chiefs, who have a strong impact on the implementation of constitutional provisions. Indeed, public participation must cope with the strong powers that are traditionally vested in the chiefs (Gaynor 2010, 803; Chihana 2008, 59) without divorcing the principles of democracy and good governance from African customary traditions (Tambulasi and Kayuni 2005, 158).

As public participation exhibits a great deal of resilience, it will probably be capable of amalgamating the two different, albeit intertwined, features exhibited by Malawian societal engagement: the participatory one, which focuses on people's involvement in decision-making processes, and the traditional one, which rests on tribal and communitarian networks. This objective, however, was already laid down in the Local Government Act 1998. Indeed, Section 5(1)(b) of the Act recognises 'Traditional Authorities and Sub-Traditional Authorities [. . .] as non-voting members *ex-officio* of local assemblies'; at the same time, Section 3 assigns to local assemblies the responsibility for consolidating and promoting local democratic institutions.

Hence, the participatory spirit may conjugate both sides of Malawian societal context (that resting on engagement and that relying on traditional law). If it is the case, this will mean that the flaws between the black-letter constitution and the living one have been overtaken and that the time for a strong constitutional democratic commitment in Malawi has come.

References

Anderson, N. (2016). 'Ephemeral Development Agendas and the Process of Priority Shifts in Malawi', *Journal of Asian and African Studies*, 51(1), 1–17.

Ank, M. (2011). 'Innovations in Democratic Governance: How Does Citizen Participation Contribute to a Better Democracy?', *International Review of Administrative Sciences*, 77(2), 275–93.

Asmal, K. (2007). 'The South African Constitution and the Transition from Apartheid: Legislating the Reconciliation of Rights in a Multi-Cultural Society', *European Journal of Law Reform*, 9(2), 155–66.

Auerbach, C. A. (1972). 'Pluralism and the Administrative Process', *Annals of the American Academy of Political and Social Science*, 400, 1–13.

Banda, S. (2009). 'Constitutional Mimicry and Common Law Reform in a Rights-Based Post-Colonial Setting: The Case of South Africa and Malawi', *Journal of African Law*, 53(1), 142–70.

Brown, S. (2008). 'The Transition from a Personal Dictatorship: Democratization and the Legacy of the Past in Malawi', in W. N. Shadrack (ed.), *The African Search for Stable Forms of Statehood: Essays in Political Criticism*, Edwin Mellen Press, Lewiston, 187–227.

Chasukwa, M. et al. (2013). 'Public Participation in Local Councils in Malawi in the Absence of Local Elected Representatives – Political Eliticism or Pluralism?', *Journal of Asian and African Studies*, 49(6), 1–16.

Chihana, P. (2008). 'Opening Space for Participation in Malawi', in P. Chihana et al. (eds.), *Towards the Consolidation of Malawi's Democracy: Essays in Honour of the Work of Albert Gisy German Ambassador in Malawi (February 2005–June 2008)*, Konrad Adenauer Stiftung, Sankt Augustin, Occasional Paper No. 11, 57–67.

Chikaya-Banda, J. (2012). 'Constitutional and Law Reform in Malawi', *Policy Voices series – Africa Research Institute*, 1–20.

Chimimba, T. P. C. (2012). 'The Search for Identity and Legitimacy: The Evolution of Malawi's Constitution', *Malawi Law Journal*, 6(1), 19–62.

Chirwa, W. C. (2014). *Malawi: Democracy and Political Participation. A review by AfriMAP and the Open Society for Southern Africa*, Open Society Foundations, New York.

Chizuda, L. (2014). 'Towards the Protection of Human Rights: Do the New Zimbabwean Constitutional Provisions on Judicial Independence Suffice?', *Potchefstroom Electronic Law Journal*, 17(1), 367–417.

Cook, A. and Sarkin, J. (2010). 'Is Botswana the Miracle of Africa? Democracy, the Rule of Law, and Human Rights Versus Economic Development', *Transnational Law & Contemporary Problems*, 19(2), 453–89.

Cottrell, J. (1991). 'The Constitution of Namibia: An Overview', *Journal of African Law*, 35(1–2), 56–78.

Dahl, R. (1992). 'Democracy and Human Rights under Different Conditions of Development', in E. Asbjørn and H. Bernt (eds.), *Human Rights in Perspective*, Blackwell, Oxford, 235–52.

Dias, N. (ed.) (2014). *Hope for Democracy: 25 Years of Participatory Budgeting Worldwide*, In loco association, Sao Bras de Alportel.

Dzimbiri, L. (1994). 'The Malawi Referendum of June 1993', *Electoral Studies*, 13(3), 229–34.

Frankenberg, G. (2012). 'Democracy', in M. Rosenfeld and A. Sajó (eds.), *The Oxford Handbook of Comparative Constitutional Law*, Oxford University Press, Oxford, 250–64.

Gaynor, N. (2010). 'Between Citizenship and Clientship: The Politics of Participatory Governance in Malawi', *Journal of Southern African Studies*, 36(4), 801–16.

Ghai, Y. (1991). 'The Role of Law in the Transition of Societies: The African Experience', *Journal of African Law*, 35(1/2), 8–20.

Green, R. H. (1989). 'Participatory Pluralism and Pervasive Poverty: Some Reflections', *Third World Legal Studies*, 8(2), 21–56.

Hara, M. H. (2007). 'Popular Involvement in Constitution-Making: The Experience of Malawi', paper presented at the World Congress of Constitutional Law, Athens, 11–15 June 2007, 15–16 (https://anayasa.tbmm.gov.tr/docs/Paper-by-Mabvuto-Herbert-Hara.pdf).

Hart, D. K. (1972). 'Theories of Government Related to Decentralization and Citizen Participation', *Public Administration Review*, 32, 603–21.

Hatchard, J. et al. (2010). *Comparative Constitutionalism and Good Governance in the Commonwealth: An Eastern and Southern African Perspective*, Cambridge University Press, Cambridge.

Huntington, S. (1991). *The Third Wave: Democratization in the Late Twentieth Century*, University of Oklahoma Press, Norman.

Hussein, M. K. (2005). 'Malawi', *South African Journal of International Affairs*, 12(1), 77–93.

Kanyongolo, F. E. (2012). 'Law, Power and the Limits of Liberal Democratic Constitutionalism in Malawi', *Malawi Law Journal*, 6(1), 1–18.

Kapindu, R. E. (2014). 'Malawi: Legal System and Research Resources', (http://www.nyulawglobal.org/globalex/Malawi1.html).

Kaufman, H. (1969). 'Administrative Decentralization and Political Power', *Public Administration Review*, 29(1), 3–15.

Manga Fombad, C. (2007). 'Challenges to Constitutionalism and Constitutional Rights in Africa and the Enabling Role of Political Parties: Lessons and Perspectives from Southern Africa', *The American Journal of Comparative Law*, 55(1), 1–45.

Manga Fombad, C. and Murray, C. (eds.) (2010). *Fostering Constitutionalism in Africa*, Pulp Pretoria.

Manga Fombad, C. (2013). 'Some Perspectives on Durability and Change Under Modern African Constitutions', *International Journal of Constitutional Law*, 11(2), 382–413.

Meinhardt, H. (2001). 'How It Began: External Actors in the Early Phase of the Democratic Transition in Malawi', *Verfassung und Recht in Übersee Law and Politics in Africa, Asia and Latin America*, 34(2), 220–40.

Mutharika, P. (1996). 'The 1995 Democratic Constitution of Malawi', *Journal of African Law*, 40(2), 205–20.

Nkhata, M. J. (2013). 'Popular Involvement and Constitution-Making: The Struggle towards Constitutionalism in Malawi', in M. M. Kiwinda and T. Ojienda (eds.), *Constitutionalism and Democratic Governance in Africa: Contemporary Perspectives from sub-Saharan Africa*, Pretoria University Law Press, Pretoria, 219–43.

Nkhata, M. J. (2016). 'The Republic of Malawi Country Report', Oxford Constitutions of the World Country Reports, (http://www.icla.up.ac.za/oxford-constitutions/country-reports).

Nicolini, M. (2015). 'Theoretical Framework and Constitutional Implications: Participatory Democracy as Decision-Making in Multilayered Italy', in F. Palermo and E. Alber (eds.). *Federalism as Decision-Making: Changes in Structures, Procedures and Policies*, Brill Publishing House, Leiden/Boston, 428–47.

Oloka-Onyango, J. (2001). *Constitutionalism in Africa: Creating Opportunities, Facing Challenges*, Fountain Publishers, Kampala, 2001.

Owen, H. (2008), *Open Space Technology: A User's Guide*, Berrett-Koehler Publishers, San Francisco.

Patel, N. (2007). *Consolidating Democratic Governance in Southern Africa: Malawi*, EISA Research Report No. 33, EISA, Johannesburg.

Patel, N. and Wahaman, M. (2015). 'The Presidential, Parliamentary and Local Elections in Malawi. May 2014', *Africa Spectrum*, 50(1), 79–92.

Pound, R. (1910). 'Law in Books and Law in Action', *American Law Review*, 44, 12–15.

Reyntjens F., (1991). 'The Winds of Change. Political and Constitutional Evolution in Francophone Africa, 1990–1991', *Journal of African Law*, 35(1/2), 44–55.

Richard, J. (1997). 'Democratization in Africa after 1989: Comparative and Theoretical Perspectives', *Comparative Politics*, 29(3), 363–82.

Rotberg, R. I. (1965). *The Rise of Nationalism in Central Africa: The Making of Malawi and Zambia, 1873–1964*, Harvard University Press, Cambridge, MA.

Roberts, S. (1964). 'The Constitution of Malawi, 1964', *Journal of African Law*, 8(3), 178–84.

Sachs, A. (1991). 'Towards a Bill of Rights for a Democratic South Africa', *Journal of African Law*, 35(1/2), 21–43.

Scholz, I. (2008). 'Introduction: Malawi's Development Course on a Knife's Edge – Do Politicians Care?', in P. Chihana et al. (eds.), *Towards the Consolidation of Malawi's Democracy: Essays in Honour of the Work of Albert Gisy German Ambassador in Malawi (February 2005–June 2008)*, Konrad Adenauer Stiftung, Sankt Augustin, Occasional Paper No. 11, 1–5.

Sintomer, Y. et al. (2012). 'Transnational Models of Citizen Participation: The Case of Participatory Budgeting', *Journal of Public Deliberation*, 8(2), Article 9.

Slinn, P. (1991). 'A Fresh Start for Africa? New African Constitutional Perspectives for the 1990s', *Journal of African Law*, 35(1/2), 1–7.

Sommermann, K.-P. (2015), 'Citizen Participation in Multi-Level Democracies: An Introduction', in C. Fraenkel-Haeberle et al. (eds.), *Citizen Participation in Multi-level Democracies*, Brill Publishing House, Leiden/Boston, 1–12.

Smith, G. (2009). *Democratic Innovations: Designing Institutions for Citizen Participation*, Cambridge University Press, Cambridge.

Stacey, R. (2010). 'Constituent Power and Carl Schmitt's Theory of Constitution in Kenya's Constitution-Making Process', *International of Journal of Constitutional Law*, 9(3–4), 587–614.

Suteu, S. (2015). 'Constitutional Conventions in the Digital Era: Lessons from Iceland and Ireland', *Boston College International and Comparative Law Review*, 3(2), 251–76.

Tambulasi, M. and Kayuni, H. (2005). 'Can African Feet Divorce Western Shoes? The Case of "Ubuntu" and Democratic Good Governance in Malawi', *Nordic Journal of African Studies*, 14, 147–61.

Trettel, M. (2015). 'The Politics of Deliberative Democracy: A Comparative Survey of the "Law in Action" of Citizen Participation', *Revista de derecho politico*, 94, 85–114.

Tushnet, M. (2014). *Advanced Introduction to Comparative Constitutional Law*, Edward Elgar Publishing, Cheltenham-Northampton.

Uganda Constitutional Commission (1991). *Guidelines on Constitutional Issues*, The Commission, Kampala.

Wampler, B. (2008). 'When Does Participatory Democracy Deepen the Quality of Democracy? Lessons from Brazil', *Comparative Politics*, 41, 61–81.

Wampler, B. and Hartz-Karp, J. (2012). 'Participatory Budgeting: Diffusion and Outcomes across the World', *Journal of Public Deliberation*, 8(2), Article 13.

Wing, A. K. (2000). 'The South African Transition to Democratic Rule: Lessons for International and Comparative Law', *Proceedings of the Annual Meeting (American Society of International Law)*, 94, 254–59.

16 Public participation and the death penalty in South Africa's constitution-making process

Heinz Klug

Introduction: Constitutions, participation and legitimacy

The dawn of the 21st century witnessed a global post-cold war moment in which democracy, the rule of law and constitution-making were embraced as international norms that would be the keys to state building, particularly in "post-conflict" societies. Even if conflict, including brutal wars and the disintegration of states – from Afghanistan to the Central African Republic, Libya, Syria, South Sudan, Somalia and counting – has become a marked feature of the early 21st century, the framework for democratic constitution-making is now embedded in the international institutions tasked with securing peace. In April 2009 the United Nations issued a *Guidance Note of the Secretary-General* laying out the "guiding principles and framework for UN engagement in constitution-making processes" (United Nations 2009: 2). A key principle is to "[s]upport inclusivity, participation and transparency" (id.). This chapter explores the limits of this principle by addressing the tension between public participation and the right to life in the context of South Africa's democratic transition and constitution-making processes.

Before describing the South African experience, however, it is important to reflect on why inclusive participation is such an important element of constitution-making processes. While there is a long tradition of elite pacts producing constitutional regimes, the question has always come down to legitimacy. Even if the founders of the American Republic met behind closed doors and negotiated the Constitution of the United States of America, it was the subsequent process of public debate and ratification, as well as subsequent renewals through an amendment process requiring intense political engagement within the States of the Union that provided the basis for its enduring legitimacy. From this perspective, participation is not just a democratic principle but is an essential part of the process of constitutional legitimation that enables a new constitutional regime to survive the challenges of its founding and lays the foundation for its hopefully successful implementation. However, if legitimacy is the goal, participation will have many forms and while it is not a single moment or activity, its breadth and depth will be important, even if continually contested.

DOI: 10.4324/9781315180540-20

In South Africa's democratic transition and constitution-making process, participation was continually contested. By first describing these processes this chapter will identify the many forms and phases of participation in the constitution-making process. Once this terrain of participation has been mapped – from the formal role of political parties and elected representatives to the less formal role of participants in constitutional conferences, public engagement programs and public demonstrations – the chapter will focus on the death penalty as a means of exploring the tension between participation and unpopular causes or segments of the society. The challenge is to throw light onto the relationship between, on the one hand the goals of deep, broad public participation and on the other hand, the rights of minorities, or even despised individuals. As South African Constitutional Court Justice Arthur Chaskalson stated in that court's now famous death penalty case: "The very reason for establishing the new legal order, and for vesting the power of judicial review of all legislation in the courts, was to protect the rights of minorities and others who cannot protect their rights adequately through the democratic process. Those who are entitled to claim this protection include the social outcasts and marginalised people of our society. It is only if there is a willingness to protect the worst and the weakest amongst us, that all of us can be secure that our own rights will be protected" (S v *Makwanyane and Mchunu* 1995: para 88).

The diversity of public participation in South Africa's constitution-making processes

South Africa's democratic transition was achieved through a two-stage process of constitution-making. The first stage in which the "interim" constitution was adopted, from approximately February 1990 until the first democratic elections in April 1994, was buffeted by violence and public protests (Klug 2001). By contrast the second stage, from the time of the elections until the adoption of the "final" constitution at the end of 1996, was formally conducted by an elected Constitutional Assembly (CA) made up of a joint-sitting of the National Assembly and the Senate of South Africa's first democratic Parliament (1993 Const. Section 68). The CA was, however, constrained by a complex set of constitutional principles contained in Schedule 4 of the "interim" constitution. It is within this context that participation in the constitution-making process must be understood.

While each of the three major parties negotiating South Africa's transition to democracy – the African National Congress (ANC), National Party (NP) government and the Inkatha Freedom Party (IFP) – negotiated for their preferred process of constitution-making, their preferences were intimately bound up with each party's substantive goals. These goals were premised on each party's particular conception of South Africa's future constitutional identity. For the ANC, a future South Africa was to be based on a common citizenship and identity which could only be achieved through a collective effort to overcome apartheid's legacies

(ANC 1994: 1–3). The NP conceived of a future South Africa in which local communities would be empowered to voluntarily choose to pursue their own living arrangements without interference from the state (NP 1991a; NP 1991b: 12). The IFP early on committed itself to the consolidation of its interests in one region of the country, KwaZulu/Natal, so as to perpetuate its existing advantage as a "Bantustan" government into the post-apartheid era (Ottaway 1993: 64–72).

The extent and nature of public participation envisioned by each party in the formulation of its own proposals was related to the character of the party's substantive goals and had a profound impact on its procedural preferences. The ANC, under pressure from its membership and the democratic movement, campaigned for an open democratic process in which a constitution would be written by an unfettered, democratically elected constituent assembly. The NP government, however, resisted calls for a democratically elected constituent assembly, envisaging instead a long transition period in which a future constitution could be negotiated between the parties. The IFP adopted an even stronger position against democratic participation, viewing the very notion of a democratically elected constituent assembly as inherently undemocratic (IFP 1992). Participation from this perspective ranged from elected representatives to party elites with very little space for public engagement.

Confronted with escalating violence, endless talks-about-talks and an apartheid government committed to a lengthy transition – including some form of power-sharing in which the white minority would continue to have a veto – the ANC and the democratic movement launched a public campaign for an interim government and a democratically elected constituent assembly. As the government in power, the NP was determined not to relinquish authority before securing effective safeguards against the future exercise of state power by the black majority. The collapse of the Codesa negotiations in mid-1992, after yet another massacre of black civilians, brought matters to a head. On the one hand, it defined the outer-limits of the NP government's ability to insist on a purely elite-driven process, as the international community pushed for progress and even the United States declared that a minority veto was unacceptable. On the other hand, the gunning down of ANC protestors outside Bisho, in the Ciskei "Bantustan", restrained those in the ANC who believed that mass popular participation and demonstrations – in what was termed the "Leipzig" option after the mass demonstrations that had brought down the East German regime in 1989 – would produce an unfettered constituent assembly. While overcoming the stalemate would require concessions from both sides, it was the post-cold war international consensus on the parameters of democratic transitions which enabled the ANC to ultimately overcome both the NP and IFP attempts to avoid an elected constituent assembly.

Despite its preference for a democratically controlled constituent assembly, the ANC recognized that the white minority would refuse to negotiate without some guarantees of the outcome (ANC 1987). With this in mind, the ANC incorporated yet another form of participation. First, in 1988 the ANC adopted a set of constitutional principles (ANC 1988: 29) which it then promoted through the Organization of African Unity (1989) until they were included in a United Nations General Assembly resolution defining the conditions that any future South African Constitution would have to meet in order to gain international acceptance (UNGA 1989). At the same time, the ANC Constitutional Committee launched a public debate on the ANC's constitutional principles and a proposed bill of rights which it published in 1990. After it returned to the country the ANC Constitutional Committee engaged in a series of broadly inclusive conferences to formulate and discuss the detail of these proposals (Klug 2000: 95–103).

Building links with a number of university-based legal institutes, which co-hosted these events, the ANC Constitutional Committee brought together a wide range of participants to discuss constitutional alternatives. Invitations went out to different ANC regions, political structures and members of the tripartite alliance – the ANC, South African Communist Party (SACP) and the Congress of South African Trade Unions (Cosatu) – ensuring the participation of a range of activists from the trade unions, nongovernment and community-based organizations. In addition, international experts and local academics were invited to present papers and to be actively involved in most of these conferences. Members of the ANC Constitutional Committee participated in these conferences and would meet at the end of each event to consider what had been learned and what needed to be done to incorporate such learning into the committee's work. These events were also used by the committee to build its own network as well as to bring its members together and ensure their own participation in the constitutional debates that were now going on at every level of the society. The format of these conferences produced a degree of participation, by both ANC aligned and independent (including foreign) participants, which was unique among the parties involved in the negotiations.

The ANC Constitutional Committee was, however, at times criticized by the ANC membership for not bringing the constitutional debates down to the grass roots, since the distribution of documents and proposals was haphazard and unreliable at the branch level. While many ANC branches in the cities held discussions or political education sessions around many of the Constitutional Committee's documents there is little evidence that these processes were characteristic of ANC branches in either the rural areas or for that matter in the urban "townships", where ongoing violence and basic organizing consumed available resources. Nevertheless, the impact of the Constitutional Committee's work profoundly reshaped the ANC's constitutional posture. Although the 1988 Constitutional Principles were ostensibly based on the ANC's political manifesto – the 1955 Freedom Charter – their elucidation by the Constitutional Committee clearly went well beyond the Freedom Charter and in retrospect involved a significant shift in the ultimate vision. This shift was made possible by the participation and engagement of activists, regional representatives and the ANC leadership itself in the discussions and debates initiated by the Constitutional Committee.

Formal participation in the negotiation process was, from the outset, premised on a notion of consensus building between contending elites. The Conference for a Democratic South Africa (Codesa), formed to negotiate the transition to a new constitutional order, reflected this elite pact-making process. Within the ANC the shift from constitutional debate to negotiations was accompanied by a demand for participation by the membership in the negotiations process itself as many felt the negotiators were becoming increasingly distanced from their democratic base. Again the ANC responded by attempting to establish negotiations fora at regional and local levels so as to keep a link between the negotiations process and membership. This too stretched the limits of resources and the representative capacities of local leadership. Meanwhile, the apartheid government argued that there could not be a non-racial election until a new constitution provided a legal basis for universal adult franchise and as holder of state power for over 40 years the NP remained determined to control the outcome, or at least to ensure certain basic property and social interests through the insulation of private power in the post-apartheid order (Friedman 1993: 26–27).

If the ANC's acceptance of a two-stage process, including a five-year government of National Unity as well as a set of sunset clauses protecting the interests of civil servants, the military and undemocratic local government structures for five years, allowed the negotiations to proceed, it also had all the hallmarks of an elite pact. When negotiations resumed in the Multi-Party Negotiating Forum in early 1993, decision-making was premised on the notion of "sufficient consensus", meaning that if agreement could be reached between the NP government and the ANC, negotiations would proceed despite disagreement from smaller negotiating parties. While this understanding enabled the constitution-making process to proceed, mass action, demonstrations and petitions represented the continuing intrusion of popular participation. Mass action, in the form of strikes, boycotts and demonstrations, played an important part in the ANC alliance's own campaign to shape the transition, while various public displays of outrage and shows of strength were employed by groups on all sides, as they tried to ensure that their concerns would be placed on the agenda at the multi-party talks. As a result, the period of the multi-party negotiations and the writing of the "interim" constitution was marked by protests, demonstrations, campaigns and even an invasion of the World Trade Center in Kempton Park, the site of the multi-party negotiations.

This mass public participation in the constitution-making process exhibited both a diversity of claims and a degree of popular frustration with an undemocratic negotiating process. A plethora of organizations and alliances gave voice to this diversity. For example, representatives of communities who were forcibly removed from their land under apartheid marched on the World Trade Center protesting the proposed constitutional protection of property, which they saw as an entrenchment of the apartheid distribution of property, and demanded constitutional recognition of their right to return to their land (Hadland 1993). The march in June 1993, in which a land rights memorandum was delivered to the negotiators, was followed by a march in central Pretoria in September 1993 in which about 600 people from 25 rural communities threatened to reoccupy land from which they had been removed by the apartheid government as a way of highlighting their demands for the unconditional restitution of land, the establishment of a land claims court and guaranteed security of tenure for farm workers and labor tenants. The Transvaal Rural Action Committee, which organized the march, also called for the rejection of the proposed property clause in the constitution. From a completely different perspective the IFP joined with two other "Bantustan" governments and ultra-rightwing white racists to demand a halt to the negotiations and the cancellation of the April 24, 1994, elections in order that the "self-determination" of different ethnic groups could be recognized.

The multiparty Women's National Coalition which came together to assert gender claims during the negotiations for the "interim" constitution provides an excellent example of a successful multi-faceted strategy of public participation. Bringing together women from all the parties who were appalled at how few women were participating in the process, the ANC's Women's League staged a sit-in at the negotiations and won the requirement that each delegation at the negotiations appoint a woman as one of its two Negotiating Council representatives. As a result, South Africa was the first case where a body negotiating a new constitutional dispensation was formally constituted by an equal number of men and women. At the same time the Women's League continued to press for greater participation within the ANC, winning a recommendation from the ANC's national working committee that one third of all ANC candidates in the April 1994 elections be women (Saturday Star 1993).

Provisions for the establishment of a Constitutional Assembly (CA) were spelled out in Chapter 5 of the "interim" constitution, which came into force on the date of the first democratic elections in April 1994. Constituted by a joint sitting of the two houses of Parliament – the National Assembly and the Senate – the CA was given two years, from the first sitting of the National Assembly, to pass a new constitutional text. At its first meeting on May 24, 1994, the Constitutional Assembly, comprised of 490 members from seven political parties, elected Cyril Ramaphosa of the ANC as its chairperson and Leon Wessels of the NP as deputy chairperson. At its second meeting in August 1994 the CA established a 44-member Constitutional Committee to serve as a steering committee and created an administrative structure to manage the process of constitution-making. In addition to the Constitutional Committee, the CA set up six theme committees in September 1994. These committees empowered legal and policy experts "to collect information, ideas, views, and submissions from political parties, interest groups, and individuals on issues that would come to form the content of the constitution" (Bell 1997: 34). The theme committees held a series of seminars and conferences that involved members of the CA, interest groups, academics and nongovernment organizations in debates over different sections of the draft constitution. In addition, a technical refinement team worked to ensure consistency throughout the fast-growing document and made certain it was written in plain language that ordinary citizens could read and understand.

Apart from these informal mechanisms, the Constitutional Assembly was also required by the interim constitution to appoint an independent panel of seven constitutional experts to provide advice to the CA and serve as a partial dead-lock-breaking mechanism if the CA was unable to achieve a two-thirds majority within the required period of time.

The CA's administrative team handled support for the assembly and among its other tasks facilitated public participation in the process. This was done under three distinct programs: a public participation program that included both written and electronic submissions; a constitutional education program; and a consti-tutional public meetings program. In addition, the CA published a newsletter, Constitutional Talk, devoted to explaining the process. Over 200 members of the CA participated in public meetings held on all nine provinces, and it "was calculated that 20,549 people attended workshops, and 717 organizations par-ticipated" (Ebrahim 1998: 244). Radio and television were also used to promote debate and educate the public about the constitution-making process. A national survey commissioned by the CA found that the CA's "media campaign reached 65 per cent of all adult South Africans in the three months between 15 January and 19 April 1995" (id.: 243).

Under the slogan "You've made your mark now have your say" the CA called on the public to submit suggestions on what they wanted included in the new constitution. Over two million submissions were received and while most of them were simply petitions over 11,000 were classified as substantive submissions (id.: 244). The CA also had a telephonic talk-line entitled Constitutional Talk-Line, which provided up-to-date briefings on progress in the CA and allowed the over 10,000 people who made use of it "to record their comments and submissions" (id.: 246). This produced one of the most iconic images of this period, a full-page newspaper advert of President Nelson Mandela standing in a driveway making his submission on a cell-phone. As Christina Murray points out, the statistics do not do justice to the program in two ways: first, they do not reflect the "vitality and energy" of the public participation program (Murray 2001: 818), and second, "they conceal the fact that its goals were not always clear" although "[o]ne goal frequently invoked was that the new constitution should be 'owned' by all South Africans" (id.: 821–22).

The degree of public exposure to the constitution-drafting process was prob-ably at that time without historical precedent anywhere in the world. Hundreds of public meetings were held to advertise the drafting of the constitution and to invite public participation in the process. The Constitutional Assembly published its own monthly newsletter, and there was an extensive publicity campaign on television and radio. Furthermore, genesis of the constitution from first draft to final product could be followed on a daily basis on the internet site of the Constitutional Assembly. In November 1995, the administrative team distributed four million copies of the working draft, which was finally approved by 87 percent of the members of the Constitutional Assembly on May 8, 1996 (Bell 1997).

The death penalty and the constitution

Colonial violence, of which capital punishment was the most symbolic, was a central feature of state society relations from long before the founding of the Union of South Africa in 1910. Nevertheless, the Annual Report of the Department of Justice described "the year of Union as a hanging year" (Chanock 2001: 536), reflecting the symbiosis between colonial rule and the exercise of capital punishment that would continue to be reflected in the coincidence between the number of hangings each year and periods of heightened resistance to colonialism and apartheid. Robert Turrell describes hanging in South Africa as "a symbolic expression of political power" (2004: 7) and how the "white men in power used the death penalty as a weapon for social discipline" (id.: 46). From 1910 until 1958 there were three crimes for which death was an available sentence – murder, treason and rape. After 1958, the legislature created "eight new capital offences" including "robbery and housebreaking with aggravating circumstances (1958), sabotage (1962), receiving training that could further the objects of communism or advocating abroad economic or social change in South Africa by violent means . . . (1963), kidnapping and childstealing (1965), and 'participation in terroristic activities' (1967)" (Dugard 1978: 127–28).

As resistance to apartheid grew in the 1980s there was a steady increase in hangings (Murray, Sloth-Nielsen and Tredoux 1989: 154). Of the approximately 4,415 death penalty executions between 1910 and the moratorium in 1989, about 80.34 percent or 3,547 took place during the apartheid years 1948–89.

Stopping the execution of prisoners on death row was one of the preliminary issues in the lead up to negotiations between the ANC and the apartheid government. By 1989 the revived Society for the Abolition of the Death Penalty was joined by a growing "Save the Patriots" campaign that focused on those on death row for political offenses (Simpson and Vogelman 1989). Responding to these pressures F. W. de Klerk, in his speech opening Parliament on February 2, 1990, stated that the government was rethinking the death penalty and declared an immediate suspension of executions pending reform (de Klerk 1990). Despite this moratorium there were two further executions in the nominally "independent" Bophuthatswana and Venda "Bantustans" in 1990 and 1991. While the 1989 Harare Declaration had called on the apartheid regime to "[c]ease all political executions" (OAU 1989: Section III, 19.5), in order to create a climate for negotiations, the ANC's proposed Bill of Rights for a New South Africa declared, under the right to life, that "[c]apital punishment is abolished and no further executions shall take place" (ANC 1990: Art 2 (3)).

Despite these developments, the parties in the Multi-Party Negotiating Forum in 1993 could not reach agreement on the abolishment of the death penalty. In their book on South Africa's Transitional Bill of Rights two members of the Technical Committee on Fundamental Rights during the Transition, Lourens du Plessis and Hugh Corder, describe how it came about that the "interim" constitution's chapter on fundamental rights includes the right to life but did not specify what this might mean for either the death penalty or abortion, both issues of concern to the parties. They point out that the ANC and its allies wanted these issues left to be decided by a "representative constitutional assembly" but agreed that the moratorium on executions should be entrenched for the duration of the transition (du Plessis and Corder 1994: 146–47). However, the NP government "disagreed with 'the entrenchment', in any form, of a moratorium on the death sentence" (id.: 146). As a result, the 1993 "interim" constitution protected the right to life but did not address the scope of this right.

One of the first cases brought to the newly established Constitutional Court challenged the constitutionality of capital punishment. In his opinion for the court, Justice Chaskalson bemoaned the fact that this contentious issue was left to the court stating that "[i]t would no doubt have been better if the framers of the Constitution had stated specifically, either that the death sentence is not a competent penalty, or that it is permissible in circumstances sanctioned by law. This, however, was not done and it has been left to this Court to decide whether the penalty is consistent with the provisions of the Constitution" (*S v Makwanyane and Mchunu* 1995: para 5). Appearing before the court the "Attorney General argued that what is cruel, inhuman or degrading depends to a large extent upon contemporary attitudes within society, and that South African society does not regard the death sentence for extreme cases of murder as a cruel, inhuman or degrading form of punishment" (id.: para 87). Responding to this claim Justice Chaskalson stated that he was "prepared to assume that it does and that the majority of South Africans agree that the death sentence should be imposed in extreme cases of murder" but argued that "[t]he question before us, however, is not what the majority of South Africans believe a proper sentence for murder should be. It is whether the Constitution allows the sentence" (id.).

Recognition that public opinion seemed to favor the retention of the death penalty posed a distinct problem for the fledgling Constitutional Court as it set out to establish its place and legitimacy as a new and unique institution in the South African legal order. Asserting its role as the protector of the constitution and human rights in a post-apartheid South Africa, the court chose this opportunity to declare that it would "not allow itself to be diverted from its duty to act as an independent arbiter of the Constitution" (*S v Makwanyane and Mchunu* 1995: para 89). Discounting the significance of public opinion to it's role, the court argued that public opinion in itself is "no substitute for the duty vested in the Courts to interpret the Constitution and to uphold its provisions without fear or favor" (id.: para 88). If public opinion were to be decisive, Justice Chaskalson declared, "there would be no need for constitutional adjudication" (id.).

The Constitutional Court's blunt dismissal of public opinion was, however, mediated by a second line of argument which appeared in a number of the concurring opinions. Here the justices justified their rejection of the death penalty, despite opposing public opinion, as based on the recognition of a national will to transcend the past and to uphold the standards of a "civilised democratic" society (id.: para 199). Society's will to break with its past and to establish a community built on values antithetical to the maintenance of capital punishment is evidenced, according to the court, in the adoption of a new constitution and bill of rights. As Justice O'Regan argued in her concurring opinion, the "new Constitution stands as a monument to this society's commitment to a future in which all human beings will be accorded equal dignity and repect" (id.: para 344). In these arguments, the court seemed to embrace the legal fiction of the 1993 Constitution's preamble which, despite its negotiated status and formal adoption by the unrepresentative tricameral Parliament, announced, "We, the people of South Africa declare that . . . [and] therefore [adopt] the following provisions . . . as the Constitution of the Republic of South Africa" (Preamble, 1993 Const).

Embracing the "altruistic and humanitarian philosophy which animates the Constitution enjoyed by us nowadays", as the true aspirations of the South African people, Justice Didcott also rejected the undue influence of public opinion. First, Justice Didcott repeated Justice Chaskalson's citation of the classic statements by Justices Powell and Jackson of the United States Supreme Court, who argued respectively that the "assessment of popular opinion is essentially a legislative, not a judicial, function", and that "the very purpose of a bill of rights is to withdraw certain subjects from the vicissitudes of political controversy, to place them beyond the reach of majorities". Then Justice Didcott went on to argue that the decision to abolish or retain capital punishment is a constitutional question, the determination of which is the duty of the Court and not of representative institutions (id.: para 188).

This concurrent rejection of public opinion and embracing of national values was repeated by Justice Kentridge. Arguing that public opinion, "even if expressed in Acts of Parliament, cannot be decisive" (id.: para 200), he suggested that while clear public opinion "could not be entirely ignored", the Court "would be abdicating [its] . . . constitutional function" if it simply deferred to public opinion (id.). Justice Kentridge then proceeded to discount any evidence of public opinion on the grounds that there had been no referendum or recent legislation (id.: para 201) and instead he suggested that the reduction in executions after 1990 and the official executive moratorium on the death penalty, "while not evidence of general opinion, do cast serious doubt on the acceptability of capital punishment in South Africa" (id.). These countermajoritarian concerns over the "appeal to public opinion" (id.) are overshadowed in the court's arguments by a reliance on the "evolving standards of civilization" (id.: para 199) which the court infers are incorporated into South African jurisprudence by the country's aspiration to be a free and democratic society (id.: paras 198–99). It is this national ambition, contained in the constitutional commitment "to promote the values which underlie an open and democratic society based on freedom and equality" (1993 Const., s 35) which the court presents as the source of social mores underlying the new constitutional dispensation. It is in this context then that Justice Kentridge concludes that the "deliberate execution of a human, however depraved and criminal his conduct, must degrade the new society which is coming into being" (*S v Makwanyane and Mchunu* 1995: para 199). A similar reliance on the constitution's inherent morality as a source of a public or national will which supercedes simple public opinion can be found in Justice Langa's argument that "implicit in the provisions and tone of the Constitution are values of a more mature society, which relies on moral persuasion rather than force; on example rather than coercion" (id.: para 222).

Conclusion: Constitutional rights and the limits of public participation

Participation in South Africa's constitution-making process took place at multiple levels over the course of the political negotiations towards an interim constitution and during the period of the Constitutional Assembly that produced the final 1996 post-apartheid Constitution. While this participation was at times essential to moving the process forward and to securing the inclusion or exclusion of particular rights, such as property and land rights, in the case of the death penalty there was a vast disjuncture between what most agreed was the common desire of people from across the political spectrum and the inability of the parties to come to any resolution of the issue during the negotiations over the interim constitution. By the time the final constitution was being negotiated the death penalty had been struck down by the Constitutional Court, which pointedly argued that popular desire was not the basis upon which the right not to be subject to inhumane treatment could be decided. Despite popular unhappiness at this decision the CA declined to make any changes to the formulation of the right to life and the right to be free of inhumane or degrading treatment, changes that might have overruled the decision of the Constitutional Court. Neither did the CA take the opportunity to explicitly declare the death penalty to be an unconstitutional punishment.

This outcome, in which the death penalty was declared by the Constitutional Court to be incompatible, in most circumstances, with the constitution's protection of the right "not to be treated or punished in a cruel, inhuman or degrading way", reveals the limits of public opinion and participation in the South African constitution-making process. This tension is not, however, unique to South Africa since the protection of "social outcasts and marginalised people" is an essential feature of constitutionalism which not only enables democracy but also protects human rights, including the rights of those who Justice Chaskalson described as the "worst and the weakest amongst us". Even as public opinion seems to favor the return of the death penalty and some politicians continue to appeal to this instinct, the fact that the CA did not respond to the court's 1995 decision and that it would now take a constitutional amendment or dramatic shift in judicial opinion to reintroduce capital punishment, indicates that there are indeed some circumstances where public participation and simple democratic majorities are not appropriate sources of decision making in the constitution-making process.

References

ANC (1987). "Statement of the National Executive Committee of the African National Congress on the Question of Negotiations", Lusaka, October 9, 1987.
ANC (1988). "Constitutional Guidelines for a Democratic South Africa", reprinted in *The Road to Peace* (ANC Dept. of Political Education, June 1990).

ANC Constitutional Committee (1990). "A Bill of Rights for a New South Africa", Bellville: University of the Western Cape, Centre for Development Studies.

ANC (1994). "The Reconstruction and Development Programme: A Policy Framework", Johannesburg: Umanyano Publications, pp. 1–3.

Bell, P. (1997). *The Making of the Constitution: The Story of South Africa's Constitutional Assembly, May 1994 to December 1996* (ed. P. Bell, March 1997), Churchill Murray Publications: South Africa.

Chanock, Martin (2001). *The Making of South African Legal Culture 1902–1936: Fear, Favour and Prejudice*, Cambridge University Press.

De Klerk, Frederik (1990). Speech at the opening of Parliament, available at: https://www.nelsonmandela.org/omalley/index.php/site/q/03lv02039/04lv02103/05lv02104/06lv02105.htm.

Dugard, John (1978). *Human Rights and the South African Legal Order*, Princeton University Press, pp. 127–28.

Du Plessis, Lourens, and Hugh Corder (1994). *Understanding South Africa's Transitional Bill of Rights*, Juta & Co: Kenwyn, South Africa.

Ebrahim, Hassen (1998). *The Soul of a Nation: Constitution-making in South Africa*, Oxford University Press: Cape Town.

Friedman, Steven ed. (1993). *The Long Journey: South Africa's quest for a negotiated settlement.*

Hadland, Adrian (1993). "Demonstrators Hand Govt Land Ultimatum", Business Day, Sept. 2, 1993.

Inkatha Freedom Party (1992). "Why the Inkatha Freedom Party Objects to the Idea of the New Constitution Being Written by a Popularly Elected Assembly (Whether called 'Constituent Assembly' or called by any other name)", undated submission to Codesa Working Group 2.

Klug, Heinz (2000). *Constituting Democracy: Law, Globalism and South Africa's Political Reconstruction*, Cambridge University Press.

Klug, Heinz (2001). "Participating in Constitution-Making: South African Aspirations and Realities", in *The Post-Apartheid Constitutions: Perspectives on South Africa's Basic Law* (Penny Andrews and Stephen Ellmann, eds,) University of the Witwatersrand Press.

Murray, Christina (2001). "A Constitutional Beginning: Making South Africa's Final Constitution", 23 *UALR L. Rev.* 809, 2000–2001.

Murray, Christina, Julia Sloth-Nielsen, and Colin Tredoux (1989). "The Death Penalty in the Cape Provincial Division 1986–1988", 5 *South African Journal on Human Rights* 154.

National Party (1991a). "Constitutional Rule in a Participatory Democracy: The National Party's framework for a democratic South Africa".

National Party (1991b). "Constitutional Plan" 11 *Nationalist* 9, p. 12.

Organization of African Unity (1989). "Harare Declaration, Declaration of the OAU Ad-hoc Committee on Southern Africa on the Question of South Africa"; Harare, Zimbabwe: August 21, 1989 reprinted in *The Road to Peace* (ANC Dept. of Political Education, June 1990) at 34.

Ottaway, Marina (1993). *South Africa: The Struggle for a New Order*, Brookings Institution: Washington D.C.

S v Makwanyane and Mchunu (1995). (3) SA 391 (CC).

Saturday Star (1993). October 16, 1993, at p.6 col.1.

Simpson, Graeme, and Lloyd Vogelman (1989). "The Death Penalty in South Africa", available at: http://www.csvr.org.za/wits/articles/artdpgl.htm.

Turrell, Robert (2004). *White Mercy: A Study of the Death Penalty in South Africa*, Praeger Publishers: Westport, CT.

United Nations (2009). "Guidance Note of the Secretary-General, United Nations Assistance to Constitution-making Processes", available at: http://www.refworld.org/pdfid/4b8648b52.pdf.

United Nations General Assembly (1989). GA Resolutions 44/27A, B and K, 22 Nov. 1989; 44 GAOR, Supp. No. 49 (A/44/49), at 34–35. See also, GA Resolution S-16/1, 14 Dec. 1989. The Declaration is reprinted in Sec.-Gen., Second Report, U.N. Doc. A/45/1052 (1991), Annex III.

17 A success story of participation?

LGBTI rights in South Africa

Veronica Federico

Introduction

"No constitution, no legislation without participation" could easily be regarded as the leitmotiv of any constitution-making and relevant law-making exercise in the first two decades of the 21st century. From Iceland to South Africa, from Bolivia to the Fiji Islands, constitution-makers and law-makers know that if the process has no participatory mechanism, it will be hard to paint it as legitimate and truly democratic. Participation may be pursued through several and very different mechanisms and institutes; it can be a sham participation or a substantial one, it can target and include solely elite, very specific and informed stakeholders, or it can be open to wider sectors of society (Allegretti, Corsi, Allegretti, 2016; Cornell, 2011; Suteu, 2015; Saati, 2015), and scholars who have recently engaged in inquiring into the concept, mechanisms, forms, levels of inclusiveness, etc. Nonetheless, participation is not the panacea and we cannot assume that as long as there has been a participatory process in the constitution-making or law-making the outputs are automatically good products, in both legal and socio-political terms. Moreover, research also highlights participation's "dark side" when specific stakeholders or social, political, religious, ethnic, etc. groups use participatory mechanisms to uphold their interests to the detriments of other groups or society as a whole (Gluck, Brandt, 2015; Moehler, 2008).

Since the democratic transition at the beginning of the 1990s, South Africa has been a laboratory for experimental participation in both constitution-making and law-making processes (but also in broader terms in policy-making) and several participatory mechanisms at the different stages of the constitution and law-making processes have been implemented. The outcomes, especially when it concerns the constitution-making processes, have been largely positive in terms of the intrinsic quality of the constitution and legislation, of the legitimacy of the single act and of the whole legal system, of inclusiveness and nation-building, and in terms of democracy. As a product of participatory mechanisms itself, the 1996 South African Constitution imposes both the National Assembly and the National Council of Provinces (the Parliament's two houses) to "facilitate public involvement in the legislative and other processes of the Assembly/Council and its committees" (Art. 59(1)(a) and 72(1)(a)).

DOI: 10.4324/9781315180540-21

The Constitutional Court, in a case concerning the role of public participation in the law-making process, maintained that

> Parliament and the provincial legislatures have broad discretion to determine how best to fulfill their constitutional obligation to facilitate public involvement in a given case. [. . .] Undoubtedly, this obligation may be fulfilled in different ways and is open to innovation on the part of the legislatures. In the end, however, the duty to facilitate public involvement will often require Parliament and the provincial legislatures to provide citizens with a meaningful opportunity to be heard in the making of the laws that will govern them. Our Constitution demands no less.
>
> (*Doctors for Life International v Speaker of the National Assembly and Others* 2006, at 146)

Despite the constitutional mandate, reinforced by the Constitutional Court case law, by the political rhetoric about participatory democracy, and by specific initiatives and programmes designed to ensure that Parliament facilitates public involvement in all its functions, enhancing participation and making it an effective tool for constitution and law-making processes is not easy, especially in very divided countries, characterised by profound cultural and political cleavages and by divergent socio-economic interests Lerner, 2011.

Against this backdrop, the chapter enquires into a successful participation story: the inclusion in the 1993 and 1996 Constitution of "sexual orientation" as listed ground in the equality clause, the repeal of the apartheid's anti-sodomy laws, and the enforcement of very progressive legislation allowing for same sex marriage and adoption rights for homosexual couples, thanks to the mobilisation of LGBTI organisations that seized any participation opportunity to lodge their claims. The purpose of the chapter is twofold. On the one hand, it critically analyses this successful story and discusses the participatory mechanisms themselves and the strategies undertaken by LGBTI organisations and movements to make their voice heard and to translate their political and cultural claims into constitutionally entrenched clauses, into acts of Parliament and into courts' judgments. On the other hand, it investigates the concrete capacity of the law, even when it is the product of participatory processes, to be a vector for social change. Doubtlessly, as regards LGBTI rights, South Africa presents one of the most progressive legal frameworks in the world, and yet the country remains deeply embedded in a culture of heteronormativity, dominated by patriarchy and homophobia. The anti-discrimination constitutional clause, legislation, and case-law have not been imposed by any alien entity; they are the direct product of bottom-up participatory processes that LGBTI organisations have proficiently used to advocate for their rights. So: anti-discrimination, same sex marriages, and adoption rights meet the needs and requests of South African LGBTI people. Nonetheless, this proved insufficient to foster a radical social change.

The outcome of very recent research shows that 72 percent of the South African population still feel that same sex activity is "morally wrong" and 70 percent feel strongly that homosexual sex and breaking gender dressing norms is "disgusting".[1] "While gay and lesbian people have been much more visible and vocal in post-apartheid South Africa [. . .] disturbing levels of violence against them have persisted and increased both in number and brutality" (The Other Foundation, 2016:10). The awful practice of "corrective rape", that is, raping lesbian and gay people to convert them to heterosexuality (Hunter-Gault, 2015),[2] and the extremely high numbers of sex-related crimes and harassment show the other side of this success story.

Participation in the constitution-making process: The inclusion of sexual orientation in Art. 9 listed grounds

"South African law has never treated gays and lesbians kindly" (Gevisser, Cameron, 1995:91). Both British rule and the Roman Dutch law, the two pillars of the white legal system, criminalised and punished homosexuality. According to the principles of the Roman Dutch law, sodomy and unnatural immoralities had to be punished by hanging and immediate burning of the body, and this perfectly fitted the typical British colonial anti-sodomy law. The criminalisation of same sex conduct was a fertile terrain for apartheid ideology, which was "based on keeping the white nation not only racially pure, but morally pure as well" (Cage, 2003:14). The state intrusion into South African private life was very pervasive and was an instrument for social control and repression of the opposition. The Sexual Offences Act of 1957 banned the private gathering of two or more gay men[3] which meant, on the one hand, that "gay clubs and restaurants were theoretically operating illegally" (Reddy, 1998:69), and, on the other hand, that the apartheid regime could use anti-sodomy legislation as an additional tool for political oppression, effectuating invasive controls on private gatherings in the name of morality (Retief, 1995). Of course, this reinforced the idea of homosexuality as a crime (da Costa Santos, 2013).

Despite the fact that homosexual activism has been present in South Africa since 1966, the democratic transition opened new political opportunities for LGBTI movements (Currier, 2012). The complex and multifaceted evolution of LGBTI organisations in South Africa is the object of an interesting literature (Currier, 2012; Gevisser, Cameron, 1995; Nicol, 2005) that we cannot discuss in this work. Suffice to recall that "the gay movement was never a cohesive phenomenon with a strong, collective voice", as "the particular fragmented forms

1 For more detail: http://mg.co.za/article/2016-09-07-new-report-reveals-south-africans-attitudes-to-homophobia-and-gender-noncomformity.
2 For a recent media report on this crime: http://www.telegraph.co.uk/women/womens-life/11608361/Corrective-rape-The-homophobic-fallout-of-post-apartheid-South-Africa.html.
3 Section 20a of the Act stated: "(1) a male person who commits with another male person at a party an act which is calculated to stimulate sexual passion or to give sexual gratification shall be guilty of an offence; (2) For the purpose of subsection (1) "a party" means any occasion when more than two persons are present".

that sexual politics have taken in the last 50 years of South African history reflect the complex interplay of sexual identity with the politics of race, class and gender" (Cock, 2005:35). LGBTI organisations were neither necessarily anti-apartheid nor multiracial, so that in 1987, at the International Lesbian and Gay Alliance (ILGA) ninth annual conference in Cologne, Germany, Alfred Siphiwe Machela, a black South African gay, described the gay community of the country as divided into two parts: "a white camp interested in gay social activities only, and a black camp which puts its weight behind all movements that are truly committed to the liberation of all South Africans" (Croucher, 2002:319).

In the context of the transition, however, LGBTI organisations proliferated, and were able to gain visibility and to make their voice heard in the constitution-making process. This could not be taken for granted, first of all because of the fragmentation and scarce politicisation of South African LGBTI movements, but also for the skepticism that the liberation movements themselves had regarding the inclusion of LGBTI rights in the new legal system.[4] Moreover, in the late 1980s and early 1990s the country remained deeply imbued with homophobia and the large majority of the African population perceived any deviation from the heterosexual paradigm as "un-African" phenomena. The inclusion of the "gay rights clause in the South Africa post-apartheid Constitution [. . .] represents a paradox, given the commitment of the post-apartheid state to mass participation in policy formulation and the high level of homophobia in South Africa" (Cock, 2005:188).

Obviously, participatory constitution and law-making processes do not necessarily mean the simple transposition in the final outcome (constitution or legislation) of mainstream public opinion views and perceptions. Furthermore, as already highlighted by Klug in the previous chapter, there might be issues that find better regulation through discussions in other arenas (i.e., for example, the courts). For other issues, as is the case for LGBTI rights, participatory mechanisms might favour specific interests and aspirations that may oppose mainstream public opinion.

> On the cusp of the democratic transition away from apartheid in the late 1980s and early 1990s, lesbian and gay activists took advantage of national liberation movement frames of equality to encourage ANC leaders to endorse lesbian and gay rights in the re-imagined, inclusive South Africa.
>
> (Currier, 2012:15)

Under the pressure of internal and international LGBTI rights organisations, in 1992 the ANC included a specific anti-discrimination provision in its political agenda, encompassing the idea of discrimination on the ground of sexual orientation in the Bill of Rights for a New South Africa prepared by the ANC

4 In August 1987, Ruth Mompati, an ANC executive member, adamantly stated, "I cannot even begin to understand why people want lesbian and gay rights. The gays have no problems. They have nice houses and plenty to eat. I don't see them suffering. [. . .] The gay issue is being brought up to take attention away from the main struggle against apartheid" (quoted in Tatchell, 2005:142).

Constitutional Committee[5] (Croucher, 2002). The Democratic Party and the Inkatha Freedom Party did the same, as most of the opposition parties and groups did, to create a distance from the LGBTI discriminatory policies of the Government of Pretoria. Moreover, by the early 1990s, the issue of the recognition of LGBTI people's rights became a topic of academic and scientific debate, so that in the scientific literature on the future of the South African legal system sexual orientation was often mentioned (Sachs, 1992; Cameron, 1993).

The constitution-making process was a complex, two-step inclusive process.[6] Very interestingly, during the long and complex negotiations that led to the enactment of the 1993 interim Constitution, the Equality Foundation[7] hired a prominent lawyer, K. Botha, as lobbyist for the gay and lesbian movement, "to spend time at the constitutional negotiations and engage with all key parties" (Bilchitz, 2015:9). In this first step, in fact, lobbying at the negotiation table was a successful strategy associated with a highly structured submission by the Equality Foundation to the Technical Committee on Fundamental Rights: the 1993 interim Constitution encompassed an enumerated equality clause that included sexual orientation.

The second step of the constitution-making process was heavily characterised by participation as strategic axis to avoid the phenomenon of "constitutions without constitutionalism"[8] and to legitimise the whole transition, as described by Klug in the previous chapter. In early 1995, the Constitutional Assembly launched an ambitious participation programme that included both written and electronic submissions, together with a constitutional educational programme and a constitutional public meeting programme (Skjelten, 2006). The challenge was to solicit a population of more than 40 million people, most of whom were illiterate with no access to print or electronic media. Without the necessary education, consultation would have been sham and meaningless. The strategy of running concomitant programmes was successful: nearly 1.7 million petitions and submissions were received. The bulk of these were petitions, whereas substantive submissions were relatively fewer in number. Both petitions and

---

5 So that section 8 on gender rights provided that:
   (1) Discrimination on the grounds of gender, single parenthood, legitimacy of birth or sexual orientation shall be unlawful.
   (2) Legislation shall provide remedies for oppression, abuse, harassment or discrimination based on gender or sexual orientation.
   (3) Educational institutions, the media, advertising and other social institutions shall be under a duty to discourage sexual and other types of stereotyping. For the full text of the ANC Bill of Rights: http://www.anc.org.za/show.php?id=231.
6 A broad literature exists on the topic. See *inter alia*: Ebrahim, 1998; Spitz, Chaskalson, 2000; Federico, Fusaro, 2006; Klug, 2010.
7 The Equality Foundation was established in 1993 as a follow up on the National Law Reform Fund with the explicit aim of lobbying for the inclusion of "sexual orientation" in the equality clause of the interim Constitution.
8 This is a typical example of what political scientists name the influence of the "political opportunity structure" on social movements and civil society organisations.

submissions dealt with a wide variety of issues, among them, LGBTI rights. Once the Constitutional Assembly had elaborated a refined working draft, this document was once again open to public comments from late November 1995 to the end of February 1996. About 250,000 submissions were received in this second phase, the vast bulk of which were petitions focusing on few topics: the death penalty, sexual orientation, and animal rights.

The success of the inclusion of the sexual orientation clause in the interim constitution had led to the creation of an umbrella organisation, the National Coalition for Gay and Lesbian Equality (NCGLE) to coordinate the participation and seize all opportunities to lobby for equality in the Constitutional Assembly.[9] Out of the almost two million submissions received by the Constitutional Assembly in the first phase of the participation programme, 7,032 were from gays, lesbians, and sympathetic persons, and about 13,000 were the signatures on petitions for the inclusion of LGBTI rights in the final constitution, whereas there were only 564 submissions opposing the inclusion of sexual orientation as listed ground (Botha, 1996). Once again, despite the hostile environment for lesbians and gays in South Africa,[10] a "virtuous confluence of many factors" allowed "the fragmented and poorly-organised lesbian and gay movement to achieve inclusion of sexual rights as part of the democratic project for South Africa" (da Costa Santos, 2013:330).

Noticeably for the purpose of this chapter, the NCGLE and other vocal LGBTI organisations were capable of producing some very focused submissions, framing their claims into the technical language of rights. In association with a number of other elements (international lobby, awareness of some prominent ANC leaders, the tension towards an inclusive rights-oriented constitution-making process) this proved to be the right approach. In fact, despite the large participation programme, the "process was an expert-dominated one", where well-structured submissions, in line with the very progressive approach of the constitution-making process, had a greater chance of being positively considered (Cock, 2005:194).

Participation in the implementation of LGBTI constitutional rights

As a cascade effect of the constitutional protection of LGBTI persons,[11] a number of post 1994 laws encompass fundamental anti-discrimination standing,

---

9   The NCGLE was launched at the end of 1994 explicitly to fight for the retention of sexual orientation in the equality clause of the constitution. At its peak, the NCGLE claimed a membership of almost 80 affiliated organisations. It disbanded in 1999, and was replaced by the Lesbian and Gay Equality Project, as will be described later in the chapter.

10 In a survey conducted contemporary with the first participation programme launched by the Constitutional Assembly and reaching respondents in all South African provinces, 48 percent identified themselves as anti-gay, 44 percent opposed granting homosexuals equal rights in the constitution, 64 percent were against recognising the right to marry, and 68 percent disagreed with any adoption rights for homosexuals (Cock, 2005:194).

11 It is important to recall that the Constitution provides for both vertical and horizontal application of its provisions, so that the anti-discrimination clause has to be enforced not only in the

among which the Labour Relations Act of 1995 defines and sanctions the discrimination on the basis of sexual orientation as an unfair labour practice, and the Employment Equity Act 55 of 1998 defines "family responsibility" as to include gay and lesbian relationships.

In the meanwhile, building on the success of the constitution-making process, the NCGLE focused on obtaining legal advancements through the implementation of the constitutional rights by the judiciary. The coalition, which later became the Lesbian and Gay Equality Project, filed a number of lawsuits that contributed towards deeply transforming the legal framework for LGBTI people. Since the landmark decision of 1998, *National Coalition for Gay and Lesbian Equality & Another v. Minister of Justice & Others*, when the Constitutional Court declared all sodomy laws inconsistent with the Constitution, "one by one the Court [has] struck down legislation which restricted the legal entitlements of people in same-sex relationships, including immigration privileges (*National Coalition for Gay and Lesbian Equality & Others v. Minister of Home Affairs & Others*, 1999), spousal benefits (*Satchwell v. President of the Republic of South Africa & Another*, 2003), adoption (*Du Toit & Another v. Minister of Welfare and Population Development & Others*, 2002), and parental rights (*J & Another v. Director General, Department of Home Affairs and Others*, 2003)" (Lee, 2010:35).

The Court's case-law strongly contributed to end the criminalisation of homosexual acts in South Africa,[12] and in 2005 it held that the common law definition of marriage that excluded same-sex couples from enjoying the same rights as heterosexual ones was discriminatory[13], and inconsistent with the Constitution (*Minister of Home Affairs and Another v. Fourie & Another*, 2005). The Court decided to suspend its judgment for twelve months to allow Parliament to amend existing marriage law, and urged Parliament to widely consult before adopting the new legislation, as the law should serve as "a great teacher, establish[ing] public norms that become assimilated into daily life and protect[ing] vulnerable people from unjust marginalisation and abuse".[14] The law-making process was complex:[15] in March 2006 the South African Law Reform Commission[16] issued its report arguing in favour of an act recognising the possibility for same-sex partnerships to choose both "civil unions" and "marriage",[17] but the first draft of the

---

relations between the State and the individual, but also in whatever private-private transaction and relationship.

12 For a more detailed discussion, see: Berger, 2008; Cameron, 2014; Cock, 2005; da Costa Santos, 2013; de Vos, 2008.

13 Marriage Act 25 of 1961.

14 *Minister of Home Affairs and Another v. Fourie & Another*, (CCT 60/04) of 1 December 2005, at 557A.

15 For an in-depth analysis, see: De Vos, Barnard, 2007.

16 The South African Law Reform Commission (SALRC) is an independent body that is accountable to the Minister of justice, and consists of nine members, appointed by the President of the Republic. Its tasks consist of making recommendations for the development, improvement, modernisation, or reform of legislation.

17 South African Law Reform Commission, *Report on Domestic Partnerships* (Project 118) (2006) at 292 para. 5.3.15, 296 para. 5.4.11, and 305 para. 5.6.2.

Civil Union Bill 26 of 2006 tabled in Parliament in September 2006 did not provide this choice, shelving the option of marriage for same-sex couples. The bill was opened to public debate. The hearings held by the Parliamentary Portfolio Committee turned out to be highly contested arenas.[18] "The public participation debates surrounding the Civil Unions Bill also revealed widely held homophobic and patriarchal attitudes that were sanctioned and promoted by citizens and religious, political and traditional leaders" (Robins, 2008:148). To contrast the homophobic atmosphere that surrounded the hearings and to redress the structural configuration of the bill, a number of constitutional lawyers filed very precise submissions[19] and LGBTI organisations mobilised to make mass-based support for the marriage-equality campaign visible to the South African public (Currier, 2012:97). At this stage, the ANC was obliged to exert its power to review the bill in order to comply with the Constitutional Court's requirements. "The Court's judgment had left the ANC in a precarious position: it had to comply with the Court's judgment while aware that the vast majority of its voters were strongly opposed to it" (De Vos, Barnard, 2007:820). The final version of the bill was signed into law by the Deputy President on 28 November 2006.

On 1 December 2006, the Civil Union Act n. 17, "Noticing that the family law dispensation as it existed after the commencement of the Constitution did not provide for same-sex couples to enjoy the status and the benefits coupled with the responsibilities that marriage accords to opposite sex couples, entered into force, "to provide for the solemnisation of civil unions, by ways of either a marriage or a civil union" (Preamble, Civil Union Act n. 17, 2006). Once again, participation was crucial to secure that the law meets LGBTI people's expectations. So, in the case of LGBTI rights in South Africa participation proved to matter.

Ten years later, the country remains the only African country to have legalised same-sex marriages. According to the most recent available statistics that date back to December 2012, from 2007 to 2011 3, 327 marriages and civil unions have been celebrated in South Africa under the Civil Union Act of 2006,[20] which is a really small number, even if weighted against the generalised low South African marriage rate, and according to estimates up until 2014 the total number has reached 6,500.

---

18 Mail & Guardian, 26 September 2006; in their analysis on the Civil Union Act, De Vos and Barnard argue that Parliament "failed to inform the public of the constitutional and legal parameters within which the consultation was supposed to take place, and this opened the door to high levels of contentiousness and to several misleading submissions" (De Vos, Barnard, 2007:814–16).

19 See *Minutes of the Home Affairs Portfolio Committee, Civil Union Dill Deliberation*, November 2007, available at: https://pmg.org.za/committee-meeting/7592/.

20 Noticeably, statistics do not make any difference between heterosexual and same-sex couples. Heterosexual couples can choose whether to get married under the Civil Union Act or under the 1961 Marriage Act. The number of celebrated marriages and civil unions is low, even considering that South Africa has one of the lowest marriage rates in the world. Reasons for this are complex, and scholars argue it is mainly due to poverty and education. For further details: http://www.statssa.gov.za/publications/P0307/P03072011.pdf.

It is controversial to evaluate the importance of the Act simply and solely against the number of marriages and civil unions celebrated,[21] and yet this is a significant datum. It is equally true, however, that the above mentioned 2015 survey on South Africans' attitudes towards homosexuality and gender non-conformity shows that "between 2012 and 2015 there has been a tenfold increase in the number of South Africans who strongly agree with allowing same-sex marriage" (The Other Foundation, 2016, ii). Does law matter, then?

Concluding remarks: From legal change to social transformation

Legal change has a substantial and concrete impact on people's lives: first and foremost, no one can any longer be arrested or legally harassed for consensual same-sex relationships in South Africa, people cannot be discriminated against in the workplace, and same-sex marriages and partnerships can claim a number of very relevant rights.

The legal framework matters in terms of rights and liberties, in terms of political opportunities, and in terms of social, political, and cultural identification and self-identification. As scholars maintain, "the legal discourses surrounding sexual orientation allow all the players to participate in the construction of their own sexual-orientation identities, and to make themselves available for interpretation along this register by others" (De Vos, 1996:272). But social change may take longer than legal change, and some even argue that "social norms are unlikely to change as a result of simple, discrete, low-cost interventions by the governments, [. . .] the only self-conscious way of changing them in a direction they seek, is to violate them. Not just to violate them, but to violate them in a public and decisive way" (Posner, 2000:8).

The whole strategy of "incremental" demand for equality and rights (from the lobby on the ANC leadership in the early 1990s to submissions and claims to include LGBTI rights in its Bill of Rights and to recognise same-sex marriages and civil unions) shows how LGBTI organisations have been able, on the one hand, to seize the opportunities for participation to avoid backlash and, on the other, to constantly renegotiate identities in both political and socio-cultural terms. But it is equally noticeable that the legalisation of same-sex marriage, together with the entire legislation granting equal rights and legal protection to LGBTI persons, seem not to have made significant strides ahead in terms of social inclusion and tolerance. If there has ever been the hope that the legalisation of same-sex marriages would foster a culture of acceptance, this has proved not to be the case. LGBTI hate crimes remain the hard reality for the majority of the LGBTI communities, especially in the poorest and

---

21 Moreover, the media report difficulties in celebrating same-sex marriages because section 5 the Civil Union Act explicitly allows religious institutions not to solemnise same-sex marriages, and section 6 allows marriage officers who work for the State and who object "on the ground of conscience, religion and belief" to same-sex marriage to refuse to solemnise same-sex marriages.

most deprived areas of the country. The awful practice of "corrective rape" still claims too many victims.

Without a progressive legal framework and recognised and enforced rights and liberties, the lives of LGBTI people in South Africa would definitely be harder. Without a massive engagement of LGBTI organisations in lobbying, advocating, filing cases, preparing learned submissions, seizing all opportunities opened by participatory mechanisms, the intrinsic quality of the legal framework and of rights and liberties would probably have been much worse. Thus, the law matters and participation does as well. Nonetheless, the South African case shows that participation may be a double-edged sword: it can definitely boost the advancement of specific rights, especially if the stakeholders have the resources (in political, cultural, and also socio-economic terms) to deliver submissions, petitions, etc. that are conceived in the same language of decision-makers. Public opinion, however, may remain far behind, with the result of widening, instead of reducing, the gap between the legal framework and society.

The solution is neither to reduce participation nor to slow down the process of rights recognition and enforcement. But the South African case clearly shows that participation does not solve, *per se*, the phenomena of inconsistency and the resulting mismatch between the legal framework and society.

References

Allegretti, U., C. Corsi, and G. Allegretti (2016). "Constituent Process and Constituent Assembly: The Making of Constitutions through the Larger Involvement of Citizens", *Forum di Quaderni Costituzionali*.

Berger, J. (2008). "Getting the Constitutional Court on Time: A Litigation History of Same-Sex Marriage", in M. Judge et al., *To Have and To Hold: The Making of Same-Sex Marriage in South Africa*. Johannesburg: Jacana Media.

Bilchitz, D. (2015). *Constitutional Change and Participation of LGBTI Groups. A case study of South Africa*. Stockholm: IDEA. Available at: http://www.constitutionnet.org/sites/default/files/constitutional-change-and-participation-of-lgbti-groups-a-case-study-of-south-africa-pdf.pdf.

Botha, K. (1996). "Profile", *Equality*, 3.

Cage, K. (2003). *Gayle: The Language of Kinks and Queens: A History and Dictionary of Gay Language in South Africa*. Johannesburg: Jacana Media.

Cameron, E. (2014)., "Dignity and Disgrace – Moral Citizenship and Constitutional Protection", in H. Corder, V. Federico, and R. Orrù (eds), *The Quest for Constitutionalism. South Africa since 1994*. Farnham: Ashgate.

Cameron, E. (1993). "Sexual Orientation and the Constitution: A Test Case for Human Rights", *SAL*, 110.

Cock, J. (2005). "Engendering Gay and Lesbian Rights: The Equality Clause in the South African Constitution", in N. Hoad, K. Martin, and G. Reid (eds), *Sex and Politics in South Africa*. Cape Town: Double Storey.

Cornell, S. (2011). "The People's Constitution vs. The Lawyer's Constitution: Popular Constitutionalism and the Original Debate over Originalism", *Yale JL & Human*, 23, p. 295.

Croucher, S. (2002). "South Africa's Democratisation and the Politics of Gay Liberation", *Journal of Southern African Studies*, 28(2), pp. 315–30.

Currier, A. (2012). *Out in Africa*. Minneapolis: University of Minnesota Press.

da Costa Santos, G. (2013). "Decriminalizing Homosexuality in Africa: Lessons from the South African Experience", in Lennox C., and M. Waites (eds), *Human Rights, Sexual Orientation and Gender Identity in the Commonwealth: Struggles for Decriminalisation and Change*. London: University of London Press.

De Vos, P. (1996). "On the Legal Construction of Gay and Lesbian Identity and South Africa's Transitional Constitution", *South African Journal on Human Rights*, 12, pp. 265–90.

De Vos, P. (2008). "A Judicial Revolution? The Court-Led Achievement of Same-Sex Marriages in South Africa", in *Utrecht Law Review*, 6(4), pp. 162–74.

De Vos, P., and J. Barnard (2007). "Same-sex Marriage, Civil Unions and Domestic Partnerships in South Africa", *South African Law Journal*, 124(4), pp. 795–826.

Ebrahim, H. (1998). *The Soul of a Nation*. Cape Town: Oxford University Press.

Federico, V., and C. Fusaro (2006). *Constitutionalism and Democratic Transitions. Lessons from South Africa*. Firenze: Florence University Press.

Gevisser, M., and E. Cameron (1995). *Defiant Desire*. London: Taylor & Francis.

Gloppen, S. (1997). *South Africa: The Battle Over the Constitution*. Farnham: Ashgate.

Gluck, J., and M. Brandt (2015). "Participatory and Inclusive Constitution Making", *Peaceworks*, 105.

Hunter-Gault, C. (2015). *Corrective Rape: Discrimination, Assault, Sexual Violence, and Murder Against South Africa's L.G.B.T. Community*. Agate Digital.

Klug, H. (2010). *The Constitution of South Africa*. Oxford: Hart Publishing.

Lee, M.Y. (2010). *Equality, Dignity and Same Sex Marriage*. Leidan: Martinus Nijhoff publishers.

Lerner, H. (2011). *Making Constitutions in Deeply Divided Societies*. Cambridge: Cambridge University Press.

Moehler, D. C. *Distrusting Democrats: Outcomes of Participatory Constitution Making*. University of Michigan Press.

Nicol, J. (2005). "If We Can't Dance to It, It's Not Our Revolution", in N. Hoad, K. Martin, G. Reid, *Sex and Politics in South Africa*. Cape Town: Double Storey Books.

The Other Foundation, Progressive Prudes. (2016). *A survey towards homosexuality and gender non-conformity in South Africa*. Pretoria: HSRC.

Posner, E. (2000). *Law and Social Norm*. Cambridge, MA: Harvard University Press.

Reddy, V. (1998). "Negotiating Gay Masculinity", in *Agenda*, 37, pp. 65–70.

Retief, G. (1995). "Keeping Sodom out of the Laager", in E. Cameron, and M. Gevisser (eds), *Defiant Desire. Gay and Lesbian Lives in South Africa*. Taylor and Francis.

Robins, S.L. (2008). *From Revolution to Rights in South Africa*. Woodbridge: James Currey.

Saati, A. (2015). *The Participation Mith*. Umea: Umea University Press.

Sachs, A. (1992). *Advancing Human Rights in South Africa*. Cape Town: Oxford University Press.

Skjelten, S. (2006). *A People's Constitution: Public Participation in the South African Constitution-making Process*. Midrand: Institute for Global Dialogue.

Spitz, R., and M. Chaskalson (2000). *The Politics of Transformation. A Hidden History of South Africa's Negotiated Transition*. Johannesburg: Wits University Press.

Suteu, S. (2015). "Developing Democracy through Citizen Engagement: The Advent of Popular Participation in the United Kingdom's Constitution-Making", *Cambridge J. Int'l & Comp. L.* 4.

Tatchell, P. (2005). "The Moment the ANC Embraced Gay Rights", in N. Hoad, K. Martin, and G. Reid (eds), *Sex and Politics in South Africa*. Cape Town: Double Storey.

List of cases

National Coalition for Gay and Lesbian Equality & Others v Minister of Home Affairs & Others (CCT10/99) of 2 December 1999.

Du Toit & Another v Minister of Welfare and Population Development & Others, (CCT40/01) of 10 September 2002.

Satchwell v President of the Republic of South Africa & Another (CCT48/02) of 17 March 2003.

J & Another v Director General, Department of Home Affairs and Others, (CCT46/02) of 28 March 2003.

Minister of Home Affairs and Another v Fourie & Another, (CCT 60/04) of 1 December 2005.

Doctors for Life International v Speaker of the National Assembly and Others (CCT12/05) of 17 August 2006.

18 The cross-cutting issue of religion in the Tunisian participatory constitution-making process

Tania Abbiate

Introduction: The challenge of the religious versus secular divide

Tensions about religion and how the state accommodates religious beliefs in the constitutional order have gained increased momentum in constitution-making processes all over the world; Africa has not remained untouched by the issue, having been interested by a wave of constitutional reform since the eighties of last century (Bâli and Lerner 2017). Remarkably, religion occupied a central place in the process which led to the adoption of 2013 Constitution of Zimbabwe, where Pentecostal churches called for the new constitution to categorically criminalise homosexuality (Manynganise 2016: 67). Similarly, in the 2010 Kenyan constitutional reform the issue of constitutional recognition of Kadhi courts applying Muslim law has been highly debated; remarkably, the issue invested also the Kenyan High Court which, in the middle of the process, declared the Kadhi to be unconstitutional, without determining whether an altered form of the Islamic courts should be included in the new constitution (Ahaya 2015). Finally, it is also worth recalling the case of Egypt, where the position of Islamic Shari'a has long been one of the most controversial ones.

Although each case presents its own peculiarity depending on local history, culture and socio-political condition, it is understandable that religion, being a fundamental element of identity, plays a role in the constitutional debate, where the founding principles of the legal order are laid down.

This aspect is reflected by the fact that out of 194 constitutions in existence today, 186 refer to the world "religion" and 183 include some forms of formal guarantee of religious freedom, while a total of 114 mention the word "God", "the divine" or other deities (Bâli and Lerner 2017: 6).

The importance of religion for national identity cannot be ignored, especially because this issue often overlaps with other sources of tension, of different nature (ethnic, linguistic, historical and so on). In these circumstances, it is particularly difficult to distinguish the specific nature of the religious debate from the other factors of material or identarian conflict. As a matter of fact, religion can operate as a sort of shroud that surrounds all matters of constitutional debate.

The Tunisian experience can be considered as representative of this complex situation because of the centrality occupied by Islamists – secularist polarisation

DOI: 10.4324/9781315180540-22

about the place of Islam in the new constitution, involving the religious-oriented governing coalition led by *Ennahda* (meaning "Renaissance" in Arabic)[1] and the secular parties – unified, since 2012, by the emergent political force *Nidaa Tounes* (meaning "Call to Tunisia" in Arabic).

The secularists wanted to preserve the achievements made in terms of civil liberties dating back to the Bourguiba era, such as women's emancipation and secularity of the public sphere; Islamists claimed the right to publicly express their religion, after decades of repression, and promoted a political agenda inspired by Islamic values. The secular perspective was supported mainly by the liberal, left-wing, largely francophone upper middle class, while the Islamic viewpoint rallied the conservative, Arabic-speaking groups with strong ties to organised religion (Honwana 2013: 8). This dichotomy, which emerged mainly following the revolution and the liberalisation of the political landscape after the public emergence of *Ennahda*, represents, however, a hyper-simplification of reality, as at closer inspection both groups had an educated middle-class (Camau and Geisser 2011: 245–46). Moreover, such a simplification hides the presence of internal divisions within each of the faction.

Nonetheless, the public debate has been dominated by the religious cleavage, also to the detriment of other compelling issues such as this socio-economic divide (Allal 2016)[2], thus confirming the argument according to which religion can surround all matters of deliberation. Even though religion has been one of the main reasons of divide within and outside the NCA, it is still questionable whether and to what extent this debate was mainly an elite bargain, disrespecting the public will. Undoubtedly, this feature of the transition represented something of a surprise, since traditionally, Tunisia had been characterised by a limited constitutionalization of Islam and, historically, it had remained far away from religious radicalisation (Houki 2015). Even during the Revolution, political Islam[3] did not have a prominent role, but it managed to emerge in a second phase thanks to its ability in using the political instrument of the elections for affirming itself. The successful emergence of the religious factor should not be considered as a surprise, but rather as a sort of reaction to the past "relegation" of religion to the private sphere.

The present chapter will shed light on the religious issues in the Tunisian constitutional transition and it will be structured as follows: Part 1 will be dedicated to the analysis of the main reasons for the conflicts and will highlight how

---

1 *Ennahda* is a political movement whose roots date back to the Islamic Tendency Movement (MTI) founded in 1981, and it is considered the Tunisian arm of the Muslim Brotherhood. It presents itself as a moderate Islamist party, but its Islamist character has been controversial since the very beginning of the transition (see further Abbiate 2015; Ozzano and Cavatorta 2013; Cavatorta and Merrone 2013).

2 Moreover, it should be noted that religion has also represented a matter of disconnect between the ideological discourse portrayed by the media and the citizenship; indeed, the latter neglects that it has represented the main issue of conflict in the Tunisian transition (see further Böckenförde 2016: 3).

3 The term "political Islam" refers to forces that declare to inspire themselves to Islam principles but do not promote a definite institutional model. They aim at strengthening the polarisation between religion and politics within the legal order that is peculiar to Islamic law (see Campanini 2012).

each group tended to its specific interests, thus provoking a situation of potential conflict between divergent, competing, opposing claims; Part 2 will deal with the results of the contestations, namely the presence of nuanced Islamic references in the constitution, alongside democratic and civic values and principles; eventually, in Part 3, some reflections on the negotiated constitution-making process will be drawn, followed by the presentation of some open questions about the future.

The most contested issues concerning religion in the constitution-making process

The presence of a deep ideological conflict which has confronted secularists and Islamists became particularly evident in some crucial points.

Among the many, the most acute concerned *Ennahda*'s initial motion of including Shari'a law as a source of legislation. This proposal contradicted the willingness claimed by the party to respect the civic character of the state and has been perceived by secularists as a proof of its real intent to impose a religious state.

Indeed, since 2011, the Islamic party has been accused of promoting a "double discourse", characterised, on one side, by the purported support to democratic values and principles and, on the other, by the hidden effort to promote an Islamization of society and the public sphere (Cavatorta and Merrone 2013).

Because of these concerns, the Shari'a proposition trigged a harsh opposition. The resistance was particularly visible during some topical moments, such as the series of demonstrations, culminating on 20 March 2012, in which supporters of and opponents to the constitutional recognition of Shari'a gathered near the National Constituent Assembly (NCA) in order to express their apprehensions (Mandraud 2012). Salafist groups[4] demonstrated in favour of instituting Shari'a and establishing an islamic state in Tunisia, and *Ennahda*, initially, was unable to distance itself from these religious maximalists. However, the hostility demonstrated by a large share of the population forced the party to promptly step back by declaring, already on 25 March after just a few months since the beginning of the constitution-making process, its adherence to Article 1 of the 1959 Constitution, which states that "Tunisia is a free, independent, sovereign state; its religion is Islam, its language Arabic, and its system is republican".[5] However, because of this decision, *Ennahda* became the target of strong criticism coming from its base. The movement's grassroots components were in fact pushing for a more visible pursuit of the Islamic project and disapproved of the Islamist leaders' pragmatism (Marks 2014: 18). The latter, however, has represented the key to success for *Ennahda*: thanks to its capability to compromise, it has been able to remain in power for a long time, despite its failure to solve the most impelling issues.

---

4 Salafism is an Islamic branch claiming a return to the Islamic origins which presents two strands: a scientific one, mainly nonviolent; and a jihadi one, which believes in and pursues armed struggle (see further Honwana 2013: 97–98; Boukhars 2014: 10).
5 See *infra* and Böckenförde 2016: 932.

Another paradigmatic focal point of the secularist-versus-Islamist conflict in the constitution-making process has been the proposal of a controversial clause in the first draft of the constitution with regard to the role of men and women in society. Art. 28 of the August 2012 draft stated indeed that women and men had a complementary role within the family, without making any reference to the equality principle, which in turn constitutes an international human rights standard. This wording raised huge criticism from secularists and women's groups who feared a contraction of the considerable recognition of their rights in the legal system. Those groups organised a massive demonstration on 13 August 2012 on the occasion of the Tunisian Women's Day, which commemorates the adoption of the Code of Personal Status (CPS) in 1956, granting several rights to women and considered to be the basis of women empowerment.[6] The large participation in the popular protest once more forced *Ennahda* to step back from its proposal, declaring that the wording had been misunderstood and that the party was instead committed to support and encourage women's equality.

Already in the second constitutional draft of December 2012 this principle was laid down in two provisions (Arts. 5 and 37), on which basis further elaboration led to the current Article 21, which explicitly mentions the application of the equality principle to male and female alike and has been praised as one of the Arab world's most liberal provisions concerning women.[7] Women's status and women's rights have been at the forefront of other disputes between secularists and Islamists: another example is represented by the issue of *hijab*. Islamic political parties supported the right of Tunisian women to wear the veil, a practice that had been banned by Law 108 of 1981 and Law 102 of 1986; in November 2011, a group of Salafists protested against the ban on wearing the *niqab* (the integral veil) at Manouba University and claimed the creation of a prayer area within the campus. The challenge sparked public turmoil and eventually the Salafists' demands were withdrawn (Debuysere 2013: 36; Dubois 2012: 20).

Another area of debate concerned the introduction of the crime of blasphemy in both the constitution and the penal code. The issue emerged in June 2012 after the opening of an art exhibition in the capital of Tunis that was considered offensive to Islam (Marks, 2012a). *Ennahda* condemned the exhibition and in a

6 CSP abolished polygamy, mandated consent by both spouses prior to marriage, set a minimum age for marriage, and gave women legal divorce and inheritance rights. Because of these provisions, it has become a symbol of women's emancipation (see further Charrad 2001; Giolo 2002; Bouguerra 2005; Ben Achour 1992).

7 Article 21 of the Constitution states: "All citizens, male and female, have equal rights and duties, and are equal before the law without any discrimination. The state guarantees freedom and individual and collective rights to all citizens, and provides all citizens with the conditions for a dignified life". The protection of the status of women is reinforced by Article 46, which expresses the state's commitment to protecting and strengthening their rights. This provision also contains an imposition on the state to guarantee equal opportunities between women and men in accessing all levels of responsibility in all domains. To this end, the state works to attain parity between women and men in elected assemblies. Finally, Article 46 requires the state to play an active role in eradicating violence against women.

statement urged the Constituent Assembly of Tunisia to add a provision to the penal code criminalizing blasphemy. In addition, the party proposed the insertion of a constitutional provision to prohibit blasphemy. The stated reason for such a proposal was to protect Tunisia's Islamic identity, albeit maintaining freedom of expression. The secular parties and civil society groups rejected both proposals submitted by the majoritarian Islamic party and eventually the constitutional proposal was dropped, but a reference to *takfir* (an Arabic word meaning to accuse someone of being a nonbeliever) was included in the constitution.

In 2013, the ideological conflict between secularists and Islamists reached its apex: the escalation was mainly caused by an unprecedented wave of political violence: on 6 February 2013, Chokri Belaid, a lawyer and left-wing opposition politician, was murdered. This assassination was followed, on 25 July 2013, by the killing of Mohamed Brahmi, an NCA member: this led almost 60 deputies to take the decision of leaving the NCA and request its dissolution. In addition, they asked for the replacement of the coalition in power represented by *Ennahda* and two secular parties (*Ettakatol* and *Congrès pour la République*) as well as for the removal of *Ennahda*-appointed governors and public officials, through a permanent sit-in named *Errahil* (meaning "departure" in Arabic) outside the NCA building. In this situation, the President of the Assembly ordered, on 6 August 2013, the suspension of the NCA's activities. This occurred in a delicate regional situation: in July 2013, as highlighted by Mohamed Abdelaal in this volume, the democratically elected Egypt President of the Republic Mohamed Morsi was dismissed, while Libya was in the middle of a tremendous civil war. This framework arose the worries of a failure of the constitutional transition in Tunisia and fostered political parties to make compromises.

This was possible thanks to the mediation of four non-institutional organisations, the Tunisian General Labour Union (*Union Générale Tunisienne du Travail*, UGTT), the Tunisian Union for Industry, Trade and Handicrafts (*Union Tunisienne de l'Industrie, du Commerce et de l'Artisanat*, UTICA), the Tunisian League for Human Rights (*Ligue Tunisienne des Droits de l'Homme*, LTDH), and the National Bar Association (*Ordre National des Avocats*, ONAT). These four organisations, which became known as the "Tunisian National Dialogue Quartet", managed to implement negotiations with the principal political parties of the country and ultimately allowed the constitution-making process to reach its conclusion. Thanks to their crucial engagement in the constitution-making process, in October 2015, they were awarded the Nobel Peace Prize for their integral role in the democratic transition.

The results of the contestations: Islamic references and liberal-democratic values at the cost of internal dissent

Despite the conflicts that emerged during the constitution-making process, secularists and Islamists have been able to reach a compromise in the constitutional text, which represents a solid basis towards the development of a culture of constitutionalism (Elkins, Ginsburg and Melton 2009). This result has been possible mainly thanks to informal meetings and the mediation of non-elected temporary institutions (Boubekeur 2015: 109). As a matter of fact the constitution-making process has been characterised by the creation of several multiparty meetings, alongside official institutions, such as the mentioned "National Dialogue" promoted by the "Quartet".

Other noteworthy evidence is the fact that both groups have sought compromises aimed at obtaining consensus in the assembly, even if that meant going against the will of much of their political grassroots. This has not only led to growing internal dissent and volatility within political alliances, but has also had the effect of alienating Tunisians from the political process as such (Boubekeur 2015: 109). The divide has affected both secularists[8] and *Ennahda*[9] and its legacy is likely to last well into the future. From a wording point of view, the compromise is evidenced by the presence of several ambiguous clauses. The most evident example of the lack of text clarity and the vagueness of the constitutional text is represented by Article 1 and Article 2.

Article 1 maintains the same wording as Article 1 of the 1959 Constitution: "Tunisia is a free, independent, sovereign state; its religion is Islam, its language is Arabic, and its system is republican". This formulation is characterised by a semantic ambiguity concerning the interpretation of Islam either as state religion, or as religion of the majority of the people (Longo 2016: 16–17).[10] The first interpretation, however, is very unlikely in the new legal framework, because this provision is meant to be integrated by Article 2, which states expressly that "Tunisia is a civil state based on citizenship, the will of the people, and the supremacy of law" (Redissi 2014). This clause is not self-explanatory, but the

8 In particular, the secularists have demonstrated to be particularly fragmented both in the 2011 election for the NCA and in the 2014 legislative elections.
9 As noted by A. Boubekeur:

Disagreement between *Ennahda* members choosing to bargain and those preferring to compete had intensified since 2011. An example is represented by the fact that, in November 2013, the members of the party's regional office in Gafsa collectively resigned, accusing *Ennahda* leaders of having abandoned the revolution's goals and having betrayed promises of social justice. In response to their grassroots' dissatisfaction and to adapt to an increasingly uncertain legislative electoral outcome, Islamist leaders encouraged their grassroots to de-politicize their networks or re-direct their mobilization potential into channels where they would not interfere with the leadership's political strategies. As a consequence, *Ennahda*'s youth started to, for example, acquire Qatari funding for civil society initiatives. To overcome the disagreement, in mid-2014 the party's Shura Council agreed on a five-year strategic plan. Among the priorities identified were the consolidation of the party's institutional position, an increase in its political influence by positioning *Ennahda* representatives in key posts in regional administrative structures, the media and the banks and countering the perception of potential Islamist dominance by limiting the number of ministerial and public administration positions it would pursue. (Boubekeur 2015: 120)

10 This double interpretation has indeed prompted a debate dating back a long time. The majoritarian doctrine deems that the reference to Islam does not entail an Islamisation of the state or of the constitution, but that, on the contrary, it facilitates the exit of religion from the public sphere. In other words, it represents an instrument to avoid the dependence of positive law on Shari'a (see further Ben Achour 1992).

reference to the will of the people and to the supremacy of the law makes clear that mere reference to Islam is not intended to open the way to the rise of a theocratic state, but aims instead at laying the foundation for a pluralist regime, compatible with the characteristics of Islamic society. Both provisions are included among those that are declared unamendable (the constitution contains four provisions that enjoy this status[11]), and this confirms their fundamental position within the new constitutional system. Together, the two provisions build a completely new framework for defining the nature of the Tunisian state. The wording of the two articles was consolidated in the third constitutional draft of April 2013 and was confirmed in the fourth draft of June 2013, which was submitted for examination to the European Commission for Democracy through Law (better known as Venice Commission).

In its opinion delivered in July 2013, the Council of Europe's advisory body on constitutional matters expressed its concerns about the existence of "tensions between, on the one hand, the predominant position given to Islam, and on the other hand, the civil nature of the Tunisian state and the principles of plurality, impartiality and non-discrimination" (Venice Commission 2013: §28). The main concern was that of a preponderance of Islam over other religions, because of the presence of several constitutional provisions making reference to Islam and because only Article 1 was declared non-amendable.

The entrenchment clause (Article 141 of the 1 June 2014 draft) was problematic also because it prohibited any modification to the status of Islam as the state religion. With this provision, it promoted an interpretation of Article 1 according to which Islam was the state religion by its own right, and not just the religion of the majority of Tunisians. This would have endangered the value of Article 2 as intended above.

The Tunisian constitution-makers therefore consented to reconsider this aspect and extended the entrenchment clause to also include Article 2.

Moreover, they also slightly modified Article 6 of the June 2013 constitutional draft, thus partly accepting the Venice Commission's advice of rewording the provision, which could have been interpreted as giving priority to Islam and thus discriminating between different religions or beliefs (Venice Commission 2013: §32).

The final version of this provision states as follows:

> The state is the guardian of religion. It guarantees freedom of conscience and belief, the free exercise of religious practices and the ban on any partisan or fanatical use of mosques and places of worship. The state acts in order to disseminate the values of moderation and tolerance, and to ensure the protection of the sacred, as well as the prohibition of all violations thereof. It equally undertakes actions with the aim of prohibiting and fighting against calls for *takfir* [an Arabic word meaning to accuse someone of being a nonbeliever], the incitement of violence and hatred.

---

11 Those are Articles 1, 2, 49 and 75 of the Constitution.

The definitive wording was modified through the approval of amendments at the very end of the drafting process, particularly to ensure the criminalization of apostasy, attacks on the sacred, and incitement to hatred and violence, and also to prevent the misuse of mosques for political purposes. The expression "the state is the guardian of religion" raises some questions, notably whether all religions are henceforth protected by the state, or only Islam. Because of the special recognition of the Islamic religion in several constitutional provisions (e.g., in the preamble and in the requirement that the President of the republic be of the Muslim faith, contained in Article 74), it might indeed be argued that it enjoys some sort of primacy over other religions. This concern is partially dismissed by the explicit mention of freedom of conscience and belief. Moreover, it has to be highlighted that the Arabic version of the text uses the plural form to indicate the "sacred", thus applying to religions in a broader sense (Bousbih and Yaalaoui 2015: 20).

A similar compromise between religion and politics is also reflected (albeit in a less evident way) in other articles, such as Article 7, stating that the family is the nucleus of society, and Article 39, stating that "the state shall also work to consolidate the Arab-Muslim identity and national conscience in the young generations, and to strengthen, promote and generalize the use of the Arabic language and openness to foreign languages, human civilizations and diffusion of the culture of human rights".

In conclusion, many provisions of the constitutional text reveal the compromise reached between Islamists and secularists and such an agreement was possible because the two had already collaborated in the period of authoritarianism to oppose authoritarianism[12]; therefore, it can be argued that there had already been some sort of consensus culture on the background which helped to overcome the challenge.

Conclusions

As has been highlighted, one of the major challenges hampering the Tunisian constitution-making process has been the religious cleavage. In particular, the constitutional transition has seen the opposition of Islamists and secularists and it has witnessed a confrontation of views, and of ideological discourses; indeed, the Islamists have worked to "reframe the secularist movement as not Muslim, or even atheist, while secularists try to depict Islamists as conservative and retrograde" (Honwana 2013: 88).

The opposition between the two fields has been amplified in the media, contributing to the spread of accusations, rumours and booklets (El-Issawi 2012: 20). It has to be noted that the secularists' accusations have found reception in the

---

12 The collaboration between secularists and Islamists dates back to the nineties: initially, the Tunisian League of Human Rights gathered political opponents of both sides, and then, on 18 October 2005 in Paris, they agreed on a set of principles which should have, but in the end has not, constituted the baseline of a democratic system (see: Collectif du 18 octobre pour les Droits et les Libertés, 2005).

Western world due to growing Islamophobia, which has been endemic since the 9/11 terrorist attacks; nevertheless, it cannot be denied that the Islamists had the explicit goal of inspiring the new legal system with Muslim principles, in contrast to the secular, liberal-democratic legal tradition of Tunisia. In addition, it should be noted that the religious cleavage – no matter how much amplified – had existed previously, and this reveals the misapprehension of Ben Ali's traditional rhetoric of national unity (Poussel 2014).

The centrality of religion in the constitution-making process reflected in public participation, as the public demonstrations in favour and against constitutional endorsement to Shari'a demonstrate. However, it can still be questionable if this debate consisted mainly in an elite bargain, with ordinary citizens being more interested in concrete issues related to everyday life.

This argument has its validity, because of the disappointment expressed by some segments of society concerning the constitution-making process.[13] However, it cannot be denied that the religious dispute has promoted mass mobilisation and active participation in the constitution-making process. Certainty, secularists and Islamists have been able to come up with a constitution that achieved national consensus. The constitutional text can be read in the form of a "national autobiography" (Ponthoreau 2008; Böckenförde 2016: 10), witnessing the struggles that opposed Tunisians during the drafting process. For this reason, it has been suggested that the adequate technique of interpreting the constitutional text would be the historic one, which consists of considering the dynamics emerged within the NCA, as well as the four constitutional drafts (Böckenförde 2016: 12).

Despite the success of the constitution-making process, it is important to also note some of its limits: firstly, political parties preferred to mobilise their supporters outside the representative institutions over the formal pattern of decision-making (Boubekeur 2015: 117); secondly, the centrality attained by religion has diverted attention from other crucial problems, such as regional demands, and the rise of a feeling of disaffection and frustration among young people; thirdly, the ability of the political leadership to reach a compromise has fostered internal disaffection towards political parties and has led to extremism among some of their components.

Nonetheless, with exclusive reference to the constitution, it must be noted that the drafting process has avoided both an installation of Islam law, and a sterile imposition of universal values with consequent losing of particularism: reference to the Arab religion, language and teaching are in fact present in the constitutional text. Such attitude concerning the place of religion in the legal system is at the origin of the "twin-tolerations" paradigm theorised by Alfred

---

13 To this effect, it is remarkable to note a qualitative survey carried out by UNDP in 2012. The survey had the aim to evaluate how the ANC was perceived by the young people between 15 and 29 years old; 57% of the participants declared to be unaware of the constitution's content, 30% declared to possess a vague knowledge of the contents, while 45% declared it did not feel as having been involved in the constitutional process (see: PNUD 2013).

Stepan: it entails a balanced relationship between politics and religion and implies, on one side, a toleration among religious citizens towards the state, and on the other, a toleration by the state towards its religious citizens (Stepan 2012: 89–90). Although this paradigm is useful for the description of the Tunisian case, some scholars disapprove, highlighting the vagueness of some constitutional provisions as far as the relationship between state and religion is concerned (Longo 2015: 116). For sure, the result in terms of constitutionalization of state-religious relationship represents a success mainly for the *Ennahda* party which, on the one hand, has been able "to secure the biggest possible Islamist imprint on the constitution" and, on the other hand, has "convinced rank-and-file *Ennahda* members to accept principles opposed to the party's original ideology" (Netterstrøm 2015: 119). This stance is representative of the existence of different orientations of Islamism and this explains also the difference in constitutional results occurred in Tunisian and other Muslim countries, such as Egypt.

If this is the situation at the level of constitutional provisions and positive laws in general, it has to be remarked that the enforcement of these norms and their concrete application is the most relevant aspect: it remains to be assessed to what extent Islam will be embedded in the ordinary legislation, in the jurisprudence, as well as in the policies of the modern state. Until the end of 2016, the constitutional implementation phase has not raised concerns of "Islamization", but it is still too early to advance any evaluation. The process is, in fact, still undergoing as demonstrated by the fact that the Constitutional Court, which will have the crucial role of interpreting the new constitution, has not been established yet.

In the meantime, a pivotal question can be raised: whether the pacts signed by the elites will be sufficient to found the basis on which to build a new democratic society (Boubekeur 2015). It is true that the consensus reached about the place of religion in the new legal system may be the indicator of a reconciliation of the two components of Tunisian society: on the one side, *Ennahda* made an attempt to impose Islamic values and this pursuit has been prevented by the engagement of the secularists[14], and on the other side, one should also recognise *Ennahda*'s ability to put forward a re-elaboration of the position of Islam in a political culture that, since the country's independence, has defined secularism as a touchstone of national identity (Honwana 2013: 9). However, some Tunisian scholars have noted that the post-election agreement for a government of national unity between *Ennahda* and *Nidaa Tounes* has dissatisfied many citizens, who have read it as a counter-revolutionary attempt aimed at reestablishing the control of the elite over the common people (Marzouki 2016b). Finally, it can never be stressed enough that, despite the obvious importance of religious issues and their centrality in the debate, "it will be the economic recovery that forms the major challenge of the post-Ben Ali era" (El-Issawi 2012: 18).

---

14 It is remarkable to note that according to Gluck and Brandt, "[p]ublic reaction to the first draft contributed to at least three substantive changes, while lobbying from civil society groups helped secure guarantees regarding separation of powers and rights and freedoms" (Gluck and Brandt 2015: 10).

Tunisia's economic situation is indeed worse than before the revolution, with an unemployment rate of more than 15% (Institut National de la Statistique 2015), and the lack of economic recovery represents a serious risk of delegitimization for the entire democratic transition. The issue is not completely detached from the religious factor, because the lack of economic and social development has made many young people turn to radical Salafism. The path forward is therefore that of tackling these challenges by building on the consensus reached over the constitution.

References

Books

Bali, A., and Lerner, H. (eds.). (2017). *Constitution Writing, Religion and Democracy*, Cambridge University Press, Cambridge.

Camau, M. and Geisser, V. (2011). *Le syndrome autoritaire: politique en Tunisie de Bourguiba à Ben Ali*, Sud Editions, Tunis.

Campanini, M. (2012). *L'alternativa islamica: aperture e chiusure del radicalismo*, Bruno Mondadori, Milano.

Charrad, M.M. (2001). *States and Women's Rights: The Making of Postcolonial Tunisia, Algeria, and Morocco*, University of California Press, Berkeley.

Elkins, Z., Ginsburg, T. and Melton, J. (2009). *The Endurance of National Constitutions*, Cambridge University Press, Cambridge.

Honwana, A. (2013). *Youth and the Revolution in Tunisia*, Zed Books, London/New York.

Houki, C. (2016). *Islam et Constitution en Tunisie*, Centre de Publication Universitaire, Manouba.

Gluck, J. and Brandt, M. (2015), *Participatory and Inclusive Constitution-Making. Giving Voice to the Demands of Citizens in the Wake of the Arab Spring*, USIP, Washington, DC.

Chapters of books

Ben Achour, Y. (1992). "Une révolution par le droit? Bourguiba et le Code du statut personnel", in Id., *Politique, Religion et droit*, Cérès Productions et Cerp, Tunis, 200 et seq.

Bouguerra, M.M. (2005). "Il codice tunisino dello statuto personale", in Horchani, F., Zolo. D. (eds.), *Mediterraneo. Un dialogo fra le due sponde*, Jouvence, Roma, 61–92.

Bousbih, E., and Yaalaoui, A. (2015). "The Interplay of Politics and Religion in the New Tunisian Constitution: A Legal Analysis", in Rousselin, M. and Smith, C. (eds.), *The Tunisian Constitutional Process: Main Actors and Key Issues*, Global Dialogues, Duisburg, 16–23.

El-Issawi, F. (2012). "The Tunisian Transition: The Evolving Face of the Second Republic", in Kitchen, N. (eds.), *After the Arab Spring: Power Shift in the Middle East?*, IDEAS reports – special reports, London School of Economics and Political Science, London, 18–22.

Longo, P. (2015). "L'Islam nella nuova Costituzione: dallo Stato neutrale allo Stato 'protettore'", in Groppi, T., and Spigno, I. (eds), Tunisia. La primavera della costituzione, Carocci, Roma, 102–116.

Longo, P. (2016). "Constitutionalism, Islam and Citizenship in Post-Revolutionary Tunisia: The NCA's Role in Building a New Culture of Consensus", in El Houssi, L., Melcangi, A., Torelli, S. and Cricco, M. (eds.), *North African Societies after the Arab Spring*, Cambridge Scholars Publishing, Newcastle upon Tyne, 4–29.

Hached, F. (2012). "La laïcité : un principe à l'ordre du jour de la IIe République Tunisienne?", in Blanc, P. (ed.), *Révoltes Arabes. Premiers Regards*, L'Harmattan, Paris, 25–32.

Manynganise, M. (2016). "We Will Chop Their Heads Off: Homosexuality versus Religio-political Grandstanding in Zimbabwe", in Van Kineke, A. and Chitando, E. *Public Religion and the Politics of Homosexuality in Africa*, Routledge, London-New York, 2016, 63ff.

Ponthoreau, M.-C. (2008). "La constitution comme structure identitaire", in Chagnollaud, D. (eds.), *Les 50 ans de la Constitution 1958–2008*, LexisNexis Litec, Paris, 31–42.

Papers

Abbiate, T. (2015). "The Revival of Political Islam in the MENA Region: The Case of Ennahda in Tunisia", *Revista Ballot*, 1(1), 67–82.

Allal, A. (2016). "Retour vers le futur. Les origines économiques de la révolution tunisienne", *Pouvoirs*, 1(156), 17–29.

Ben Achour, Y. (1992). "Islam et laïcité: propos sur la composition d'un système de normativité", *Pouvoirs*, 62(9), 15–30.

Ben Salem, M. (2015). "Social, Economic and Political Dynamics in Tunisia and the Related Short- to Medium-Term Scenarios", *IAI Working Paper*, 15, 1–18.

Böckenförde, M. (2016). "From Constructive Ambiguity to Harmonious Interpretation: Religion-Related Provisions in the Tunisian Constitution", *American Behavioural Scientist*, 1(22), 1–22.

Boubekeur, A. (2015). "Islamists, Secularists and Old Regime Elites in Tunisia: Bargained Competition", Mediterranean Politics, 21(1), 107–27.

Boukhars, A. (2014). "In the Crossfire. Islamists' Travails in Tunisia", *Carnegie Endowment for Peace*, 2014, 10ss.

Cavatorta, F. and Merrone, F. (2013). "Moderation Through Exclusion? The Journey of the Tunisian Ennahda from Fundamentalist to Conservative Party", *Democratization*, 20(5), 857–75.

Giolo, O. (2002). "Donne in Tunisia. La tutela giuridica dei diritti tra universalità dei principi e le specificità culturali", *Annali dell'Università di Ferrara – Scienze giuridiche*, XVI, 253–306.

Hamed, C. (2015). "Au-délà de l'exception tunisienne: les failles et les risques du processus révolutionnaire", *Pouvoirs*, 156, 137–47.

Marks, M. (2014). "Convince, Coerce or Compromise? Ennahda's Approach to Tunisia's Constitution", *Brooking Doha Centre Analysis Paper*, 1–30.

Marzouki, N. (2016a). "La transition tunisienne : du compromis démocratique à la réconciliation forcée", Pouvoirs, 1, 83–94.

Netterstrøm, K.L. (2015). "After the Arab Spring: The Islamists' Compromise in Tunisia", *Journal of Democracy*, 26(4), 110–24.

Ozzano, L. and Cavatorta, F. (2013). "Introduction: Religiously Oriented Parties and Democratization", *Democratization*, 20(5), 799–806.

Poussel, S. (2014). "Pluralism and Minorities in Post-Revolutionary Tunisia", *Middle East Law and Governance*, 6(1), 53–62.

Stepan, A. (2012). "Tunisia's Transition and the Twin Tolerations", *Journal of Democracy*, 23(2), 89–103.

Theses

Ahaya, L.O. (2015). "The Secular State Premise and the Kadhi Court Debate During Kenya's Constitutional Review Moment", Unpublished PhD Thesis, Moi University, Eldoret.

Debuysere, L. (2013). "The Women's Movement in Tunisia: Fault Lines in a Post-Revolutionary Context", Master thesis in Conflict and Development, University of Gent.

Dubois, A. (2012). "Tunisie: l'engagement des femmes pour leurs droits. Paroles de femmes dans la transition tunisienne", Mémoire de recherche, Faculté de Sciences Politiques de l'Université de Toulouse.

Website pages

Hamid, S. (2011). "The Rise of the Islamists", (https://www.foreignaffairs.com/articles/north-africa/2011-04-03/rise-islamists).

Mandraud, I. (2012). "La place de la charia dans la Constitution divise la Tunisie", (http://www.lemonde.fr/tunisie/article/2012/03/17/la-place-de-la-charia-dans-la-constitution-divise-la-tunisie_1671383_1466522.html#XXVVH45ofyQZzGot.99).

Marks, M. (2012a). "Speaking on the Unspeakable: Blasphemy and the Tunisian Constitution", (http://carnegieendowment.org/2012/09/04/speaking-on-unspeakable-blasphemy-tunisian-constitution/drca).

Marzouki, N. (2016b). "En Tunisie, on assiste à un mouvement de restauration qui s'est produit de manière démocratique", (http://www.lorientlejour.com/article/981957/en-tunisie-on-assiste-a-un-mouvement-de-restauration-qui-sest-produit-de-maniere-democratique.html).

NDI (2013). "Prioritizing Patriotism: Tunisian Citizens Express Their Views", (https://www.ndi.org/files/Tunisia-priortizing-patriotism-focus-groups-june-2013.pdf).

PNUD (2013). "Enquête nationale sur les attentes des jeunes à l'égard du processus constitutionnel et de la transition démocratique en Tunisie", Rapport de synthèse, (http://www.undp.org/content/dam/tunisia/docs/Projets/Gouvernance%20D%C3%A9mocratique/Publications/UNDP_TN_Rapport%20Gouvernance.pdf).

Redissi, H. (2014). "La constitution tunisienne de 2014", (http://www.esprit.presse.fr/news/frontpage/news.php?code=331).

Other publications

Enquête nationale sur l'emploi, Tunis, 1er trimestre 2015.

Institut National de la Statistique, "Mesure de la pauvreté, des inégalités et de la polarisation en Tunisie 2000–2010", Tunis.

Conclusion

Does participation help to foster constitutionalism in Africa?

H. Kwasi Prempeh

Constitution-making is not a new phenomenon in Africa. Beginning in the 1960s, as one state after another emerged from colonialism, Africa's new leaders, with Ghana's Nkrumah taking the lead,[1] jettisoned their "independence constitutions" as ill-fitting colonial garb and embarked on a fresh round of constitution drafting.[2] Defended in the name of *autochthony*, this initial wave of constitution remaking exercises in postcolonial Africa involved little to no credible public participation. Africa's first generation of leaders, hailed by their people as messiahs for freeing them from European colonial domination, carried an abundant reservoir of "founding father" legitimacy with which they underwrote their constitution-writing and other projects; public participation in these exercises was presumed unnecessary. Moreover, Africans, their leaders argued, had emerged from colonialism poor, uneducated, disease-plagued, and generally economically backward. What they needed, the argument went, was not constitutions or civil liberties; what mattered was "development"—a "war" on poverty, illiteracy, disease, and unemployment.[3] The primary instrument for delivering this would be the development plan, not constitutions.[4] Where it was felt politically expedient to involve the people in these early post-independence constitution-making exercises, public participation typically took the form of a referendum to approve a regime-authored text, with the outcome of the vote a foregone conclusion.

In the two to three decades that followed, nearly all of these homegrown, post-independence constitutions would undergo a series of amendments and

---

1 Kwame Nkrumah, who had led the Gold Coast (Ghana) to become sub-Saharan Africa's first state to emerge from colonialism, disparaged Africa's independence constitutions as neocolonial devices designed to ensure "the preservation of imperial interests in the newly emergent state" (The Editors of the Spark, 1965: 39).

2 Between 1960 and 1962 alone, thirteen newly independent African states, beginning with Ghana, amended or replaced their independence constitutions.

3 See, e.g., "[T]he Independence Constitution of Tanganyika was neither particularly suited to the needs of development nor was it entirely ours" (Nyerere, 1973: 174).

4 In the words of Tanzania's Nyerere, speaking in a 1964 defense of a new preventive detention law, "Development must be considered first. . . . Our question with regard to any matter—even the issue of fundamental freedom—must be, 'How does this affect the progress of the Development Plan?'" (Austin, 1984: 32) (quoting Nyerere).

DOI: 10.4324/9781315180540-23

revisions—and some suspensions, in those instances where military juntas intervened. As before, public participation was not a familiar feature of these later constitution rewriting exercises in any meaningful sense. Together, these initial and subsequent constitutional changes installed or enabled the pattern of political arrangements for which Africa would become known: authoritarian presidents with no term limits; one-party parliaments; central government-appointed local administration; executive-controlled judiciaries; and rights and freedoms that remained vulnerable to routine legislative and executive override. The late Kenyan legal scholar Okoth-Ogendo aptly described the products of Africa's successive post-independence constitution-making exercises as "constitutions without constitutionalism" (Okoth-Ogendo, 1993: 65).

This picture began to change in the 1990s. As the democratic wave unleashed by the ending of the Cold War swept across the globe, Africa's long-serving authoritarian rulers, like their counterparts in Eastern and Central Europe, became vulnerable to regime change. Thirty years after independence, the promise of development, which had been held up as reason enough why democracy and political freedoms must wait, had failed to materialize. Instead of development, decades of authoritarian and exclusionary politics in Africa had brought material prosperity for a politically influential few and impoverishment for the majority, with attendant corruption, economic decline, social division, and, in a good many cases, armed conflict. The founding father mystique, where it still mattered, had worn off, and with ruling elites having failed to deliver their end of the authoritarianism/development bargain, a crisis of legitimacy ensued.[5] With the old bases of legitimacy eroded and untenable, Africa's old guard leaders could no longer deny or resist growing domestic—and international—demand for multiparty elections and related constitutional reforms.

The issue of public participation in constitution-making has thus emerged in contemporary Africa, as elsewhere, in the context of the abject failure of the authoritarian project of the first three decades after independence and ensuing popular demand for a renewal of state legitimacy along democratic lines. In that regard, democracy in the contemporary African context has come to mean not merely the right of the people to vote in and vote out who may govern them but also the right of the people to a voice—and a vote—in the making and adoption of the new "rules of the game" according to which the state shall be governed. Spearheading this movement for public participation is a once-repressed African civil society that has since liberated itself from the shackles of the *ancien regime* as the latter has suffered an erosion of popular legitimacy. Then there is the important fact that public participation in constitution-making has matured into a new international norm (Hart, 2010: 20) making it at least politically

---

5 "The quest for legitimacy was an important feature of postindependence politics, and authoritarian rule did not diminish the centrality of this quest, as power was justified on the ability and willingness of the political authorities to promote public welfare" (Mkandawire, 1999: 124).

obligatory for the sake of international acceptability of the outcome, especially for polities and regimes that must negotiate a transition from an authoritarian or a conflict-ridden past.

The case studies in this volume present a variegated picture of public participation in constitution-making in Africa. In many, the constitution-making projects have run their course, at least for the time being. In a few others, notably Libya, Somalia, and South Sudan, they are still inchoate, as the related political transition remains fluid and its future not entirely certain, giving conflict resolution and peace building greater urgency and prominence and complicating the search for constitutionalism. The constitution-making exercises discussed in the case studies all were associated with countries or regimes in some form of political transition or crisis, but not all involved the same degree of crisis or threat to the legitimacy of the system or political class. As would be expected, the role and prominence of public participation in these various processes, as well as their success or failure, have varied widely.

Does participation matter?

Against the backdrop of these disparate case studies, the question to be answered in this concluding chapter is whether public participation in constitution-making can be said to have helped advance the cause of constitutionalism in Africa. This is a fair question; after all, the recent democratic revival that has necessitated the rewriting of many of Africa's constitutions was, in large part, a reaction against a long history of constitutions without constitutionalism. Thus, it is reasonable to expect that these latest constitution-making exercises, attended by an unprecedented degree of public participation, would usher in a different kind of constitution and, for that matter, a new era of constitutionalism.

Indeed, the attitude and conduct of both public and elite participants in these exercises suggest that, on all sides, there is a common expectation or understanding that public participation matters—or, at least, *must* matter. Thus, for example, where citizens have doubted the good faith commitment of political actors to meaningful public participation or have not felt their views sufficiently consulted or considered in the constitution-making process or reflected in its outcome, they have boycotted parts of the process in large numbers or voted to reject the resulting draft constitution. Zimbabwe, Kenya, and Zambia offer examples of these.

In Zimbabwe's 1999–2000 constitution-making exercise, which had been set in motion by President Mugabe on the basis of the Inquiries Act, the president's decision to exercise his discretion under the Act to reject certain key recommendations of the constitutional commission contained in the resulting draft constitution led to public rejection of the proposed constitution in the ensuing referendum (Mmonzora, Chapter 9). Similarly, Kenyans overwhelming (by roughly one million votes) rejected the so-called Wako draft constitution in the 2005 referendum. The Wako draft, reflecting regime and political class preferences, had substantially revised and departed from an earlier draft (the so-called "Bomas draft") that included certain popular provisions curbing presidential power and effecting a federal-like devolution of power to subnational communities. Consequently, the resulting document (i.e., the Wako draft), which was submitted to a referendum, was widely regarded as an elite pact that lacked the benefit of public participation and was thus rejected (Macharia and Ghai, Chapter 6).

These are two examples of cases where the *absence* of meaningful public participation in the pre-referendum stages of constitution-making have worked to deny popular legitimacy to and acceptance of the resulting draft and, arguably, delayed a transition toward constitutionalism. They also point to a new reality about public participation in contemporary African constitution-making: Not only are referendum outcomes no longer a foregone conclusion, but, as an index of public participation in constitution-making, the referendum is seen in contemporary Africa as necessary but not sufficient; public participation has become politically obligatory in the pre-referendum stages as well. Constitution drafters' awareness or anticipation that a failure to take on board significant public and civil society preferences might cause public rejection of the resulting draft likely partly explains, for example, the post-2008 changes that were made in Kenya to bridge the gap between the 2004 Bomas draft and the previously rejected 2005 Wako draft and restore in the "Harmonized draft" some of the key constitutional design preferences of civil society. With the experience of the failed 2005 referendum in mind, anticipation of an upcoming referendum in 2010 arguably served as a "downstream constraint" on the choices and decisions of elite actors in reaching agreement on the new Kenyan Constitution (Elster, 1995).

In his chapter on the Tunisian constitution-making process, Cherif details the deliberate steps which the popularly elected National Constituent Assembly (NCA) took so as to demonstrate the constitution drafters' good faith commitment to public participation and reassure public participants that their submissions or input mattered. The steps included documenting and showing in what specific ways public participants' voice had been captured in the resulting text of the draft constitution (Cherif, Chapter 5). But elite and constitution makers have not always acknowledged or demonstrated their recognition of the importance or transformative possibilities of public participation in such positive terms. Often, especially where elites or regimes feel insecure or are uncertain as to where or how far public participation might lead them, they have tried to tightly manage or control, or in some cases even subvert, the public participation process. This happened with Zimbabwe's more recent constitution-making process initiated in the context of the Global Political Agreement (GPA). Having lost control this time of the constitution-making initiative, which under the GPA was located in Parliament (now dominated by opposition politicians), President Mugabe deployed his regime's repressive resources against the participatory process, including using the regime-controlled national broadcaster to try to dampen public interest in the process. Insecure regimes are quite well aware that public participation in constitution-making, particularly when regime legitimacy stands on slippery ground, involves a risk, a ceding of power that could threaten the regime's own hold on power. In a sense, Morocco's King Mohammed VI's impromptu initiation of constitutional reform in March 2011 was a preemptive move designed to seize the momentum for constitution change from the youth and the streets and bring it within the control of the royal court, rather than wait and risk being overtaken by events and being forced to lead a constitution-making process from behind (Biagi, Chapter 4).

Despite the fact that elite and public attitudes and reactions to public participation in constitution-making suggest a common recognition of the transformative potential (or risk) of an open and inclusive process, the question whether public participation in fact helps to foster constitutionalism in Africa does not necessarily yield a definite or an unqualified yes answer. Tentativeness is warranted for a variety of reasons. The case studies highlight at least two of them.

First, while it may be reasonable to assume that participatory constitution-making projects in Africa, occurring against the background of failed authoritarian rule, are inherently anti-authoritarian, one cannot, on that account alone, proceed on the further assumption that "constitutionalism" as the end goal enjoys a strong consensus across the board or among public participants, whether in a given country or from one country to the next. Participants, whether elite, public, or civil society, frequently have divergent, sometimes opportunistic, agendas in relation to the constitution-making exercise; they do not all participate situated behind a Rawlsian "veil of ignorance" evaluating issues only on the basis of "general considerations" without thought of self (Rawls, 1971: 136–42). In many instances, regime opponents participating in constitution-making in Africa are driven more by a desire for immediate regime change—and the near-term prospecting of being in government themselves—than by a sincere commitment to a fundamental restructuring of the character and distribution of state power. Among public participants, too, especially the jobless youth, material and livelihood concerns understandably often trump constitutionalism as the primary motivation driving their participation in the process. Cherif reports, for example, that in May 2014, following adoption of the draft constitution by the Tunisian National Constituent Assembly, the NCA organized a public outreach event in the city of Sidi Bouzid, famous for being the "birthplace of the Tunisian uprising," in order to introduce the draft to the people. This event was, however, met with protests, the protesters "calling not for a constitution but for employment and development" and eventually preventing the constitution drafters led by the NCA president from going ahead with the program (Cherif, Chapter 5). Similar events in other towns were met with low attendance. As Cherif observes, "The fact that those who attended the meetings did comment as much (and sometimes more) on the political and economic situation as on the constitutional text itself clearly indicates that the constitution was eventually not everyone's main issue of concern" (Cherif, Chapter 5: 98).

Second, there is the related issue that public participation is vulnerable to populist capture—or what, writing in regard to the rights of sexual minorities in South Africa, V. Federico has called "participation's dark side": the ability of certain (often majoritarian) social forces to mobilize, in the name of public participation, to preserve interests that place the rights of other social groups in jeopardy (Federico, Chapter 17). Indeed, there may be an inherent tension between public participation in constitution-making, which may incline toward majoritarian preferences, and the idea of constitutions and constitutionalism as *supra*-majoritarian (and in some cases, even deliberately *counter*-majoritarian) projects. Both Federico and Klug discuss how this tension between majority preferences and the rights or interests of unpopular minorities has played out in the South African context; with regard to the LGBT rights, on the one hand, and the death penalty, on the other. Although in both instances, the countermajoritarian position eventually prevailed (but not without help from post-constitution making judicial review), the risk of illiberal, populist capture underscores some of the ways in which public participation may lead to perverse outcomes.

Ultimately, as the case studies show, public participation necessarily occurs within a very specific transition dynamic and country context, implicating, in each instance, a multiplicity and diversity of actors and variables unique to each context. In short, each case of public participation is different. It is thus impossible or at least hazardous to theorize or formulate universally valid propositions about the relationship of public participation to constitutionalism in Africa on the basis of these case studies. What is possible, however, is to isolate, on the basis of the available evidence, what factors or conditions—at least some key ones—that make public participation likely to impact favorably on prospects for constitutionalism in Africa.

Conditions for impactful public participation

Not all participations are equal; some are more meaningful—and impactful—than others. This is the essential insight from Saati's contribution in this volume. If we are interested in evaluating the likely impact of public participation on prospects for constitutionalism in Africa, we must, following Saati, unpack the concept of "public participation" and differentiate participation into types. Saati cautions that a failure to do so, evident in the tendency to speak of public participation in monolithic terms, leads to the common mistake of construing participation "as an issue primarily concerned with quantity, implying that the more people that have been involved in the making of the constitution, the more participatory it has been." For Saati, however, what makes participation participatory—and, for that matter, meaningful—is not the raw numbers of people who are thus enabled to make submissions to the drafting committee but the "possibility for the public to influence the process of making the constitution as well as the content of the actual document."

Building on Saati's point, it is fair to say that a constitution-making process that does not afford public participants the ability to *influence* outcomes fails to satisfy the minimum condition for meaningful public participation—or for participation that can foster constitutionalism. Influence is, of course, a necessarily qualitative measure, and, drawing on her empirical study, Saati puts forth four factors associated with constitution-making that operate interactively to determine the degree of influence of participation. These are the initiators of the process, the forms of communication, the degree of inclusion, and who holds final authority.

The last of these factors, who gets to decide the fate of the draft constitution, calls up discussion of the referendum, which has become in Africa practically obligatory as the final act of public participation in constitution-making. Markus Böckenförde examines this subject in his chapter, querying whether the referendum ought to be used the way it is ordinarily used in Africa and elsewhere, as the final obligatory act that validates or invalidates a draft constitution, or whether it would not serve a more useful, if limited, purpose at some in-between stage to break a political impasse. He is skeptical of the absolute necessity of a terminal referendum particularly where a popularly elected constituent assembly has been in the driver's seat the rest of the way.

Böckenförde does raise a very interesting point, and his proposal of an alternative way of using the referendum in the constitution-making process, which is as a conditional impasse-breaker where necessary, is a thoughtful and creative one. Saati is similarly not absolutist in her insistence on a referendum as a *sine qua non* measure of public participation. However, she does consider the presence or absence of a "decisive" referendum as a "relevant" consideration in evaluating how much influence a given case of public participation has on constitution-making outcomes. Still, there is much to be said for having an obligatory and decisive terminal referendum in the context of immediate post-authoritarian transitional democracies, which is where most of the African case studies covered in this volume find themselves. The opportunity to vote to approve the document that shall bind a polity as the supreme law of the land (as opposed to voting to elect persons to form a government), being an opportunity that presents itself infrequently and episodically in any democracy, the case for retaining it, even where a popularly elected constituent assembly is involved in the constitution drafting, remains a strong one. In the African context, where public trust in elites is understandably low, public enthusiasm and willingness to participate in other phases of a constitution-making project are likely to suffer substantially if the decisive referendum were removed from the terminal phase of the process.

To return to the first of Saati's four factors, *who initiates* the constitution-making process, the initiation phase is not specifically or separately mentioned as one of the stages in Jennifer Widner's famous (five) phases of constitution-making (Widner, 2005: 503–18). Yet, how and by whom the constitution-making process is triggered matter greatly, not only because initiators and those who influence the initiation decision set the agenda or "terms of reference" for the ensuing process, they also determine the nature and scope—and likely influence—of public participation in the process.

In the case studies covered in this volume, the recent successive failed attempts at constitutional revision in Zambia and Zimbabwe's two recent contrasting experiences of constitution-making illustrate the importance of who initiates.

In Zambia, the promise of a "people-driven constitution" has remained a promise unredeemed, in part because successive presidents have followed long-standing tradition and practice in Zambia whereby constitution-making exercises are set in motion by a president invoking the Inquiries Act to set up a commission of inquiry. Under this law, called "Commissions of Inquiry Act" in other common law jurisdictions, the president, as the commissioning authority, reserves the right to accept or reject any or all of the recommendations proposed by the constitutional commission, effectively allowing the president to dictate the constitutional reform agenda. Under these circumstances, it is not entirely surprising that Zambia's fitful constitutional reform exercises have yielded little result. Similarly, Zimbabwe's 1999–2000 constitution-making process was initiated by President Mugabe, invoking his powers under the Commissions of Inquiry Act. This allowed him to pack the drafting commission with ZANU partisans. He also proceeded, as he was statutorily entitled to do, once the commission had completed its work and submitted its recommendations, to vary the commission's recommendations, which led eventually to public rejection of the proposed constitution in the 2000 referendum.

In contrast, the 2008–9 Zimbabwe constitution-making process was initiated under the terms of the power-sharing agreement (the so-called "Global Political Agreement" or GPA) reached between the contesting parties to settle the dispute 2008 elections, effectively taking it out of Mugabe's hands. Article 6 of the GPA set forth the ground rules for the crafting of a new constitution. The power to appoint the drafting committee now resided with Parliament, and the composition of the committee was to reflect the political parties' respective representation in Parliament. This shifted the balance of power away from Mugabe's ZANU (PF) to the opposition parties, which now controlled a legislative majority. The GPA also affirmed the "fundamental right and duty of the Zimbabwean people to make a constitution by themselves and for themselves" and mandated a process "owned and driven by the people," the outcome of which must "[deepen] democratic values and principles and the protection of the equality of all citizens, particularly the enhancement of full citizenship and equality of women." The resulting process was more deliberately participatory in terms of public outreach, consultation, and input in both the pre-draft and the post-draft stages, and included substantial civil society representation on thematic subcommittees—this despite persistent regime intimidation of public participants and civil society. Inclusive public participation elicited important counter-authoritarian proposals, including presidential term limits—although the regime successfully negotiated to not have this apply retrospectively to Mugabe. The final draft won multiparty acceptance and approval of 95 percent of vote at referendum.

The third of Saati's four conditions for meaningful participation is the form of communication. Participation is more effective and meaningful in constitution-making processes that ensure a two-way flow of communication, informing people about the process but, more importantly, seeking and receiving from the public input that is to influence the outcome of deliberations and drafting.

The ability of the public to participate meaningfully in a constitution-making process, such as make input of the kind and quality likely to influence outcomes, is partly a function of the ability of everyday citizens to understand the issues at stake. Saati thus suggests not merely a two-way communication but what she calls "a two-way model of communication with proactive measures." By this she means deliberate steps to educate the population about the issues and choices involved in the making of a constitution. This necessity to include "constitutional education programs" in constitution-making projects is particularly salient in the African context, where general literacy, let alone constitutional literacy, remains a stark challenge for vast numbers of people. As Saati notes, "quite a few countries that are in transition either from protracted conflict or from authoritarian rule, have populations that are perhaps only vaguely familiar with the concept of constitutionalism; an issue that must somehow be remedied if genuine participation is to be possible."

The Egyptian case exemplifies this last point. Despite the fact that public consultation was undertaken "throughout the constitutional drafting process" and additional opportunity provided for citizens to transmit their input to the drafters via the constituent assembly's website, turnout in the ensuing referendum to approve the constitution was a dismal 32.9 percent, and less than one percent of Egypt's civilian population submitted comments by means of the assembly's website (Abdelaal, Chapter 3). Abdelaal faults the "mechanism adopted in consulting the public" for the low rate of public participation. Although nominally two-way, the mode of public consultation in the process of making the 2014 Egyptian Constitution lacked the additional preparatory "proactive measures" suggested by Saati. As a consequence, the constitution-making process failed to alleviate or tackle the problem of "the high illiteracy rate among the Egyptian population, which consequently entails digital illiteracy" (Abdelaal, Chapter 3: 51).

With regard to "degree of inclusion," the last of her four factors, Saati is concerned primarily as to "whether or not all groups in society have actually been allowed (and accepted) to participate." This seems a rather minimalist standard, requiring little more than an equal opportunity for all social constituencies to participate freely in all phases of the process. In practice, it is common knowledge that not all social groups are equally situated in their ability or capacity to access an opportunity made nominally available to all on equal terms. Thus, to assure meaningful inclusion and participation of *all* groups, some additional or targeted "affirmative action" may be necessary to get *some* groups, notably socially, economically, and politically marginalized groups, to participate. Especially if the goal is to advance constitutionalism values, the constitution-making process must enable and encourage, and, where necessary, assist social and political minorities—those likely to be disfavored by majoritarian politics—to use the process to articulate and advance their interests. Of course, not all majority-disfavored groups are disadvantaged in their ability to participate meaningfully in constitution-making processes. In fact, public participation in contemporary constitution-making processes in Africa has frequently favored organizationally better-resourced groups and civic formations, regardless of their numerical strength. In many instances, it is these primarily ideational civil society groups that have often pushed constitutionalism norms and helped to educate and mobilize public support behind those values. Aware of this, some regimes in Africa, such as Zimbabwe's Mugabe, have tried to draw a distinction between the "people" and "civil society" and to frustrate the participation of the latter in participatory constitution-making processes. However, it is crucial if public participation is to enhance or foster constitutionalism that constitution-making processes not deliberately disadvantage organized civil society.

Beyond Saati's four factors, the case studies in this volume also provide enlightenment on other conditions that might make for meaningful public participation. One of them is right *timing*. Participatory constitution-making is more likely to show transformative potential if national political conditions or state of affairs signal that the country is in a "constitutional moment," so to speak. As constitutional change is an irregular occurrence often brought on by pressing necessity, political elites and regimes are likely to prevaricate in the face of demands for substantial reform of the rules of the game unless and until the social and political dynamic is auspicious for such change, such as when a regime or political class is confronted with a severe crisis of legitimacy, making the *status quo* politically untenable and unsustainable. Such defining moments are moments both of exceptional vulnerability and exceptional opportunity for change (including constitutional change), and if not timely seized might spell greater social disaster.

The 2008 post-election mayhem in Kenya may be said to have precipitated just such a constitutional moment in that country, one that shook the Kenyan political class out of its complacency and rendered "business as usual" politics untenable and a new constitutional order inevitable. The success of the post-2008 Kenyan constitution-making process may be attributed to this common realization that the nation was at a defining moment and needed to seize the window of opportunity. In contrast, the 2004–5 Kenyan constitutional reform process arguably failed in part because the regime and political class may not have felt the urgency of the moment. Similarly, the attitude of successive presidents of post-Kaunda Zambia in paying lip service to promises of a "people-driven" constitution, as well as civil society's persistent failure to cause the political class to yield, may be due to the fact that Zambia's constitutional moment has not yet arrived—or else the last one may have passed with the fall of Kenneth Kaunda. Assertions by Zambia government leaders that "Zambia was not in a constitutional crisis and that the country had a functional and democratic constitution" (Chembe, chapter 8) should be seen in this light. When the late Zambia President Sata stated that "Zambia does not need a new constitution but needs to amend the current one," he was similarly stating his conviction, apparently shared by an influential segment of the political class, that a constitutional moment was not at hand.

Lastly, meaningful public participation, if it is to have an enduring impact on constitutionalism, must not end with the conclusion of the constitution-making process and the coming into effect of a new constitution. The political struggles that characterize constitution-making do not disappear once the process is over and a new constitution has been adopted; the struggles are merely brought back down to be fought in the rough and tumble of everyday politics. The gains made and enshrined in the constitutional text, especially on behalf of unpopular minorities, do not become irreversible or eternally secure by the mere fact of their inclusion in a constitution; they remain vulnerable to attack and reversal by legislative majorities. Moreover, as constitutions are not self-enforcing documents, they cannot in and of themselves effect what behavior modification on the part of political and bureaucratic duty-bearers may be envisioned by its new provisions. Furthermore, public participation may well be immediately successful in terms of influencing the design and content of the constitution, yet distortions and reversals may occur in the practice and implementation of the constitution, including in the form of perverse judicial interpretation and an ossified political and bureaucratic culture, which could frustrate or delay the translation of constitutional intention and text into meaningful change and transformation on the ground. For all of the above reasons, public participation remains necessary even after a constitution has been adopted, so as to monitor, defend, and enforce the bargains made and rights secured in the constitution-making process.

In the United States, for example, it took a campaign of litigation waged through the federal courts over many decades (from the 1930s through to the 1970s) and backed in the post-World War II period by political mobilization in the form of the Civil Rights Movement, culminating in judicial victories like *Brown v. Board of Education of Topeka*[6] and the passage of laws like the Civil Rights Act (1964) and the Voting Rights Act (1965), before black Americans could realize the right to equal citizenship guaranteed under the "equal protection clause" of the Fourteenth Amendment to the U.S. Constitution adopted in 1868 in the aftermath of the American Civil War. In the South African context, Federico observes that despite the inclusion of "sexual orientation" among the prohibited grounds of discrimination in Article 9 (equality clause) of the 1996 Constitution, a large majority of the South African population remains hostile or opposed to same-sex activity, identity, and rights. As a result, South Africa's LGBT community has remained organizationally active in the defense of LGBT rights over two decades after the adoption of the constitution, using a combination of constitutional litigation and political lobbying and mobilization to rid the country's statute books of a host of laws denying or restricting the legal entitlements of persons in same-sex relationships.

The fact that gains made in the constitution-making process remain vulnerable to post-adoption bureaucratic noncompliance and legislative reversal and, therefore, may require further judicial or political action to enforce, protect, and secure them underscores the need to demand and extend participation (and participation rights) beyond constitution-making to include ordinary law-making

6 [1954] 347 U.S. 483.

and judicial processes. In the area of judicial enforcement, many contemporary African constitutions, notably in the common law jurisdictions, encourage recourse to the courts to vindicate constitutional rights through liberal *locus standi* provisions. The South African and Kenyan constitutions also promote regular citizen engagement with politics and the legislative process by guaranteeing a right of public participation in the legislative and other business of Parliament and its committees. Finally, by making provision for constitutional amendment by "popular initiative," as an alternative to amendment by parliamentary initiative, the Kenyan Constitution has secured a firm place for public participation in future constitutional changes, including in the very important matter of who gets to initiate and set the agenda for constitutional reform.

References

Austin, D. (1984), *Politics in Africa*, University Press of New England, Hanover/New Hampshire.

Elster, J. (1995), "Forces and Mechanisms in the Constitution-Making Process," *Duke Law Journal* 45(2), 364–96.

Hart, V. (2010), "Constitution Making and the Right to Take Part in a Public Affair," in Miller, L.E. (eds.), *Framing the State in Times of Transition: Case Studies in Constitution Making*, United States Institute of Peace, Washington D.C., 20–56.

Mkandawire, T. (1999), "Crisis Management and the Making of Choiceless Democracies," in Joseph, R. (eds.), *State, Conflict, and Democracy in Africa*, Lynne Rienner, Boulder CO/London, 119–36.

Nyerere, J. (1973), *Freedom and Development/Uhuru Na Maendeleo*, Oxford University Press, Oxford.

Okoth-Ogendo, H.W.O. (1993), "Constitutions without Constitutionalism: Reflections on an African Political Paradox," in Greenberg, D. et al. (eds.), *Constitutionalism and Democracy: Transitions in the Contemporary World*, Oxford University Press, Oxford, 65ff.

Rawls, J. (1971), *A Theory of Justice*, Harvard University Press, Cambridge, MA, 136–42.

The Editors of the Spark (1965), *Some Essential Features of Nkrumaism*, International Publishers, New York.

Widner, J. (2005), "Constitution Writing and Conflict Resolution," *The Round Table* 94(381), 503–18.

Index

Page numbers in bold refer to information in tables. Those followed by 'n' refer to notes where the number following 'n' is the note number.

For Product Safety Concerns and Information please contact our EU
representative GPSR@taylorandfrancis.com
Taylor & Francis Verlag GmbH, Kaufingerstraße 24, 80331 München, Germany